AN EVIL VERSION OF CAPTAIN AMERICA LED TH... STRUCTION. THE ORIGINAL CAPTAIN AMERICA RETURNED IN TI... K LEGACY OF THE SECRET EMPIRE LINGERS ON — A TRUTH FELT ... ROGERS HIMSELF. CAN STEVE FIND HIS PLACE IN A WORLD THAT HAS BEEN MADE TO FEAR CAPTAIN AMERICA?

CAPTAIN AMERICA

HOME OF THE BRAVE

MARK WAID & **CHRIS SAMNEE**
STORYTELLERS

MATTHEW WILSON
COLOR ARTIST

VC's JOE CARAMAGNA
LETTERER

CHRIS SAMNEE & **MATTHEW WILSON**
COVER ARTISTS

ALANNA SMITH
ASSISTANT EDITOR

TOM BREVOORT
EDITOR

"THE GANTLET!"

MARK WAID
(BASED UPON MATERIAL BY STAN LEE & JACK KIRBY)
STORY

JACK KIRBY
PENCILER

FRANK GIACOIA
INKER

MATTHEW WILSON
COLOR ARTIST

FERRAN DELGADO
WITH **ARTIE SIMEK**
& **SAM ROSEN**
LETTERERS

MICHAEL KELLEHER
ART CLEANUP

SPECIAL THANKS TO **JOHN ROGERS** FOR THE **FIVE MAGIC WORDS**

CAPTAIN AMERICA CREATED BY **JOE SIMON** & **JACK KIRBY**

COLLECTION EDITOR **MARK D. BEAZLEY** ASSISTANT EDITOR **CAITLIN O'CONNELL**
ASSOCIATE MANAGING EDITOR **KATERI WOODY** SENIOR EDITOR, SPECIAL PROJECTS **JENNIFER GRÜNWALD**
VP PRODUCTION & SPECIAL PROJECTS **JEFF YOUNGQUIST** SVP PRINT, SALES & MARKETING **DAVID GABRIEL**
BOOK DESIGNER **JAY BOWEN**

EDITOR IN CHIEF **C.B. CEBULSKI** CHIEF CREATIVE OFFICER **JOE QUESADA**
PRESIDENT **DAN BUCKLEY** EXECUTIVE PRODUCER **ALAN FINE**

CAPTAIN AMERICA BY WAID & SAMNEE: HOME OF THE BRAVE. Contains material originally published in magazine form as CAPTAIN AMERICA #695-700. First printing 2018. ISBN 978-1-302-90992-5. Published by MARVEL WORLDWIDE, INC., a subsidiary of MARVEL ENTERTAINMENT, LLC. OFFICE OF PUBLICATION: 135 West 50th Street, New York, NY 10020. **Printed in the U.S.A.** DAN BUCKLEY, President, Mar-vel Entertainment; JOHN NEE, Publisher; JOE QUESADA, Chief Creative Officer; TOM BREVOORT, SVP of Publishing; DAVID BOGART, SVP of Business Affairs & Opera-tions, Publishing & Partnership; DAVID GABRIEL, SVP of Sales & Marketing, Publish-ing; JEFF YOUNGQUIST, VP of Production & Special Projects; DAN CARR, Executive Director of Publishing Technology; ALEX MORALES, Director of Publishing Opera-tions; DAN EDINGTON, Managing Editor; SUSAN CRESPI, Production Manager; STAN LEE, Chairman Emeritus. For information regarding advertising in Marvel Com-ics or on Marvel.com, please contact Vit DeBellis, Custom Solutions & Integrated Ad-vertising Manager, at vdebellis@marvel.com. For Marvel subscription inquiries, please call 888-511-5480. **Manufactured between 4/13/2018 and 5/15/2018 by LSC COMMUNICATIONS INC., KENDALLVILLE, IN, USA.**

10 9 8 7 6 5 4 3 2 1

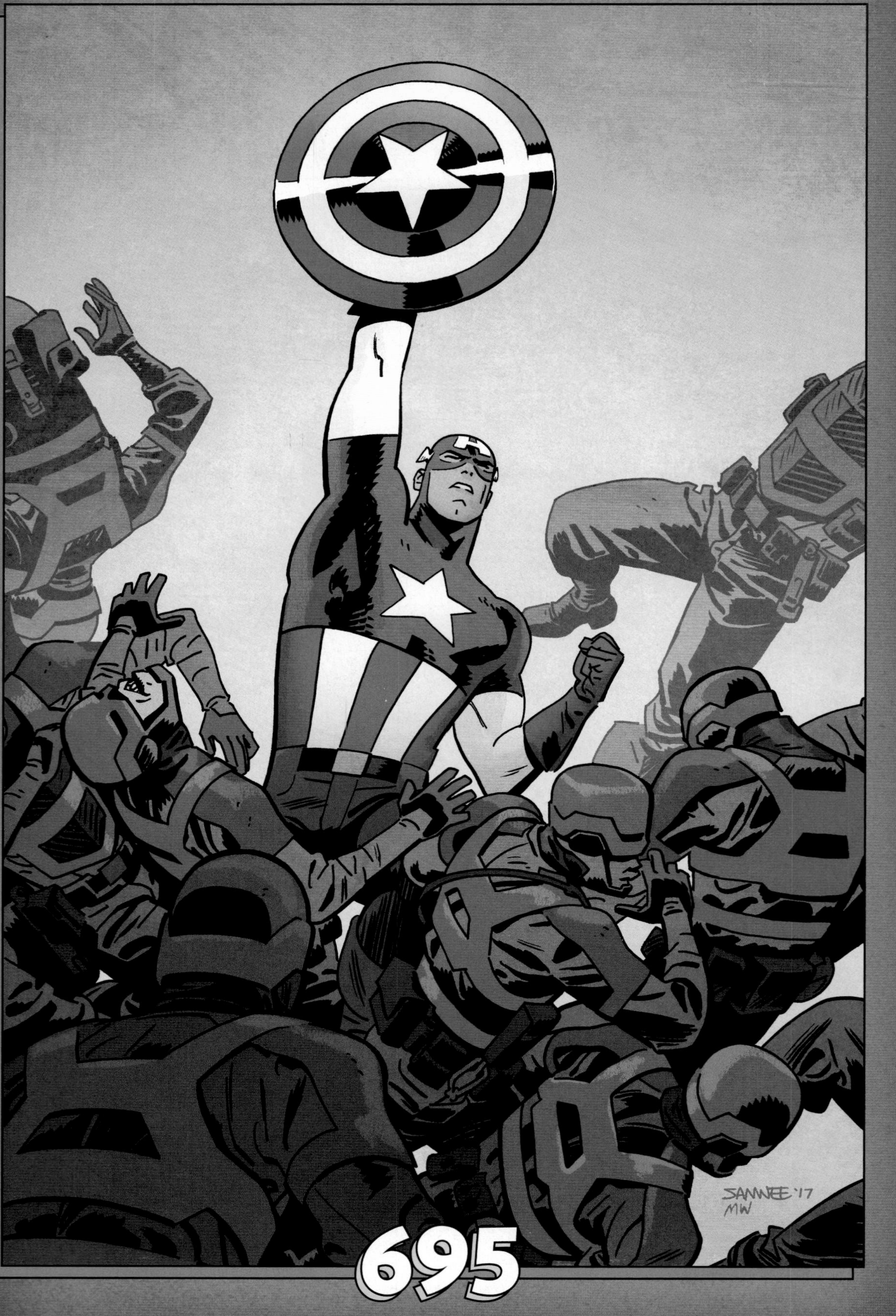
SAMNEE '17
MW
695

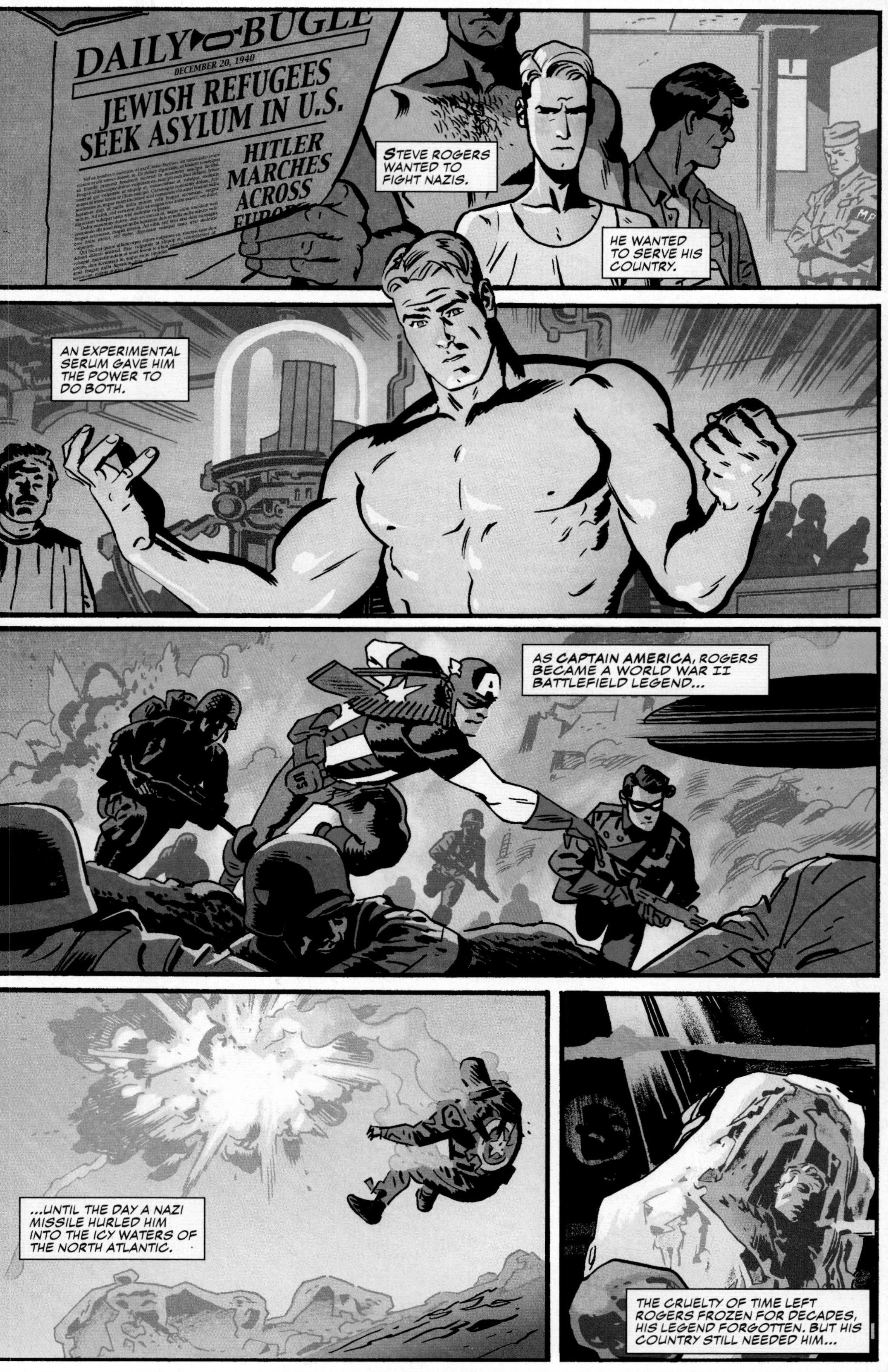
DAILY BUGLE
DECEMBER 20, 1940
JEWISH REFUGEES SEEK ASYLUM IN U.S.
HITLER MARCHES ACROSS
STEVE ROGERS WANTED TO FIGHT NAZIS.
HE WANTED TO SERVE HIS COUNTRY.
AN EXPERIMENTAL SERUM GAVE HIM THE POWER TO DO BOTH.
AS CAPTAIN AMERICA, ROGERS BECAME A WORLD WAR II BATTLEFIELD LEGEND...
...UNTIL THE DAY A NAZI MISSILE HURLED HIM INTO THE ICY WATERS OF THE NORTH ATLANTIC.
THE CRUELTY OF TIME LEFT ROGERS FROZEN FOR DECADES, HIS LEGEND FORGOTTEN. BUT HIS COUNTRY STILL NEEDED HIM...

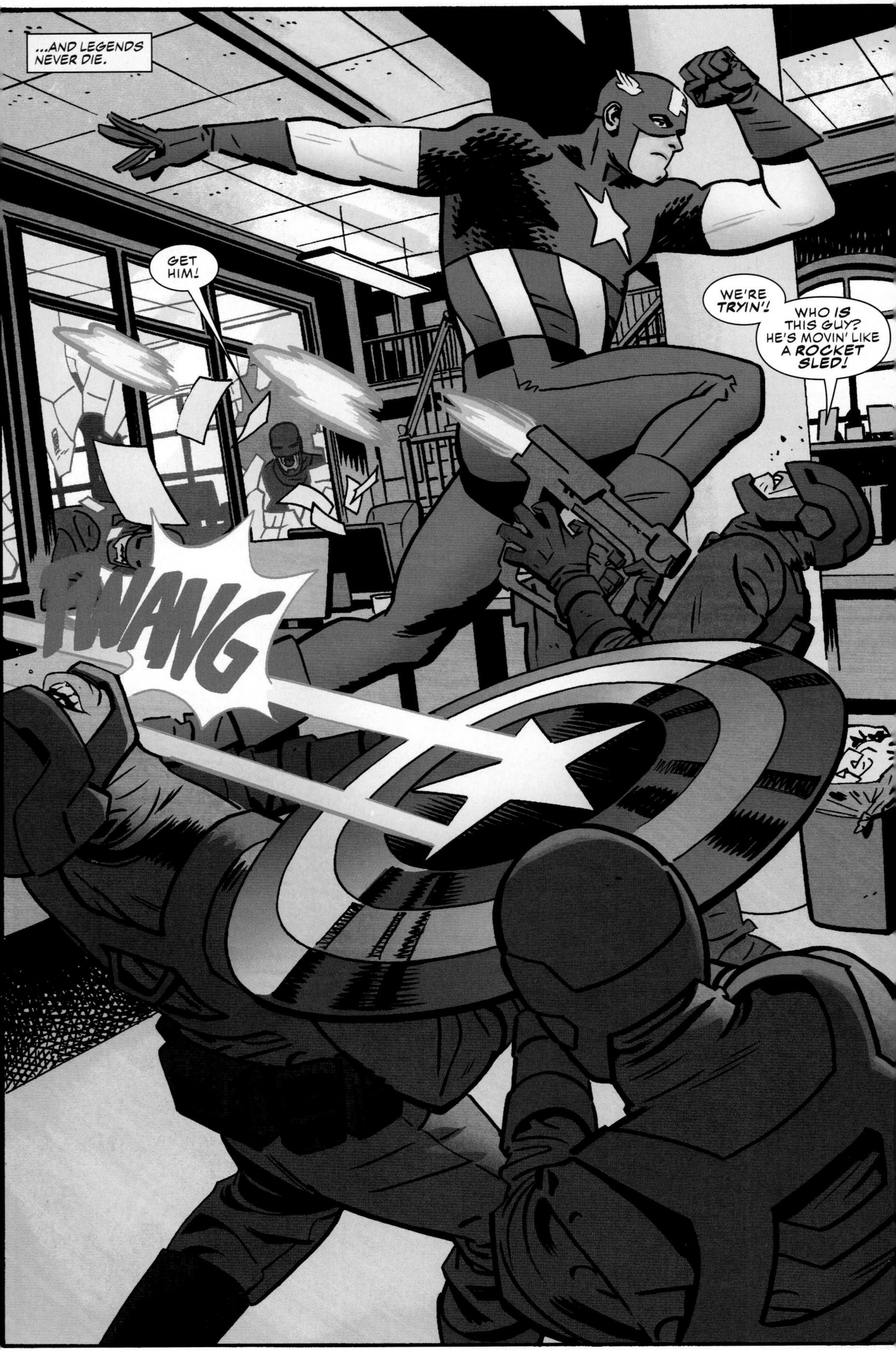
...AND LEGENDS NEVER DIE.
GET HIM!
WE'RE TRYIN'!
WHO IS THIS GUY? HE'S MOVIN' LIKE A ROCKET SLED!
PWANG

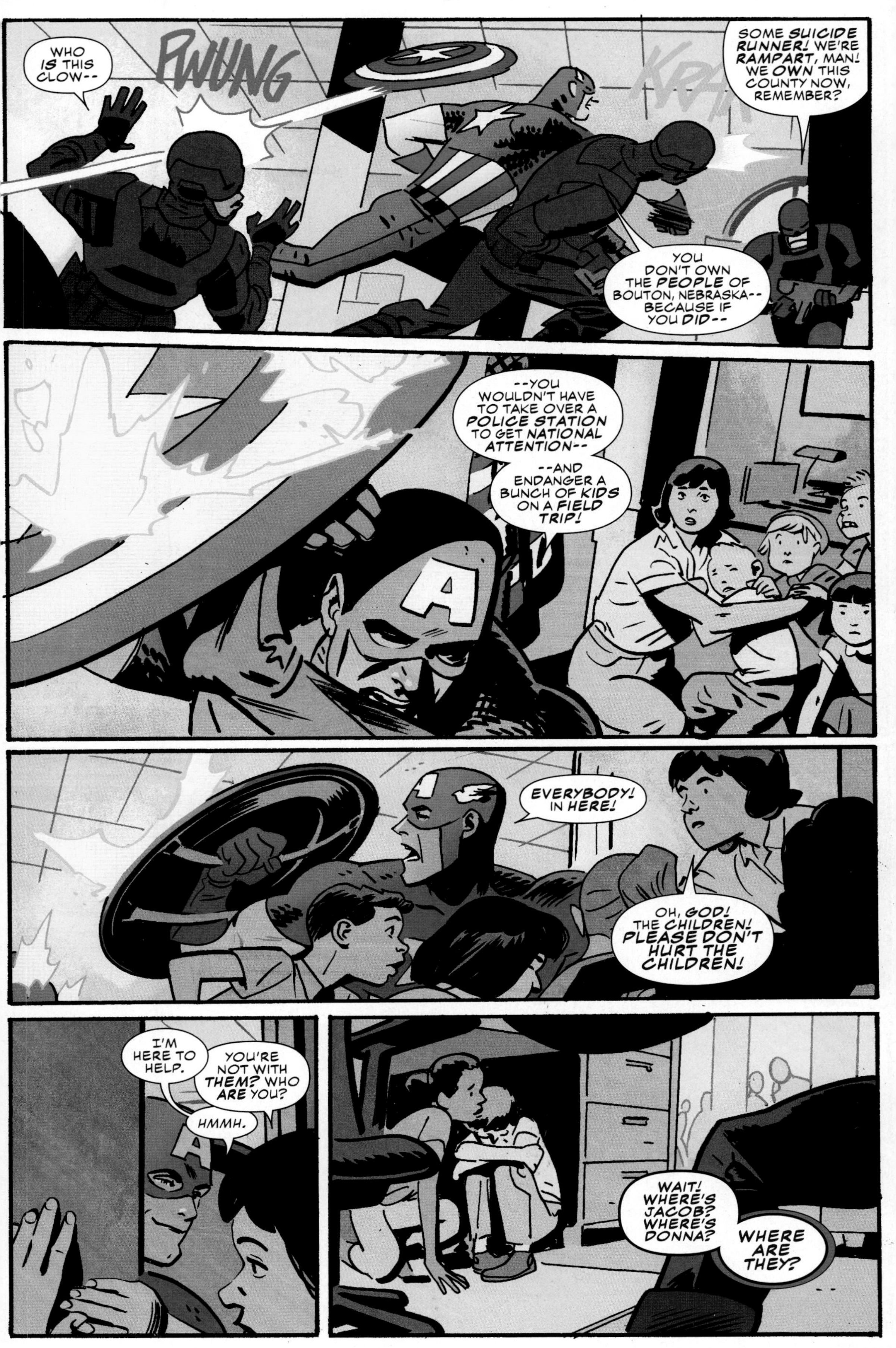

WHO IS THIS CLOW--
PWUNG
SOME SUICIDE RUNNER! WE'RE RAMPART, MAN! WE OWN THIS COUNTY NOW, REMEMBER?
YOU DON'T OWN THE PEOPLE OF BOUTON, NEBRASKA-- BECAUSE IF YOU DID--
--YOU WOULDN'T HAVE TO TAKE OVER A POLICE STATION TO GET NATIONAL ATTENTION--
--AND ENDANGER A BUNCH OF KIDS ON A FIELD TRIP!
EVERYBODY! IN HERE!
OH, GOD! THE CHILDREN! PLEASE DON'T HURT THE CHILDREN!
I'M HERE TO HELP.
YOU'RE NOT WITH THEM? WHO ARE YOU?
HMMH.
WAIT! WHERE'S JACOB? WHERE'S DONNA?
WHERE ARE THEY?

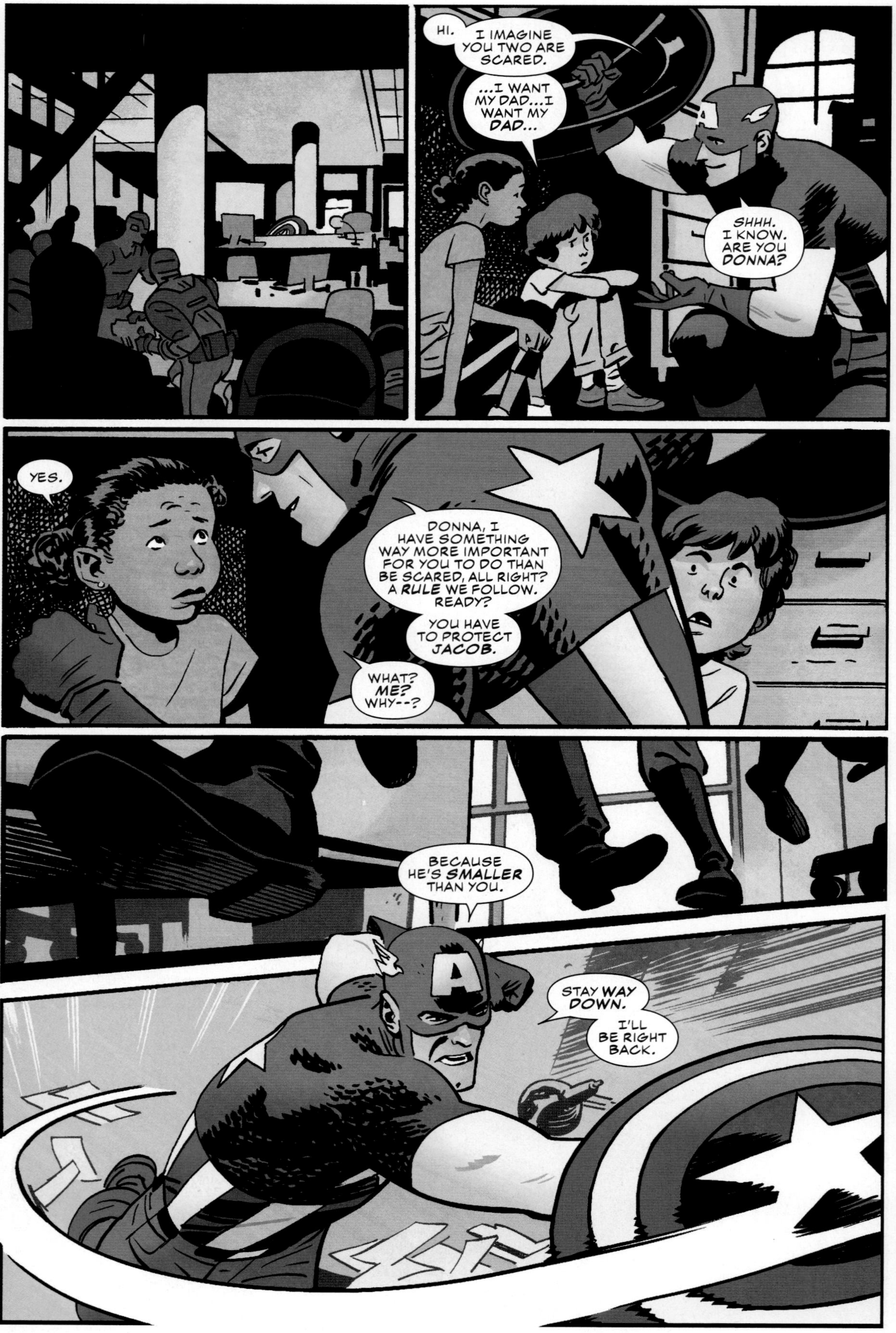
HI.
I IMAGINE YOU TWO ARE SCARED.
...I WANT MY DAD...I WANT MY DAD...
SHHH. I KNOW. ARE YOU DONNA?
YES.
DONNA, I HAVE SOMETHING WAY MORE IMPORTANT FOR YOU TO DO THAN BE SCARED, ALL RIGHT? A RULE WE FOLLOW. READY?
YOU HAVE TO PROTECT JACOB.
WHAT? ME? WHY--?
BECAUSE HE'S SMALLER THAN YOU.
STAY WAY DOWN.
I'LL BE RIGHT BACK.

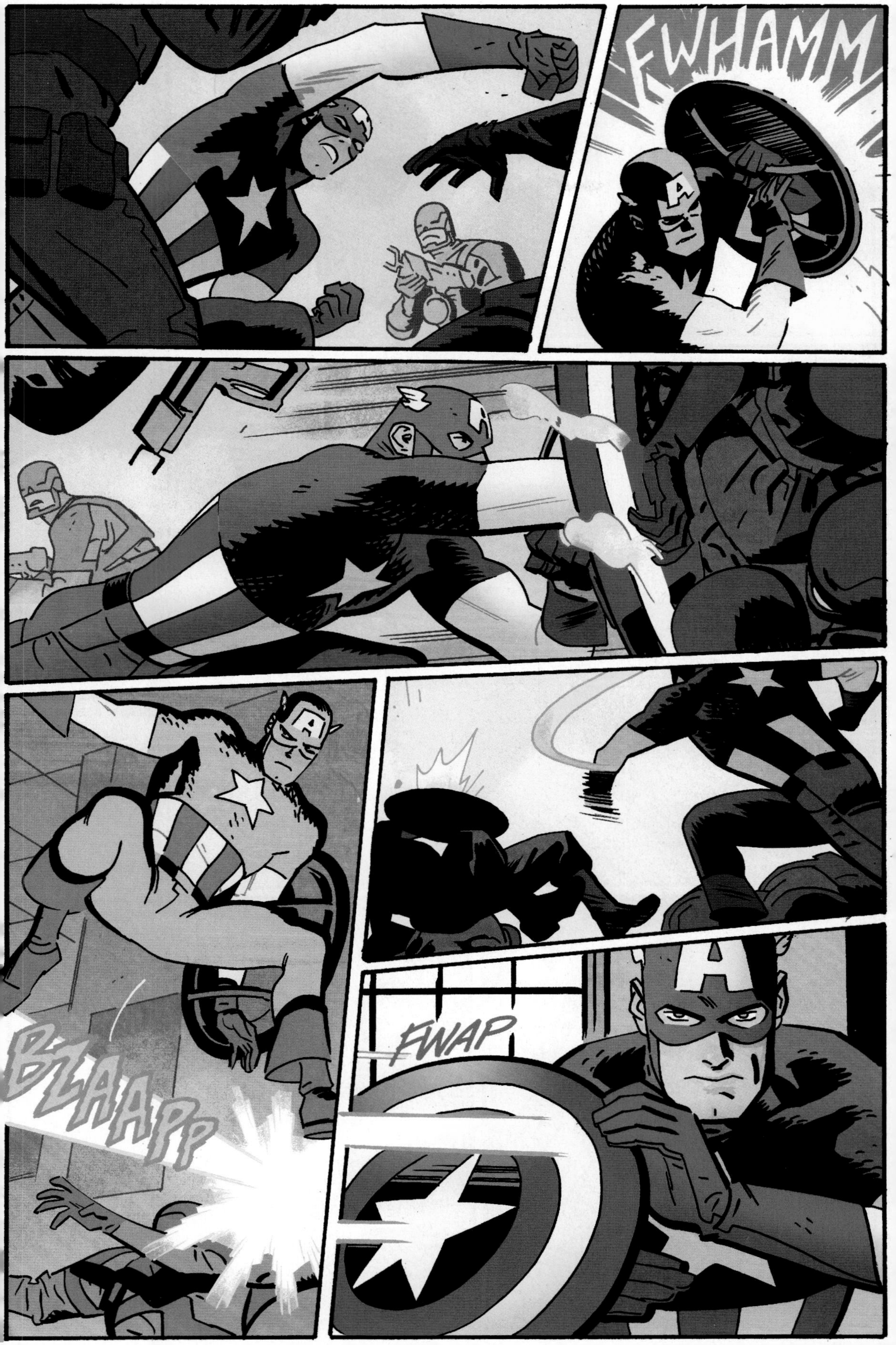

FWHAMM
BZLAAPP
FWAP

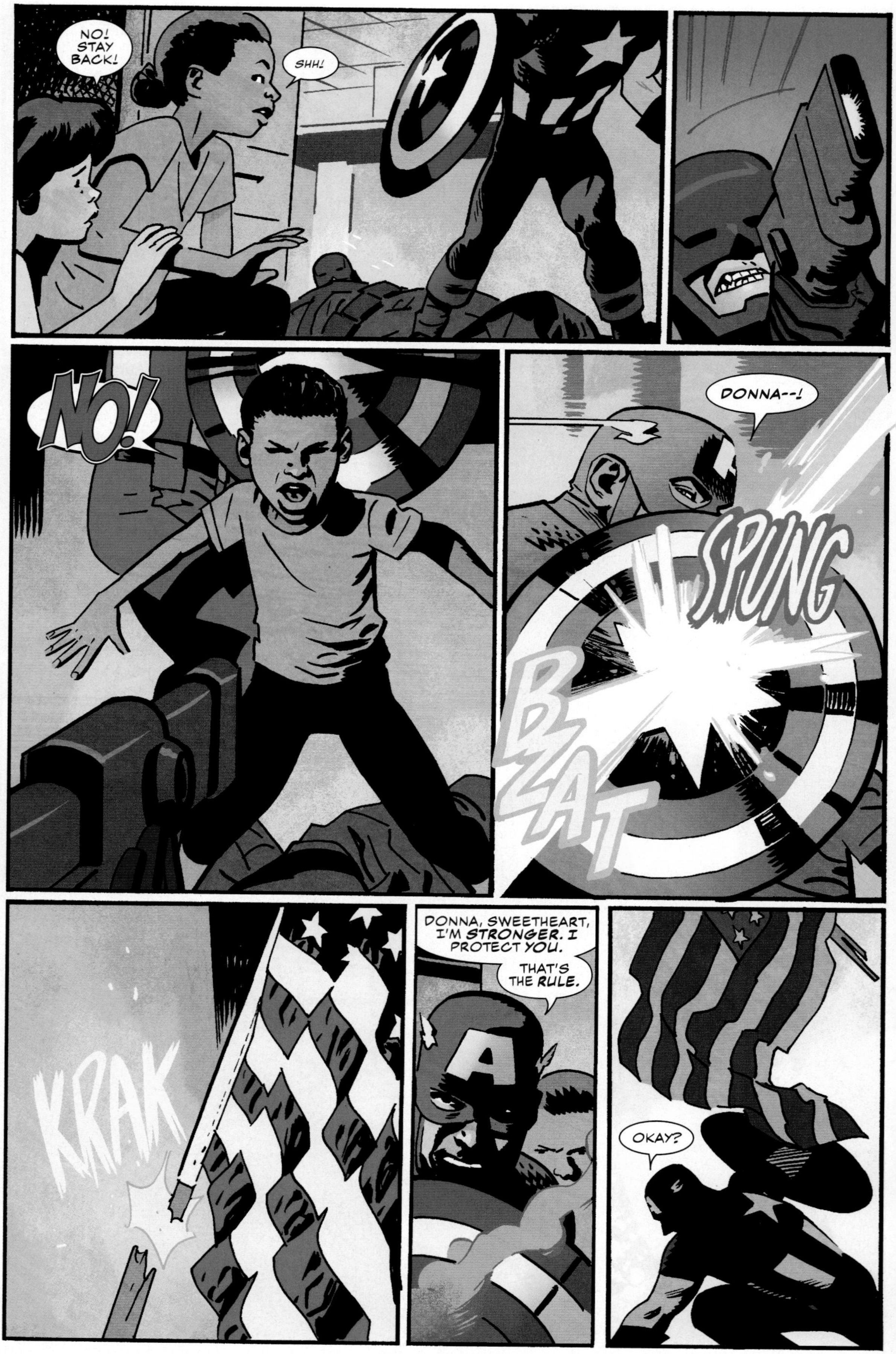
NO! STAY BACK!
SHH!
NO!
DONNA--!
SPUNG
BLAT
KRAK
DONNA, SWEETHEART, I'M STRONGER. I PROTECT YOU.
THAT'S THE RULE.
OKAY?

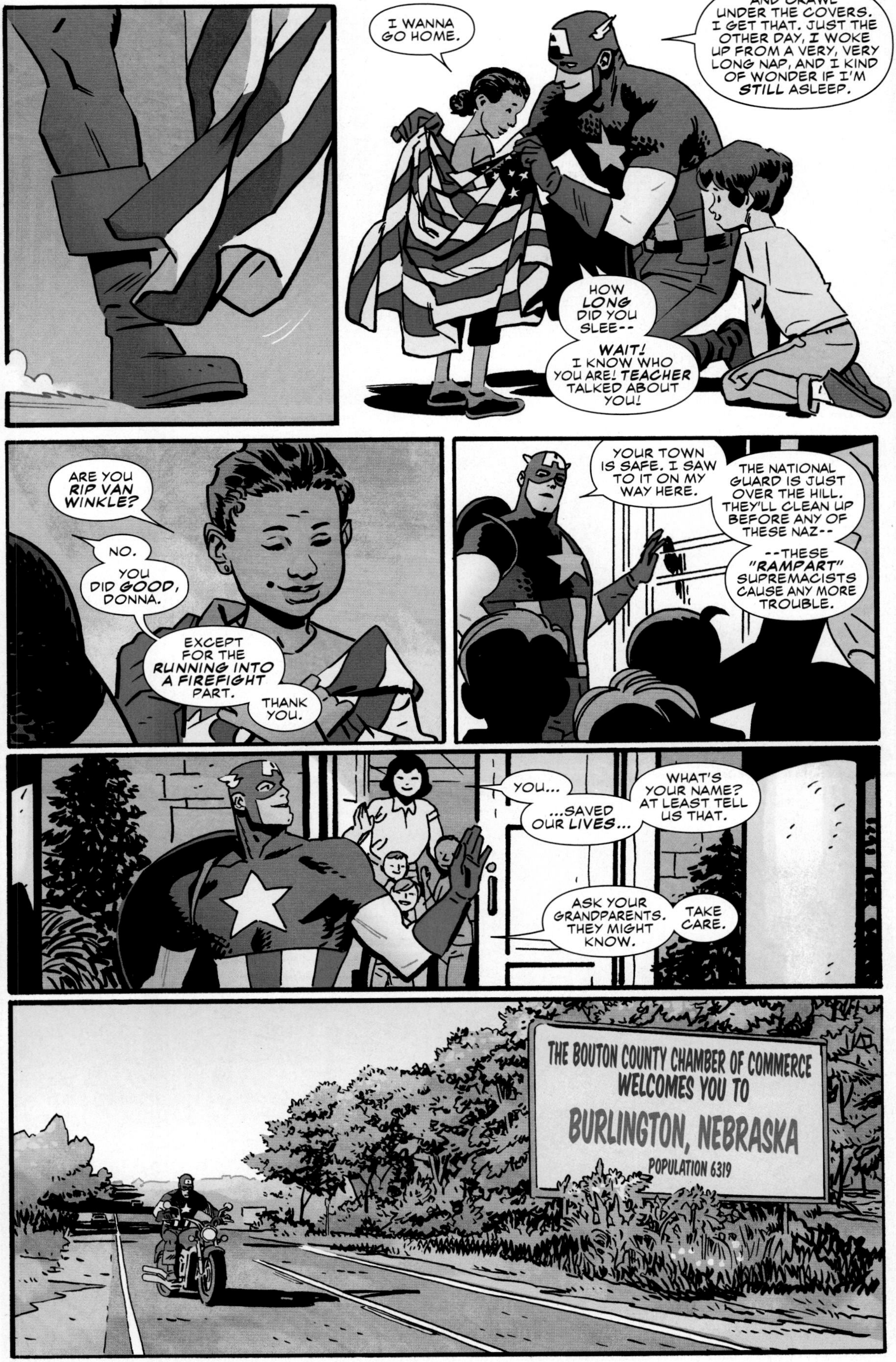
I WANNA GO HOME.
AND CRAWL UNDER THE COVERS. I GET THAT. JUST THE OTHER DAY, I WOKE UP FROM A VERY, VERY LONG NAP, AND I KIND OF WONDER IF I'M STILL ASLEEP.
HOW LONG DID YOU SLEE--
WAIT! I KNOW WHO YOU ARE! TEACHER TALKED ABOUT YOU!
ARE YOU RIP VAN WINKLE?
NO.
YOU DID GOOD, DONNA.
EXCEPT FOR THE RUNNING INTO A FIREFIGHT PART.
THANK YOU.
YOUR TOWN IS SAFE. I SAW TO IT ON MY WAY HERE.
THE NATIONAL GUARD IS JUST OVER THE HILL. THEY'LL CLEAN UP BEFORE ANY OF THESE NAZ--
--THESE "RAMPART" SUPREMACISTS CAUSE ANY MORE TROUBLE.
YOU...
...SAVED OUR LIVES...
WHAT'S YOUR NAME? AT LEAST TELL US THAT.
ASK YOUR GRANDPARENTS. THEY MIGHT KNOW.
TAKE CARE.
THE BOUTON COUNTY CHAMBER OF COMMERCE
WELCOMES YOU TO
BURLINGTON, NEBRASKA
POPULATION 6319

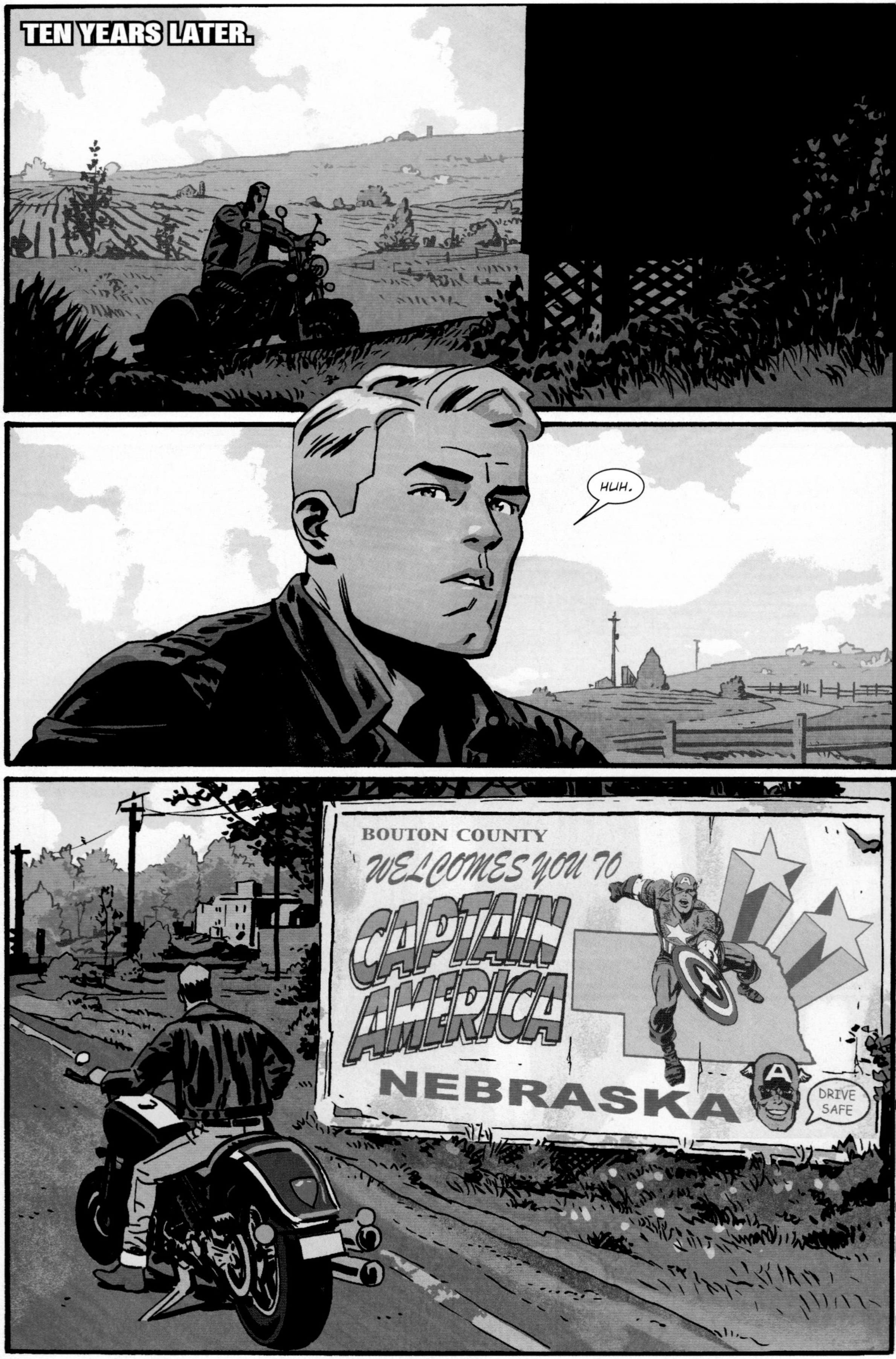
TEN YEARS LATER.
HUH.
BOUTON COUNTY
WELCOMES YOU TO
CAPTAIN AMERICA
NEBRASKA
DRIVE SAFE

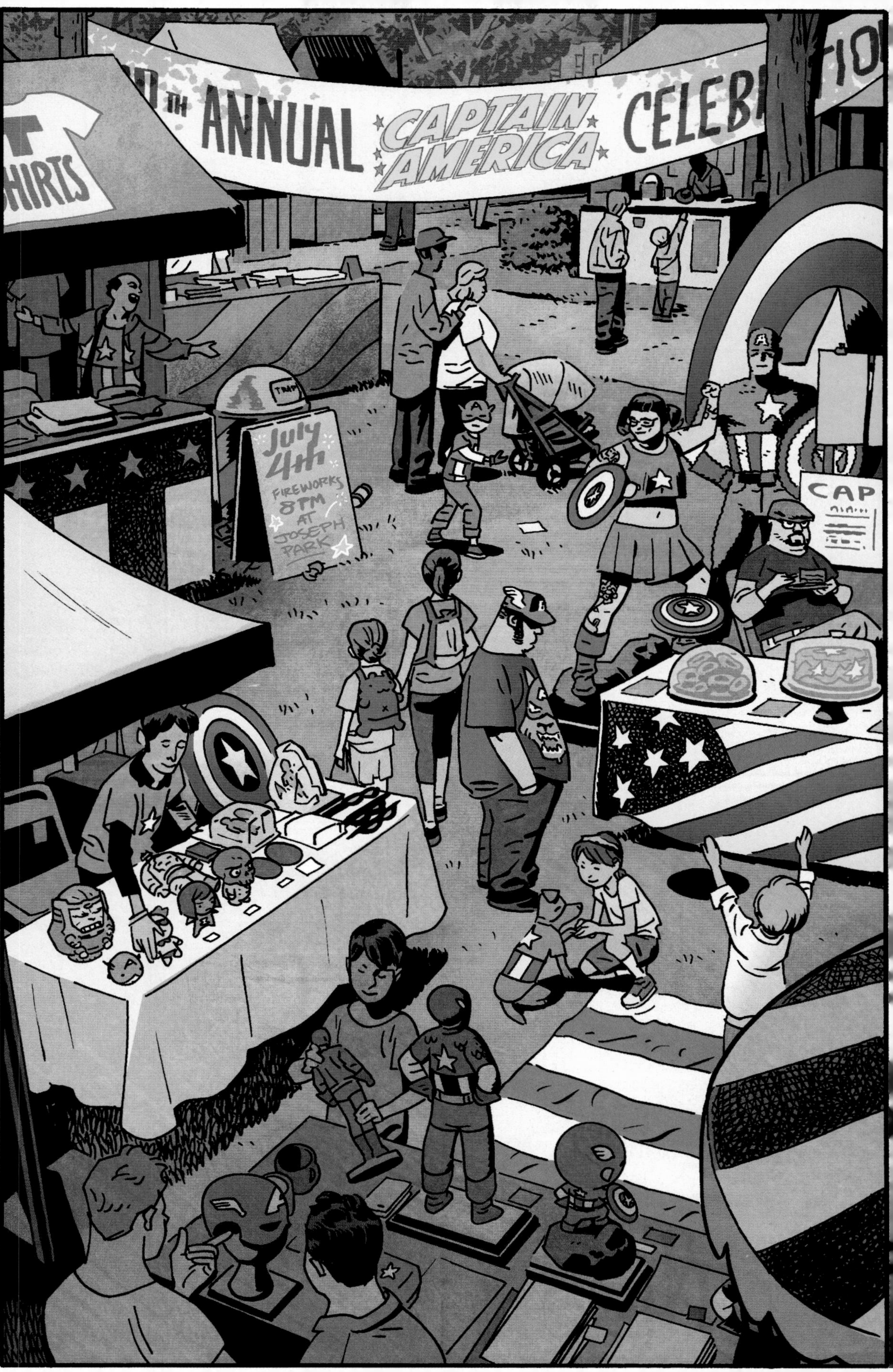
TH ANNUAL CAPTAIN AMERICA CELEB
HIRTS
July 4th
FIREWORKS 8PM AT JOSEPH PARK
CAP

CLANK

ANNUAL *CAPTAIN AMERICA* CELEBR—

WOW.

YOU'RE *HIM*.

PARDON?

AWESOME *COSPLAY*, "STEVE." YOU SHOULD CHECK OUT THE *CONTEST* AT *NOON*.

CAPTAIN AMERICA MUSEUM AND GIFT SHOP

THERE'S A *CONTEST*?

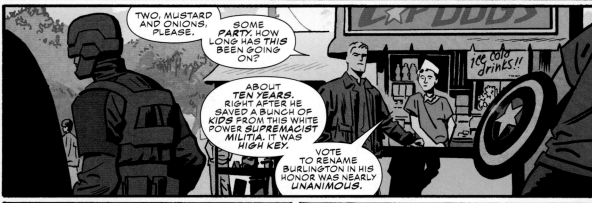

TWO, MUSTARD AND ONIONS, PLEASE.

SOME *PARTY*. HOW LONG HAS *THIS* BEEN GOING ON?

ABOUT *TEN YEARS*. RIGHT AFTER HE SAVED A BUNCH OF *KIDS* FROM THIS WHITE POWER *SUPREMACIST MILITIA*. IT WAS *HIGH KEY*.

VOTE TO RENAME BURLINGTON IN HIS HONOR WAS NEARLY *UNANIMOUS*.

HUH.

IS THIS RIGHT AFTER HE CAME OUT OF THE *ICE*?

OH. YOU'RE AN *ICER*. GOTCHA.

"*ICER*"?

BELIEVES THAT STUFF ABOUT THE AVENGERS FINDING HIM *FROZEN*.

AS OPPOSED TO...?

WELL, C'MON. THAT'S LIKE *ABRAHAM LINCOLN* WAKING UP. EXCEPT KIDS HAD *HEARD* OF LINCOLN.

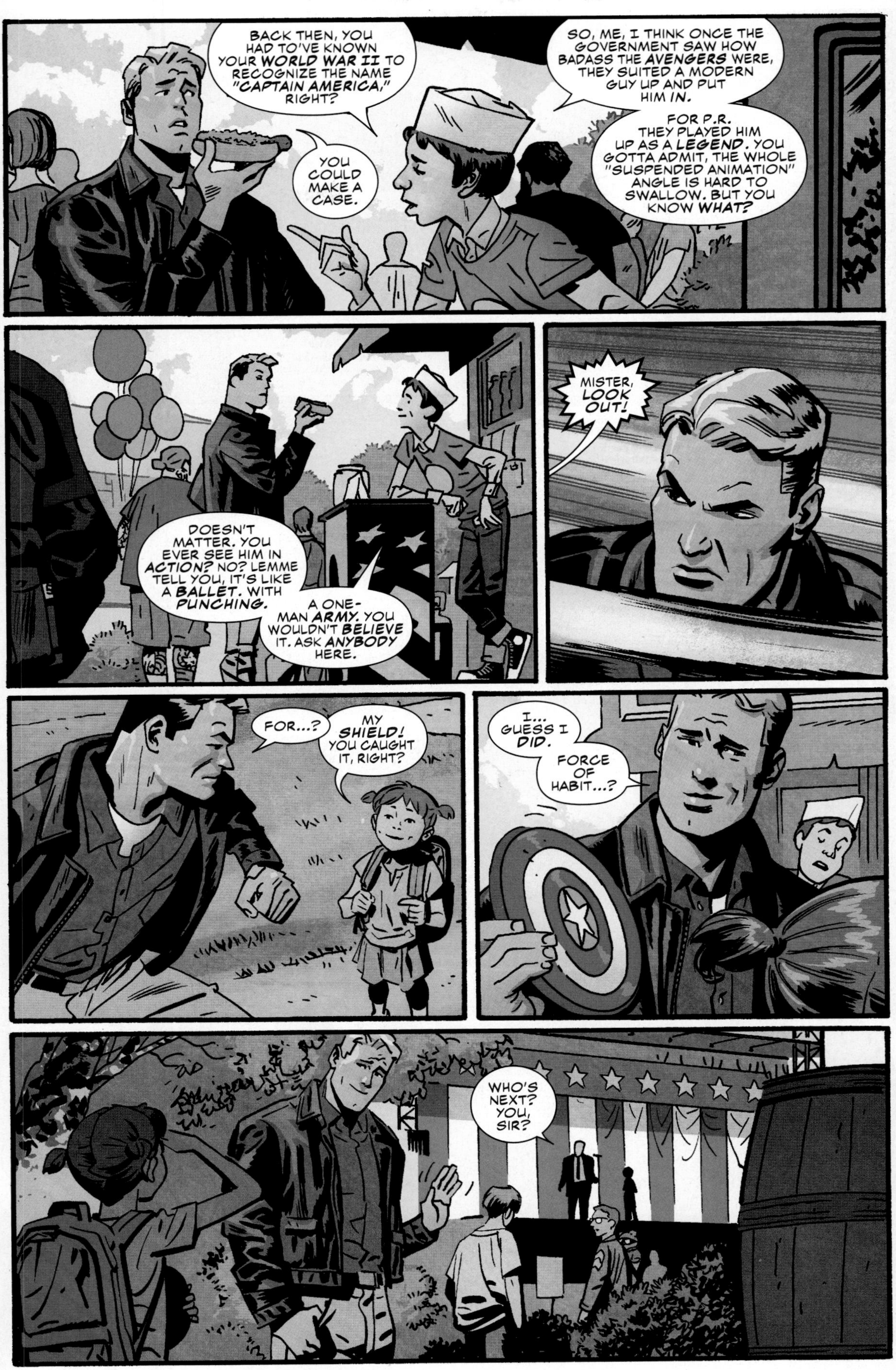
BACK THEN, YOU HAD TO'VE KNOWN YOUR WORLD WAR II TO RECOGNIZE THE NAME "CAPTAIN AMERICA," RIGHT?
YOU COULD MAKE A CASE.
SO, ME, I THINK ONCE THE GOVERNMENT SAW HOW BADASS THE AVENGERS WERE, THEY SUITED A MODERN GUY UP AND PUT HIM IN.
FOR P.R. THEY PLAYED HIM UP AS A LEGEND. YOU GOTTA ADMIT, THE WHOLE "SUSPENDED ANIMATION" ANGLE IS HARD TO SWALLOW. BUT YOU KNOW WHAT?
DOESN'T MATTER. YOU EVER SEE HIM IN ACTION? NO? LEMME TELL YOU, IT'S LIKE A BALLET. WITH PUNCHING.
A ONE-MAN ARMY. YOU WOULDN'T BELIEVE IT. ASK ANYBODY HERE.
MISTER, LOOK OUT!
FOR...?
MY SHIELD! YOU CAUGHT IT, RIGHT?
I... GUESS I DID.
FORCE OF HABIT...?
WHO'S NEXT? YOU, SIR?

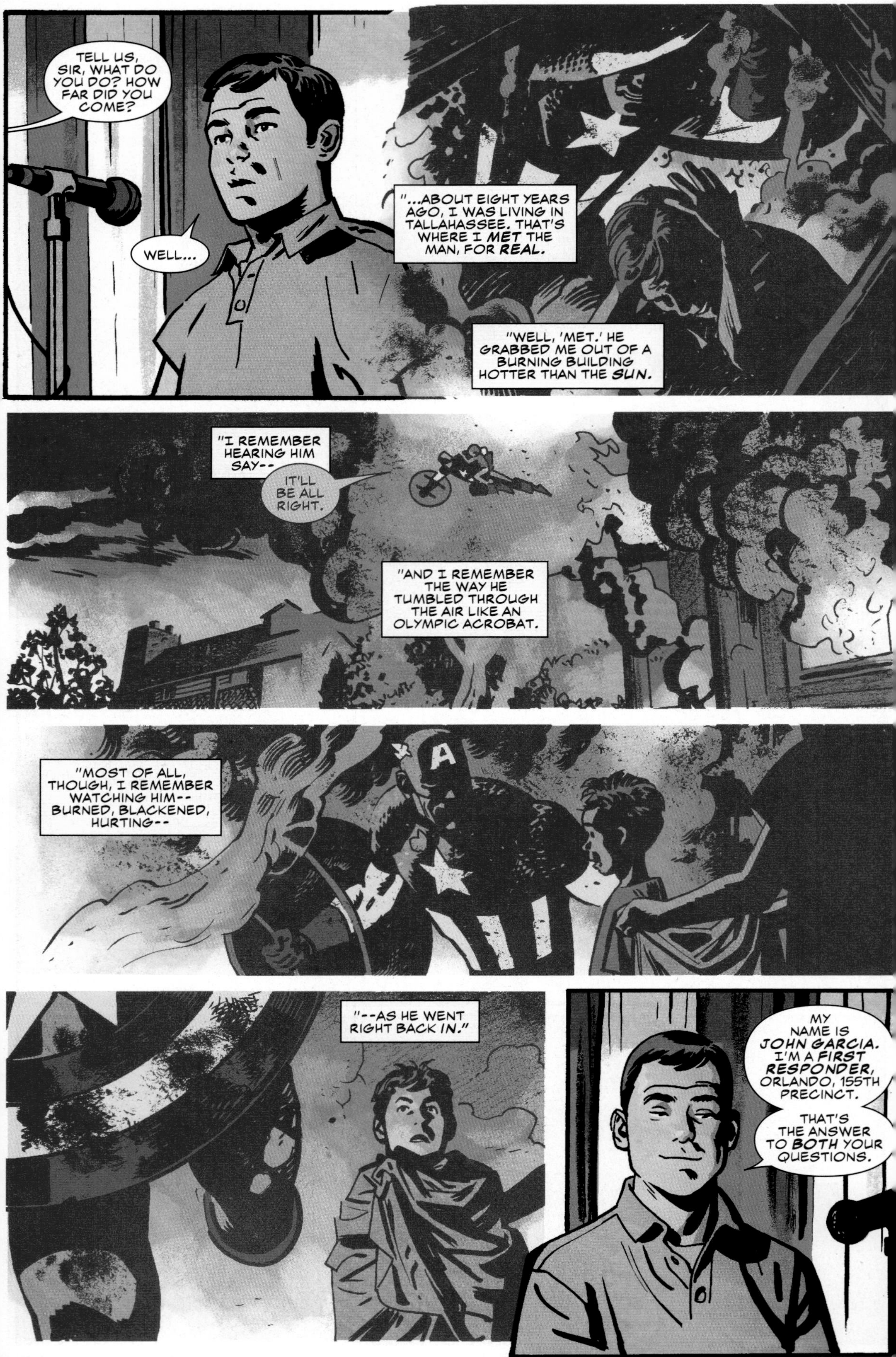
TELL US, SIR, WHAT DO YOU DO? HOW FAR DID YOU COME?
WELL...
"...ABOUT EIGHT YEARS AGO, I WAS LIVING IN TALLAHASSEE. THAT'S WHERE I MET THE MAN, FOR REAL.
"WELL, 'MET.' HE GRABBED ME OUT OF A BURNING BUILDING HOTTER THAN THE SUN.
"I REMEMBER HEARING HIM SAY--
IT'LL BE ALL RIGHT.
"AND I REMEMBER THE WAY HE TUMBLED THROUGH THE AIR LIKE AN OLYMPIC ACROBAT.
"MOST OF ALL, THOUGH, I REMEMBER WATCHING HIM-- BURNED, BLACKENED, HURTING--
"--AS HE WENT RIGHT BACK IN."
MY NAME IS JOHN GARCIA. I'M A FIRST RESPONDER, ORLANDO, 155TH PRECINCT.
THAT'S THE ANSWER TO BOTH YOUR QUESTIONS.

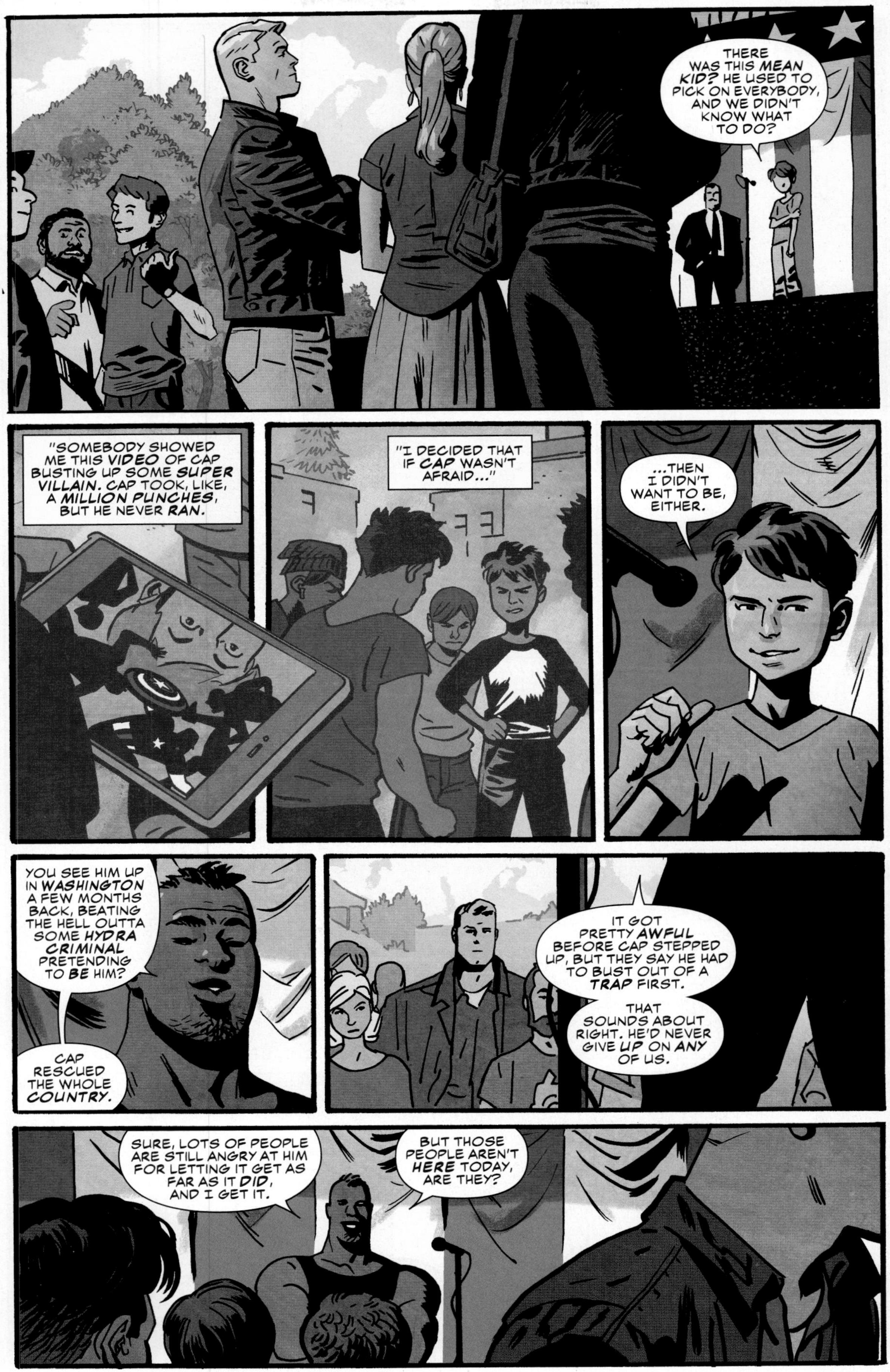
THERE WAS THIS MEAN KID? HE USED TO PICK ON EVERYBODY, AND WE DIDN'T KNOW WHAT TO DO?
"SOMEBODY SHOWED ME THIS VIDEO OF CAP BUSTING UP SOME SUPER VILLAIN. CAP TOOK, LIKE, A MILLION PUNCHES, BUT HE NEVER RAN.
"I DECIDED THAT IF CAP WASN'T AFRAID..."
...THEN I DIDN'T WANT TO BE, EITHER.
YOU SEE HIM UP IN WASHINGTON A FEW MONTHS BACK, BEATING THE HELL OUTTA SOME HYDRA CRIMINAL PRETENDING TO BE HIM?
CAP RESCUED THE WHOLE COUNTRY.
IT GOT PRETTY AWFUL BEFORE CAP STEPPED UP, BUT THEY SAY HE HAD TO BUST OUT OF A TRAP FIRST.
THAT SOUNDS ABOUT RIGHT. HE'D NEVER GIVE UP ON ANY OF US.
SURE, LOTS OF PEOPLE ARE STILL ANGRY AT HIM FOR LETTING IT GET AS FAR AS IT DID, AND I GET IT.
BUT THOSE PEOPLE AREN'T HERE TODAY, ARE THEY?

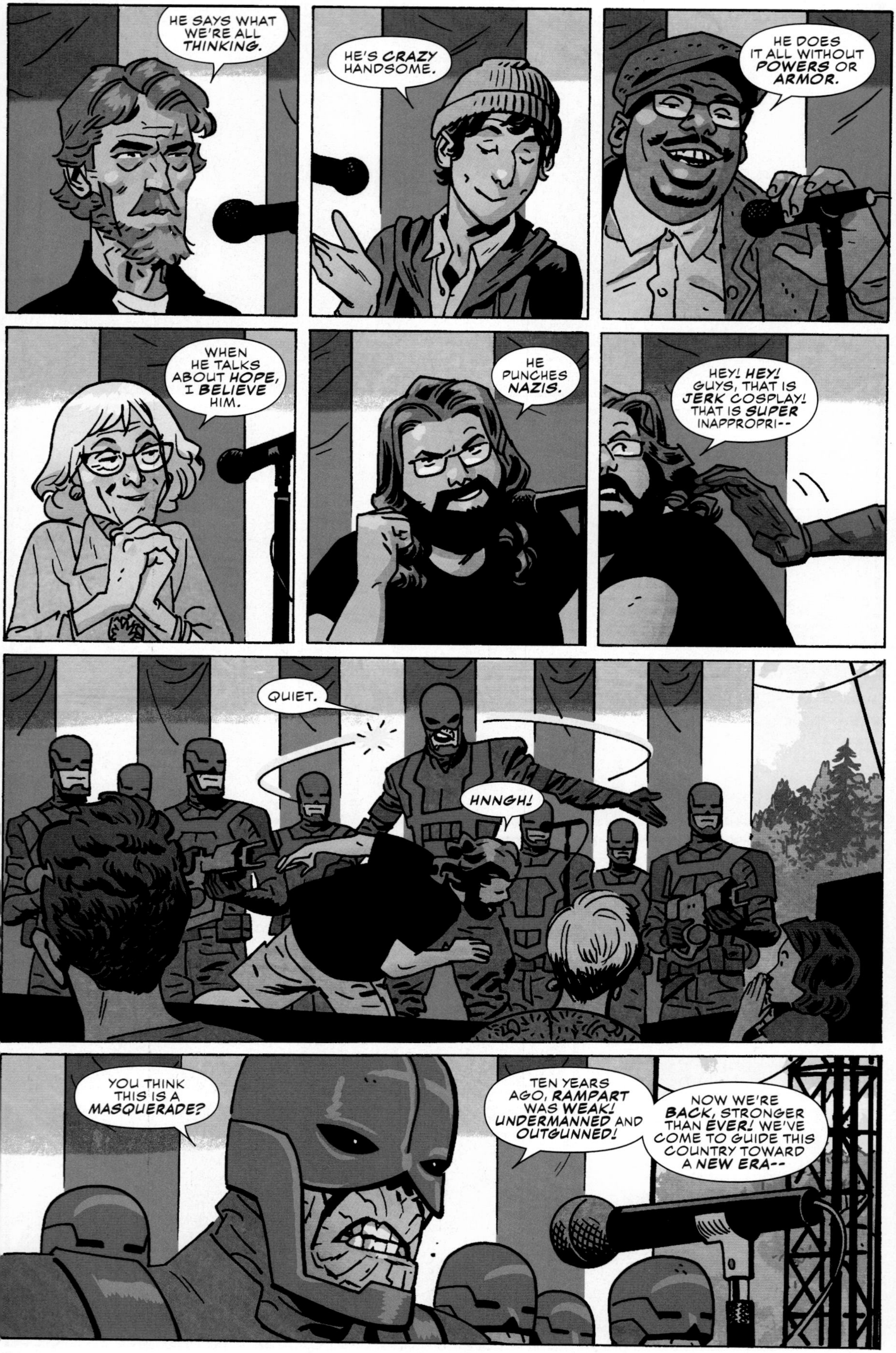
HE SAYS WHAT WE'RE ALL THINKING.
HE'S CRAZY HANDSOME.
HE DOES IT ALL WITHOUT POWERS OR ARMOR.
WHEN HE TALKS ABOUT HOPE, I BELIEVE HIM.
HE PUNCHES NAZIS.
HEY! HEY! GUYS, THAT IS JERK COSPLAY! THAT IS SUPER INAPPROPRI--
QUIET.
HNNGH!
YOU THINK THIS IS A MASQUERADE?
TEN YEARS AGO, RAMPART WAS WEAK! UNDERMANNED AND OUTGUNNED!
NOW WE'RE BACK, STRONGER THAN EVER! WE'VE COME TO GUIDE THIS COUNTRY TOWARD A NEW ERA--

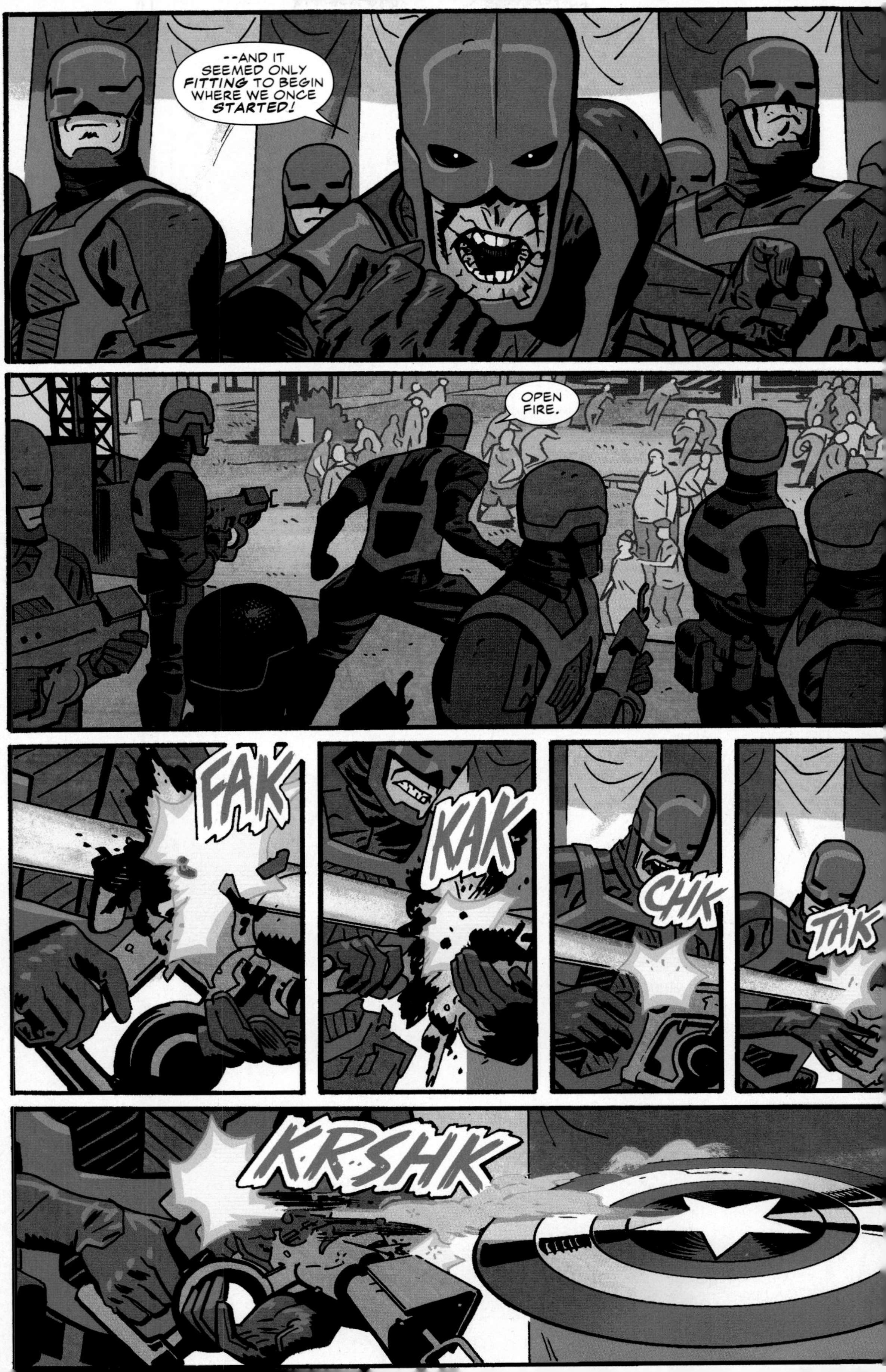
--AND IT SEEMED ONLY FITTING TO BEGIN WHERE WE ONCE STARTED!
OPEN FIRE.
FAK
KAK
CHK
TAK
KRSHK

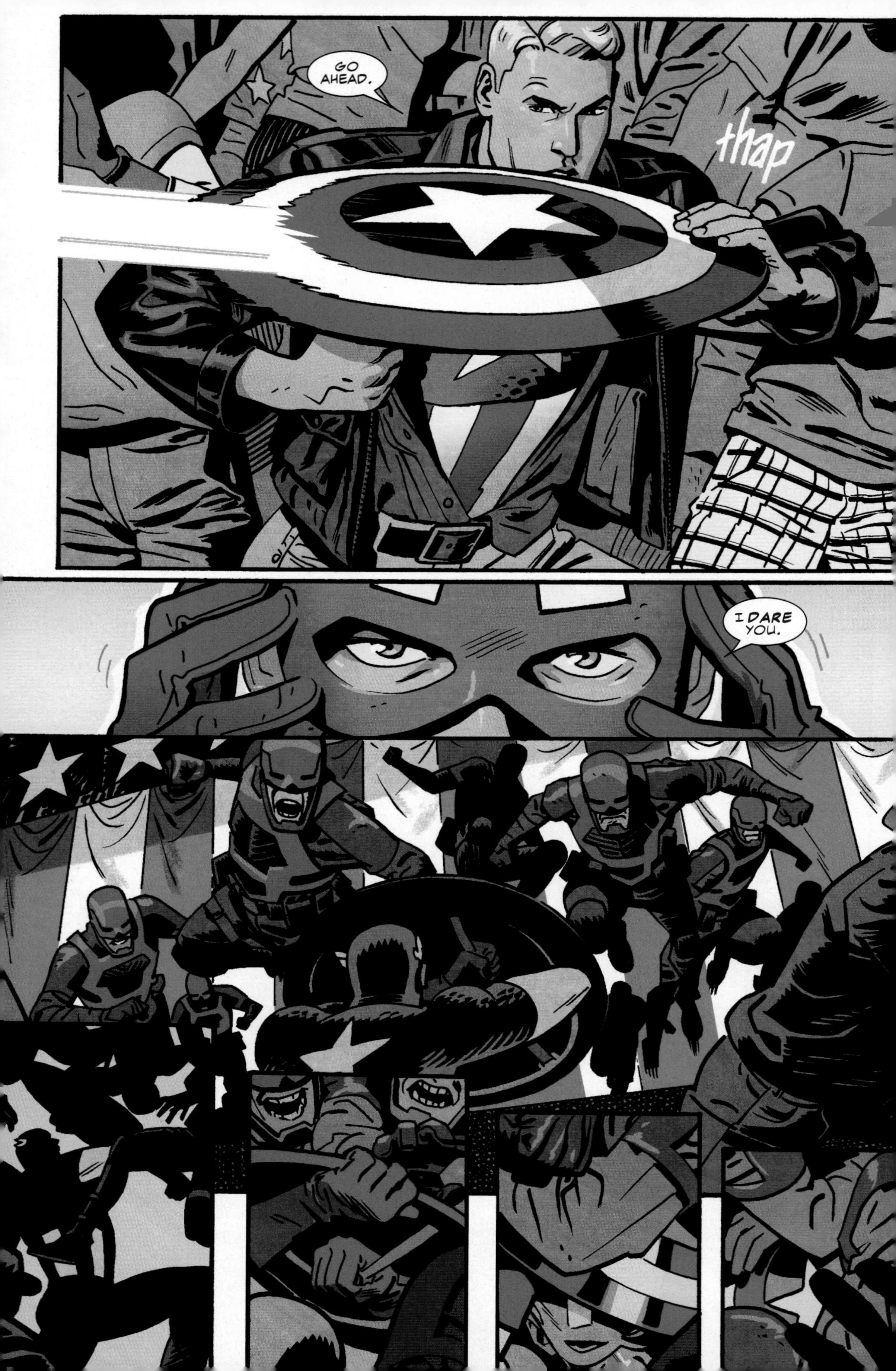
GO AHEAD.
thap
I DARE YOU.

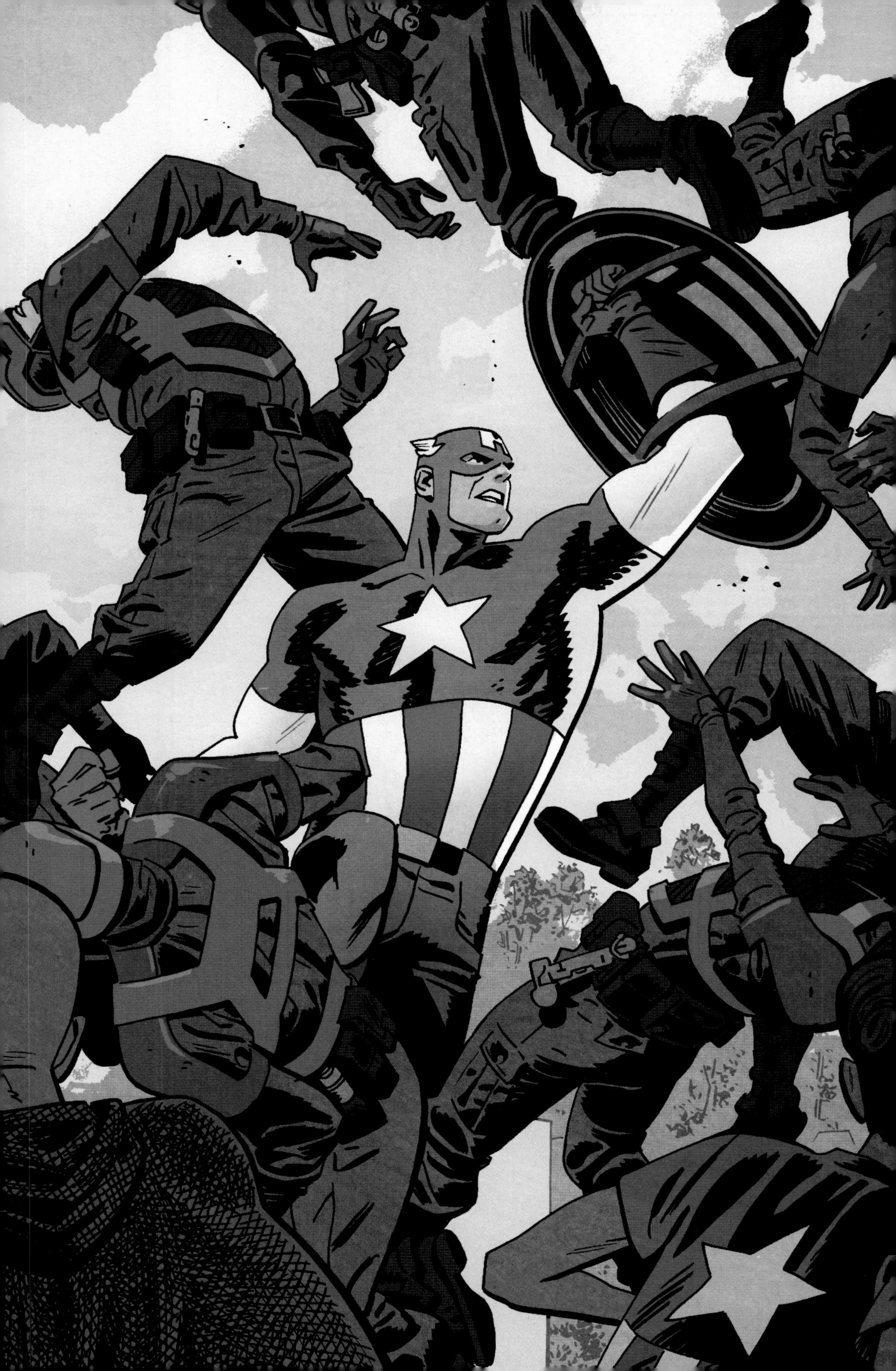

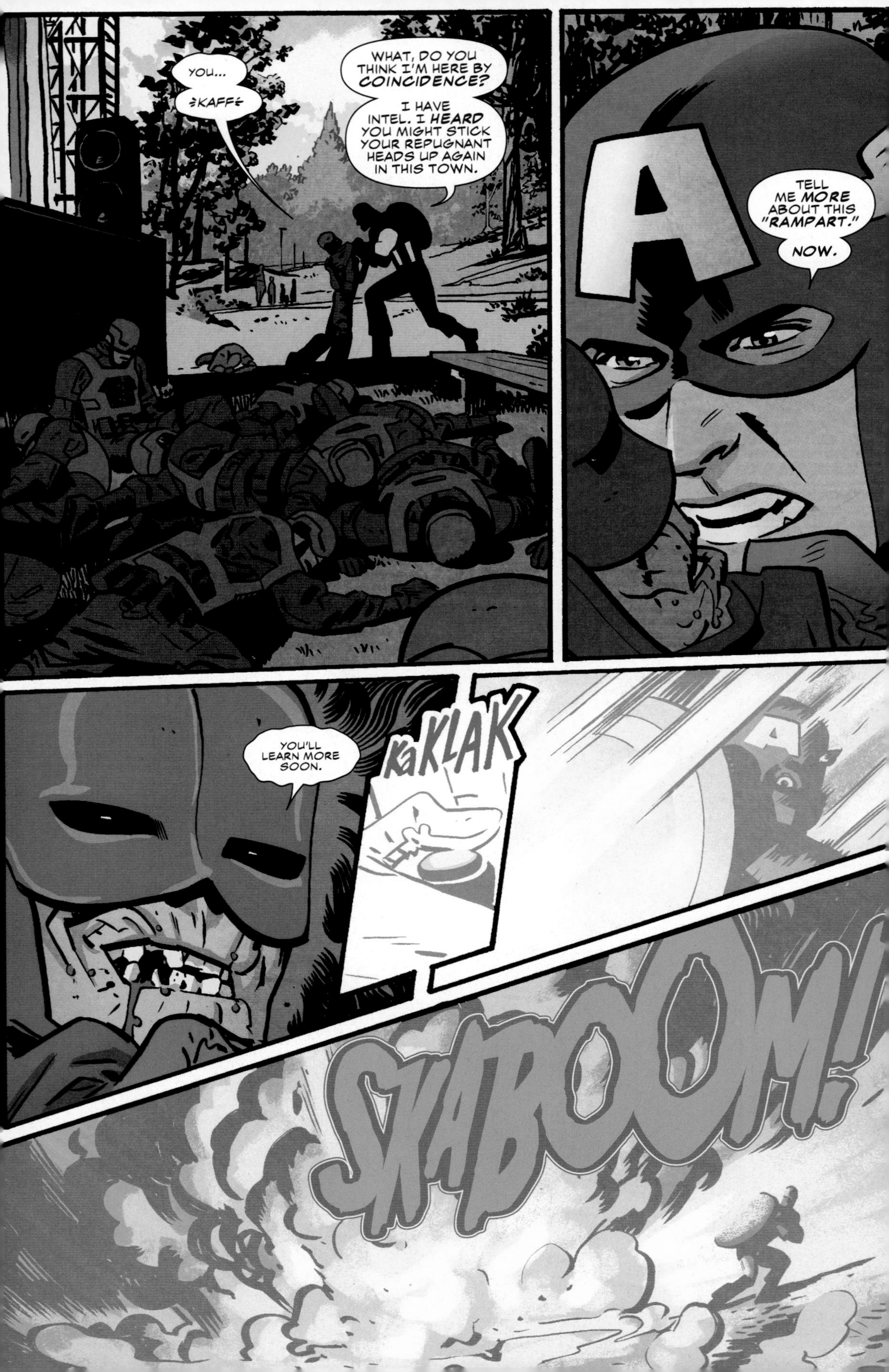
YOU... =KAFF=
WHAT, DO YOU THINK I'M HERE BY COINCIDENCE?
I HAVE INTEL. I HEARD YOU MIGHT STICK YOUR REPUGNANT HEADS UP AGAIN IN THIS TOWN.
TELL ME MORE ABOUT THIS "RAMPART."
NOW.
YOU'LL LEARN MORE SOON.
KaKLAK
SKABOOM!

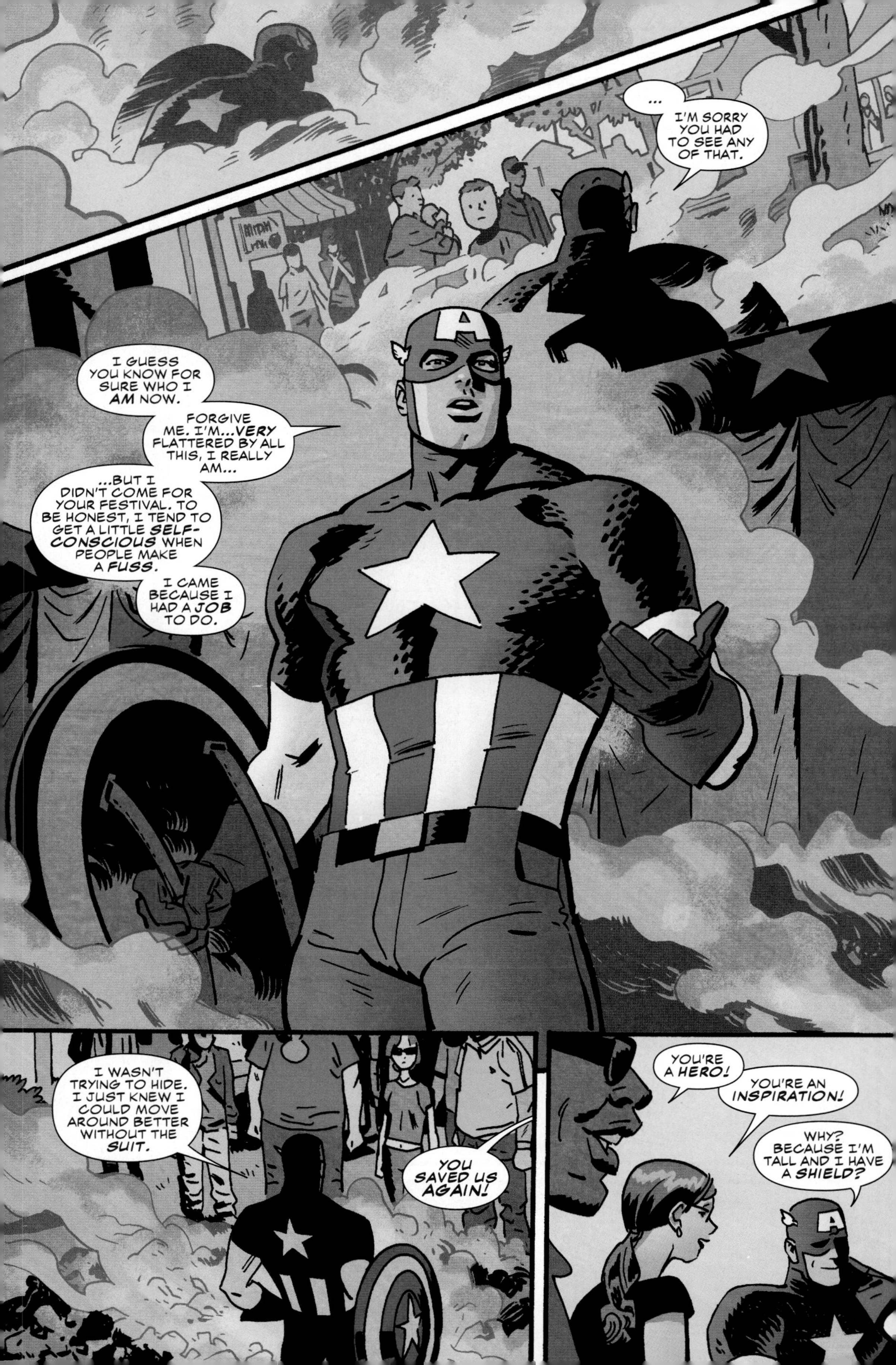
...
I'M SORRY YOU HAD TO SEE ANY OF THAT.
I GUESS YOU KNOW FOR SURE WHO I AM NOW.
FORGIVE ME. I'M...VERY FLATTERED BY ALL THIS, I REALLY AM...
...BUT I DIDN'T COME FOR YOUR FESTIVAL. TO BE HONEST, I TEND TO GET A LITTLE SELF-CONSCIOUS WHEN PEOPLE MAKE A FUSS.
I CAME BECAUSE I HAD A JOB TO DO.
I WASN'T TRYING TO HIDE. I JUST KNEW I COULD MOVE AROUND BETTER WITHOUT THE SUIT.
YOU SAVED US AGAIN!
YOU'RE A HERO!
YOU'RE AN INSPIRATION!
WHY? BECAUSE I'M TALL AND I HAVE A SHIELD?

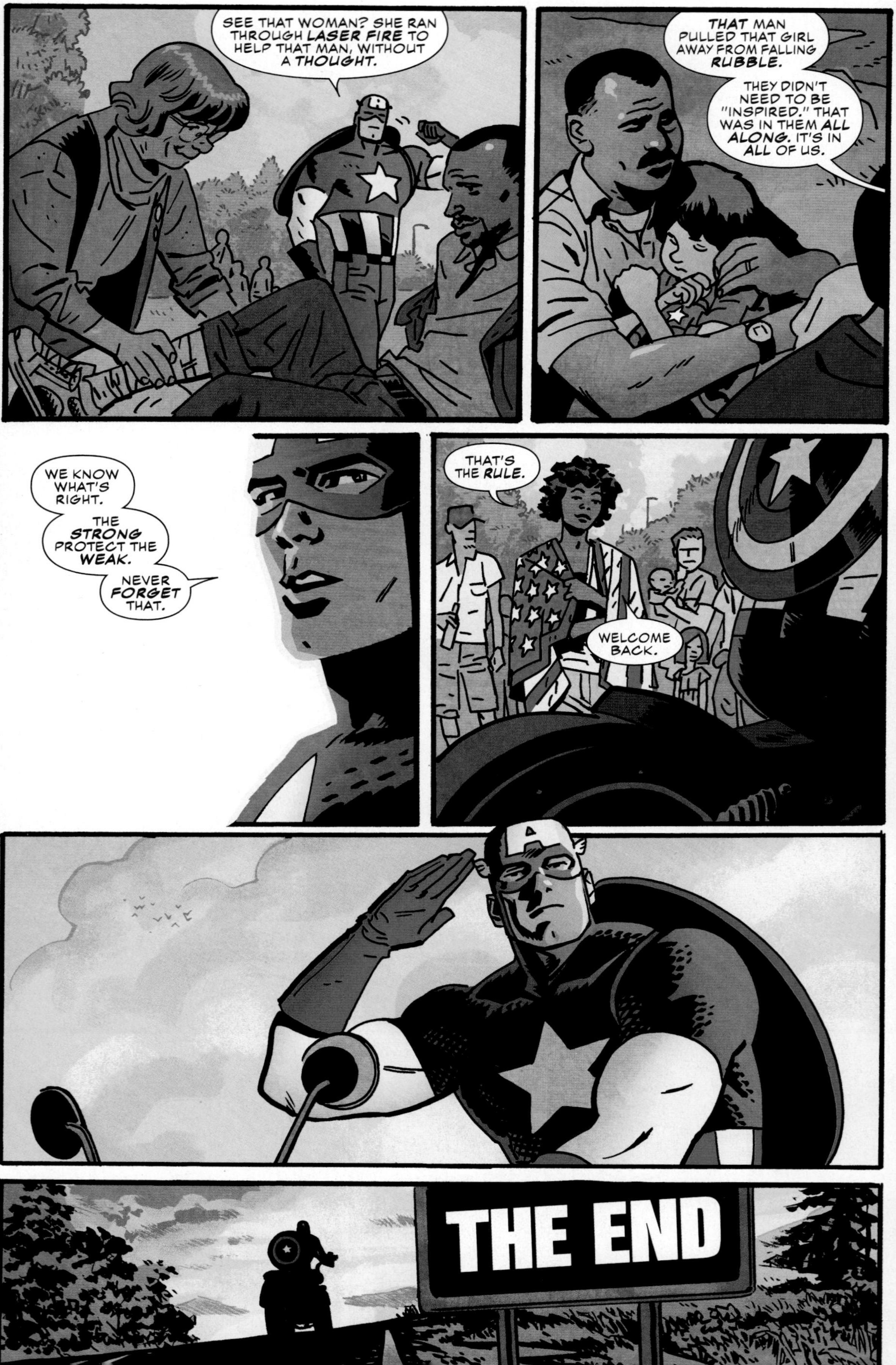

SEE THAT WOMAN? SHE RAN THROUGH LASER FIRE TO HELP THAT MAN, WITHOUT A THOUGHT.
THAT MAN PULLED THAT GIRL AWAY FROM FALLING RUBBLE.
THEY DIDN'T NEED TO BE "INSPIRED." THAT WAS IN THEM ALL ALONG. IT'S IN ALL OF US.
WE KNOW WHAT'S RIGHT.
THE STRONG PROTECT THE WEAK.
NEVER FORGET THAT.
THAT'S THE RULE.
WELCOME BACK.
THE END

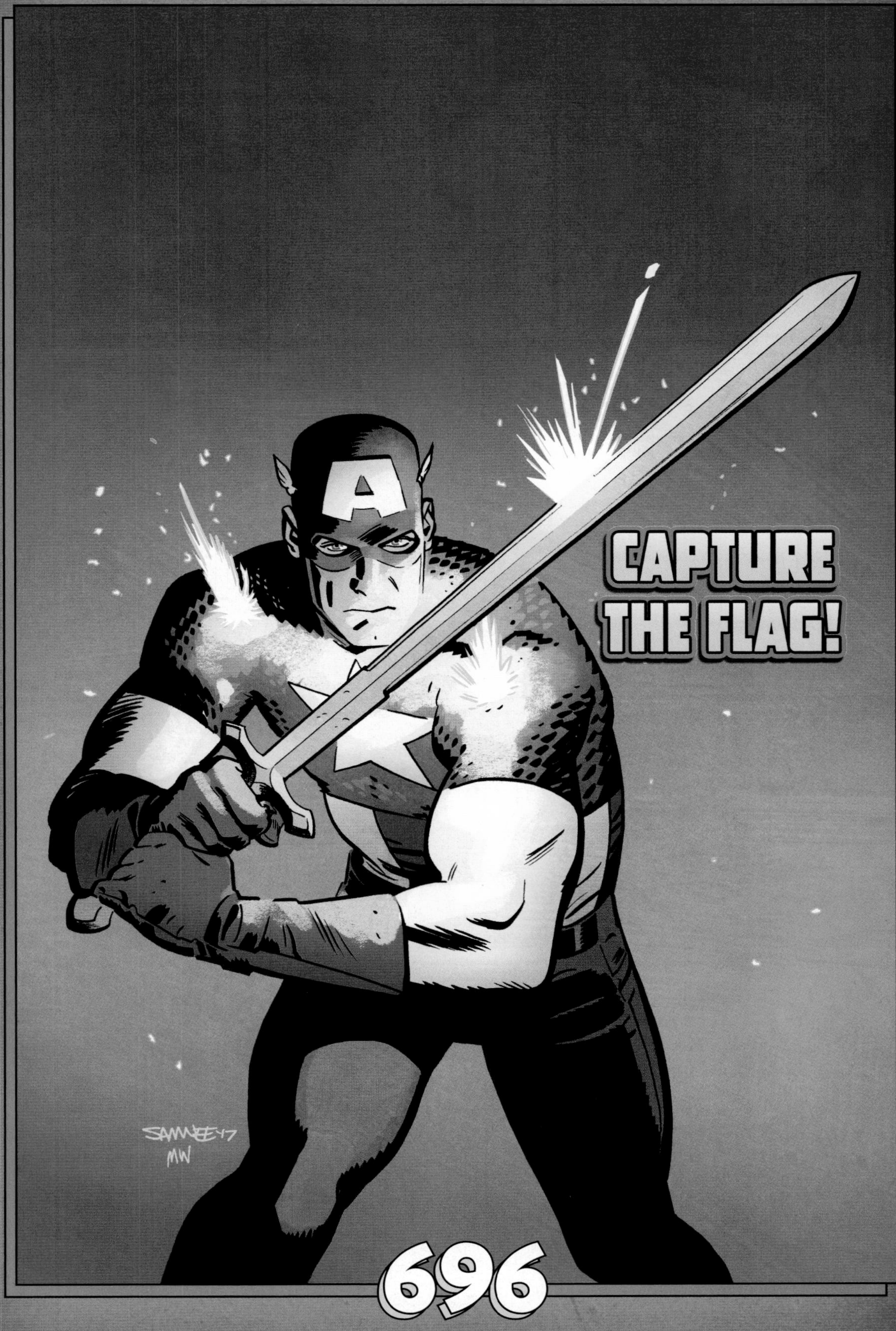
CAPTURE THE FLAG!
SAMNEE '17
MW
696

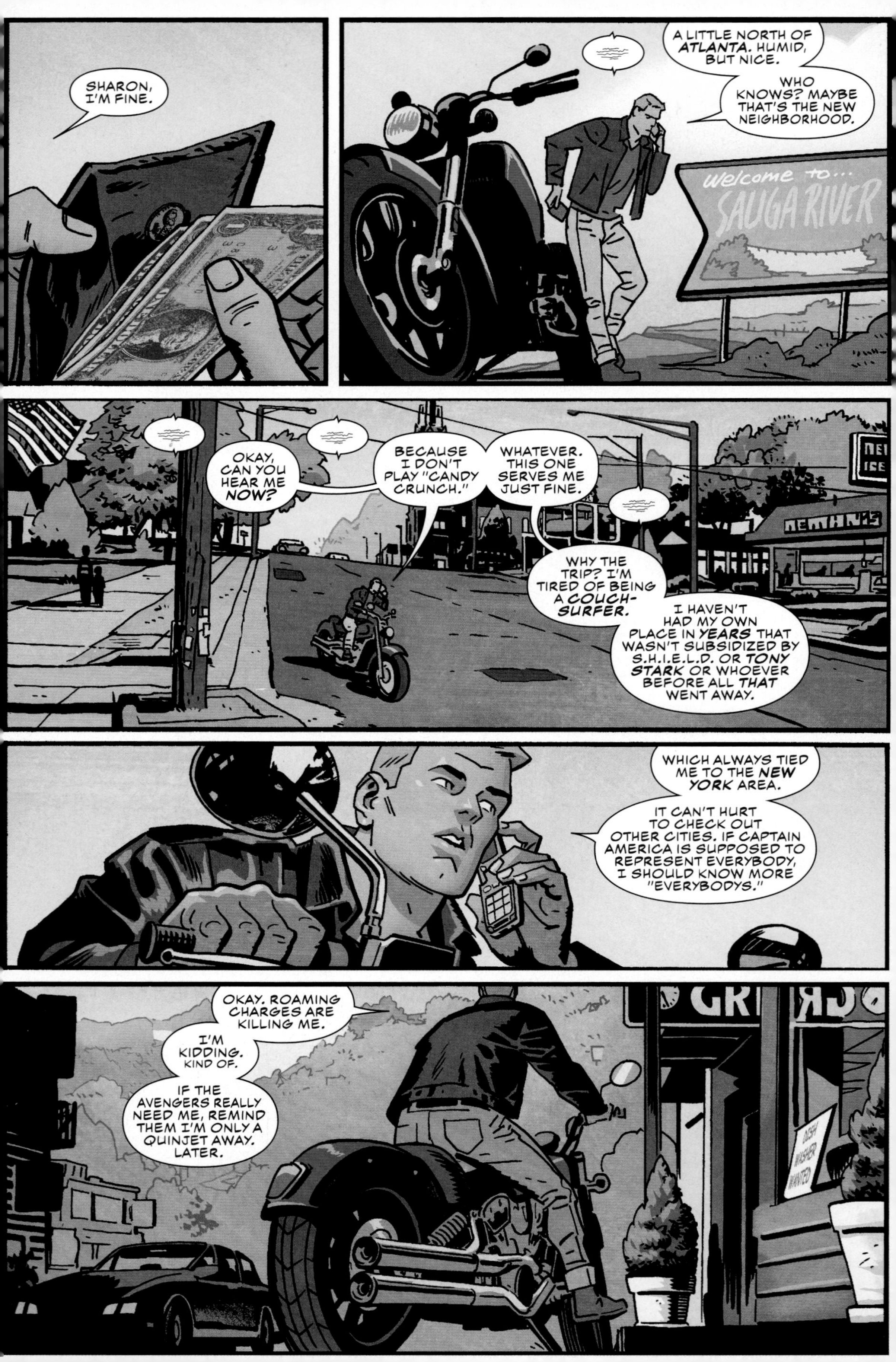
SHARON, I'M FINE.
A LITTLE NORTH OF ATLANTA. HUMID, BUT NICE.
WHO KNOWS? MAYBE THAT'S THE NEW NEIGHBORHOOD.
Welcome to... SAUGA RIVER
OKAY, CAN YOU HEAR ME NOW?
BECAUSE I DON'T PLAY "CANDY CRUNCH."
WHATEVER. THIS ONE SERVES ME JUST FINE.
WHY THE TRIP? I'M TIRED OF BEING A COUCH-SURFER.
I HAVEN'T HAD MY OWN PLACE IN YEARS THAT WASN'T SUBSIDIZED BY S.H.I.E.L.D. OR TONY STARK OR WHOEVER BEFORE ALL THAT WENT AWAY.
WHICH ALWAYS TIED ME TO THE NEW YORK AREA.
IT CAN'T HURT TO CHECK OUT OTHER CITIES. IF CAPTAIN AMERICA IS SUPPOSED TO REPRESENT EVERYBODY, I SHOULD KNOW MORE "EVERYBODYS."
OKAY. ROAMING CHARGES ARE KILLING ME.
I'M KIDDING. KIND OF.
IF THE AVENGERS REALLY NEED ME, REMIND THEM I'M ONLY A QUINJET AWAY. LATER.
DISH WASHER WANTED

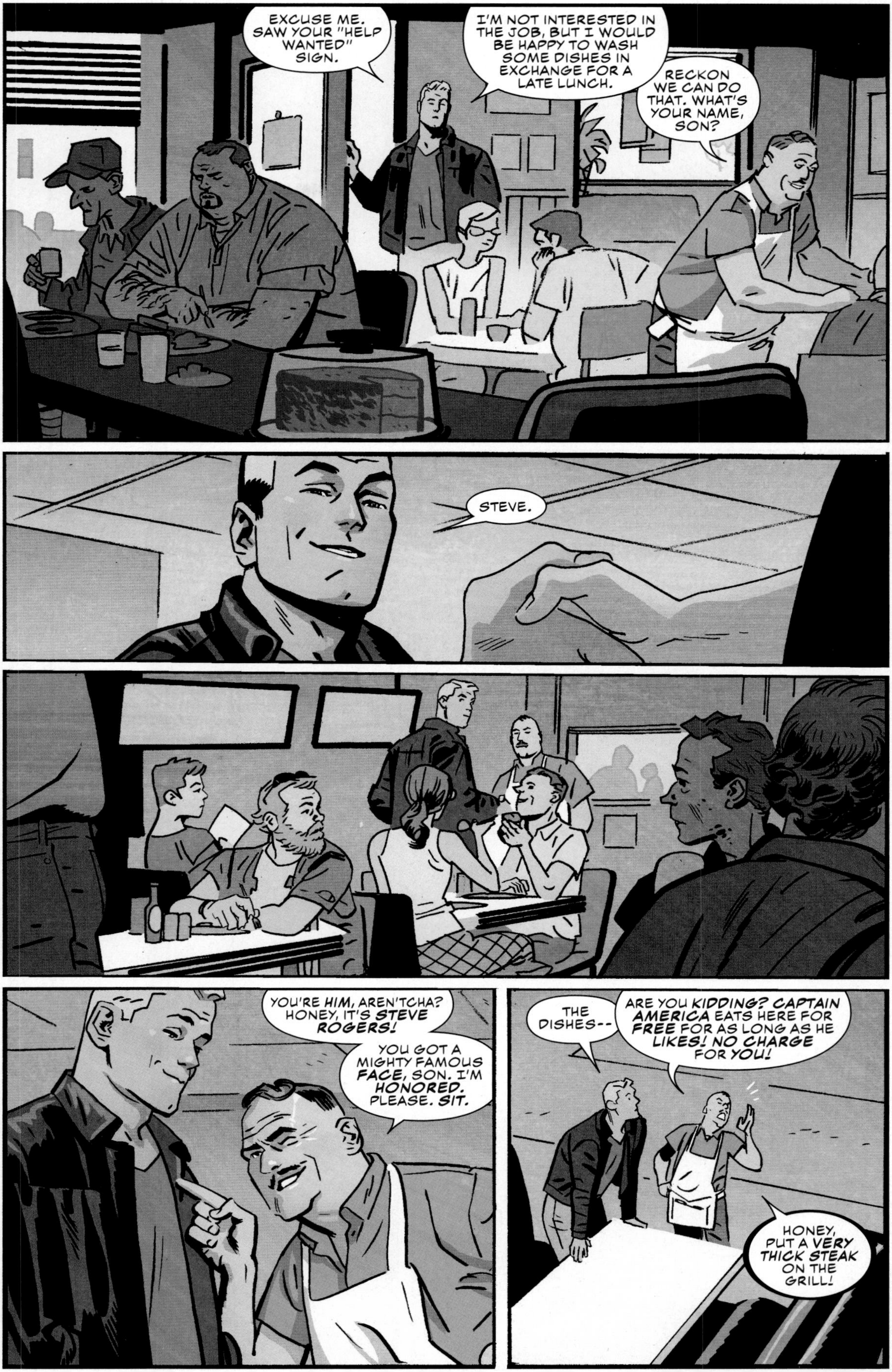

EXCUSE ME. SAW YOUR "HELP WANTED" SIGN.
I'M NOT INTERESTED IN THE JOB, BUT I WOULD BE HAPPY TO WASH SOME DISHES IN EXCHANGE FOR A LATE LUNCH.
RECKON WE CAN DO THAT. WHAT'S YOUR NAME, SON?
STEVE.
YOU'RE HIM, AREN'TCHA? HONEY, IT'S STEVE ROGERS!
YOU GOT A MIGHTY FAMOUS FACE, SON. I'M HONORED. PLEASE. SIT.
THE DISHES--
ARE YOU KIDDING? CAPTAIN AMERICA EATS HERE FOR FREE FOR AS LONG AS HE LIKES! NO CHARGE FOR YOU!
HONEY, PUT A VERY THICK STEAK ON THE GRILL!

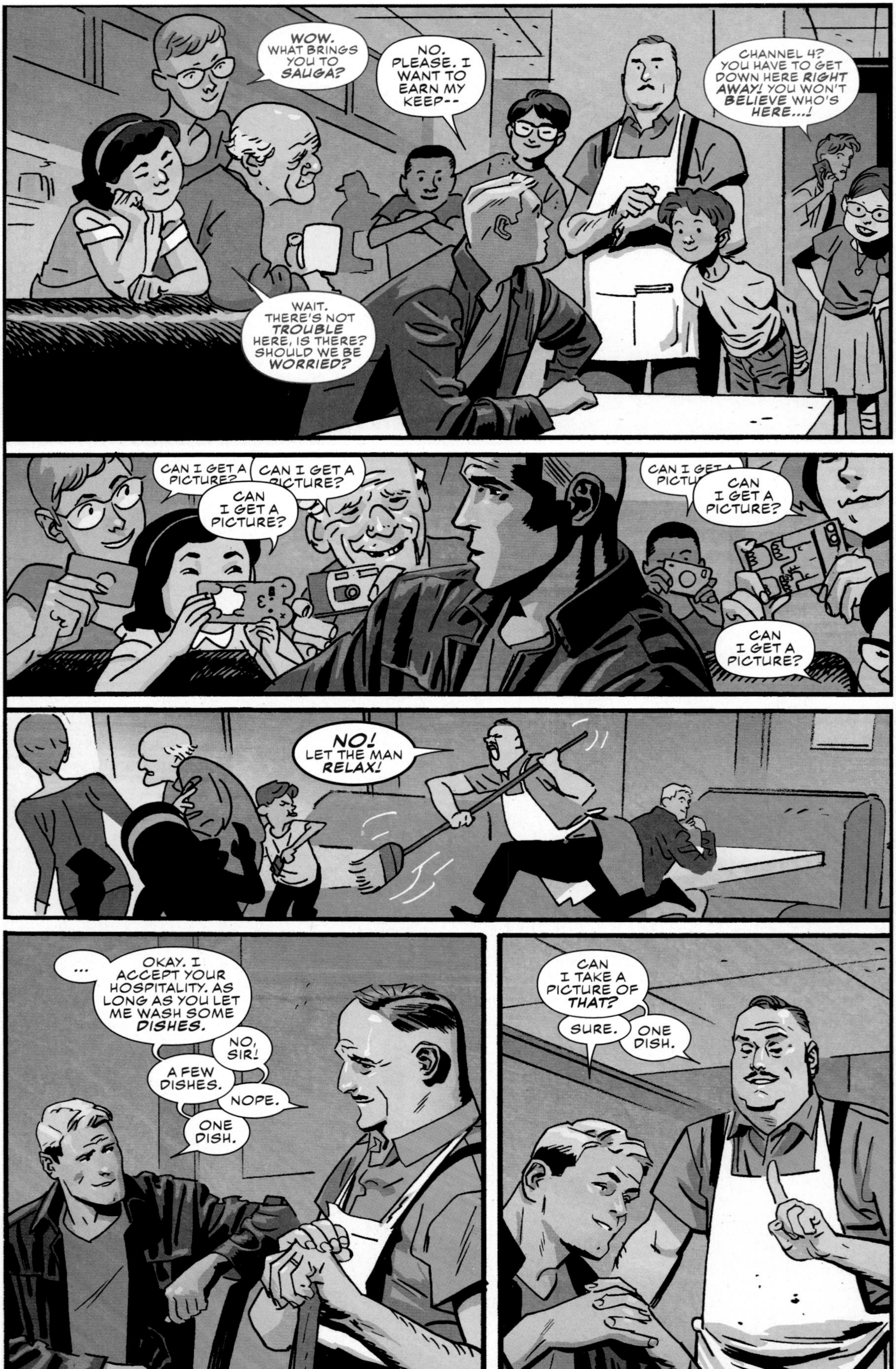
WOW. WHAT BRINGS YOU TO SAUGA?
NO. PLEASE. I WANT TO EARN MY KEEP--
CHANNEL 4? YOU HAVE TO GET DOWN HERE RIGHT AWAY! YOU WON'T BELIEVE WHO'S HERE...!
WAIT. THERE'S NOT TROUBLE HERE, IS THERE? SHOULD WE BE WORRIED?
CAN I GET A PICTURE?
CAN I GET A PICTURE?
CAN I GET A PICTURE?
CAN I GET A PICTURE?
CAN I GET A PICTURE?
CAN I GET A PICTURE?
NO! LET THE MAN RELAX!
...
OKAY. I ACCEPT YOUR HOSPITALITY. AS LONG AS YOU LET ME WASH SOME DISHES.
NO, SIR!
A FEW DISHES.
NOPE.
ONE DISH.
CAN I TAKE A PICTURE OF THAT?
SURE.
ONE DISH.

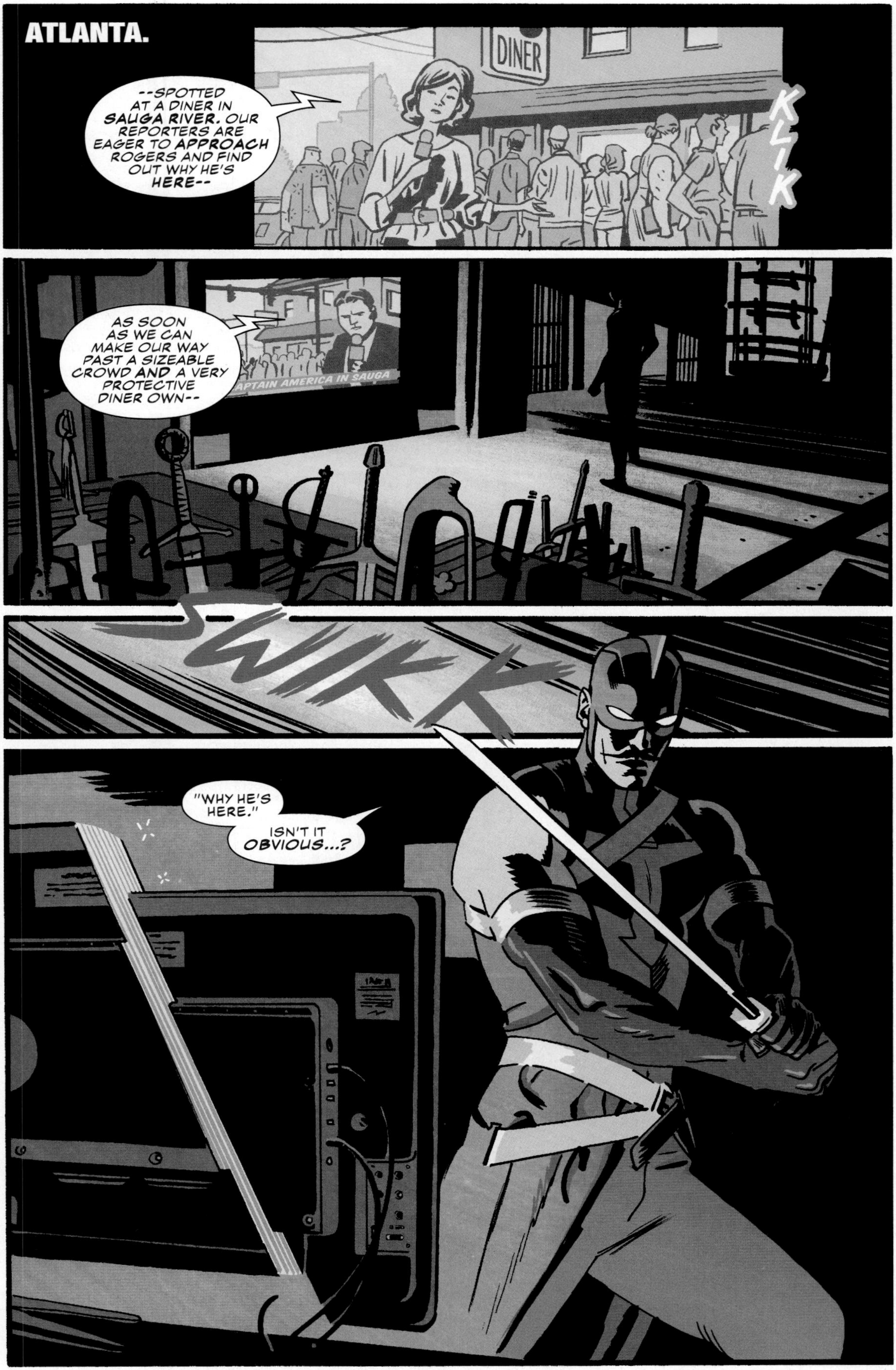
ATLANTA.
--SPOTTED AT A DINER IN SAUGA RIVER. OUR REPORTERS ARE EAGER TO APPROACH ROGERS AND FIND OUT WHY HE'S HERE--
DINER
KLIK
AS SOON AS WE CAN MAKE OUR WAY PAST A SIZEABLE CROWD AND A VERY PROTECTIVE DINER OWN--
CAPTAIN AMERICA IN SAUGA
SWIKK
"WHY HE'S HERE."
ISN'T IT OBVIOUS...?

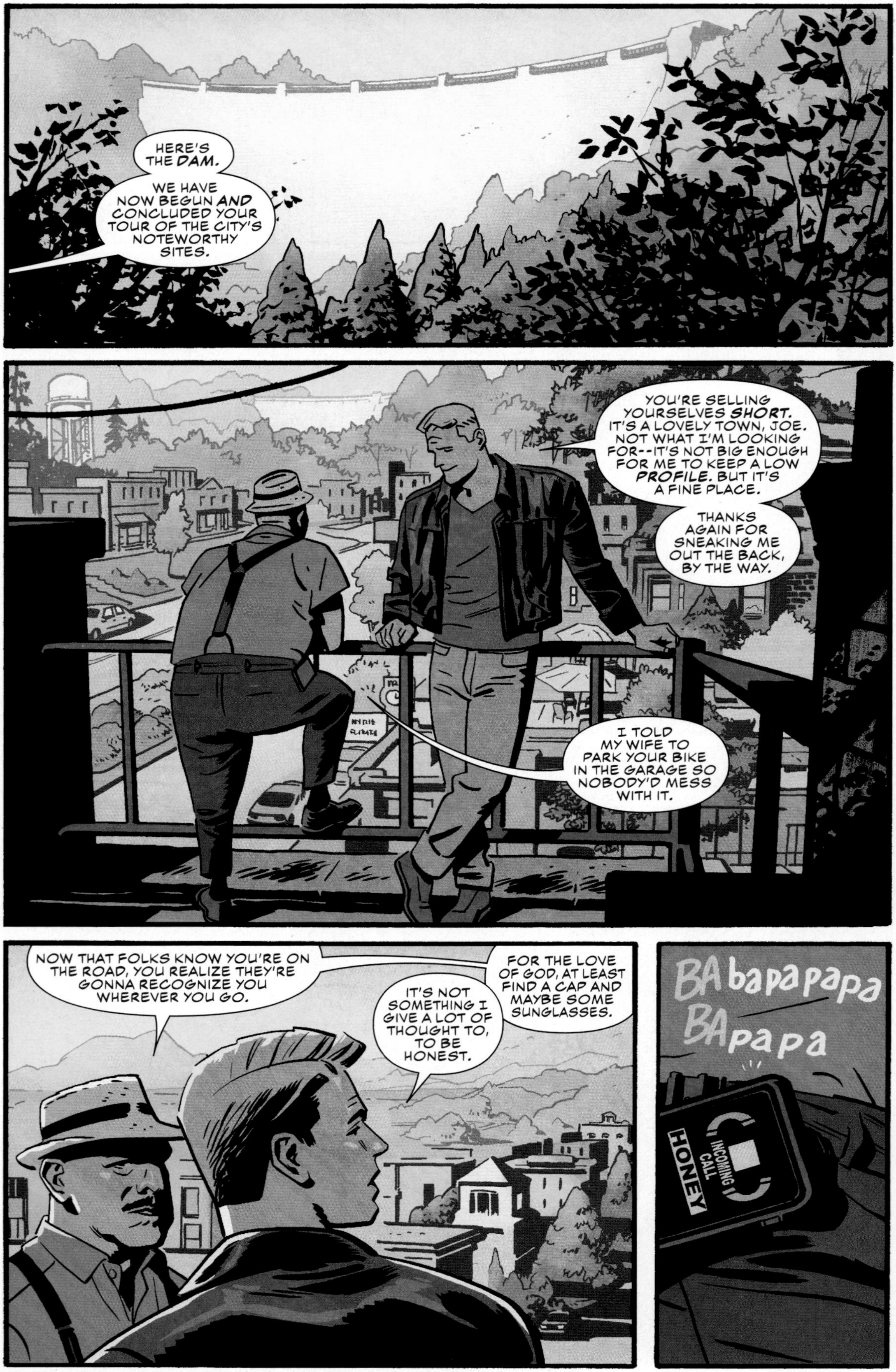
HERE'S THE DAM.
WE HAVE NOW BEGUN AND CONCLUDED YOUR TOUR OF THE CITY'S NOTEWORTHY SITES.
YOU'RE SELLING YOURSELVES SHORT. IT'S A LOVELY TOWN, JOE. NOT WHAT I'M LOOKING FOR--IT'S NOT BIG ENOUGH FOR ME TO KEEP A LOW PROFILE. BUT IT'S A FINE PLACE.
THANKS AGAIN FOR SNEAKING ME OUT THE BACK, BY THE WAY.
I TOLD MY WIFE TO PARK YOUR BIKE IN THE GARAGE SO NOBODY'D MESS WITH IT.
NOW THAT FOLKS KNOW YOU'RE ON THE ROAD, YOU REALIZE THEY'RE GONNA RECOGNIZE YOU WHEREVER YOU GO.
IT'S NOT SOMETHING I GIVE A LOT OF THOUGHT TO, TO BE HONEST.
FOR THE LOVE OF GOD, AT LEAST FIND A CAP AND MAYBE SOME SUNGLASSES.
BA bapapapa
BA papa
INCOMING CALL
HONEY

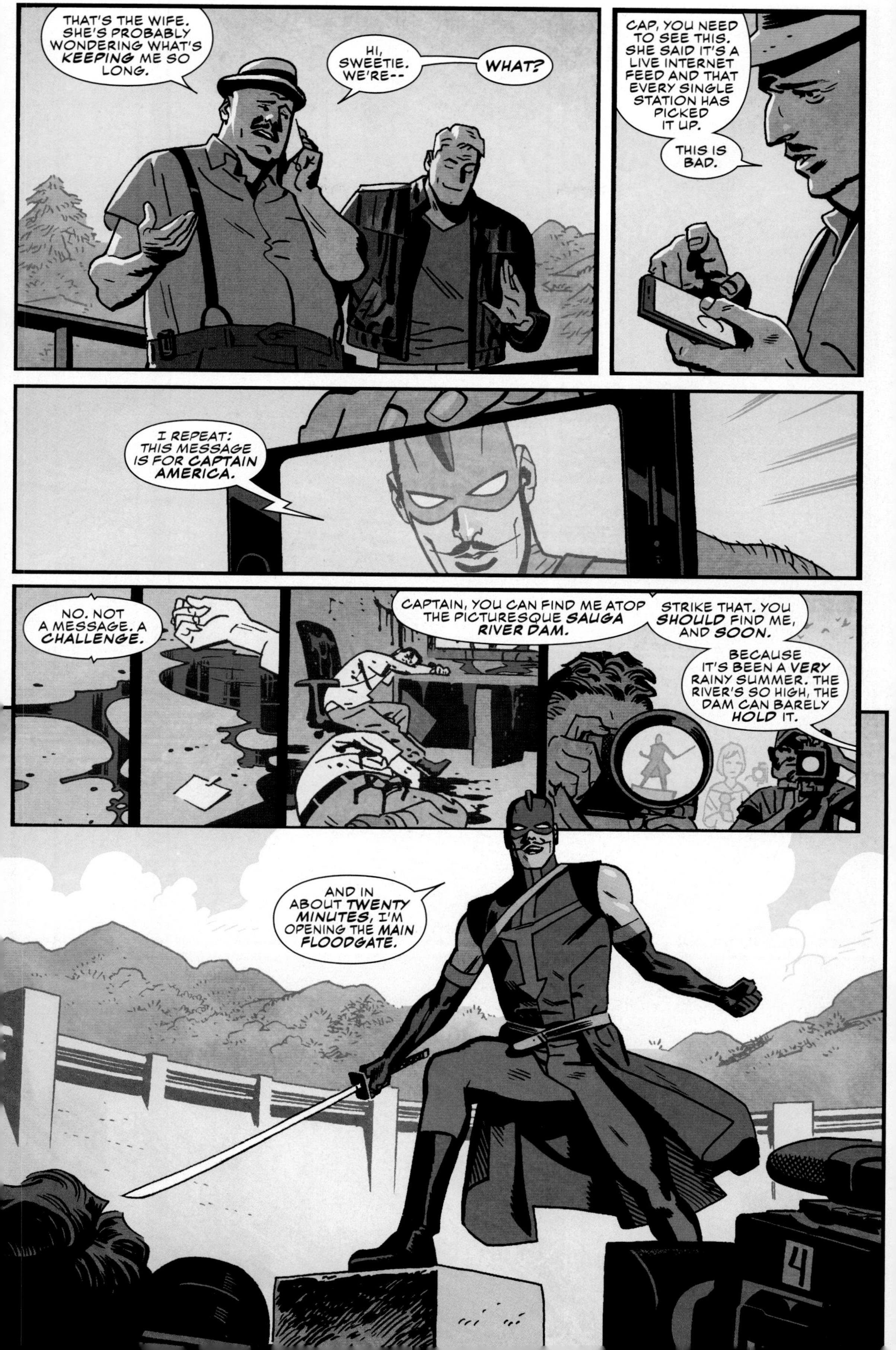
THAT'S THE WIFE. SHE'S PROBABLY WONDERING WHAT'S KEEPING ME SO LONG.
HI, SWEETIE. WE'RE--
WHAT?
CAP, YOU NEED TO SEE THIS. SHE SAID IT'S A LIVE INTERNET FEED AND THAT EVERY SINGLE STATION HAS PICKED IT UP.
THIS IS BAD.
I REPEAT: THIS MESSAGE IS FOR CAPTAIN AMERICA.
NO. NOT A MESSAGE. A CHALLENGE.
CAPTAIN, YOU CAN FIND ME ATOP THE PICTURESQUE SAUGA RIVER DAM.
STRIKE THAT. YOU SHOULD FIND ME, AND SOON.
BECAUSE IT'S BEEN A VERY RAINY SUMMER. THE RIVER'S SO HIGH, THE DAM CAN BARELY HOLD IT.
AND IN ABOUT TWENTY MINUTES, I'M OPENING THE MAIN FLOODGATE.
4

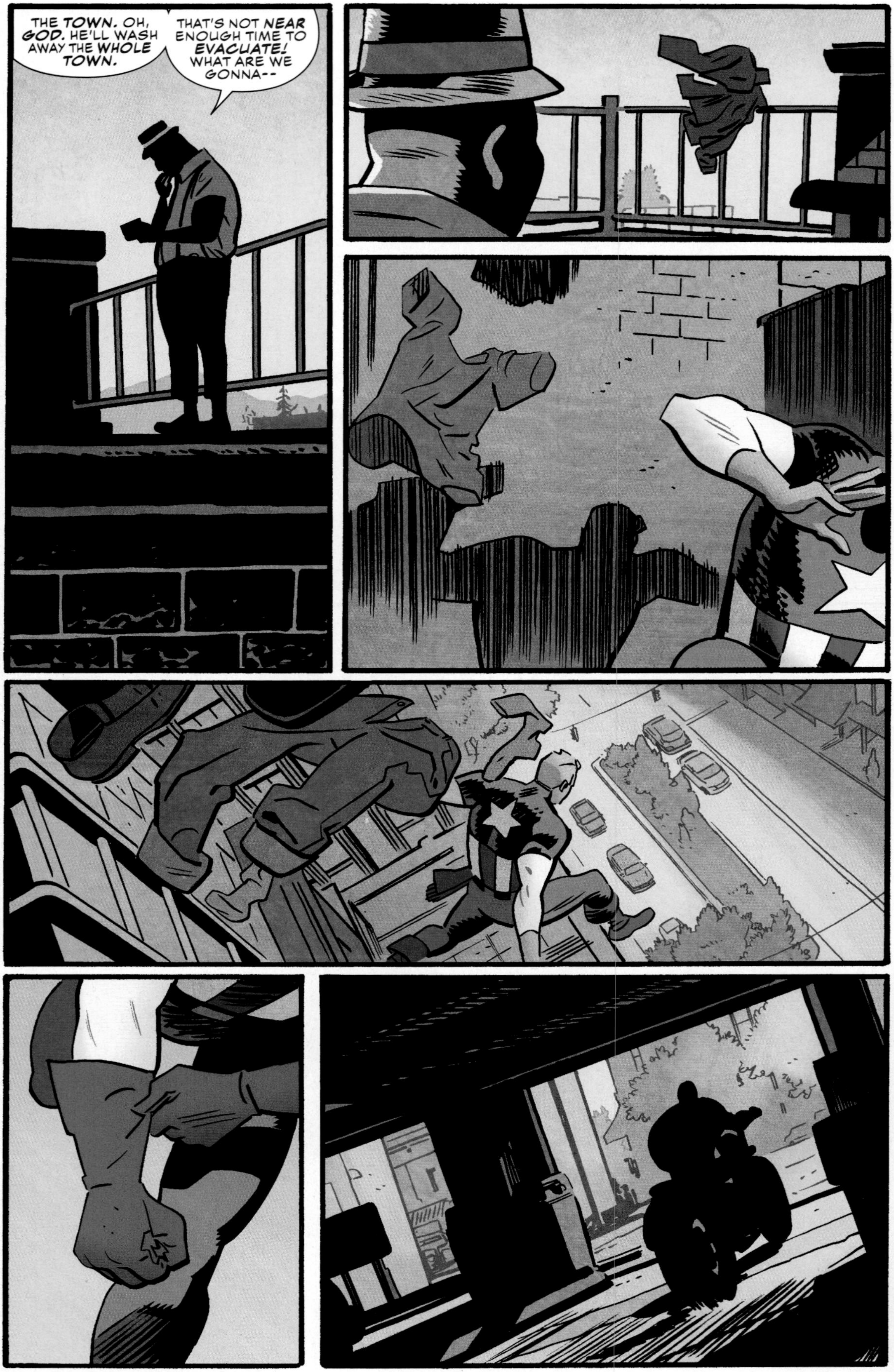
THE TOWN. OH, GOD. HE'LL WASH AWAY THE WHOLE TOWN.
THAT'S NOT NEAR ENOUGH TIME TO EVACUATE! WHAT ARE WE GONNA--

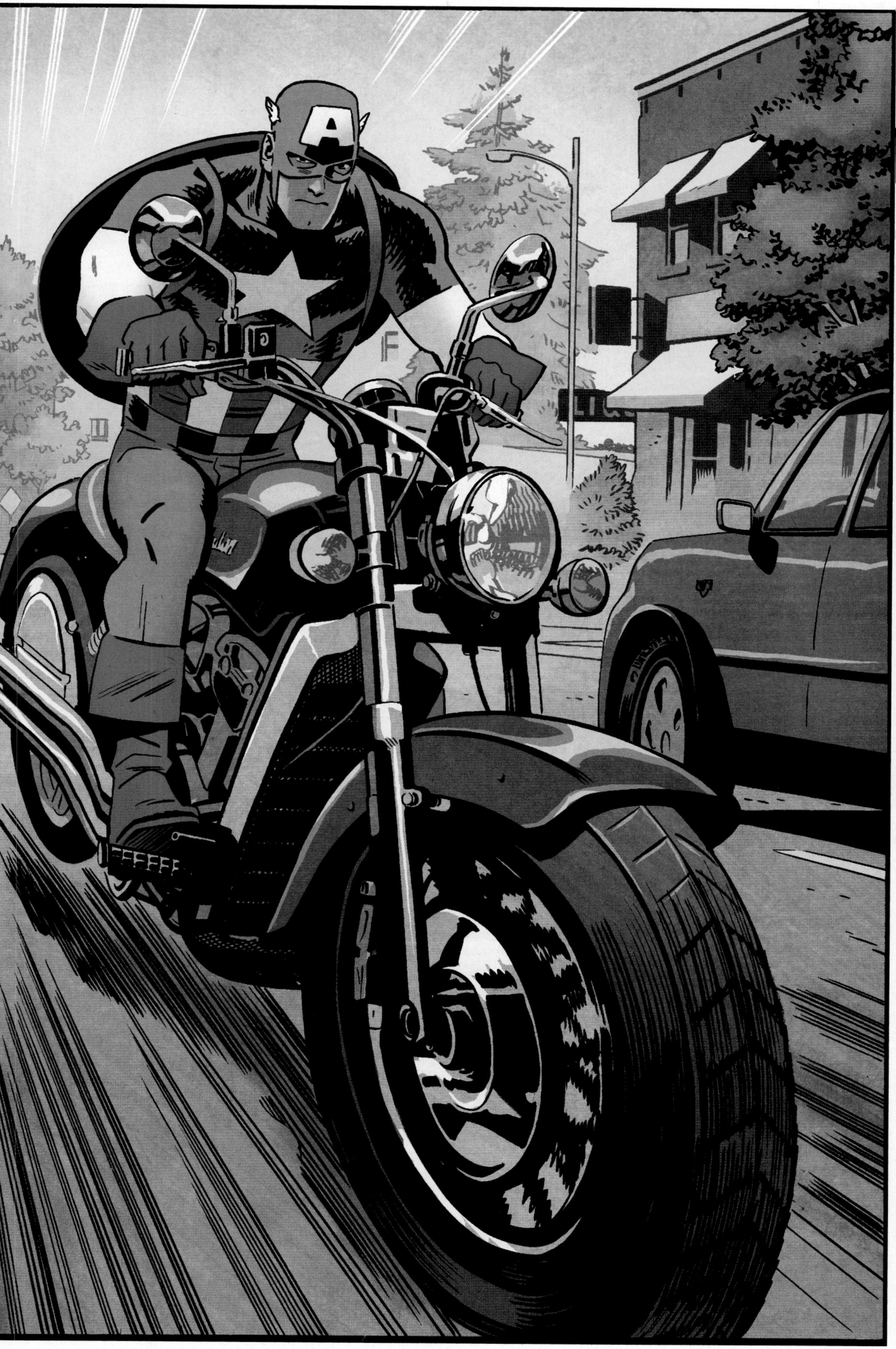

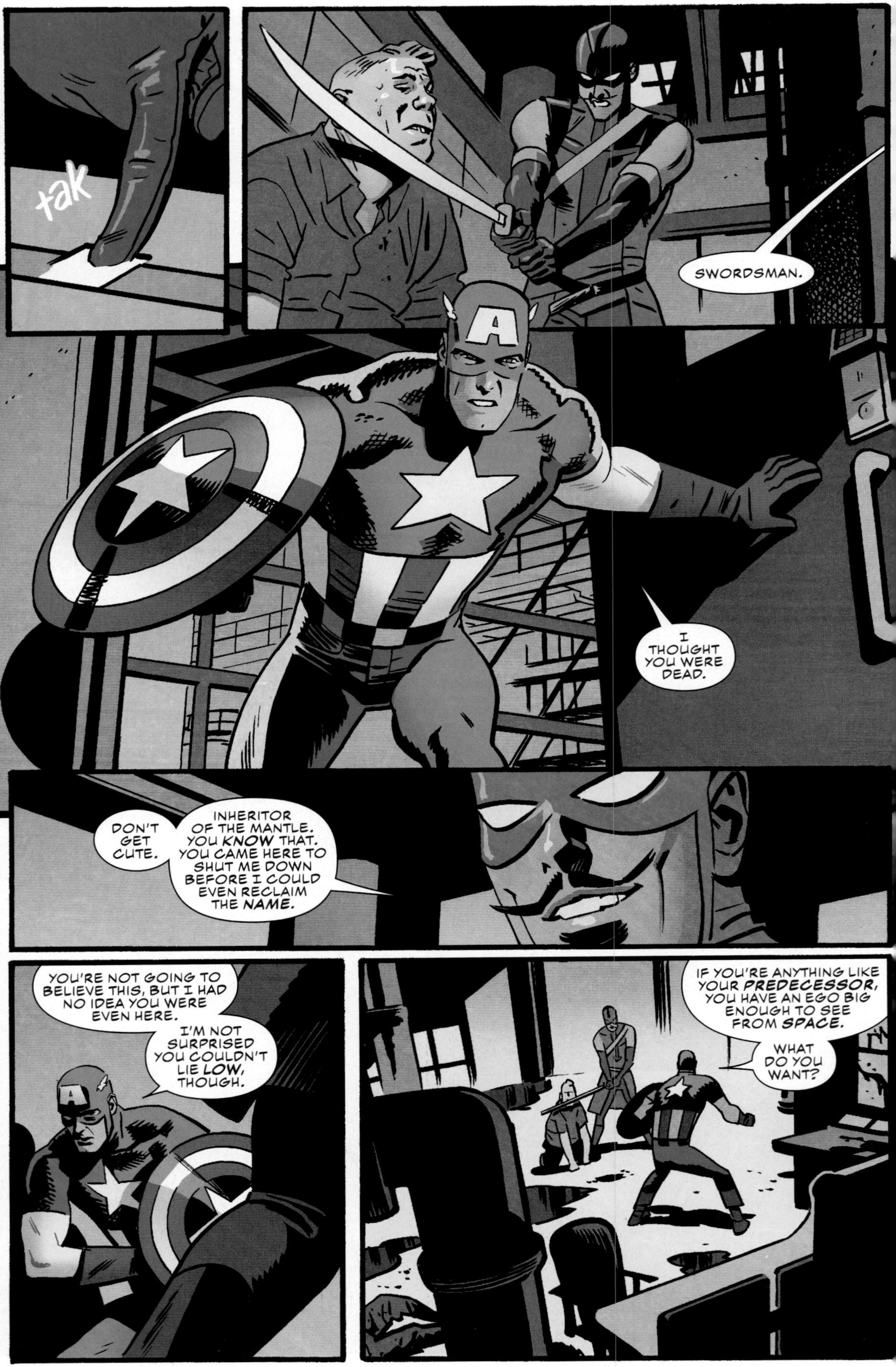
tak
SWORDSMAN.
I THOUGHT YOU WERE DEAD.
DON'T GET CUTE.
INHERITOR OF THE MANTLE. YOU KNOW THAT. YOU CAME HERE TO SHUT ME DOWN BEFORE I COULD EVEN RECLAIM THE NAME.
YOU'RE NOT GOING TO BELIEVE THIS, BUT I HAD NO IDEA YOU WERE EVEN HERE.
I'M NOT SURPRISED YOU COULDN'T LIE LOW, THOUGH.
IF YOU'RE ANYTHING LIKE YOUR PREDECESSOR, YOU HAVE AN EGO BIG ENOUGH TO SEE FROM SPACE.
WHAT DO YOU WANT?

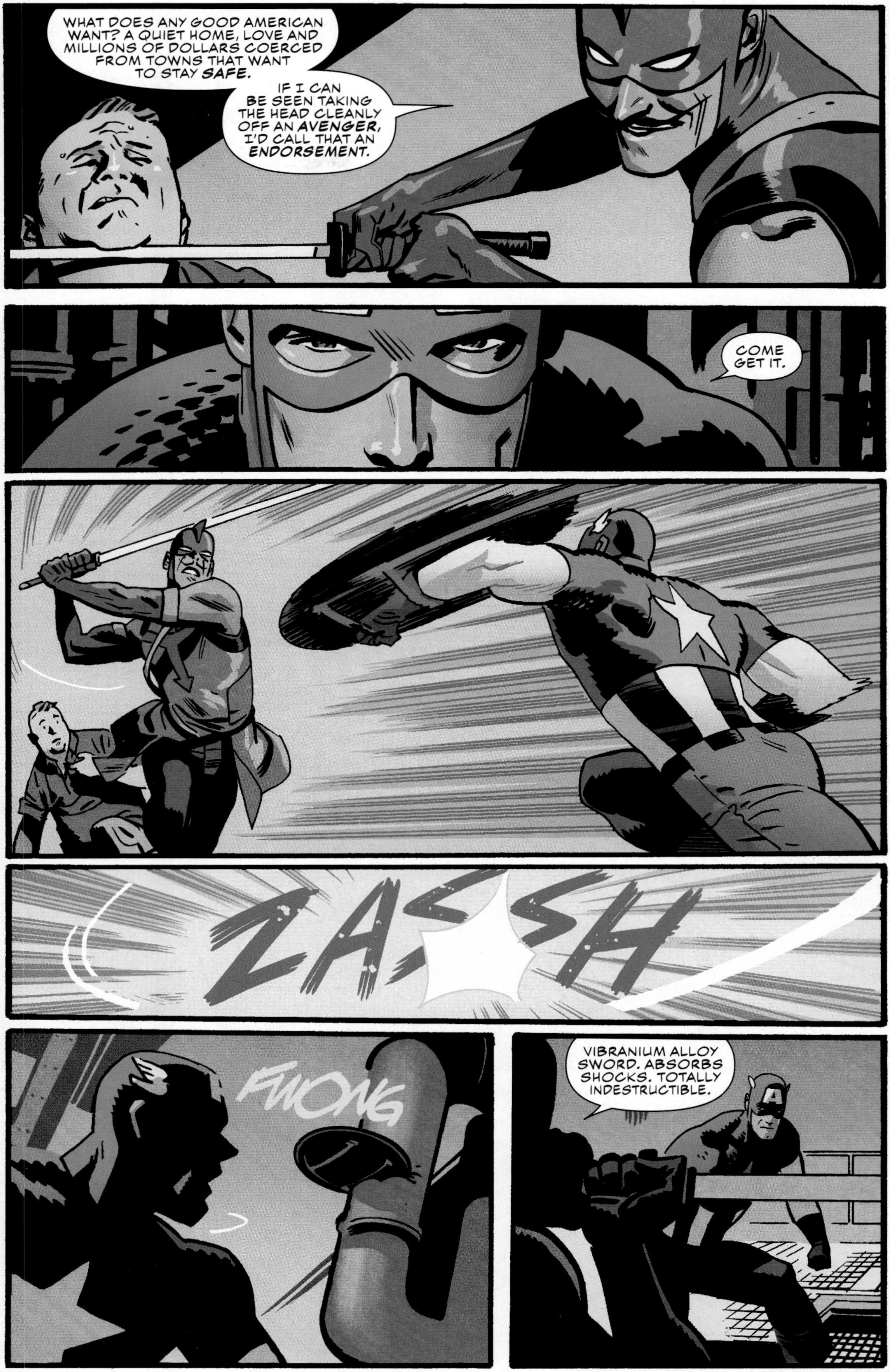
WHAT DOES ANY GOOD AMERICAN WANT? A QUIET HOME, LOVE AND MILLIONS OF DOLLARS COERCED FROM TOWNS THAT WANT TO STAY SAFE.
IF I CAN BE SEEN TAKING THE HEAD CLEANLY OFF AN AVENGER, I'D CALL THAT AN ENDORSEMENT.
COME GET IT.
ZASSH
FWONG
VIBRANIUM ALLOY SWORD. ABSORBS SHOCKS. TOTALLY INDESTRUCTIBLE.

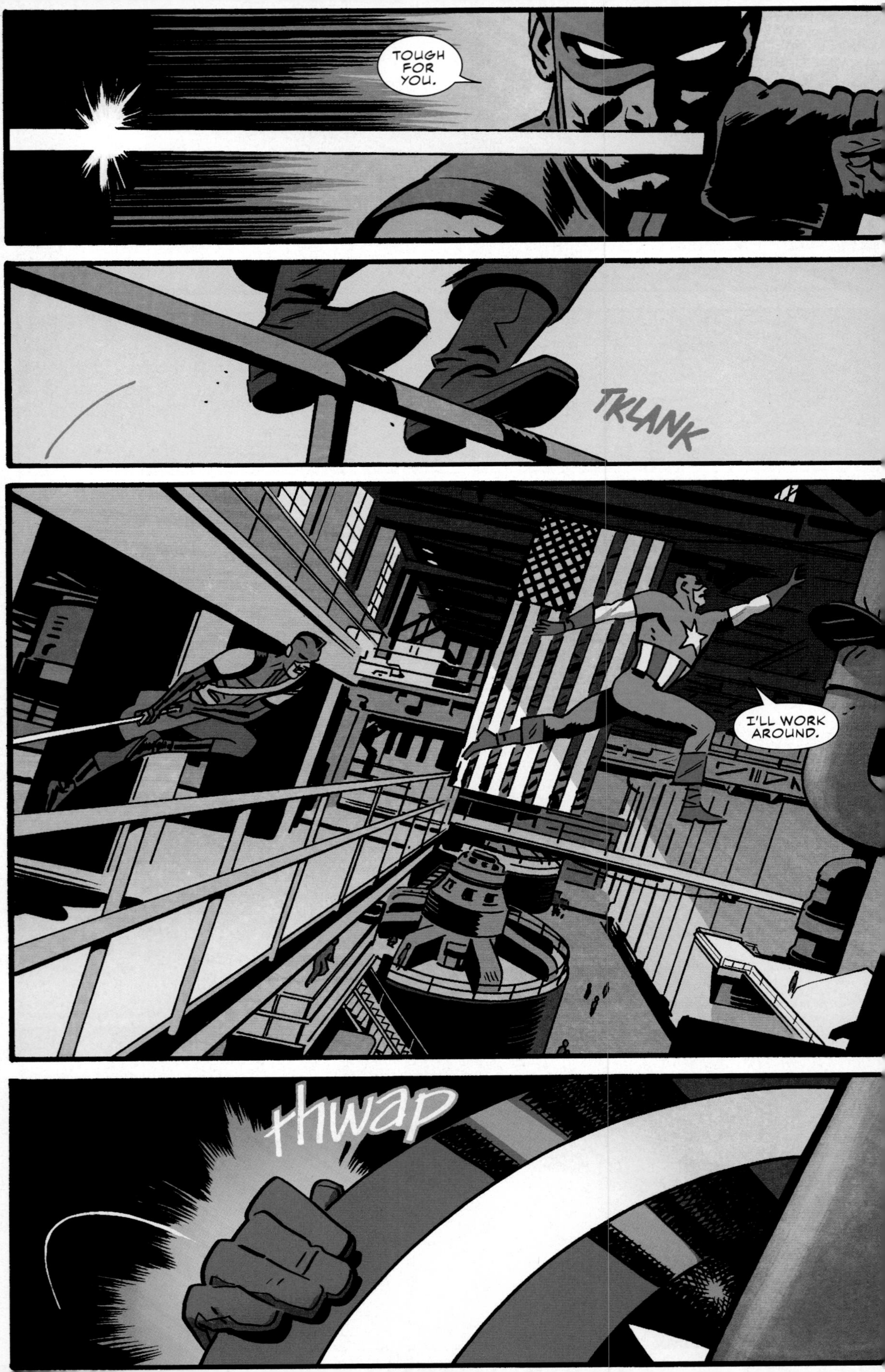
TOUGH FOR YOU.
TKLANK
I'LL WORK AROUND.
thwap

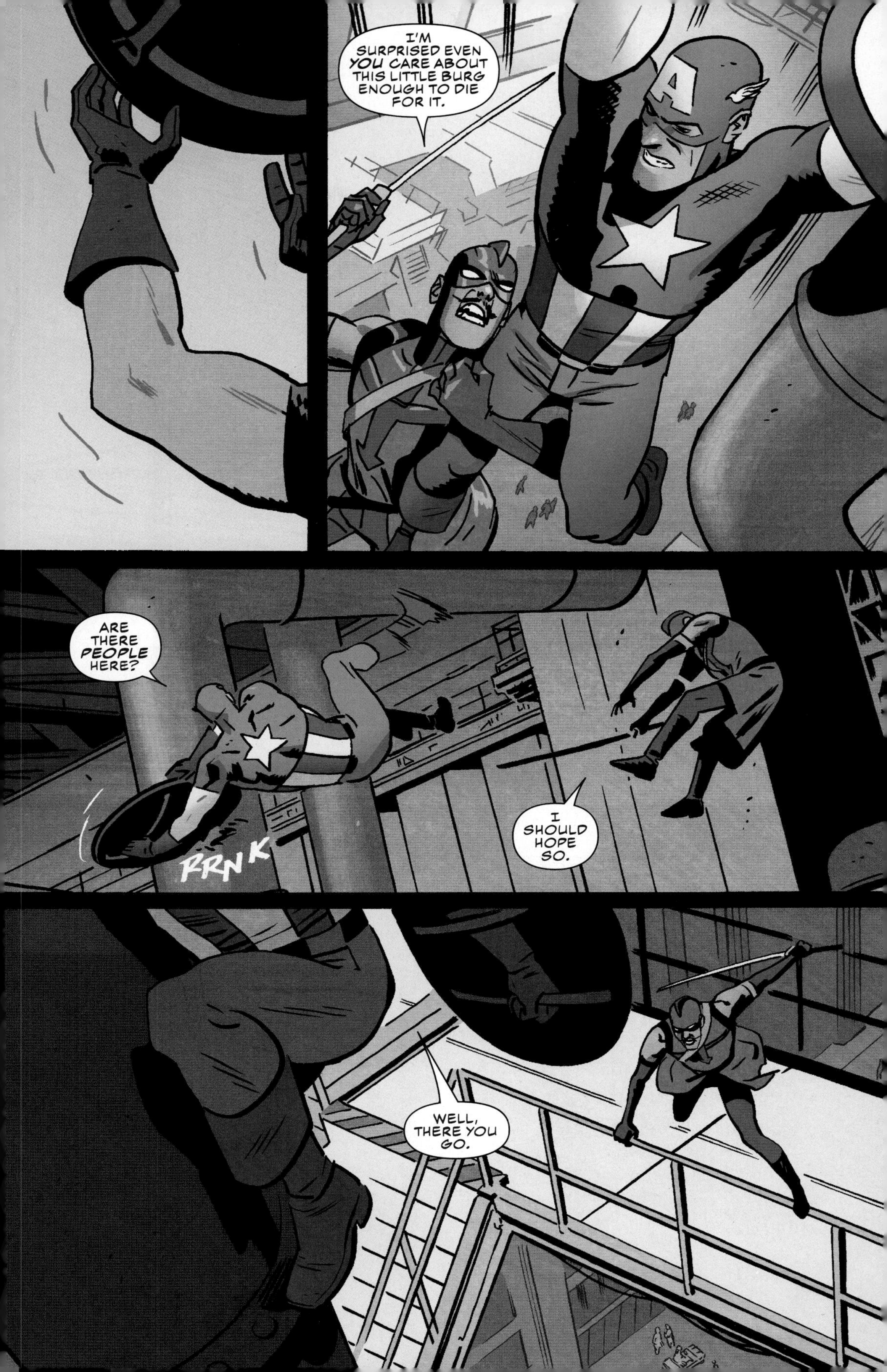
I'M SURPRISED EVEN YOU CARE ABOUT THIS LITTLE BURG ENOUGH TO DIE FOR IT.
ARE THERE PEOPLE HERE?
RRNK
I SHOULD HOPE SO.
WELL, THERE YOU GO.

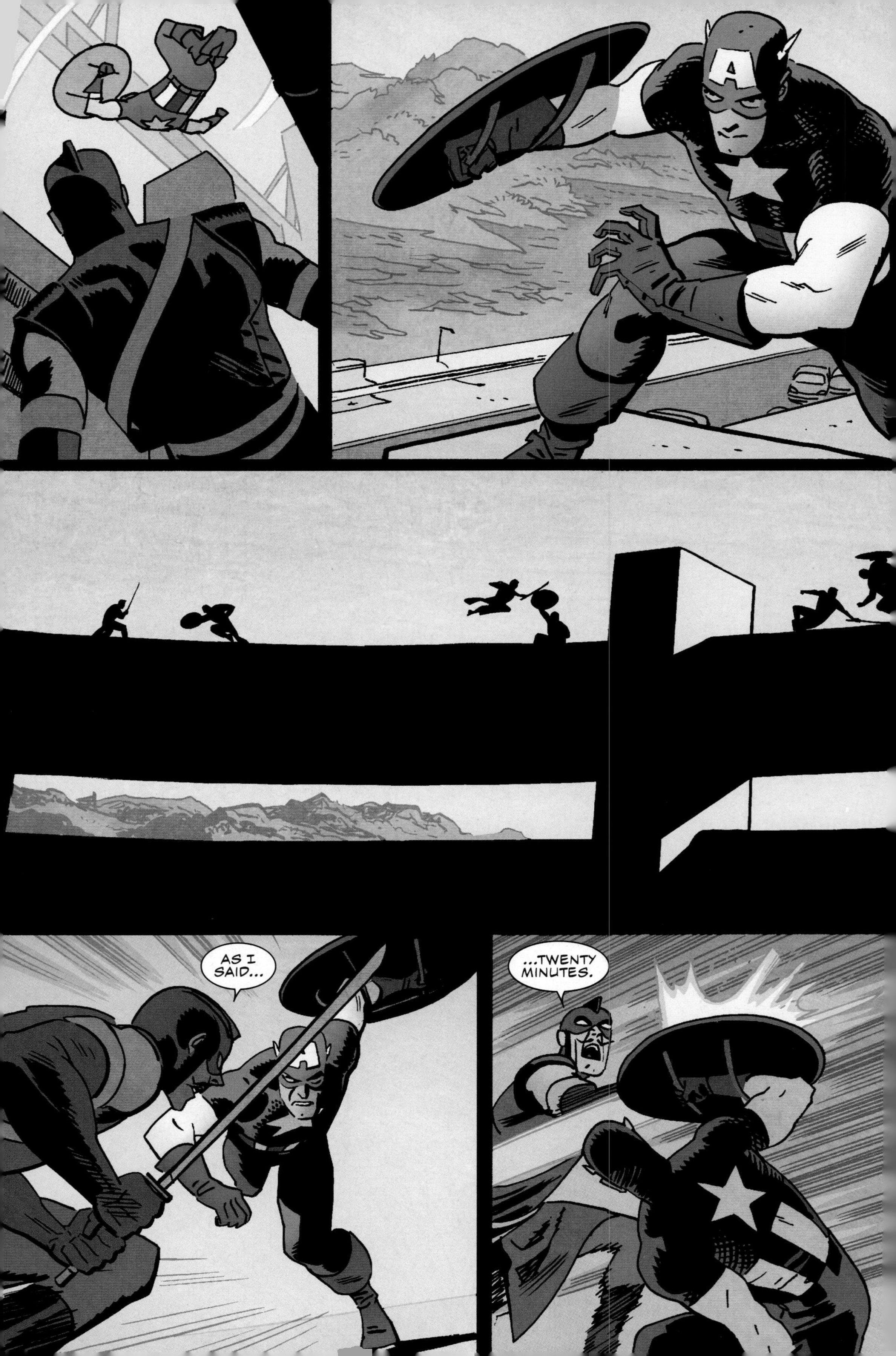
AS I SAID...
...TWENTY MINUTES.

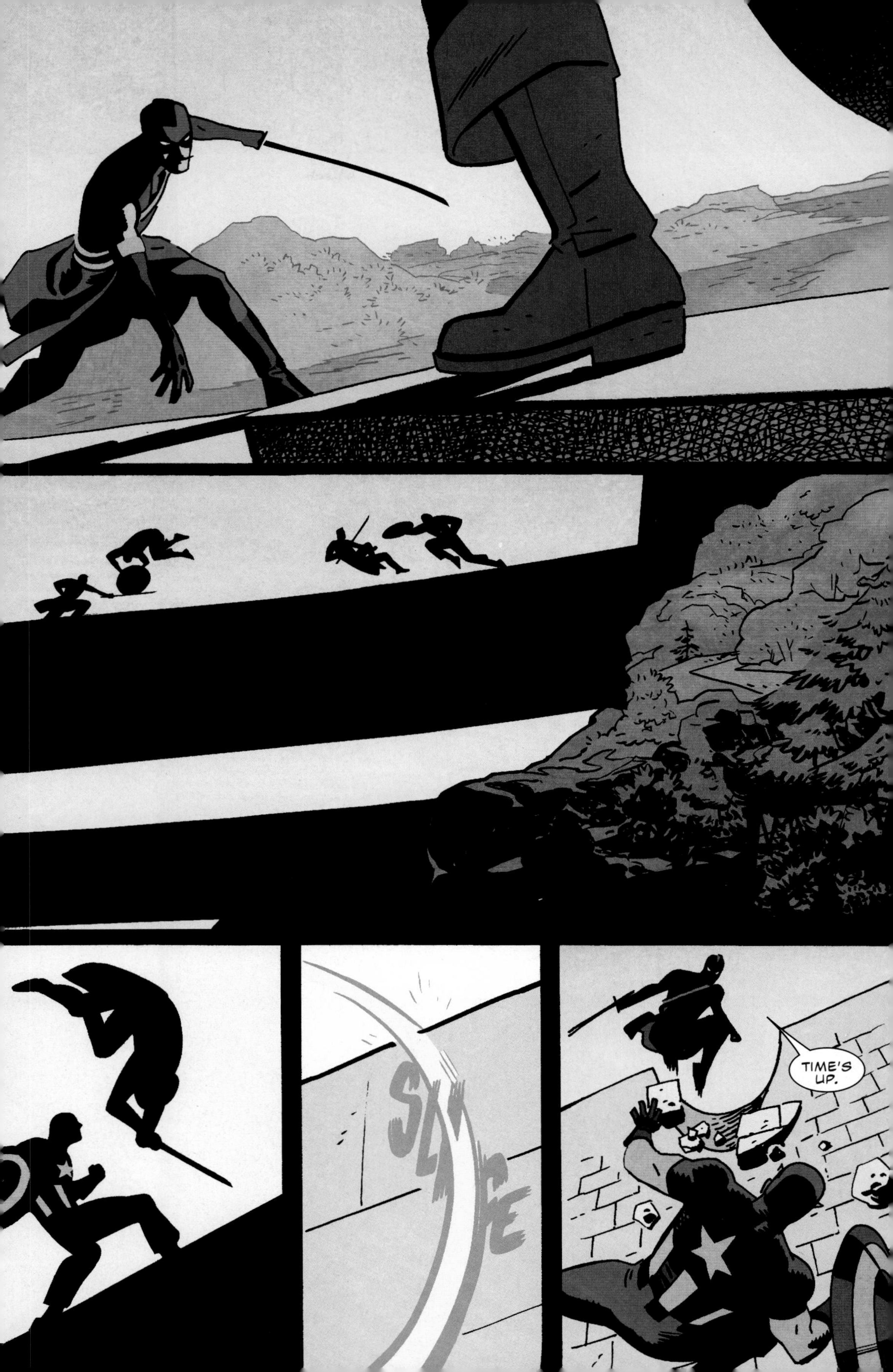
TIME'S UP.

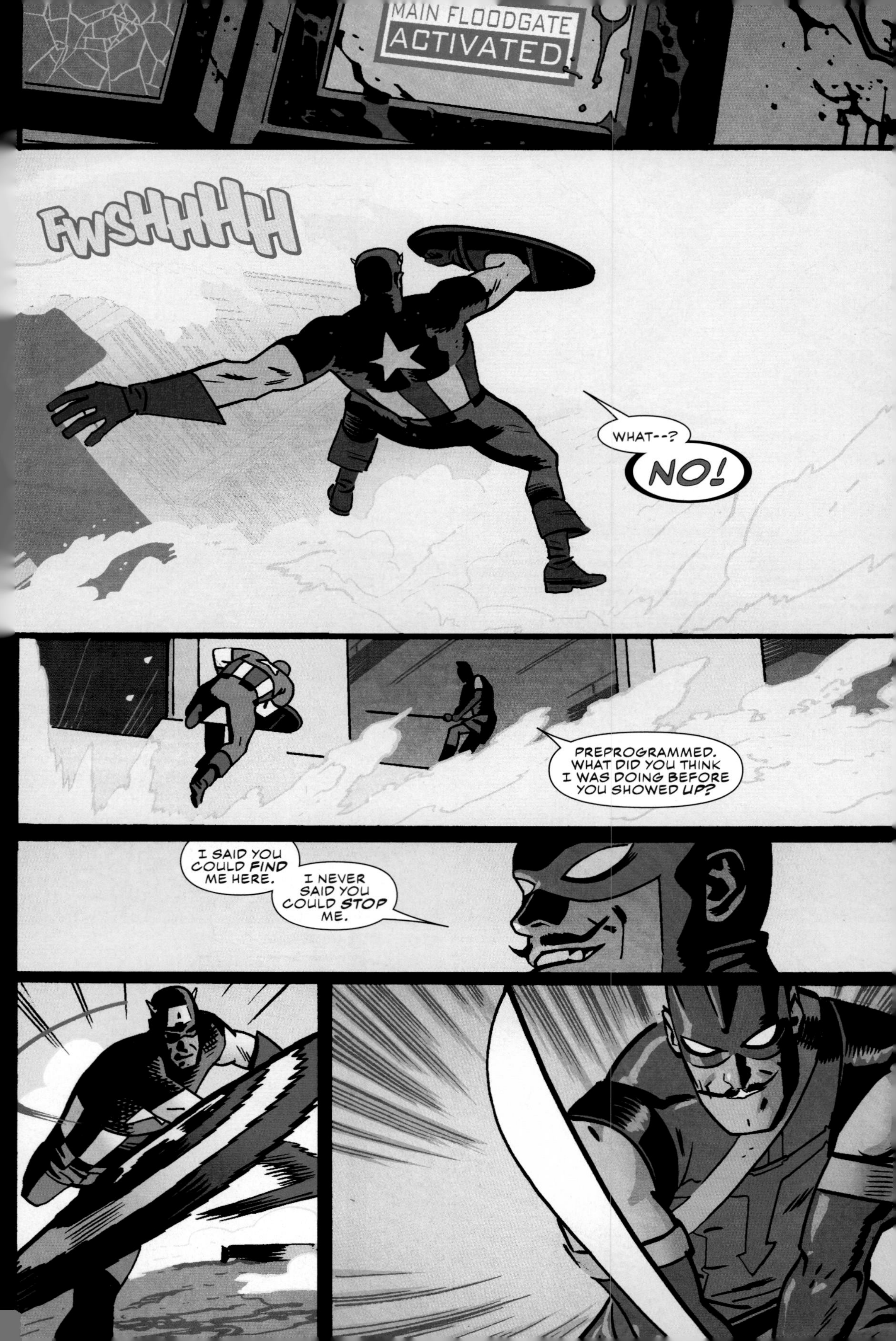
MAIN FLOODGATE ACTIVATED
FWSHHHHH
WHAT--?
NO!
PREPROGRAMMED. WHAT DID YOU THINK I WAS DOING BEFORE YOU SHOWED UP?
I SAID YOU COULD FIND ME HERE.
I NEVER SAID YOU COULD STOP ME.

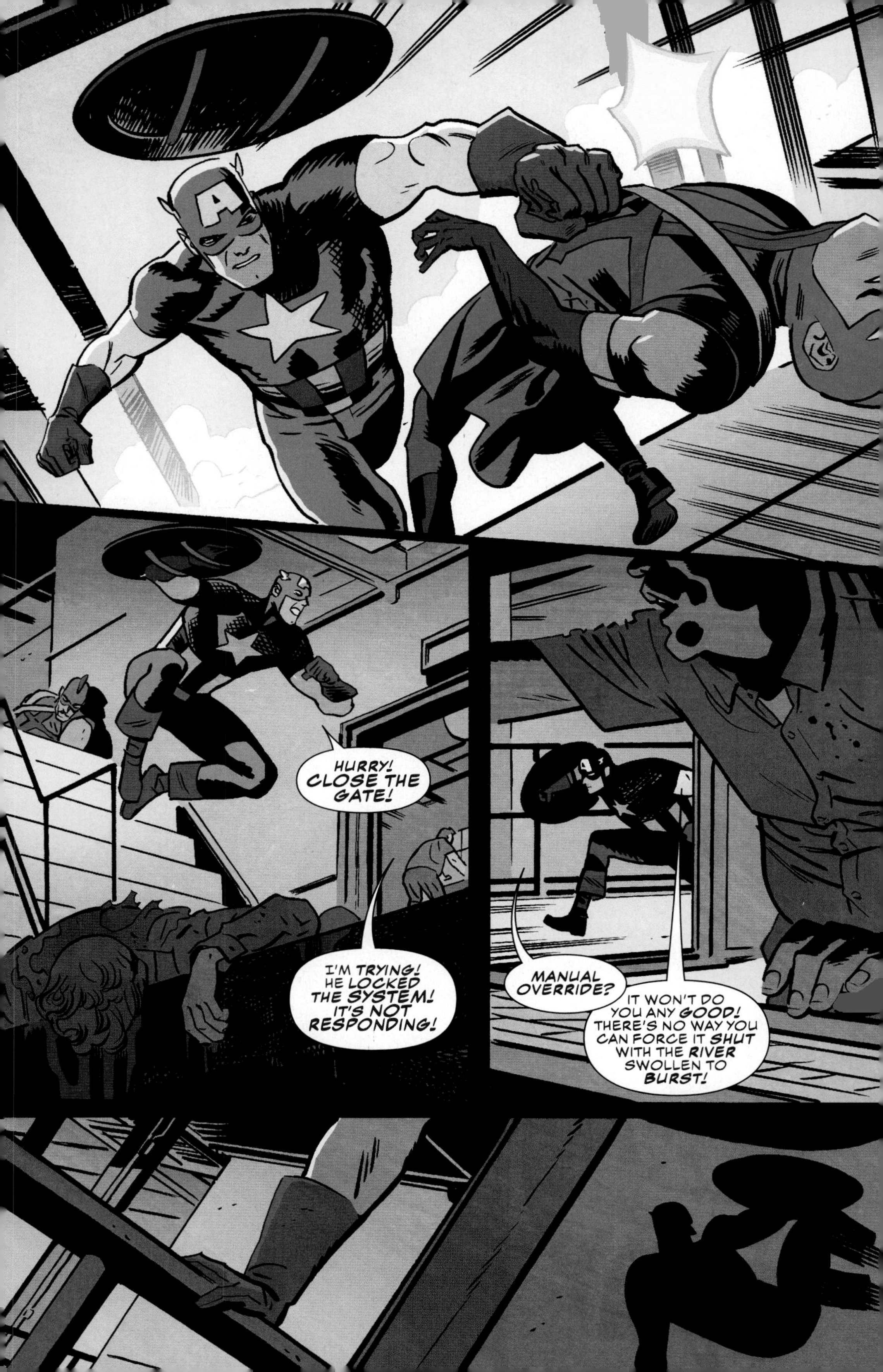
HURRY! CLOSE THE GATE!
I'M TRYING! HE LOCKED THE SYSTEM! IT'S NOT RESPONDING!
MANUAL OVERRIDE?
IT WON'T DO YOU ANY GOOD! THERE'S NO WAY YOU CAN FORCE IT SHUT WITH THE RIVER SWOLLEN TO BURST!

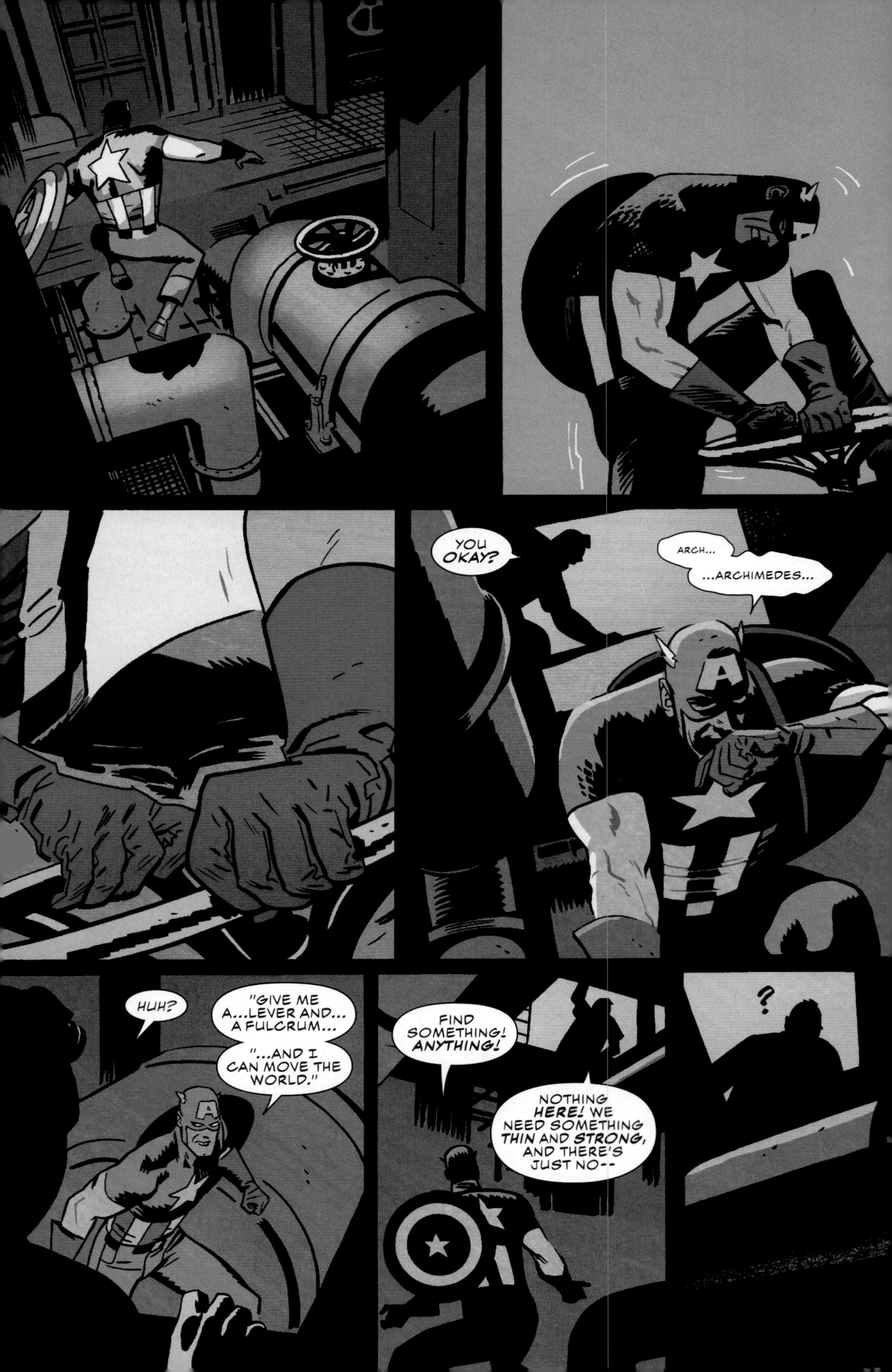
YOU OKAY?
ARCH...
...ARCHIMEDES...
HUH?
"GIVE ME A...LEVER AND... A FULCRUM...
"...AND I CAN MOVE THE WORLD."
FIND SOMETHING! ANYTHING!
NOTHING HERE! WE NEED SOMETHING THIN AND STRONG, AND THERE'S JUST NO--
?

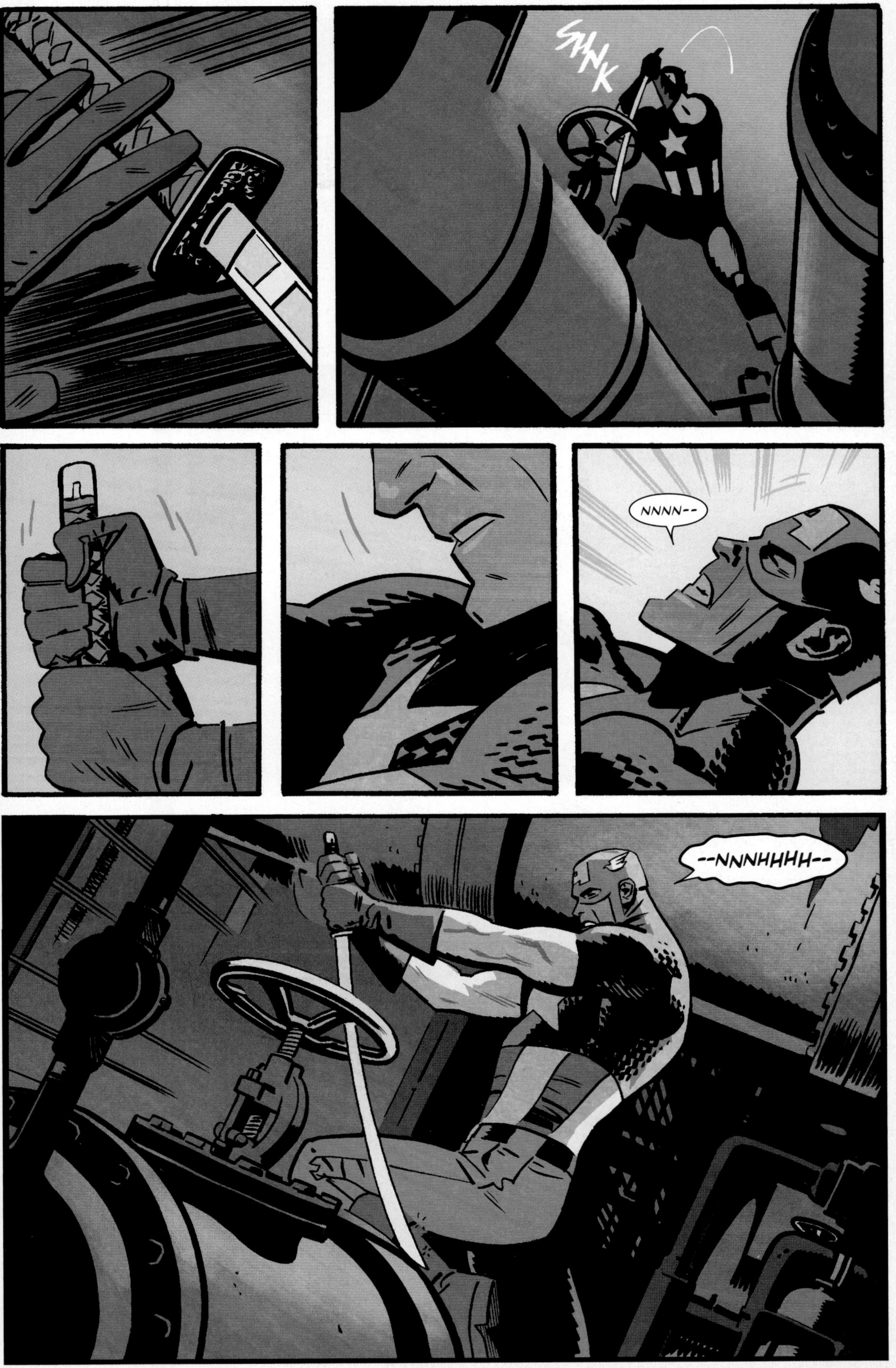
SHNK
NNNN--
--NNNHHHH--

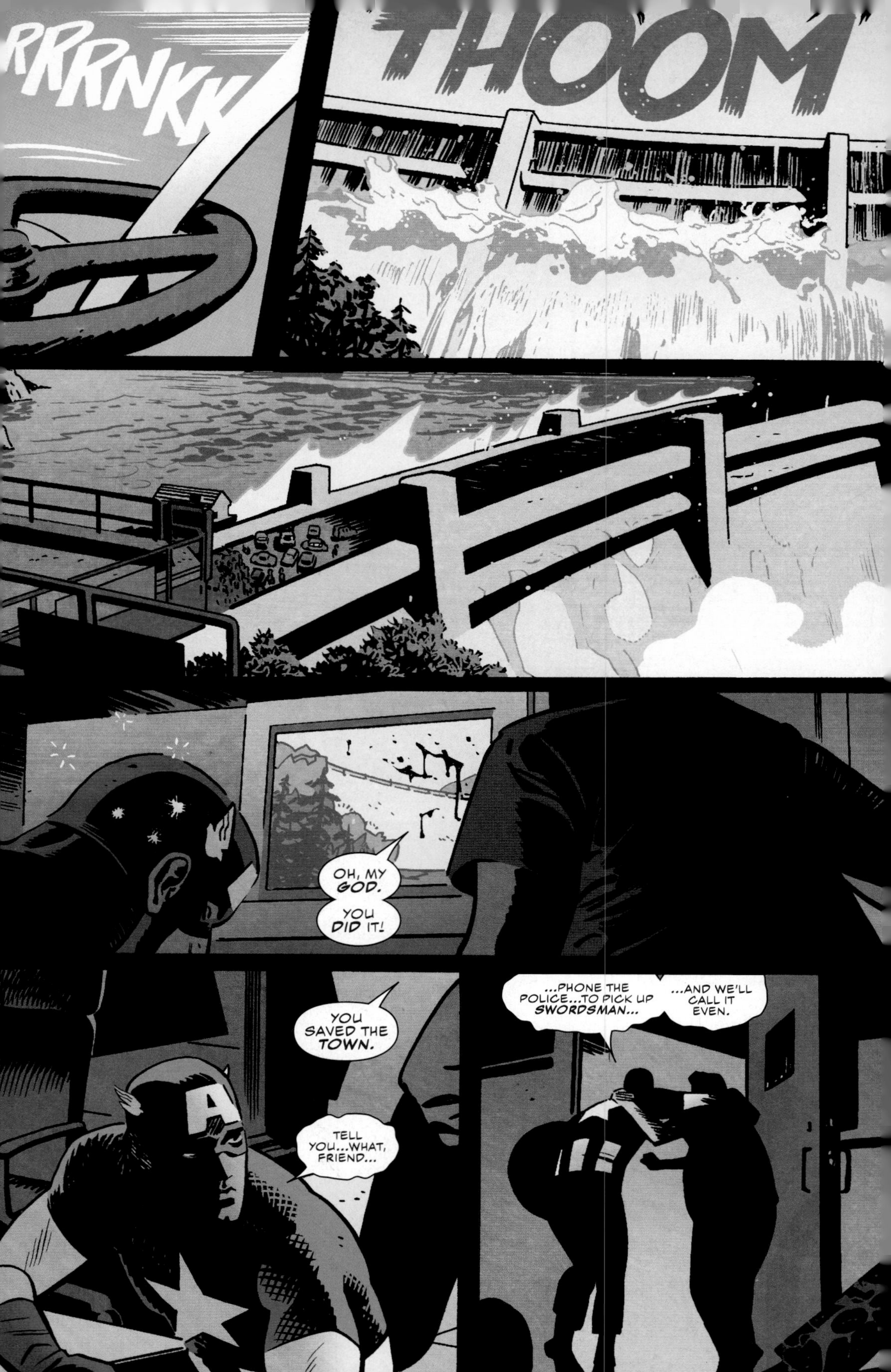
RRRNKK
THOOM
OH, MY GOD.
YOU DID IT!
YOU SAVED THE TOWN.
TELL YOU...WHAT, FRIEND...
...PHONE THE POLICE...TO PICK UP SWORDSMAN...
...AND WE'LL CALL IT EVEN.

...LOST A COUPLE OF **BASEMENTS** AND A **PLAYGROUND.** THAT'S IT. IF YOU'RE READY TO MOVE ON, DO IT BEFORE WE THROW YOU A **PARADE.**

YOU GONNA BE OKAY?

FEELS LIKE I JUST BENCHED THE **HULK,** BUT YES.

WHAT'S THIS?

FOR THE ROAD. WIFE'S **SPECIALTY.** HOPE YOU LIKE **CHILI.**

WHAT DO I OWE YOU?

ALL RIGHT. FAIR TRADE. THIS ONE TIME.

TAKE CARE.

CITY LIMIT
SAUGA RIVER

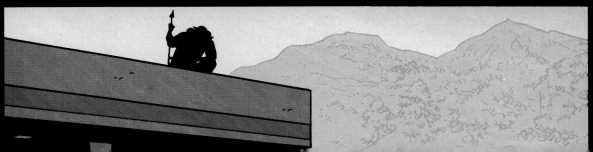

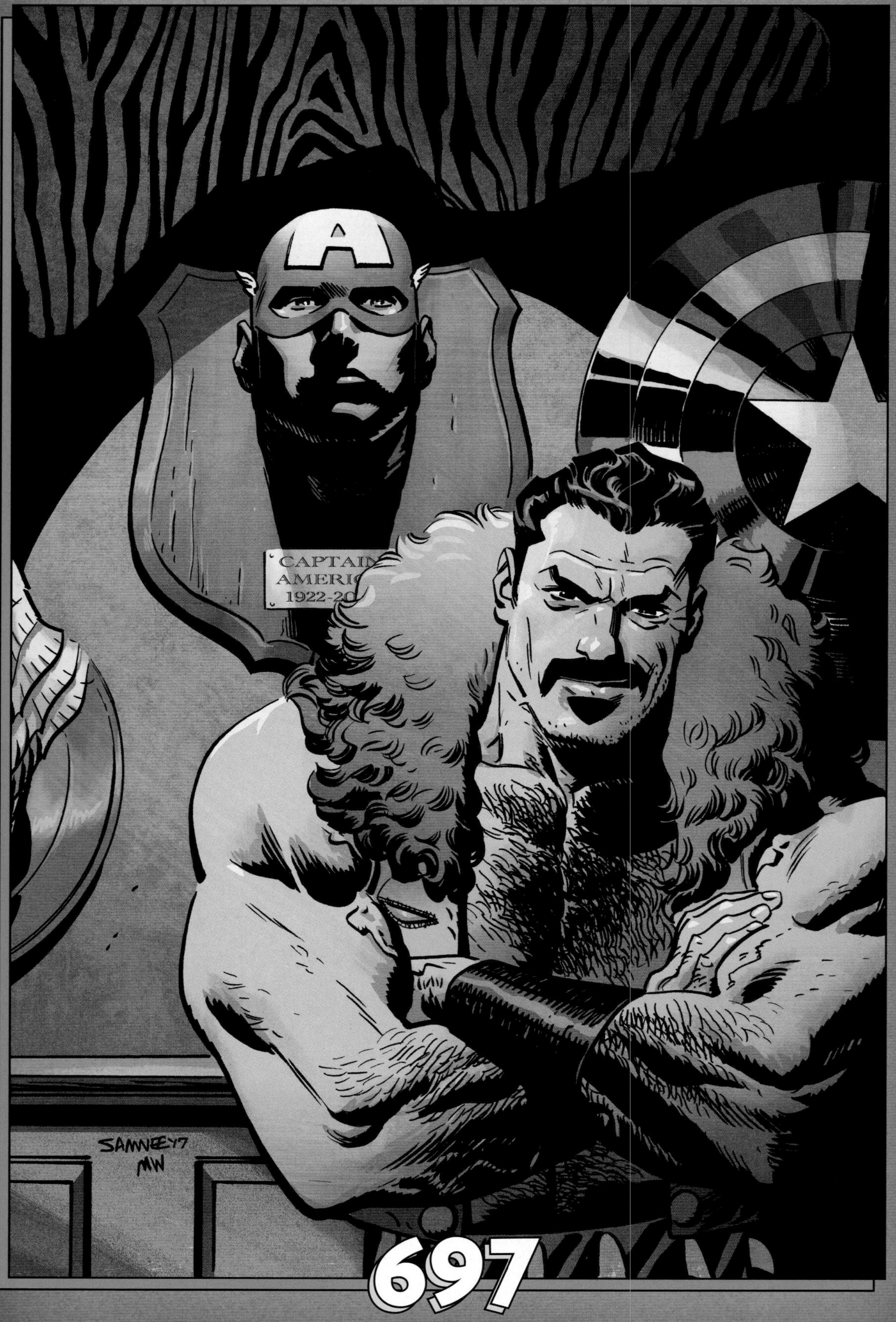

CAPTAIN
AMERIC
1922-20
SAMNEE'17
MW
697

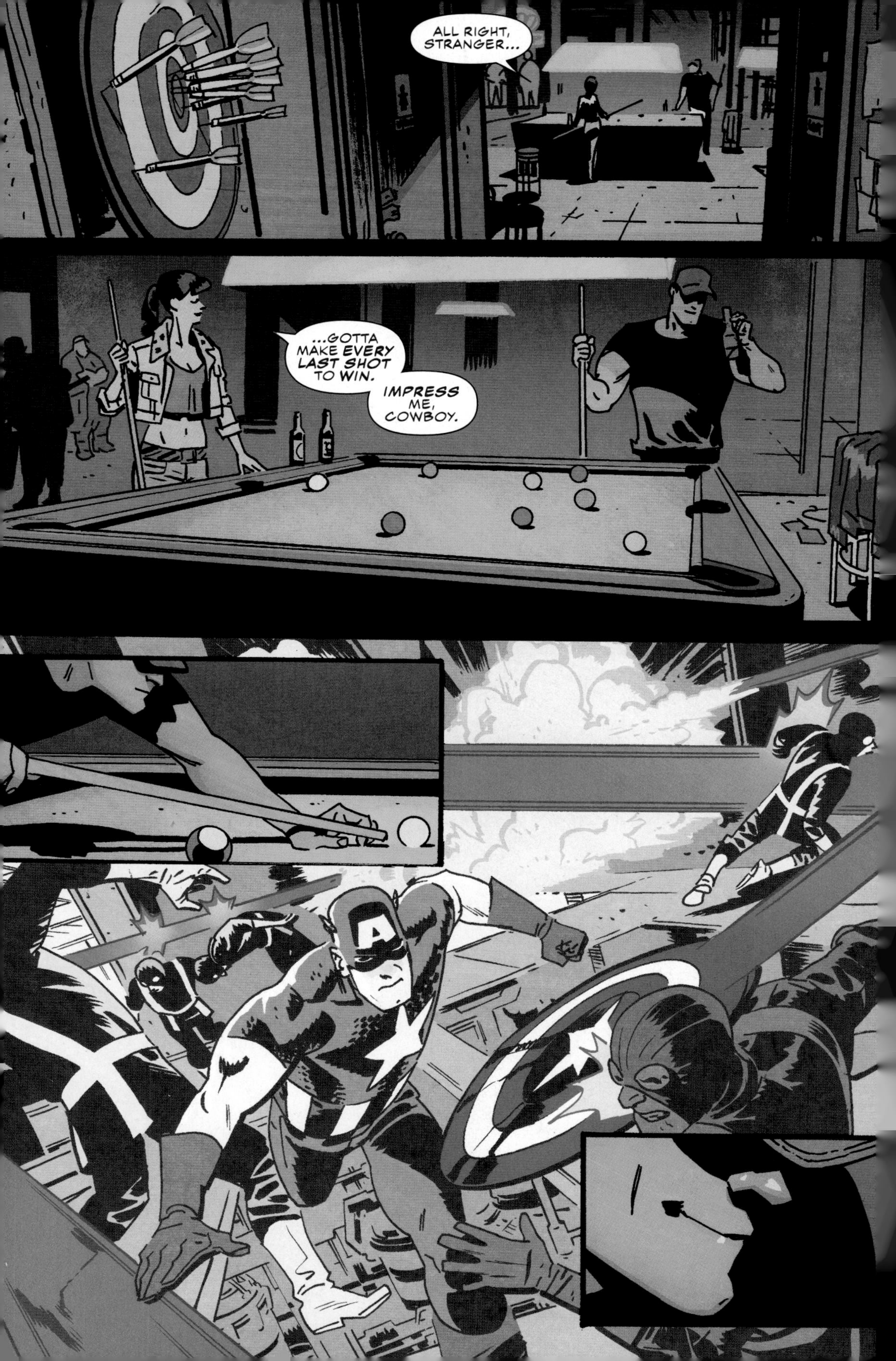
ALL RIGHT, STRANGER...
...GOTTA MAKE EVERY LAST SHOT TO WIN.
IMPRESS ME, COWBOY.

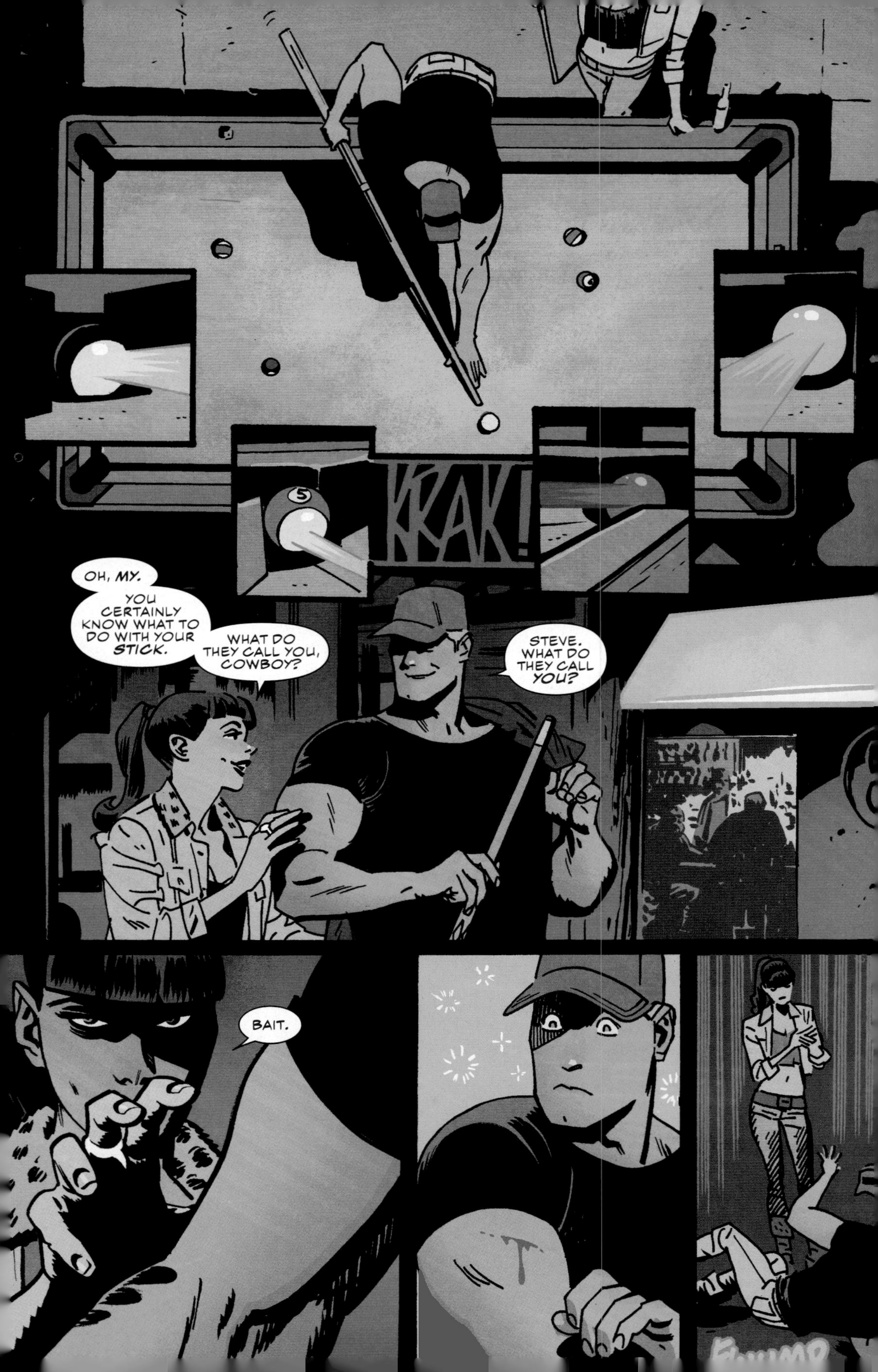
KRAK!
OH, MY.
YOU CERTAINLY KNOW WHAT TO DO WITH YOUR STICK.
WHAT DO THEY CALL YOU, COWBOY?
STEVE. WHAT DO THEY CALL YOU?
BAIT.

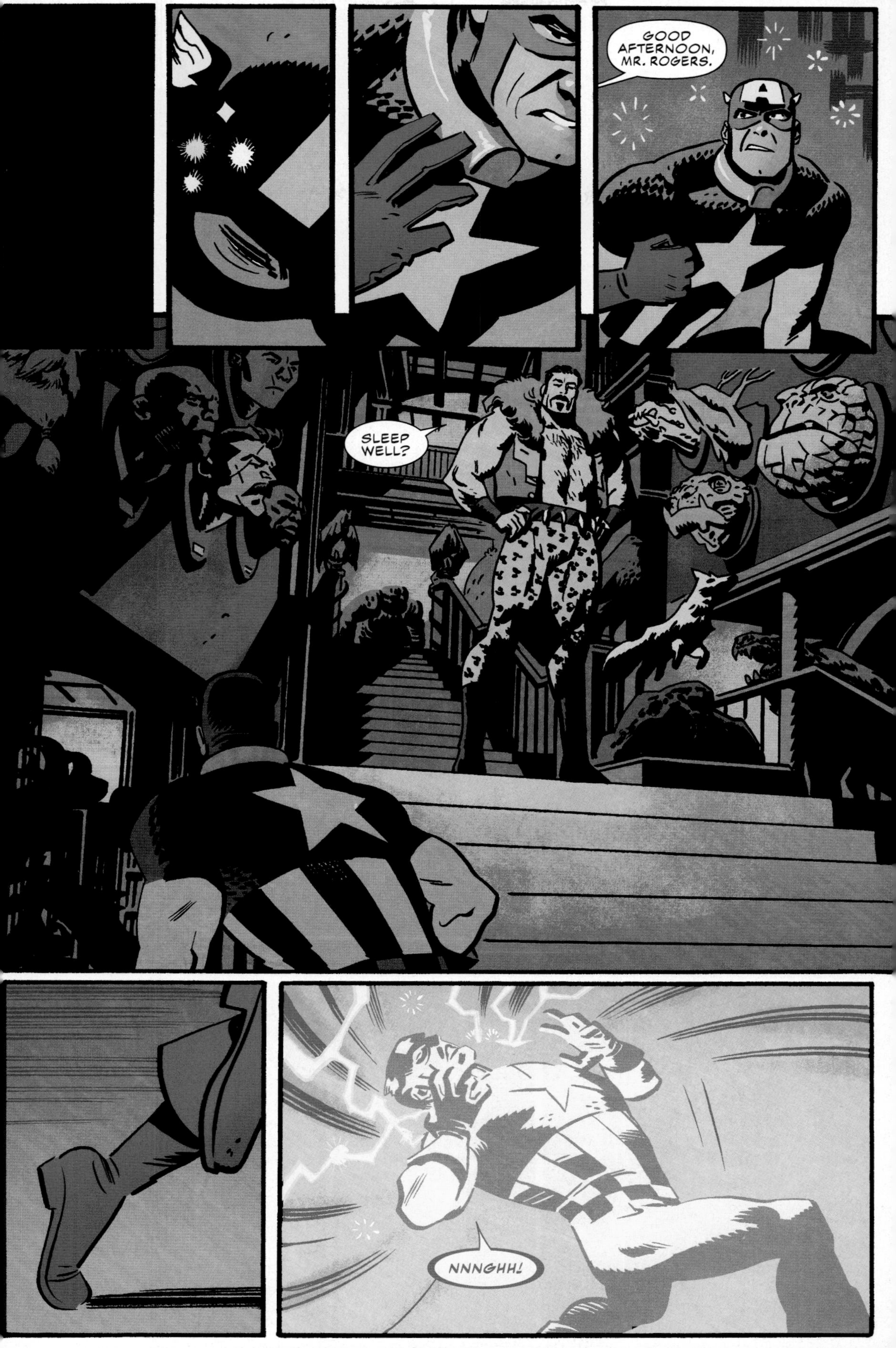
GOOD AFTERNOON, MR. ROGERS.
SLEEP WELL?
NNNGHH!

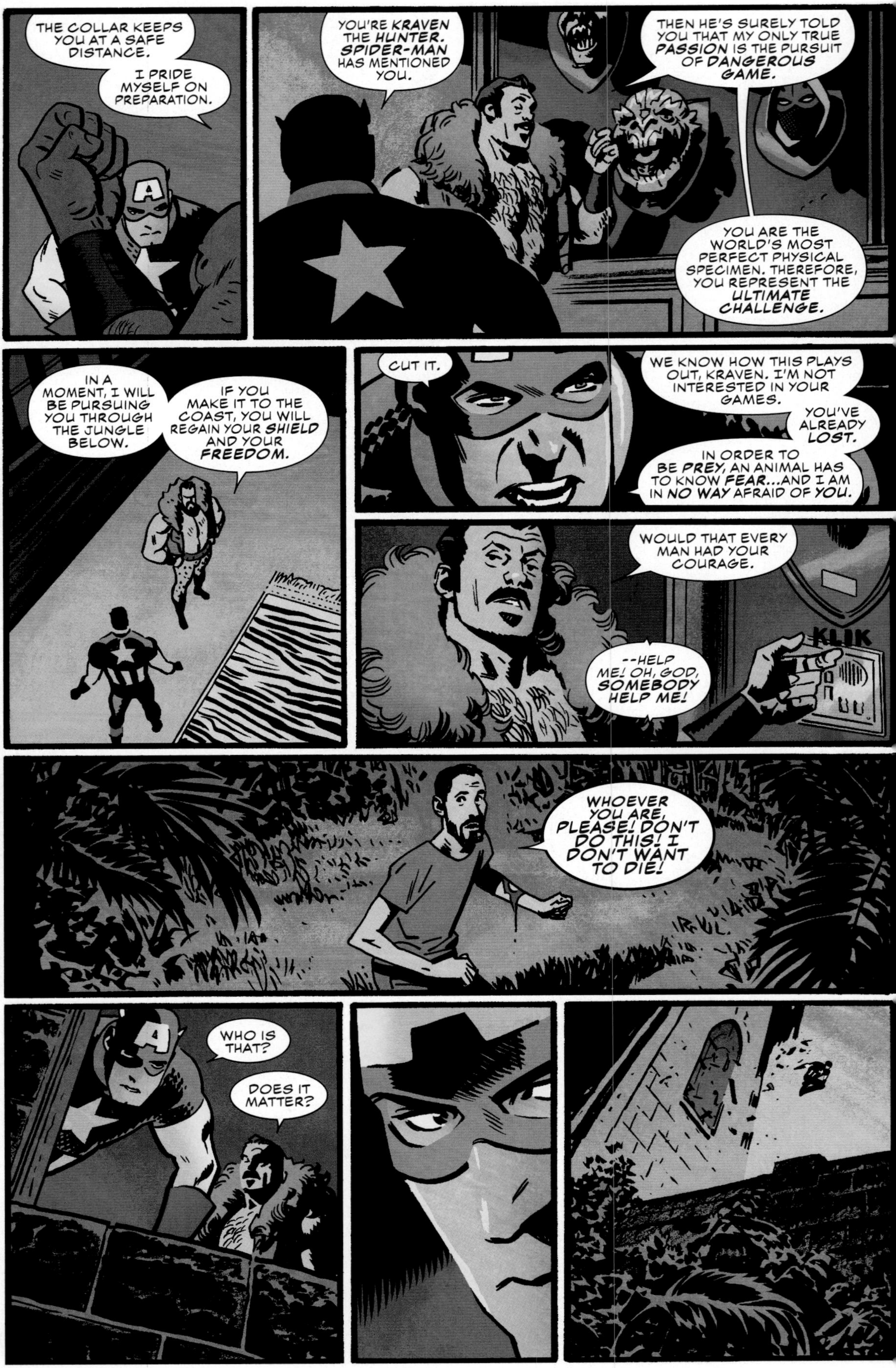
THE COLLAR KEEPS YOU AT A SAFE DISTANCE.
I PRIDE MYSELF ON PREPARATION.
YOU'RE KRAVEN THE HUNTER. SPIDER-MAN HAS MENTIONED YOU.
THEN HE'S SURELY TOLD YOU THAT MY ONLY TRUE PASSION IS THE PURSUIT OF DANGEROUS GAME.
YOU ARE THE WORLD'S MOST PERFECT PHYSICAL SPECIMEN. THEREFORE, YOU REPRESENT THE ULTIMATE CHALLENGE.
IN A MOMENT, I WILL BE PURSUING YOU THROUGH THE JUNGLE BELOW.
IF YOU MAKE IT TO THE COAST, YOU WILL REGAIN YOUR SHIELD AND YOUR FREEDOM.
CUT IT.
WE KNOW HOW THIS PLAYS OUT, KRAVEN. I'M NOT INTERESTED IN YOUR GAMES.
YOU'VE ALREADY LOST.
IN ORDER TO BE PREY, AN ANIMAL HAS TO KNOW FEAR...AND I AM IN NO WAY AFRAID OF YOU.
WOULD THAT EVERY MAN HAD YOUR COURAGE.
KLIK
--HELP ME! OH, GOD, SOMEBODY HELP ME!
WHOEVER YOU ARE, PLEASE! DON'T DO THIS! I DON'T WANT TO DIE!
WHO IS THAT?
DOES IT MATTER?

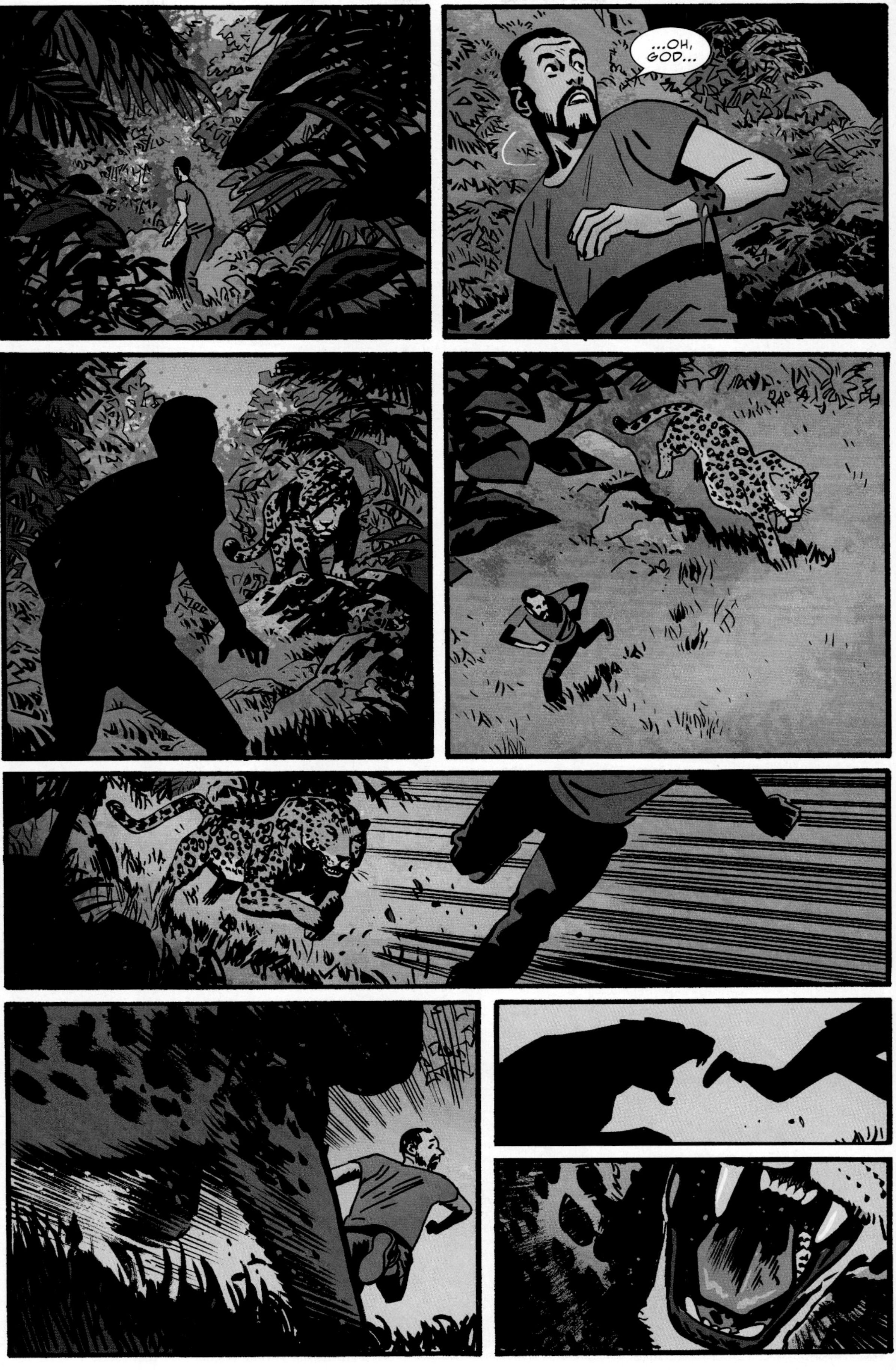
...OH, GOD...

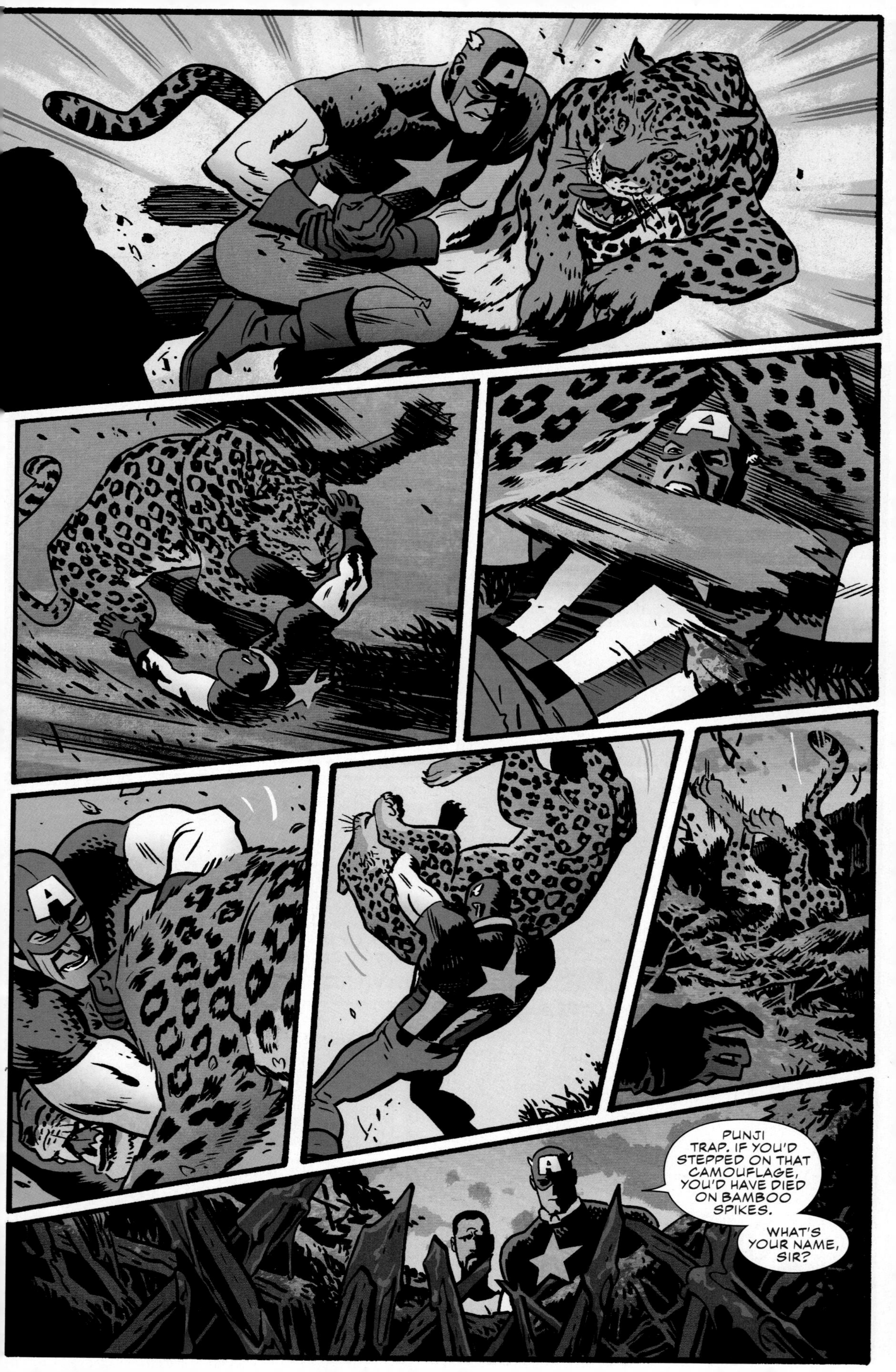
PUNJI TRAP. IF YOU'D STEPPED ON THAT CAMOUFLAGE, YOU'D HAVE DIED ON BAMBOO SPIKES.
WHAT'S YOUR NAME, SIR?

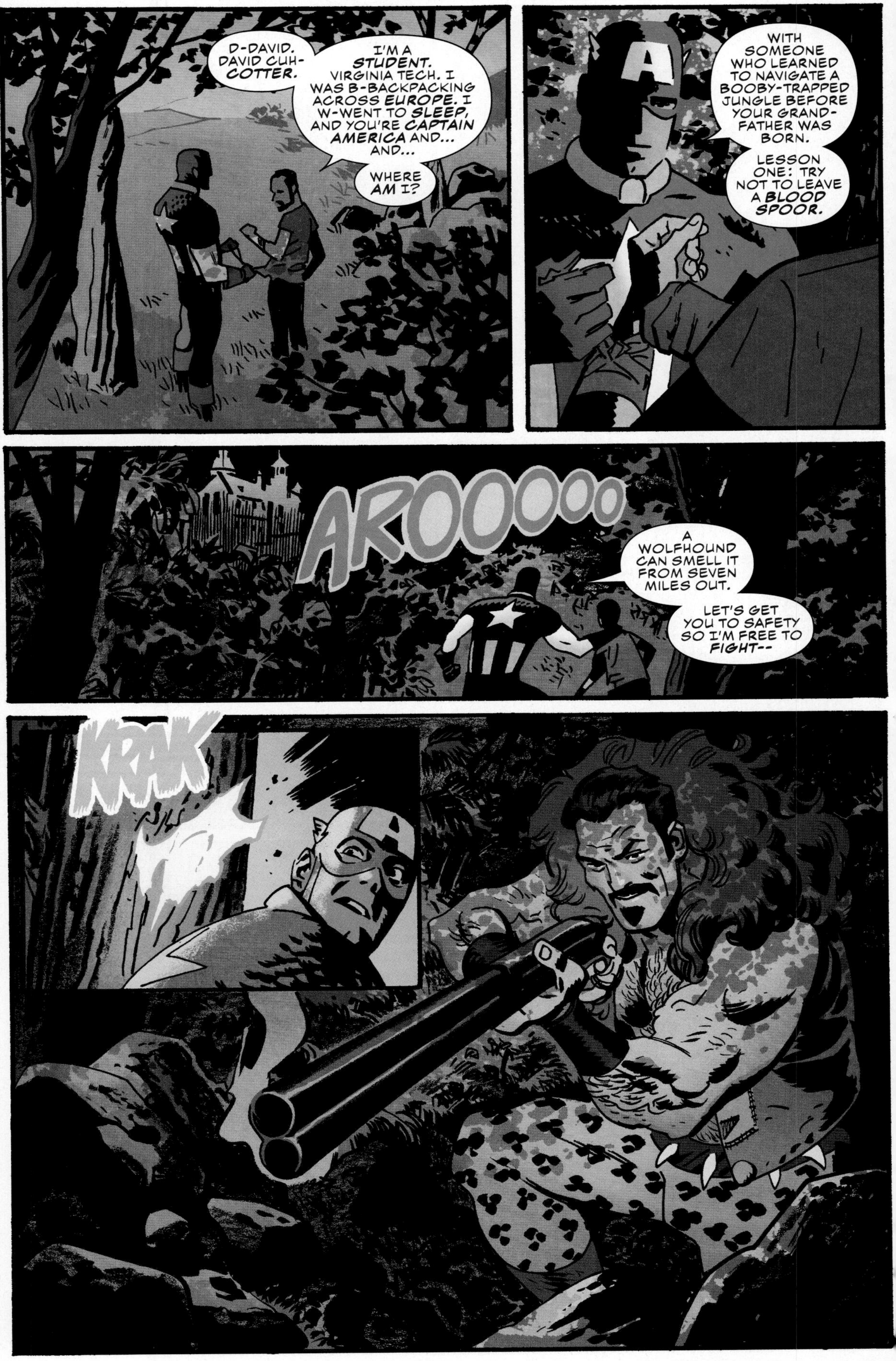
D-DAVID. DAVID CUH-COTTER.
I'M A STUDENT. VIRGINIA TECH. I WAS B-BACKPACKING ACROSS EUROPE. I W-WENT TO SLEEP, AND YOU'RE CAPTAIN AMERICA AND... AND...
WHERE AM I?
WITH SOMEONE WHO LEARNED TO NAVIGATE A BOOBY-TRAPPED JUNGLE BEFORE YOUR GRAND-FATHER WAS BORN.
LESSON ONE: TRY NOT TO LEAVE A BLOOD SPOOR.
AROOOOO
A WOLFHOUND CAN SMELL IT FROM SEVEN MILES OUT.
LET'S GET YOU TO SAFETY SO I'M FREE TO FIGHT--
KRAK

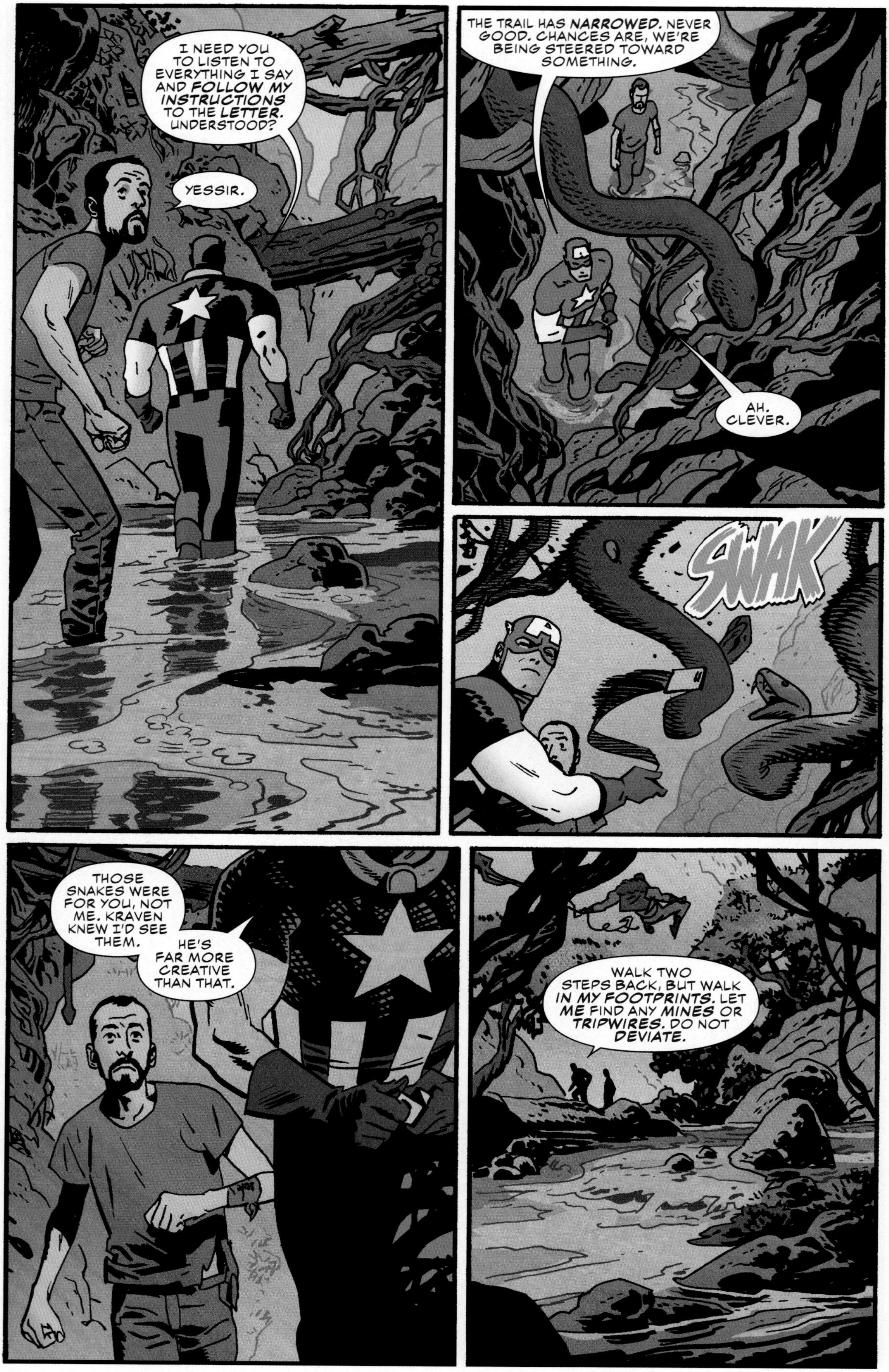
I NEED YOU TO LISTEN TO EVERYTHING I SAY AND FOLLOW MY INSTRUCTIONS TO THE LETTER. UNDERSTOOD?
YESSIR.
THE TRAIL HAS NARROWED. NEVER GOOD. CHANCES ARE, WE'RE BEING STEERED TOWARD SOMETHING.
AH. CLEVER.
SWAK
THOSE SNAKES WERE FOR YOU, NOT ME. KRAVEN KNEW I'D SEE THEM.
HE'S FAR MORE CREATIVE THAN THAT.
WALK TWO STEPS BACK, BUT WALK IN MY FOOTPRINTS. LET ME FIND ANY MINES OR TRIPWIRES. DO NOT DEVIATE.

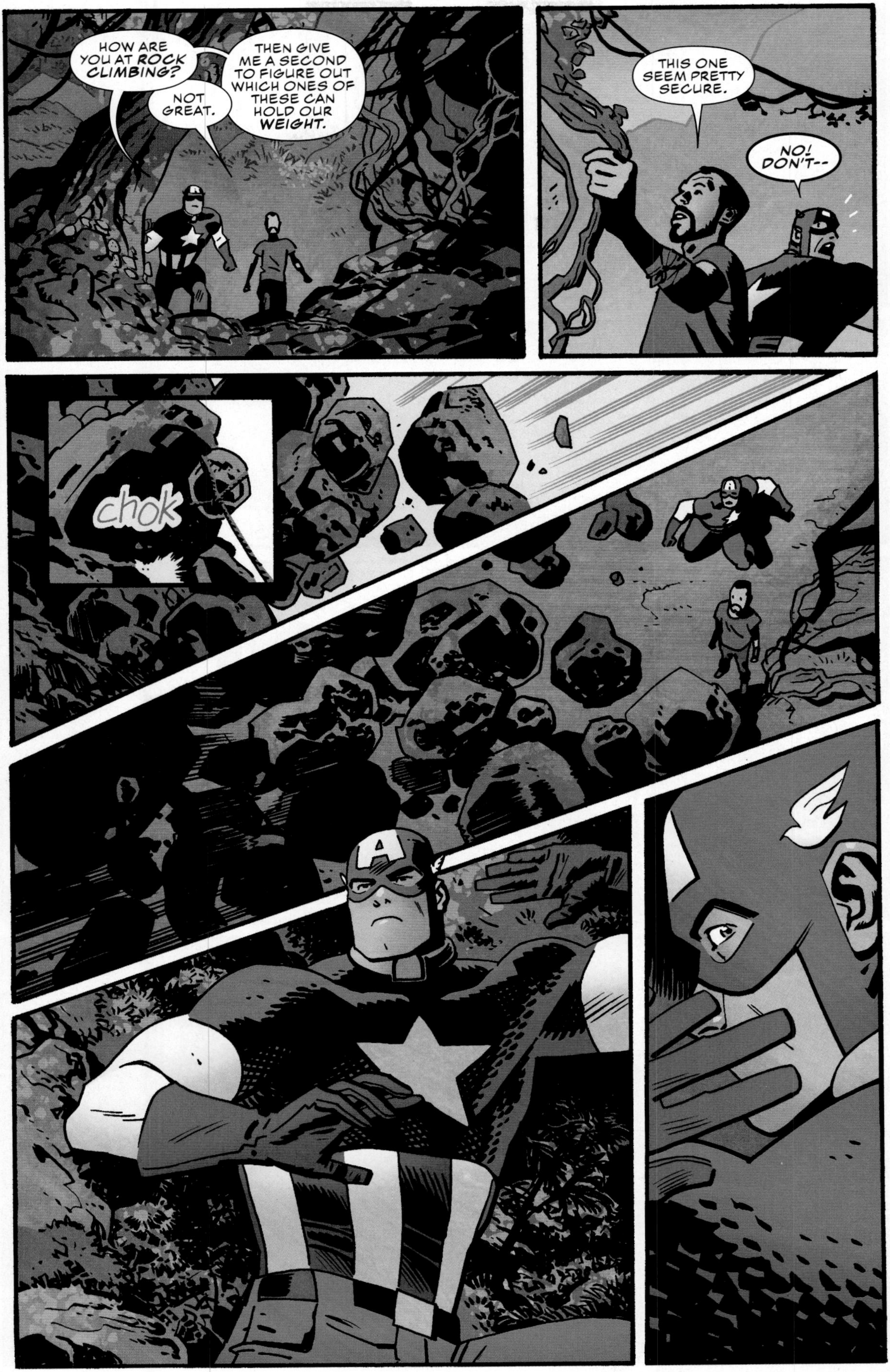
HOW ARE YOU AT ROCK CLIMBING?
NOT GREAT.
THEN GIVE ME A SECOND TO FIGURE OUT WHICH ONES OF THESE CAN HOLD OUR WEIGHT.
THIS ONE SEEM PRETTY SECURE.
NO! DON'T--
chok

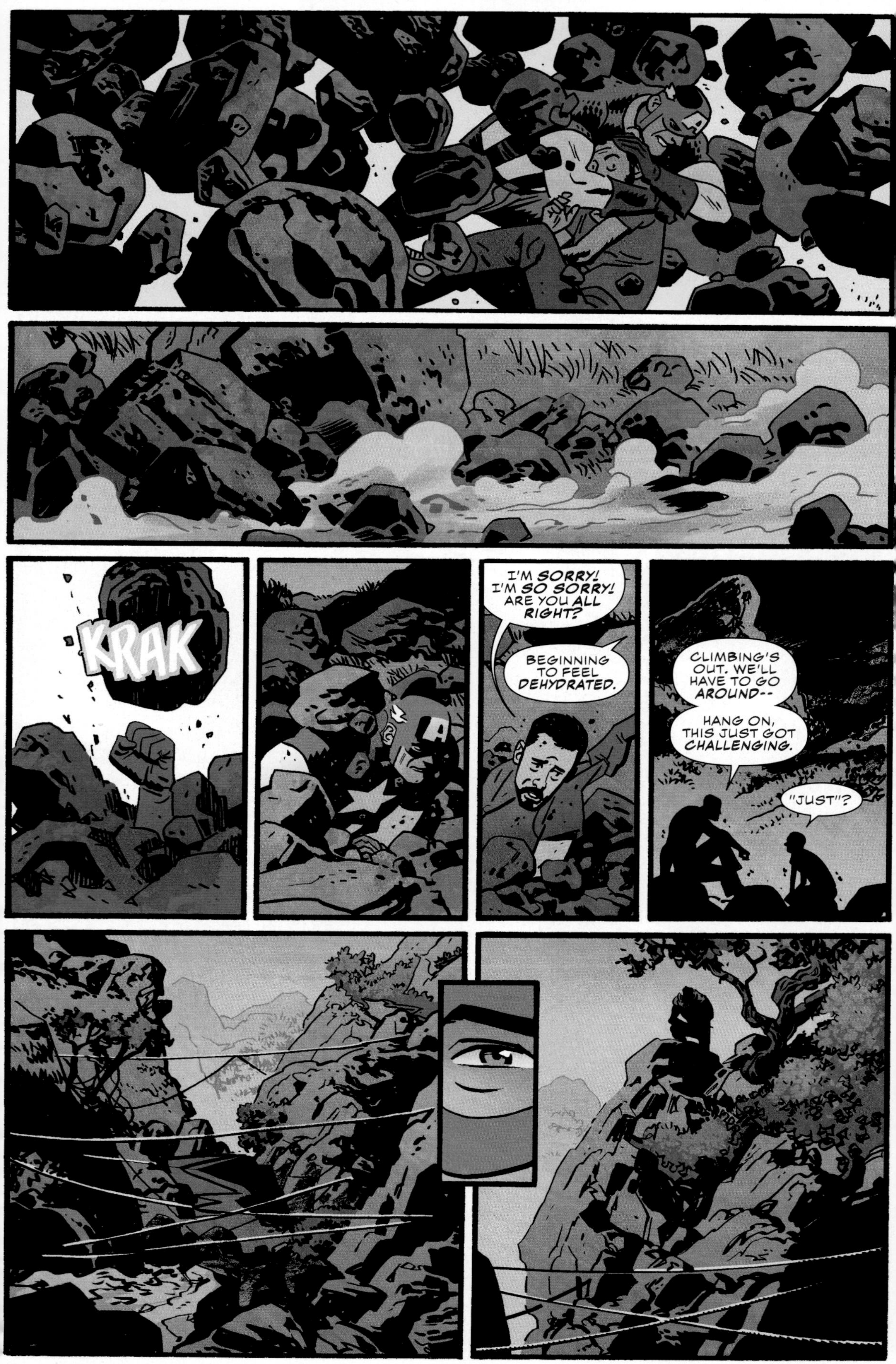
KRAK
I'M SORRY! I'M SO SORRY! ARE YOU ALL RIGHT?
BEGINNING TO FEEL DEHYDRATED.
CLIMBING'S OUT. WE'LL HAVE TO GO AROUND--
HANG ON, THIS JUST GOT CHALLENGING.
"JUST"?

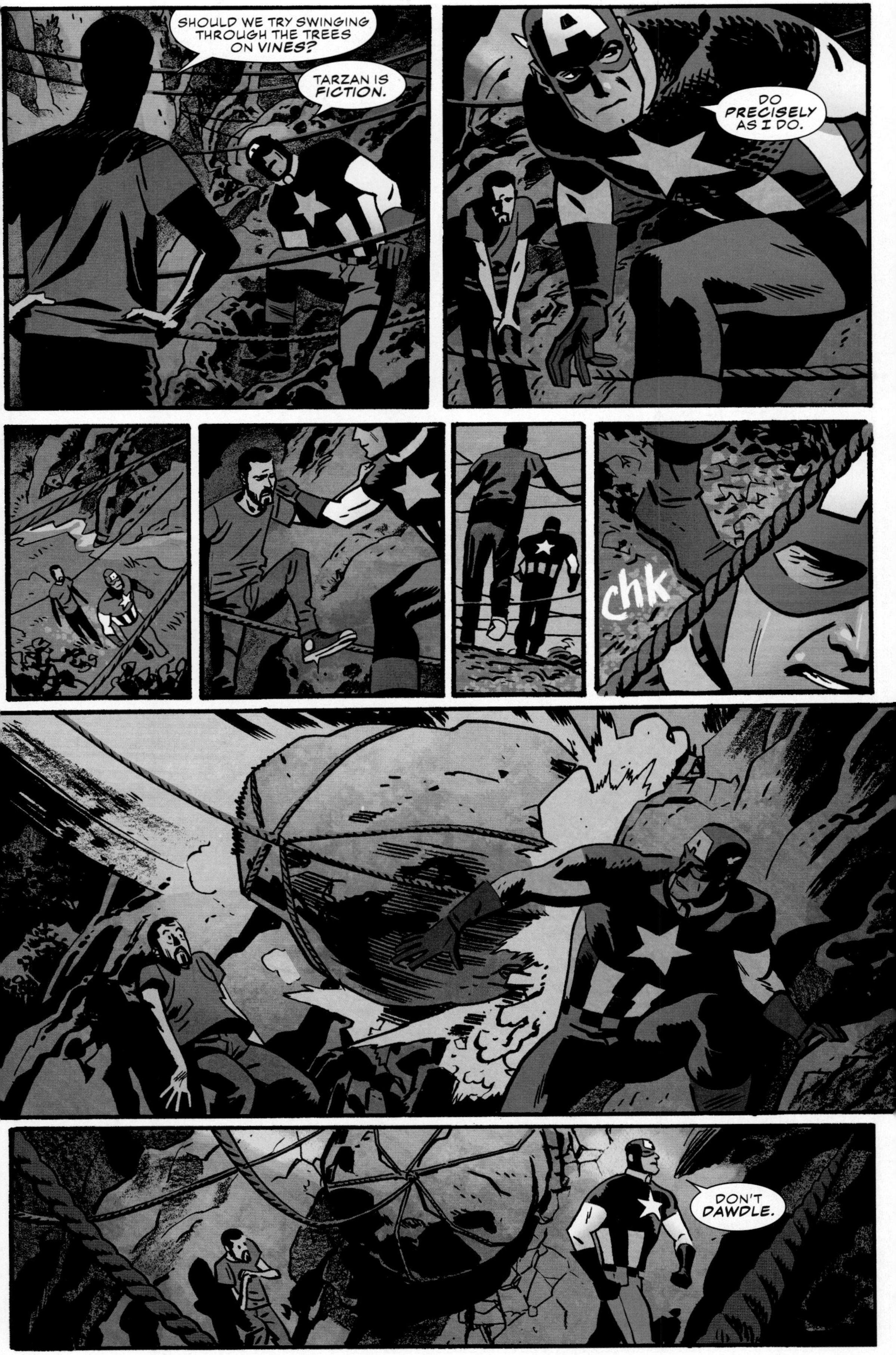
SHOULD WE TRY SWINGING THROUGH THE TREES ON VINES?
TARZAN IS FICTION.
DO PRECISELY AS I DO.
CHK
DON'T DAWDLE.

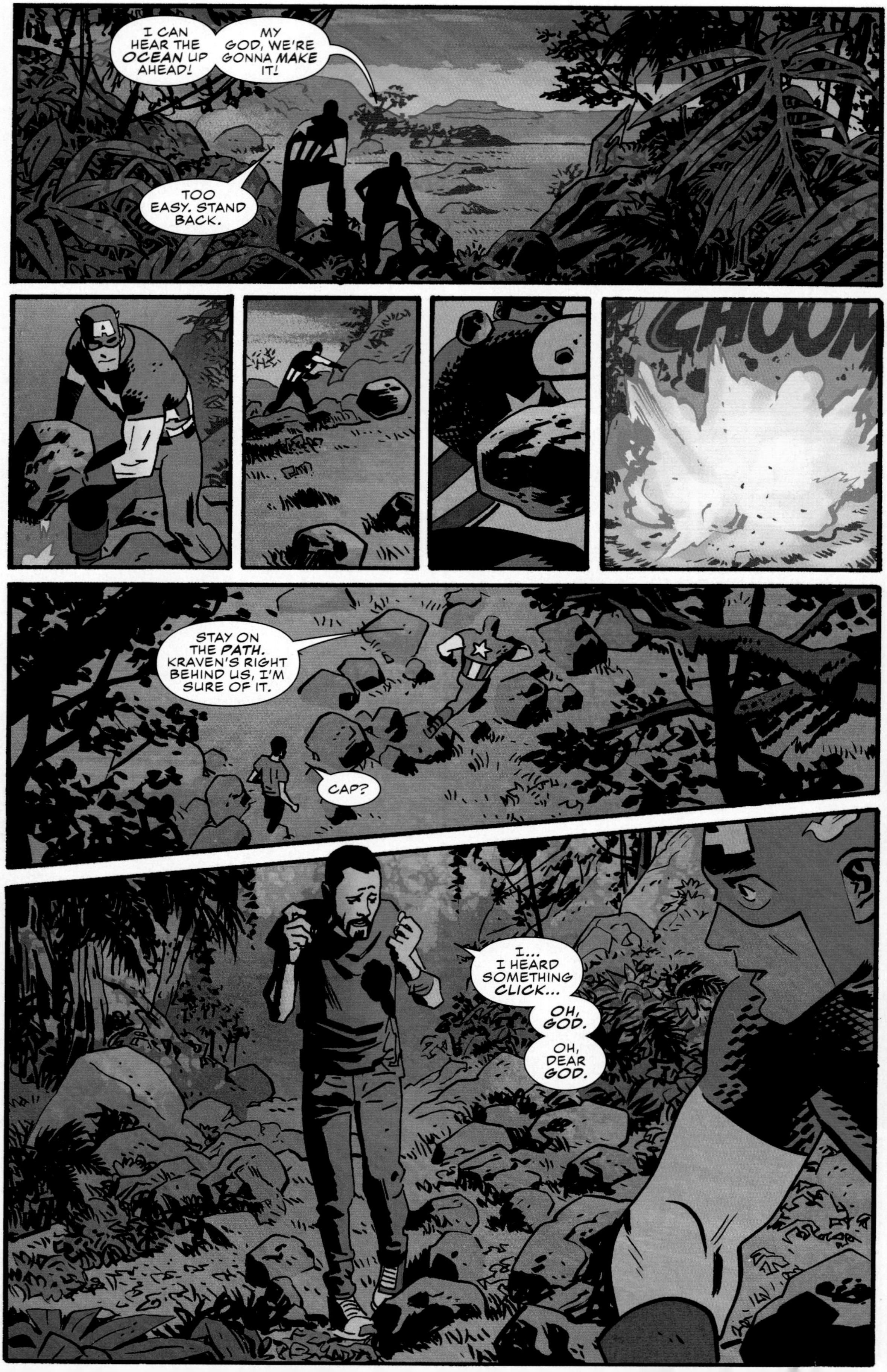
I CAN HEAR THE OCEAN UP AHEAD!
MY GOD, WE'RE GONNA MAKE IT!
TOO EASY. STAND BACK.
CHOOM
STAY ON THE PATH. KRAVEN'S RIGHT BEHIND US, I'M SURE OF IT.
CAP?
I... I HEARD SOMETHING CLICK...
OH, GOD.
OH, DEAR GOD.

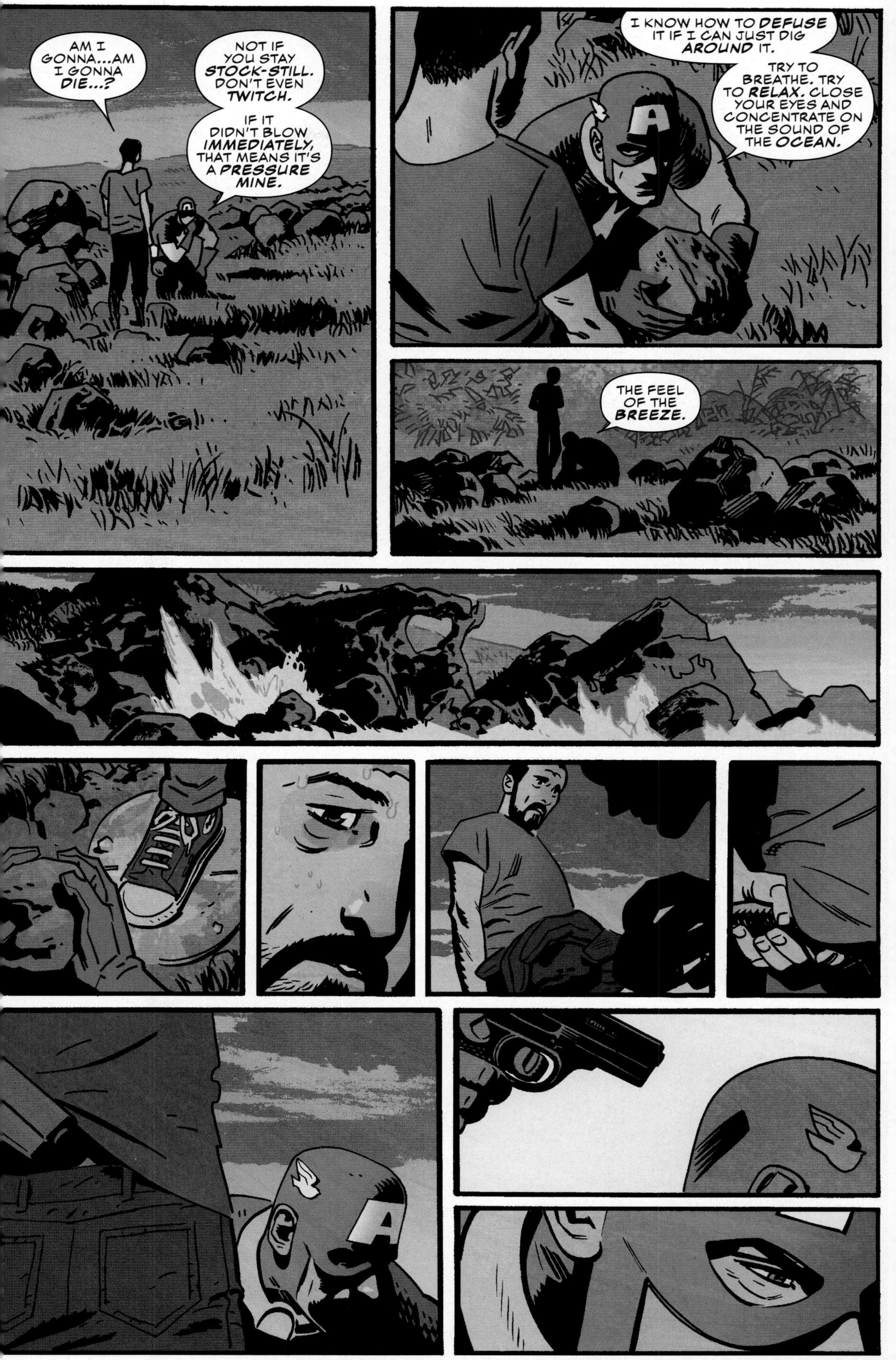
AM I GONNA...AM I GONNA DIE...?
NOT IF YOU STAY STOCK-STILL. DON'T EVEN TWITCH.
IF IT DIDN'T BLOW IMMEDIATELY, THAT MEANS IT'S A PRESSURE MINE.
I KNOW HOW TO DEFUSE IT IF I CAN JUST DIG AROUND IT.
TRY TO BREATHE. TRY TO RELAX. CLOSE YOUR EYES AND CONCENTRATE ON THE SOUND OF THE OCEAN.
THE FEEL OF THE BREEZE.

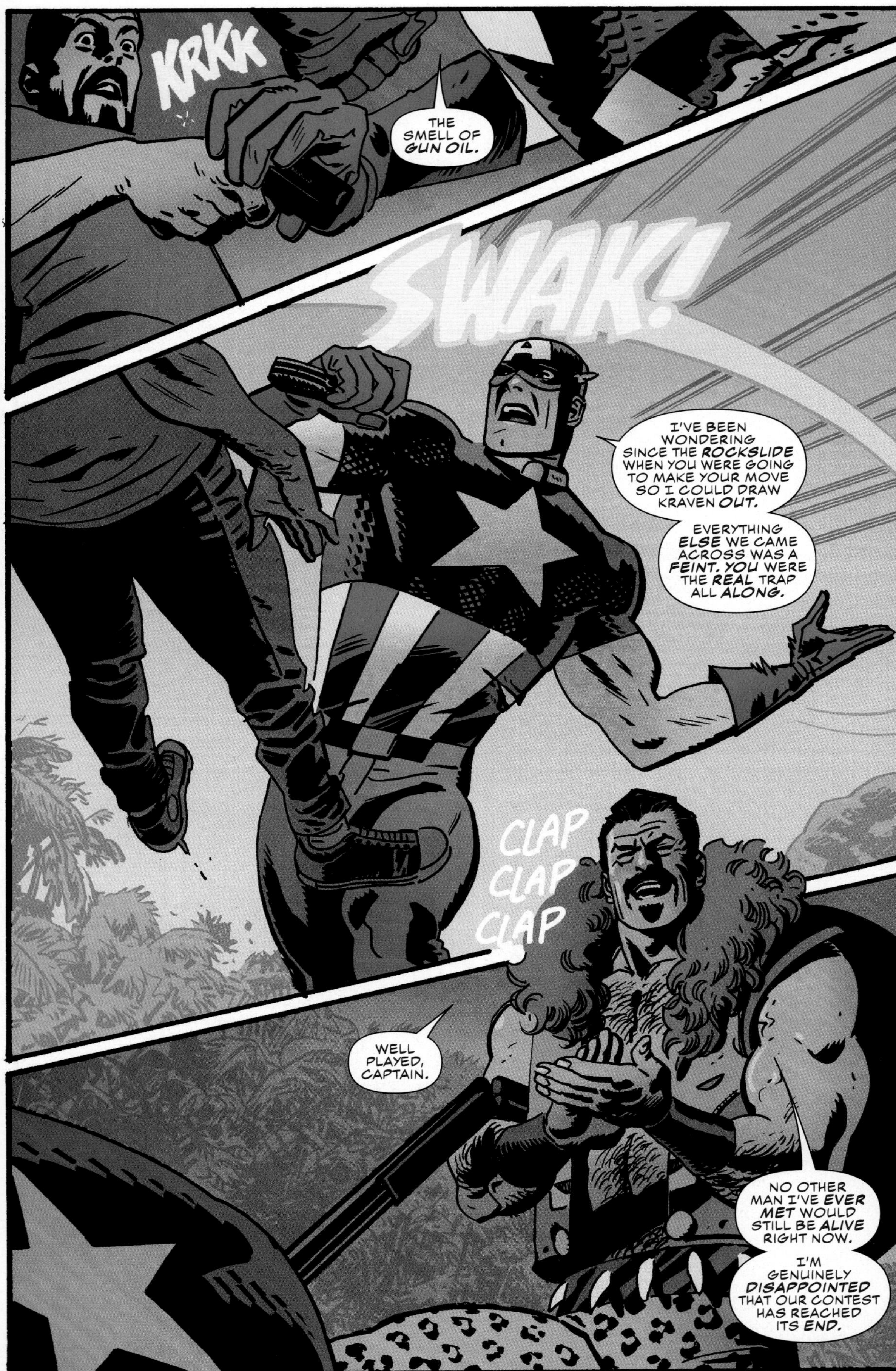
KRKK
THE SMELL OF GUN OIL.
SWAK!
I'VE BEEN WONDERING SINCE THE ROCKSLIDE WHEN YOU WERE GOING TO MAKE YOUR MOVE SO I COULD DRAW KRAVEN OUT.
EVERYTHING ELSE WE CAME ACROSS WAS A FEINT. YOU WERE THE REAL TRAP ALL ALONG.
CLAP CLAP CLAP
WELL PLAYED, CAPTAIN.
NO OTHER MAN I'VE EVER MET WOULD STILL BE ALIVE RIGHT NOW.
I'M GENUINELY DISAPPOINTED THAT OUR CONTEST HAS REACHED ITS END.

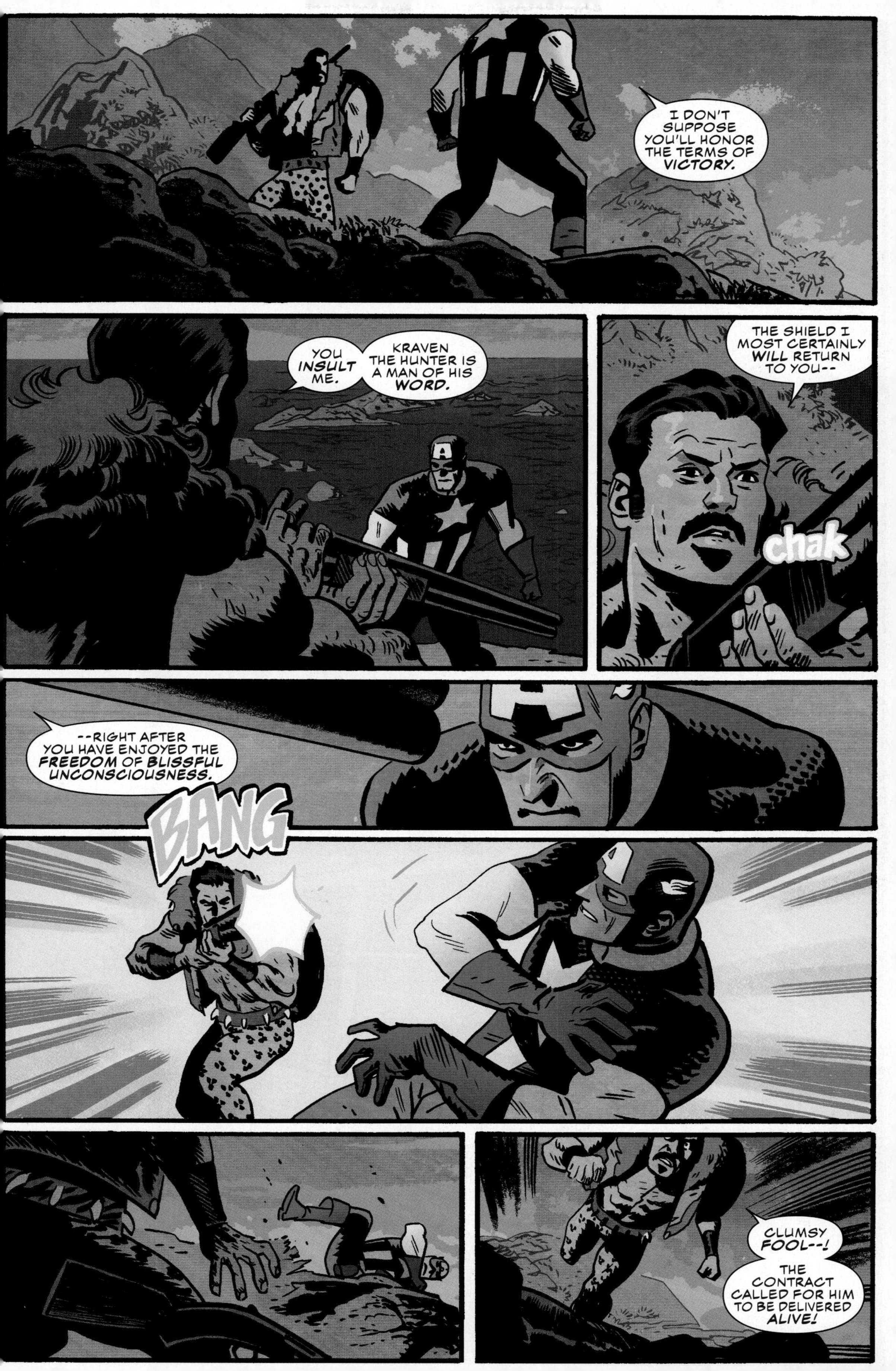
I DON'T SUPPOSE YOU'LL HONOR THE TERMS OF VICTORY.
YOU INSULT ME.
KRAVEN THE HUNTER IS A MAN OF HIS WORD.
THE SHIELD I MOST CERTAINLY WILL RETURN TO YOU--
chak
--RIGHT AFTER YOU HAVE ENJOYED THE FREEDOM OF BLISSFUL UNCONSCIOUSNESS.
BANG
CLUMSY FOOL--!
THE CONTRACT CALLED FOR HIM TO BE DELIVERED ALIVE!

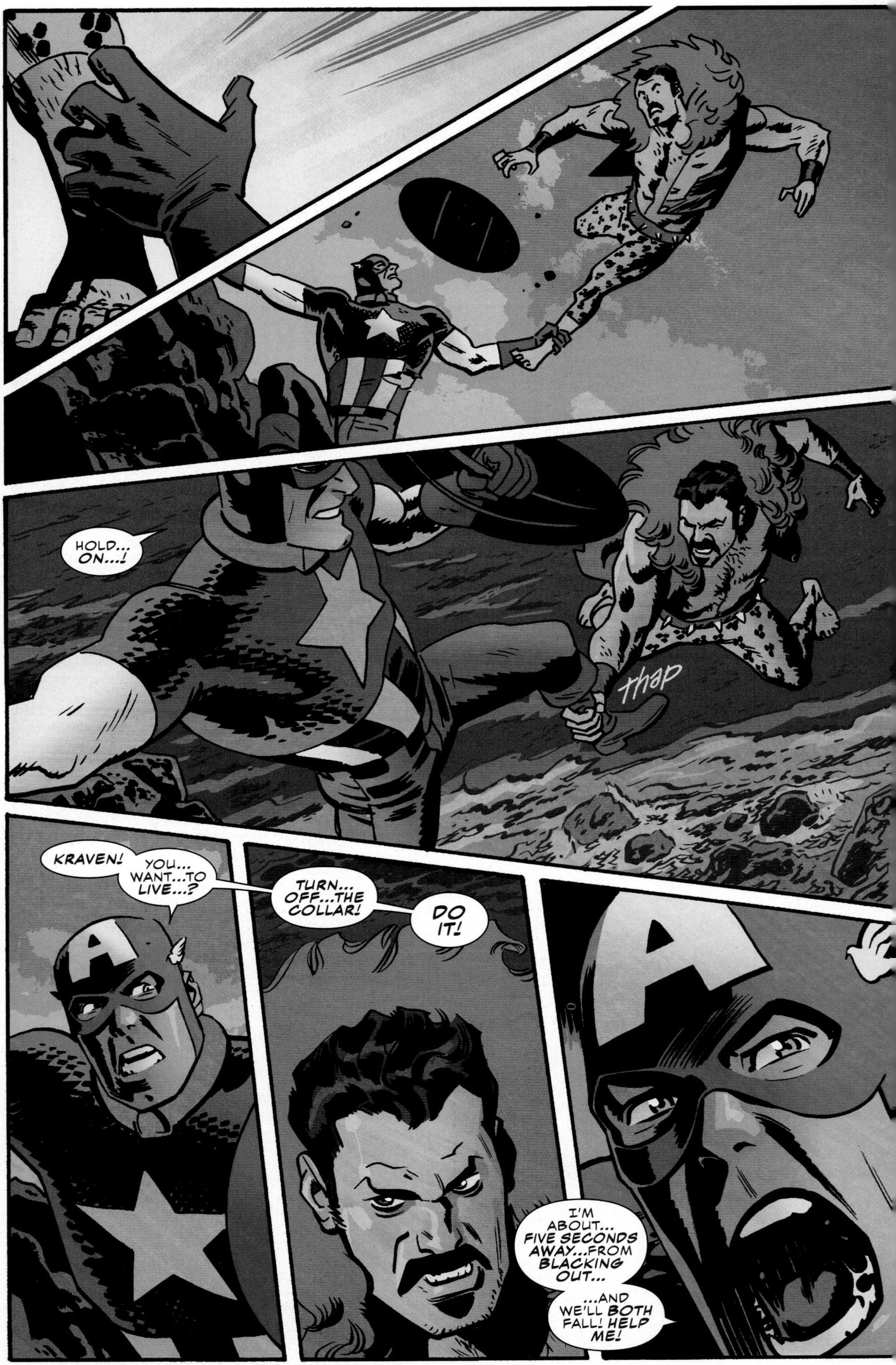
HOLD... ON...!
thap
KRAVEN!
YOU... WANT...TO LIVE...?
TURN... OFF...THE COLLAR!
DO IT!
I'M ABOUT... FIVE SECONDS AWAY...FROM BLACKING OUT...
...AND WE'LL BOTH FALL! HELP ME!

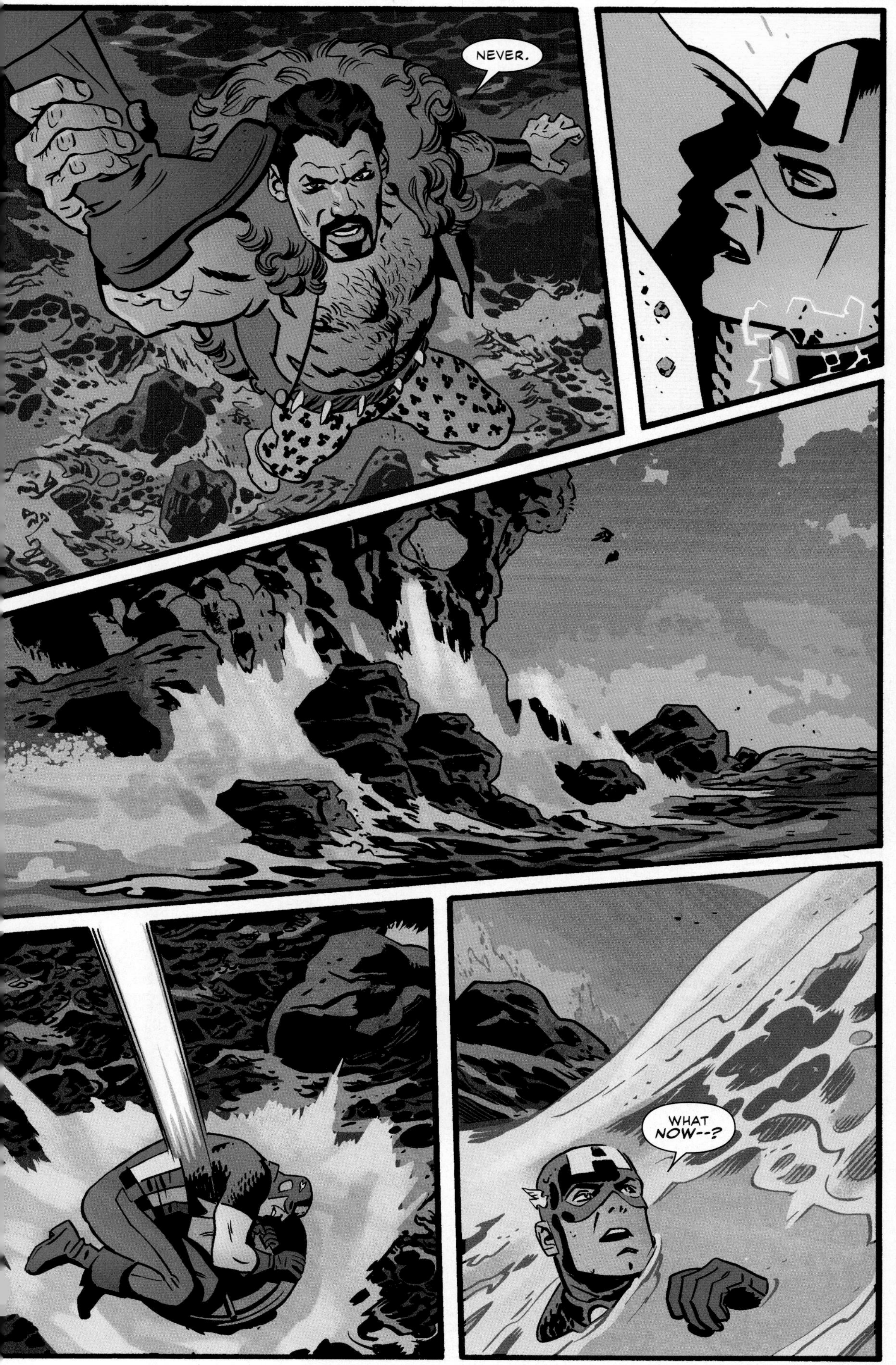
NEVER.
WHAT NOW--?

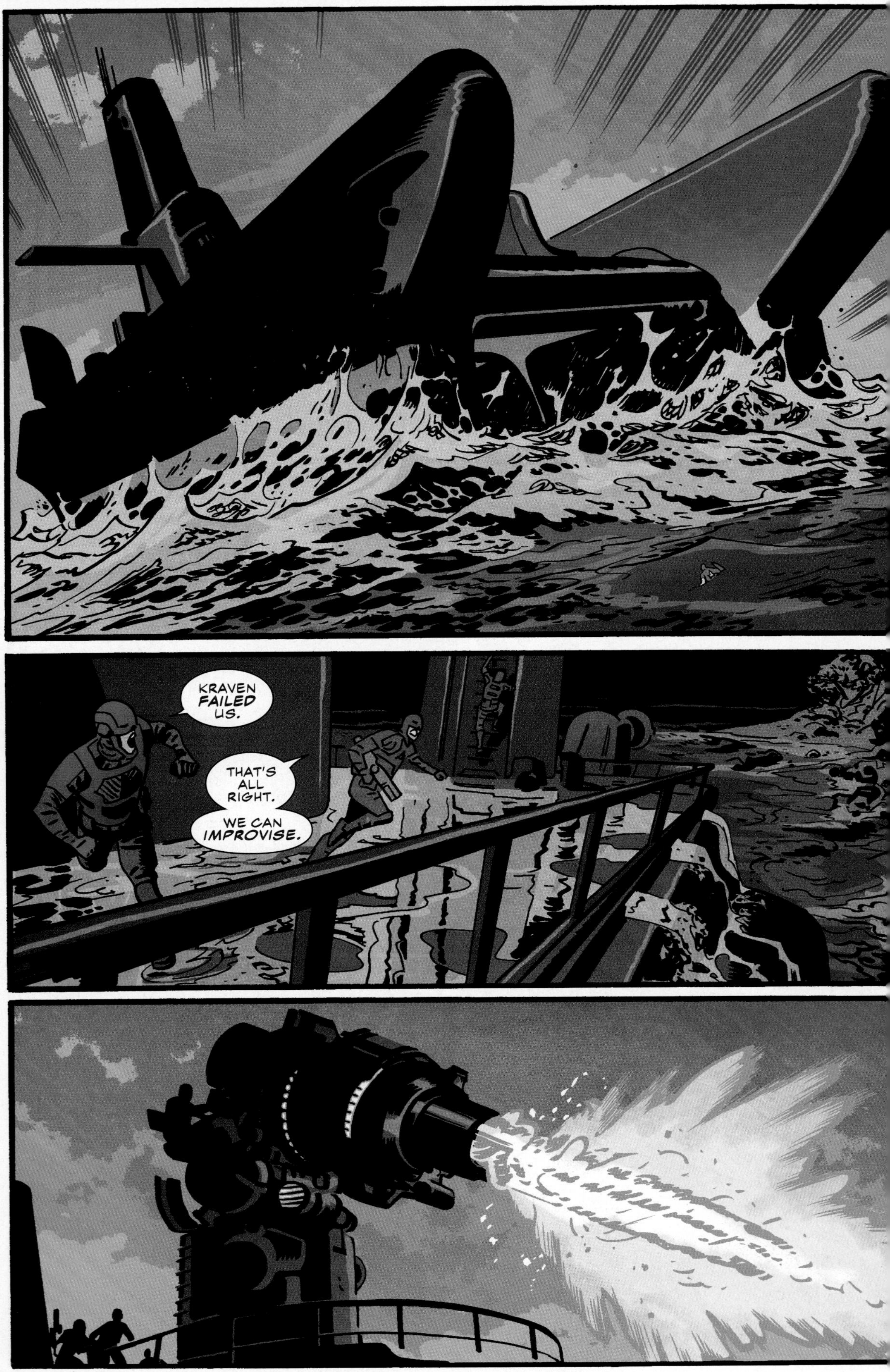
KRAVEN FAILED US.
THAT'S ALL RIGHT.
WE CAN IMPROVISE.

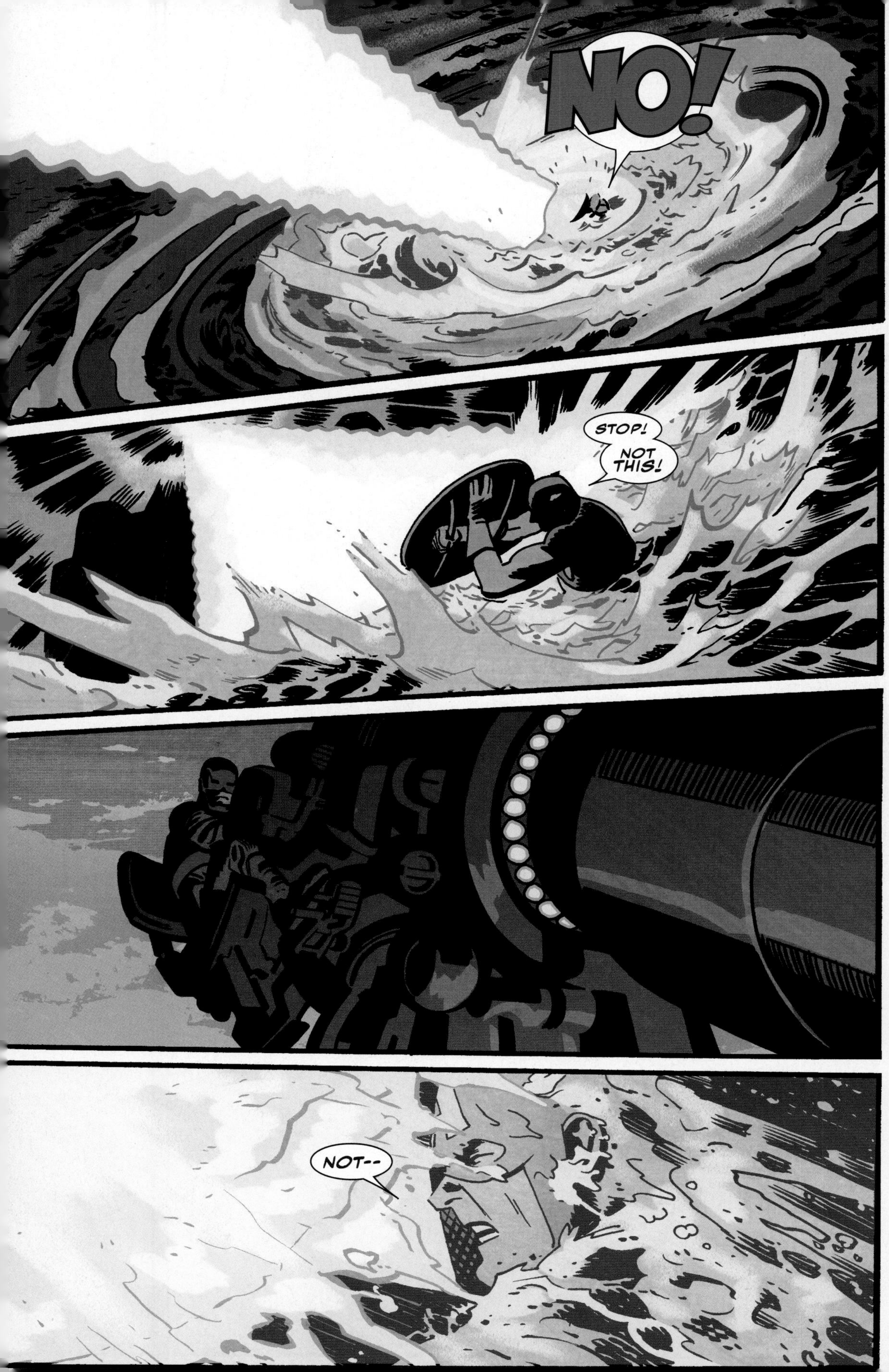
NO!
STOP! NOT THIS!
NOT--

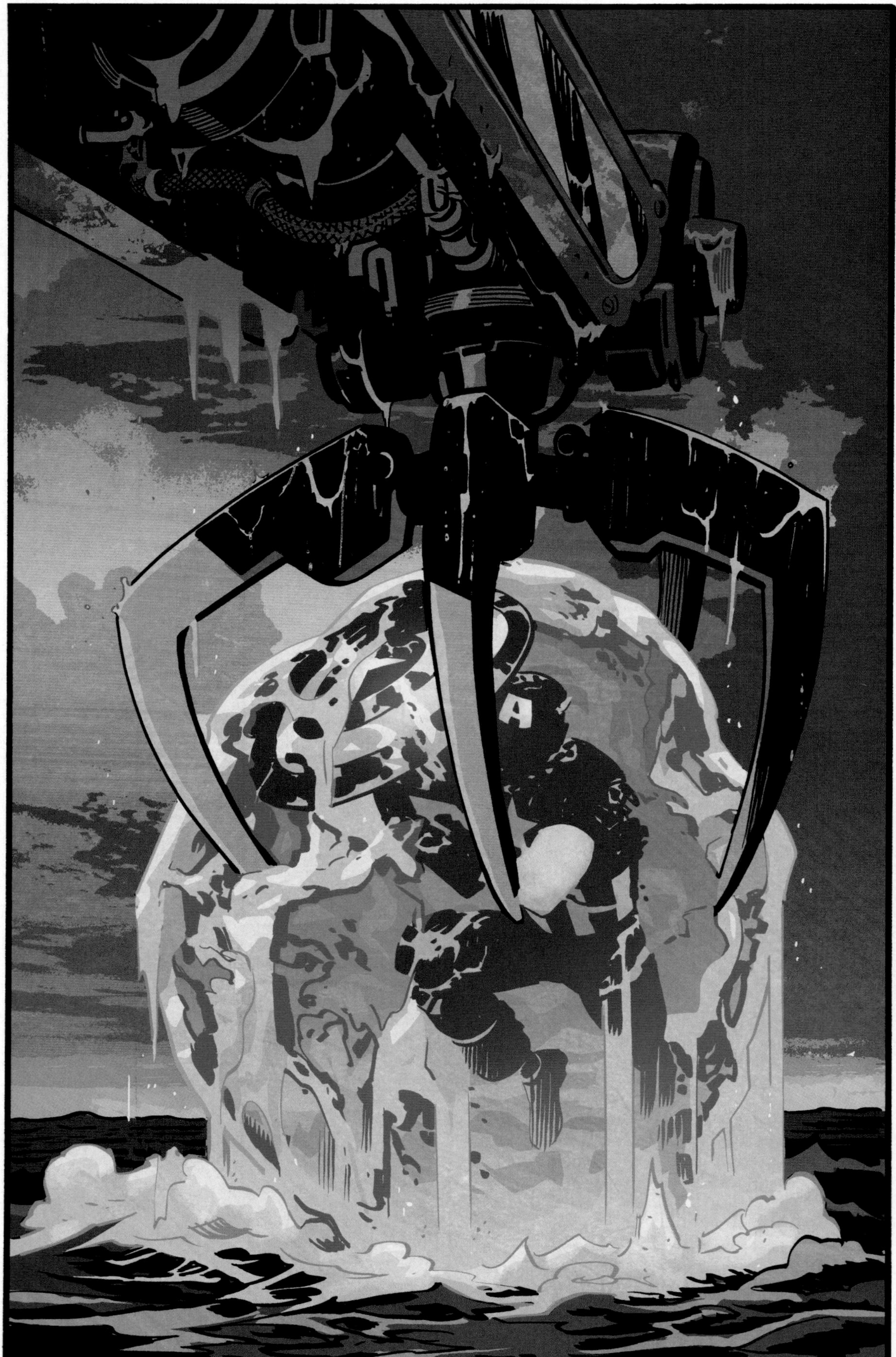

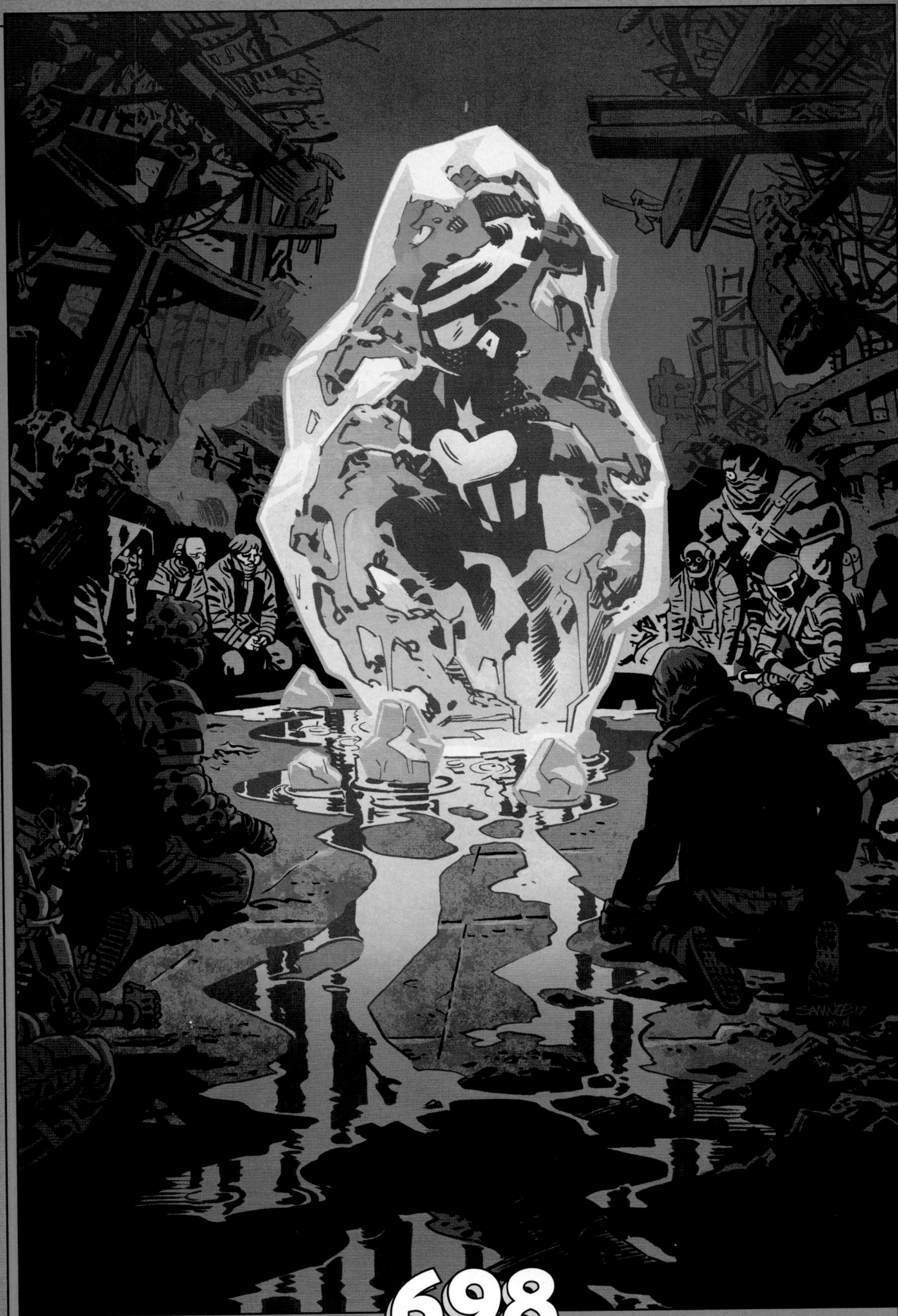
698

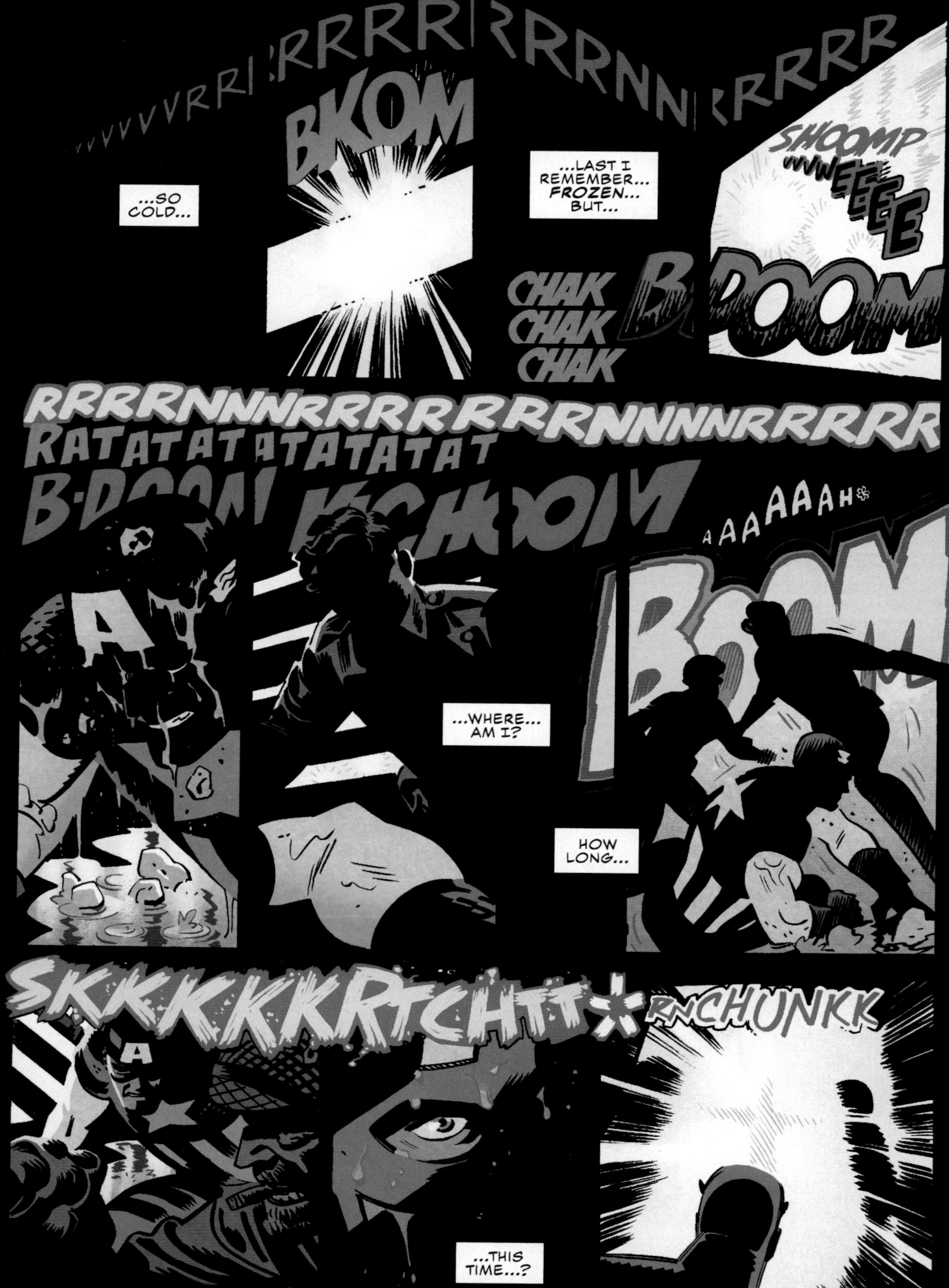
COLD...
VVVVVVVRRRRRRRRRRRRRNNRRRRR
BKOM
...SO COLD...
...LAST I REMEMBER... FROZEN... BUT...
SHOOMP
WWWEEEEE
CHAK CHAK CHAK
BDOOM
RRRRNNNNRRRRRRRRRRNNNNNRRRRR
RATATATATATATATAT
B-DOOM
KCHOOM
AAAAAAH
BOOM
...WHERE... AM I?
HOW LONG...
SKKKKKRTCHTT
RNCHUNKK
...THIS TIME...?

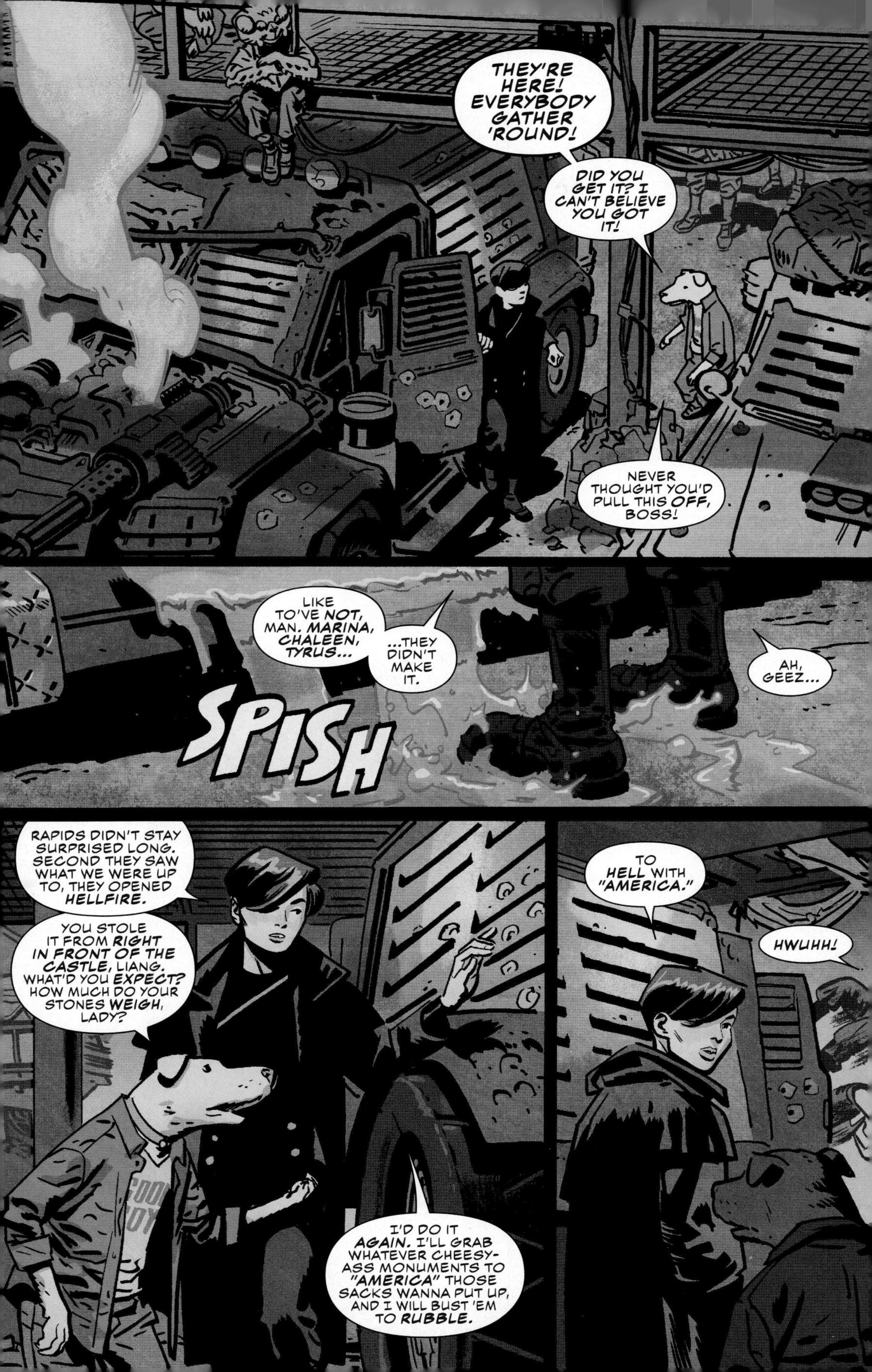
THEY'RE HERE! EVERYBODY GATHER 'ROUND!
DID YOU GET IT? I CAN'T BELIEVE YOU GOT IT!
NEVER THOUGHT YOU'D PULL THIS OFF, BOSS!
LIKE TO'VE NOT, MAN. MARINA, CHALEEN, TYRUS...
...THEY DIDN'T MAKE IT.
AH, GEEZ...
SPISH
RAPIDS DIDN'T STAY SURPRISED LONG. SECOND THEY SAW WHAT WE WERE UP TO, THEY OPENED HELLFIRE.
YOU STOLE IT FROM RIGHT IN FRONT OF THE CASTLE, LIANG. WHAT'D YOU EXPECT? HOW MUCH DO YOUR STONES WEIGH, LADY?
I'D DO IT AGAIN. I'LL GRAB WHATEVER CHEESY-ASS MONUMENTS TO "AMERICA" THOSE SACKS WANNA PUT UP, AND I WILL BUST 'EM TO RUBBLE.
TO HELL WITH "AMERICA."
HWUHH!

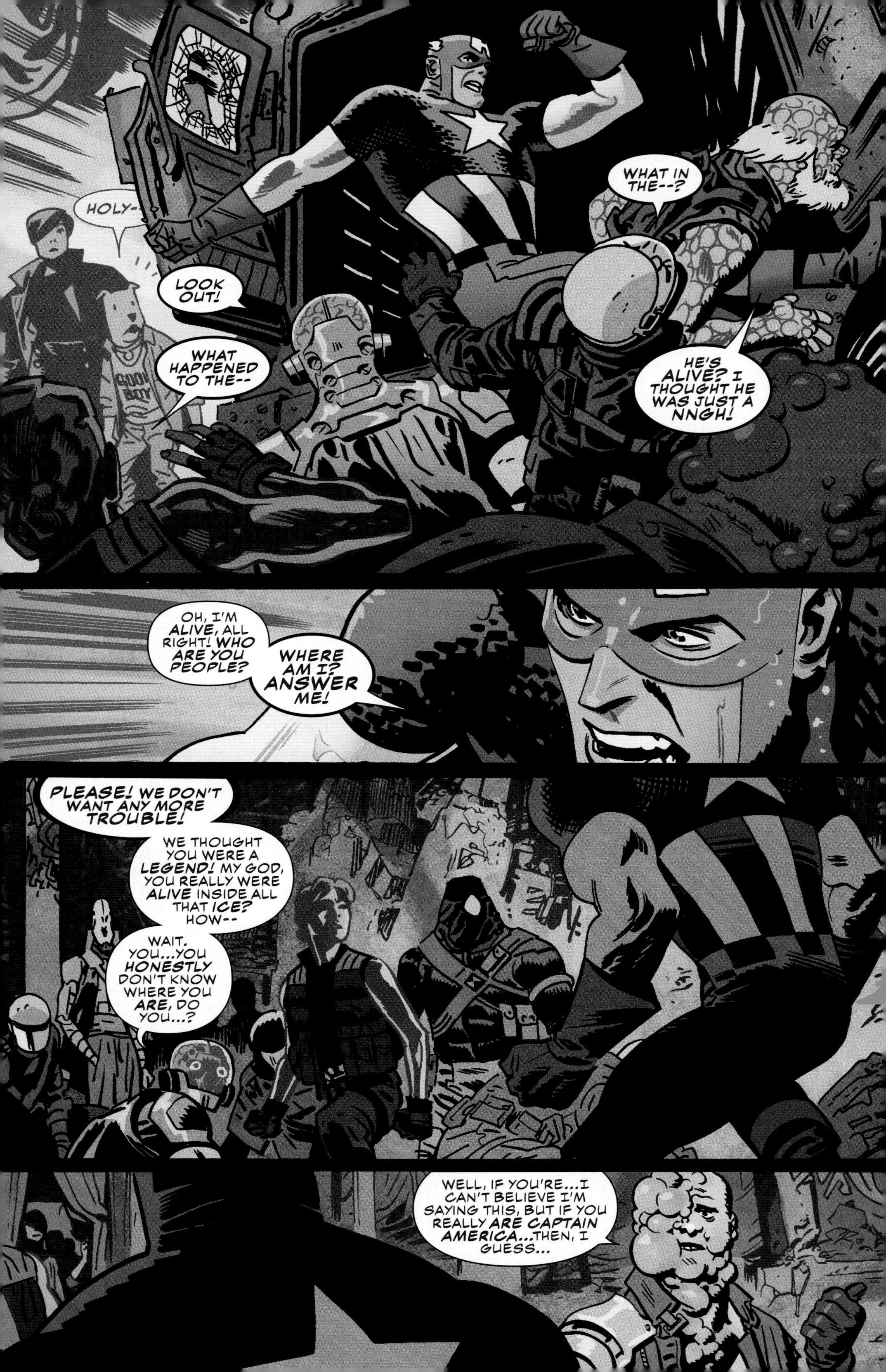
HOLY--
LOOK OUT!
WHAT HAPPENED TO THE--
WHAT IN THE--?
HE'S ALIVE? I THOUGHT HE WAS JUST A NNGH!
OH, I'M ALIVE, ALL RIGHT! WHO ARE YOU PEOPLE?
WHERE AM I? ANSWER ME!
PLEASE! WE DON'T WANT ANY MORE TROUBLE!
WE THOUGHT YOU WERE A LEGEND! MY GOD, YOU REALLY WERE ALIVE INSIDE ALL THAT ICE? HOW--
WAIT. YOU...YOU HONESTLY DON'T KNOW WHERE YOU ARE, DO YOU...?
WELL, IF YOU'RE...I CAN'T BELIEVE I'M SAYING THIS, BUT IF YOU REALLY ARE CAPTAIN AMERICA...THEN, I GUESS...

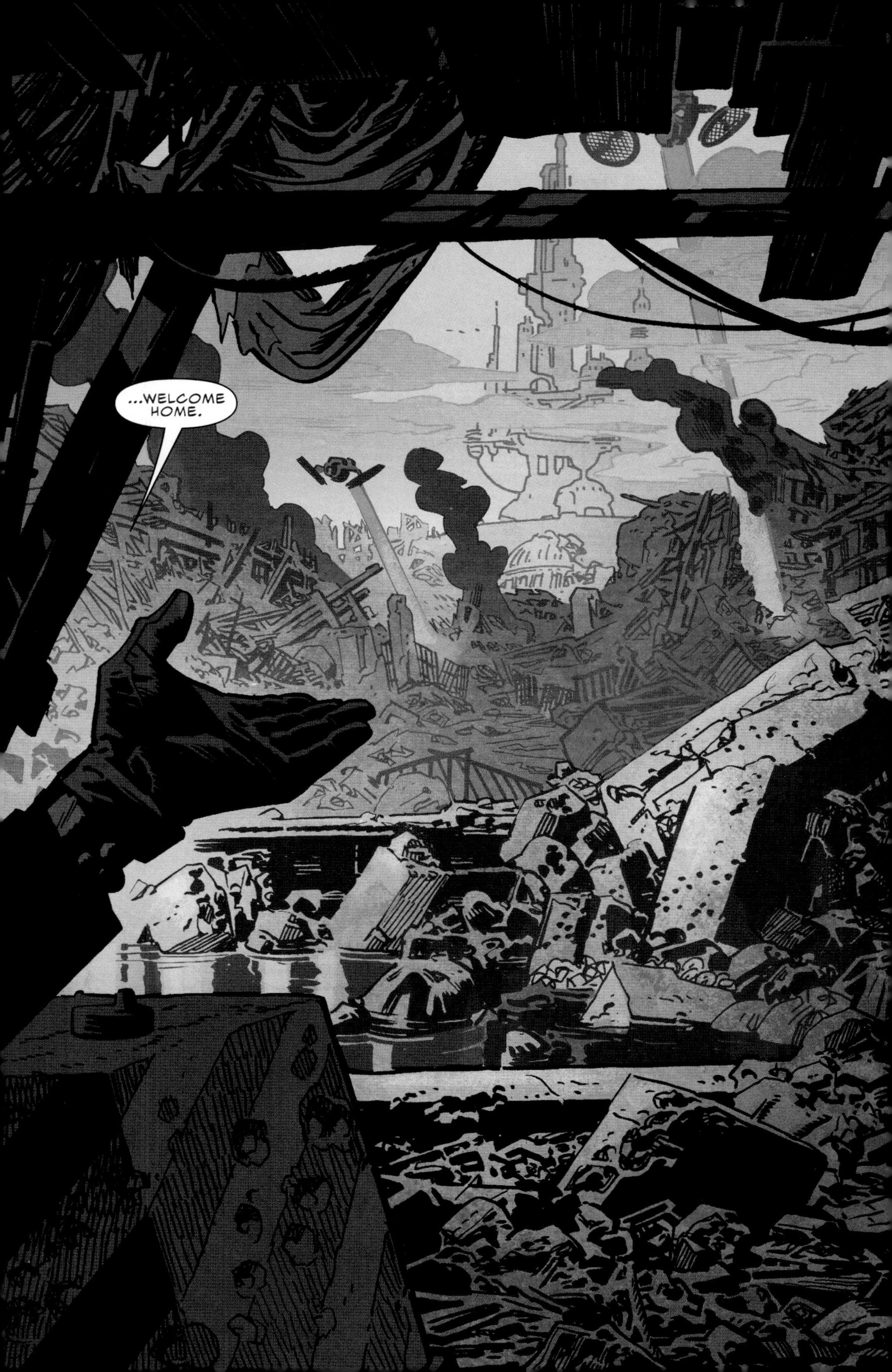
...WELCOME HOME.

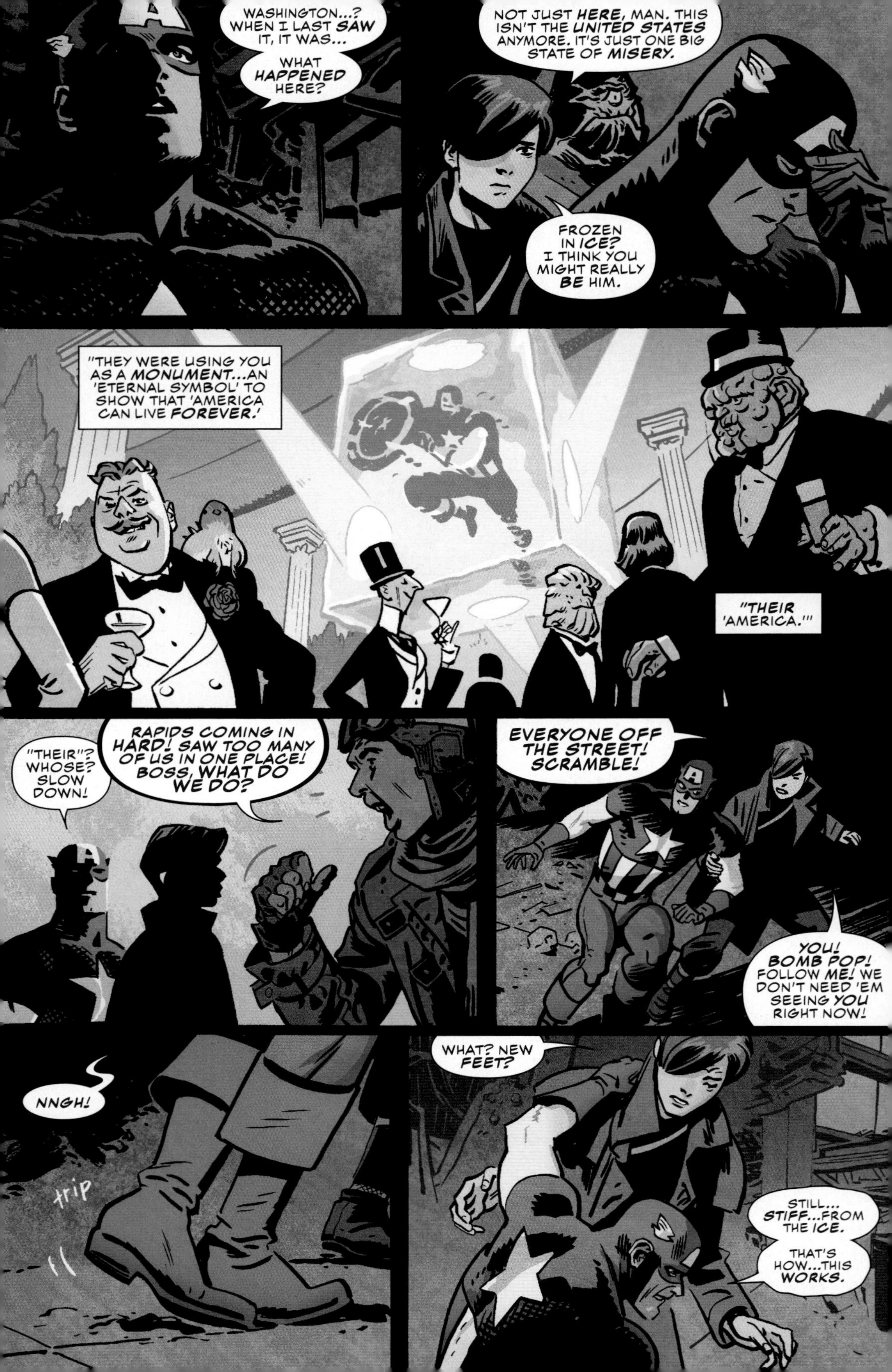
WASHINGTON...? WHEN I LAST SAW IT, IT WAS...
WHAT HAPPENED HERE?
NOT JUST HERE, MAN. THIS ISN'T THE UNITED STATES ANYMORE. IT'S JUST ONE BIG STATE OF MISERY.
FROZEN IN ICE? I THINK YOU MIGHT REALLY BE HIM.
"THEY WERE USING YOU AS A MONUMENT...AN 'ETERNAL SYMBOL' TO SHOW THAT 'AMERICA CAN LIVE FOREVER.'
"THEIR 'AMERICA.'"
"THEIR"? WHOSE? SLOW DOWN!
RAPIDS COMING IN HARD! SAW TOO MANY OF US IN ONE PLACE! BOSS, WHAT DO WE DO?
EVERYONE OFF THE STREET! SCRAMBLE!
YOU! BOMB POP! FOLLOW ME! WE DON'T NEED 'EM SEEING YOU RIGHT NOW!
NNGH!
trip
WHAT? NEW FEET?
STILL... STIFF...FROM THE ICE.
THAT'S HOW...THIS WORKS.

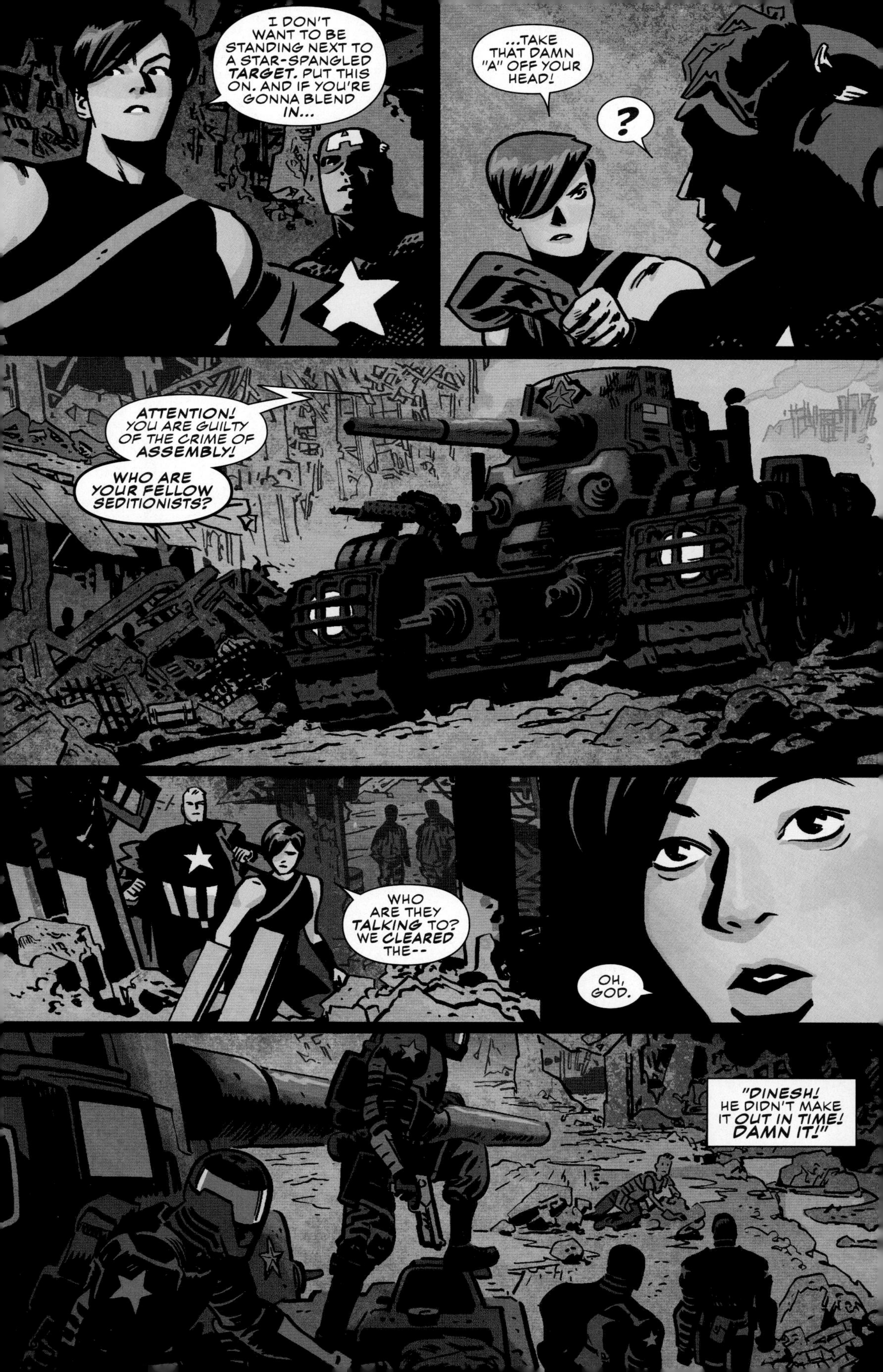
I DON'T WANT TO BE STANDING NEXT TO A STAR-SPANGLED TARGET. PUT THIS ON. AND IF YOU'RE GONNA BLEND IN...
...TAKE THAT DAMN "A" OFF YOUR HEAD!
?
ATTENTION! YOU ARE GUILTY OF THE CRIME OF ASSEMBLY!
WHO ARE YOUR FELLOW SEDITIONISTS?
WHO ARE THEY TALKING TO? WE CLEARED THE--
OH, GOD.
"DINESH! HE DIDN'T MAKE IT OUT IN TIME! DAMN IT!"

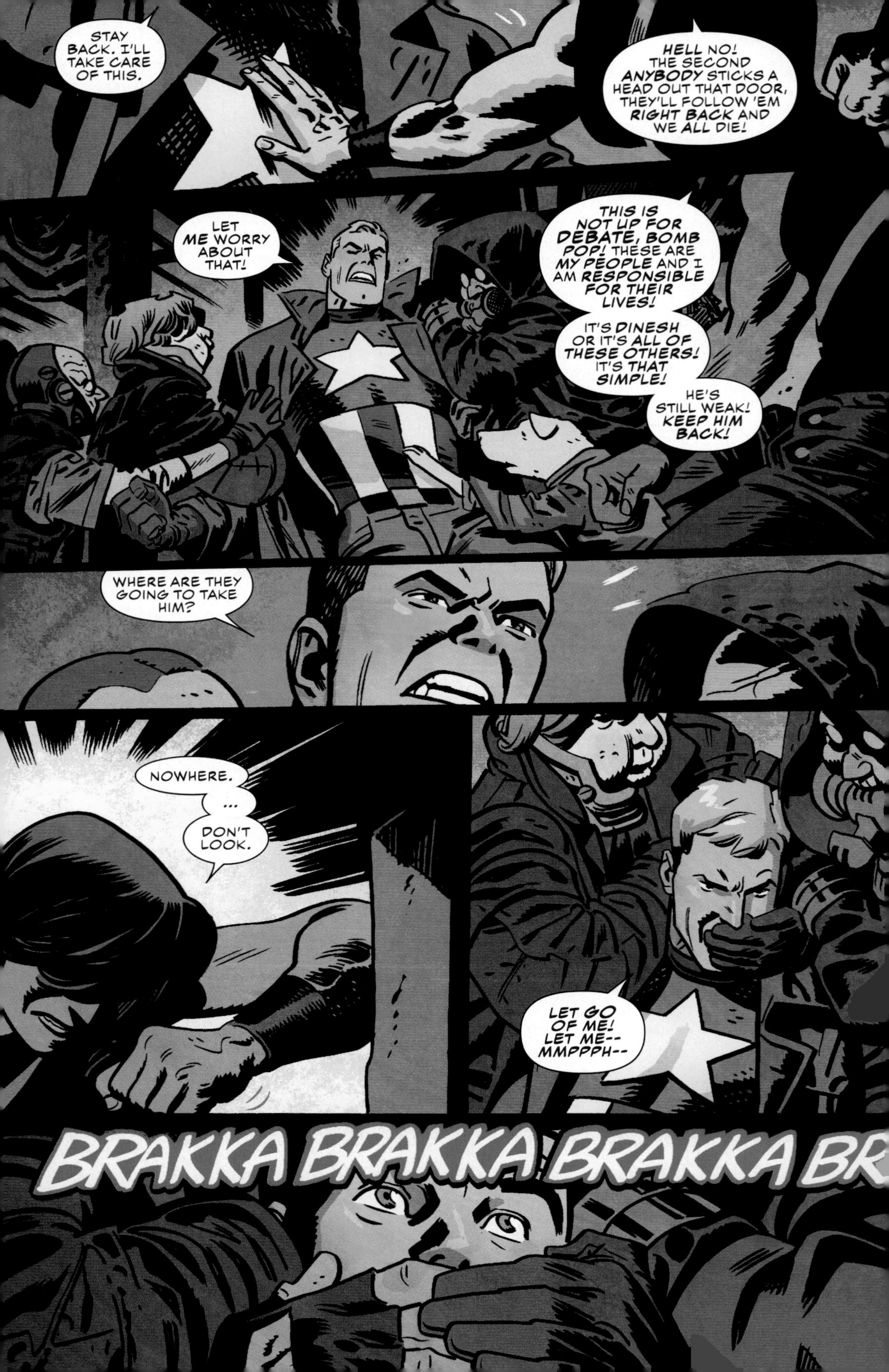
STAY BACK. I'LL TAKE CARE OF THIS.
HELL NO! THE SECOND ANYBODY STICKS A HEAD OUT THAT DOOR, THEY'LL FOLLOW 'EM RIGHT BACK AND WE ALL DIE!
LET ME WORRY ABOUT THAT!
THIS IS NOT UP FOR DEBATE, BOMB POP! THESE ARE MY PEOPLE AND I AM RESPONSIBLE FOR THEIR LIVES!
IT'S DINESH OR IT'S ALL OF THESE OTHERS! IT'S THAT SIMPLE!
HE'S STILL WEAK! KEEP HIM BACK!
WHERE ARE THEY GOING TO TAKE HIM?
NOWHERE.
...
DON'T LOOK.
LET GO OF ME! LET ME-- MMPPPH--
BRAKKA BRAKKA BRAKKA BR

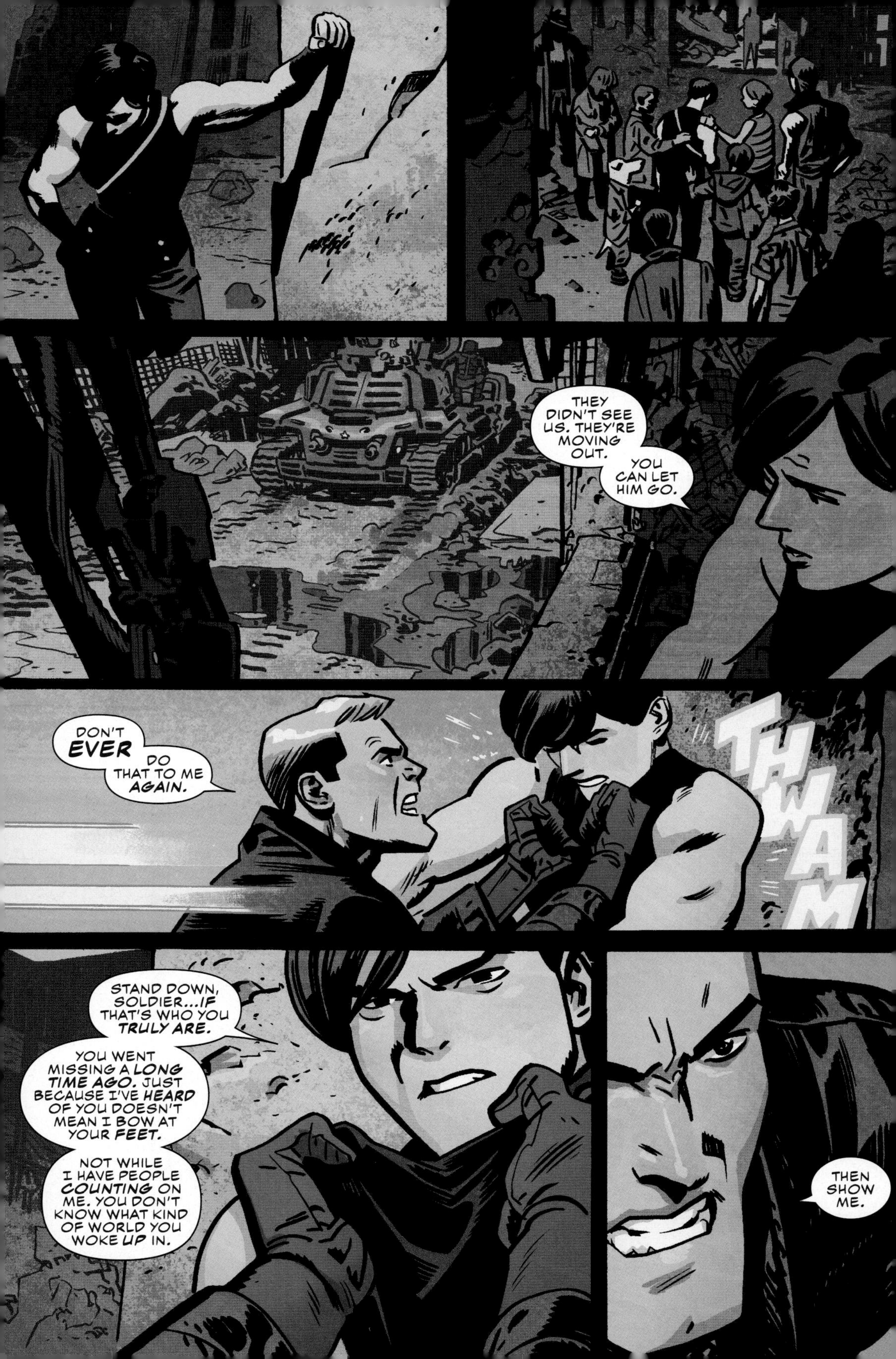
THEY DIDN'T SEE US. THEY'RE MOVING OUT.
YOU CAN LET HIM GO.
DON'T EVER DO THAT TO ME AGAIN.
THWAM
STAND DOWN, SOLDIER...IF THAT'S WHO YOU TRULY ARE.
YOU WENT MISSING A LONG TIME AGO. JUST BECAUSE I'VE HEARD OF YOU DOESN'T MEAN I BOW AT YOUR FEET.
NOT WHILE I HAVE PEOPLE COUNTING ON ME. YOU DON'T KNOW WHAT KIND OF WORLD YOU WOKE UP IN.
THEN SHOW ME.

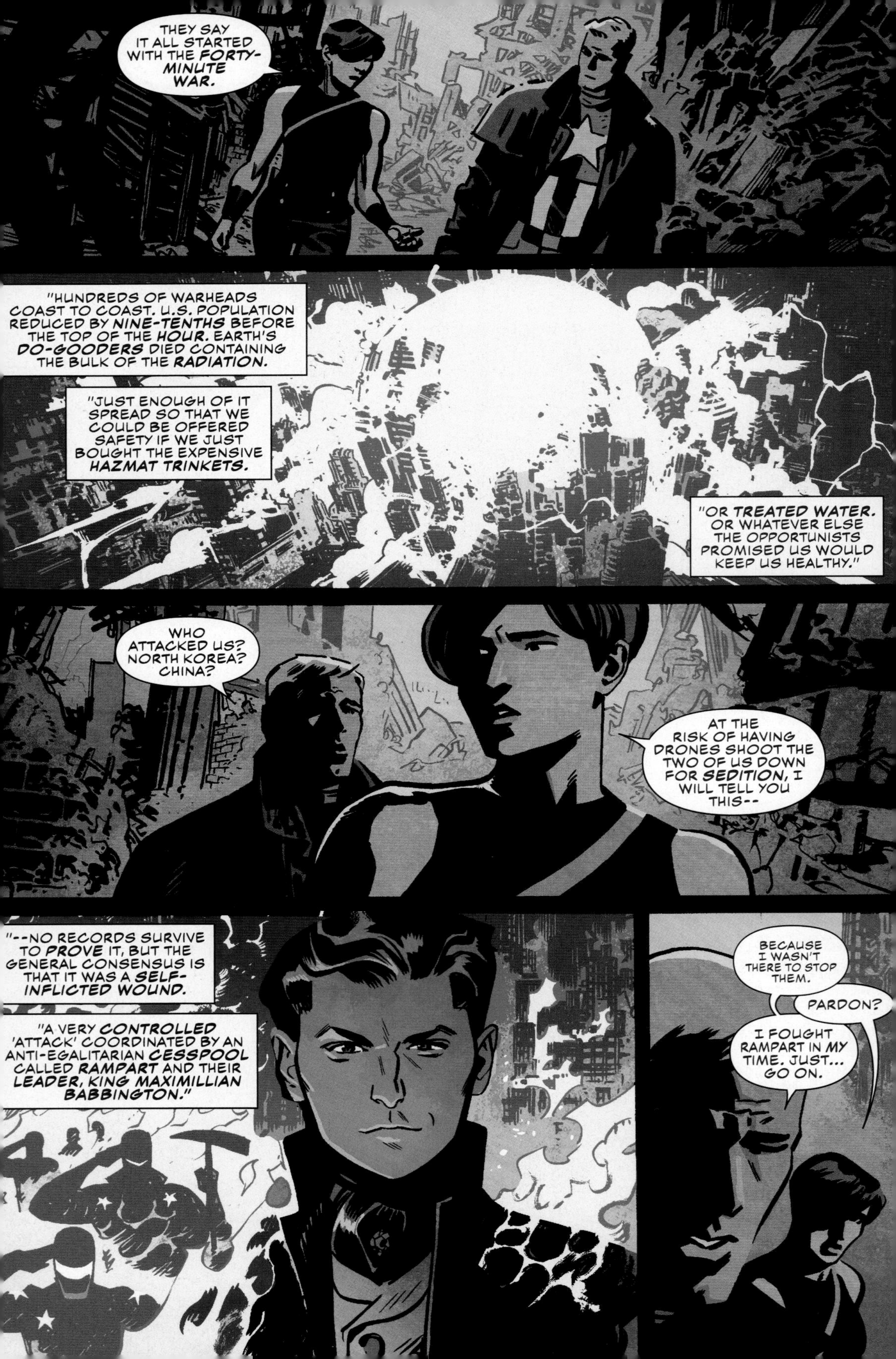

THEY SAY IT ALL STARTED WITH THE FORTY-MINUTE WAR.
"HUNDREDS OF WARHEADS COAST TO COAST. U.S. POPULATION REDUCED BY NINE-TENTHS BEFORE THE TOP OF THE HOUR. EARTH'S DO-GOODERS DIED CONTAINING THE BULK OF THE RADIATION.
"JUST ENOUGH OF IT SPREAD SO THAT WE COULD BE OFFERED SAFETY IF WE JUST BOUGHT THE EXPENSIVE HAZMAT TRINKETS.
"OR TREATED WATER. OR WHATEVER ELSE THE OPPORTUNISTS PROMISED US WOULD KEEP US HEALTHY."
WHO ATTACKED US? NORTH KOREA? CHINA?
AT THE RISK OF HAVING DRONES SHOOT THE TWO OF US DOWN FOR SEDITION, I WILL TELL YOU THIS--
"--NO RECORDS SURVIVE TO PROVE IT, BUT THE GENERAL CONSENSUS IS THAT IT WAS A SELF-INFLICTED WOUND.
"A VERY CONTROLLED 'ATTACK' COORDINATED BY AN ANTI-EGALITARIAN CESSPOOL CALLED RAMPART AND THEIR LEADER, KING MAXIMILLIAN BABBINGTON."
BECAUSE I WASN'T THERE TO STOP THEM.
PARDON?
I FOUGHT RAMPART IN MY TIME. JUST... GO ON.

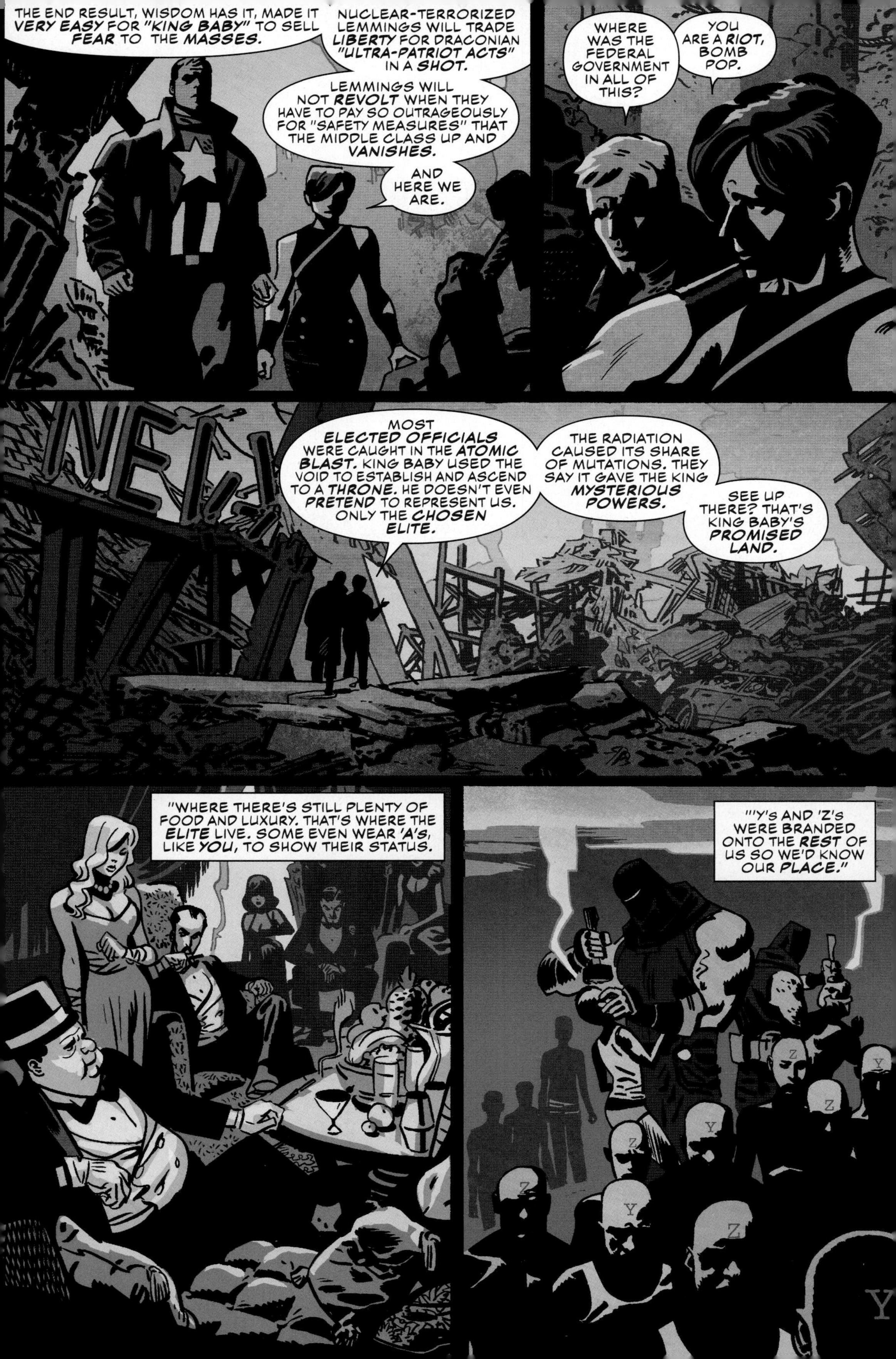
THE END RESULT, WISDOM HAS IT, MADE IT VERY EASY FOR "KING BABY" TO SELL FEAR TO THE MASSES.
NUCLEAR-TERRORIZED LEMMINGS WILL TRADE LIBERTY FOR DRACONIAN "ULTRA-PATRIOT ACTS" IN A SHOT.
LEMMINGS WILL NOT REVOLT WHEN THEY HAVE TO PAY SO OUTRAGEOUSLY FOR "SAFETY MEASURES" THAT THE MIDDLE CLASS UP AND VANISHES.
AND HERE WE ARE.
WHERE WAS THE FEDERAL GOVERNMENT IN ALL OF THIS?
YOU ARE A RIOT, BOMB POP.
MOST ELECTED OFFICIALS WERE CAUGHT IN THE ATOMIC BLAST. KING BABY USED THE VOID TO ESTABLISH AND ASCEND TO A THRONE. HE DOESN'T EVEN PRETEND TO REPRESENT US. ONLY THE CHOSEN ELITE.
THE RADIATION CAUSED ITS SHARE OF MUTATIONS. THEY SAY IT GAVE THE KING MYSTERIOUS POWERS.
SEE UP THERE? THAT'S KING BABY'S PROMISED LAND.
"WHERE THERE'S STILL PLENTY OF FOOD AND LUXURY. THAT'S WHERE THE ELITE LIVE. SOME EVEN WEAR 'A'S, LIKE YOU, TO SHOW THEIR STATUS.
"'Y'S AND 'Z'S WERE BRANDED ONTO THE REST OF US SO WE'D KNOW OUR PLACE."

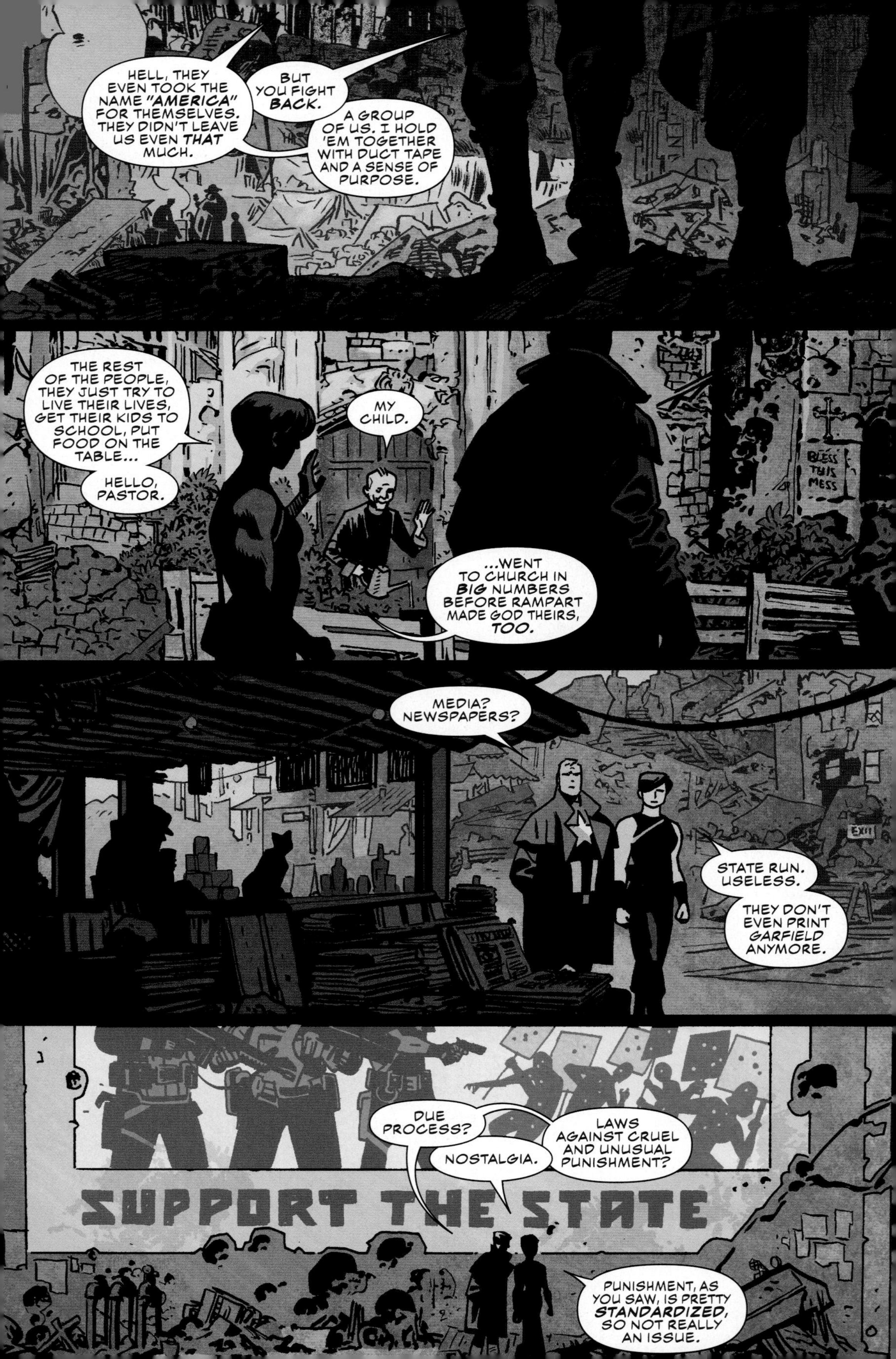
HELL, THEY EVEN TOOK THE NAME "AMERICA" FOR THEMSELVES. THEY DIDN'T LEAVE US EVEN THAT MUCH.
BUT YOU FIGHT BACK.
A GROUP OF US. I HOLD 'EM TOGETHER WITH DUCT TAPE AND A SENSE OF PURPOSE.
THE REST OF THE PEOPLE, THEY JUST TRY TO LIVE THEIR LIVES, GET THEIR KIDS TO SCHOOL, PUT FOOD ON THE TABLE...
HELLO, PASTOR.
MY CHILD.
BLESS THIS MESS
...WENT TO CHURCH IN BIG NUMBERS BEFORE RAMPART MADE GOD THEIRS, TOO.
MEDIA? NEWSPAPERS?
EXIT
STATE RUN. USELESS.
THEY DON'T EVEN PRINT GARFIELD ANYMORE.
DUE PROCESS?
NOSTALGIA.
LAWS AGAINST CRUEL AND UNUSUAL PUNISHMENT?
SUPPORT THE STATE
PUNISHMENT, AS YOU SAW, IS PRETTY STANDARDIZED, SO NOT REALLY AN ISSUE.

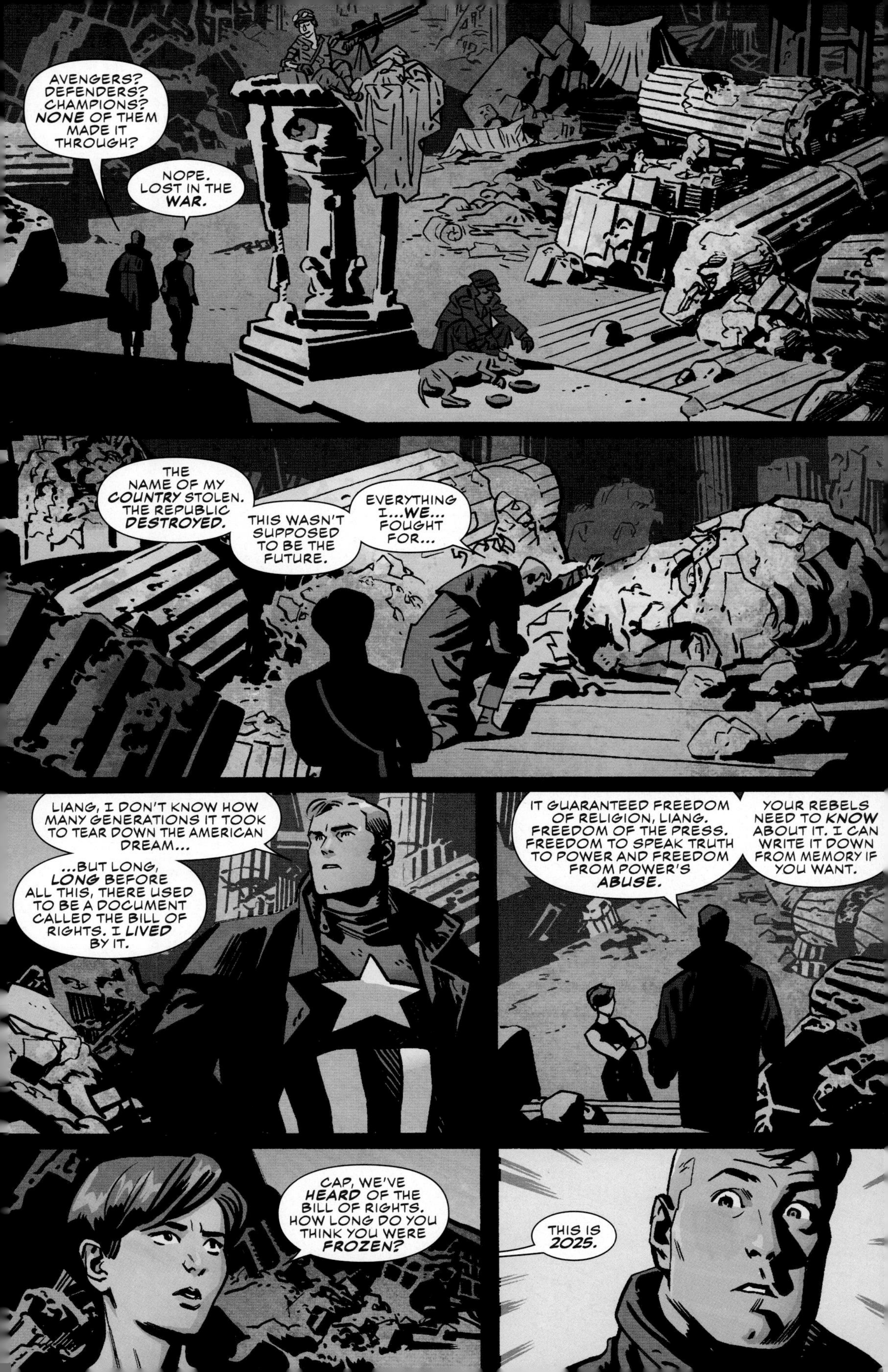
AVENGERS? DEFENDERS? CHAMPIONS? NONE OF THEM MADE IT THROUGH?
NOPE. LOST IN THE WAR.
THE NAME OF MY COUNTRY STOLEN. THE REPUBLIC DESTROYED.
THIS WASN'T SUPPOSED TO BE THE FUTURE.
EVERYTHING I...WE... FOUGHT FOR...
LIANG, I DON'T KNOW HOW MANY GENERATIONS IT TOOK TO TEAR DOWN THE AMERICAN DREAM...
...BUT LONG, LONG BEFORE ALL THIS, THERE USED TO BE A DOCUMENT CALLED THE BILL OF RIGHTS. I LIVED BY IT.
IT GUARANTEED FREEDOM OF RELIGION, LIANG. FREEDOM OF THE PRESS. FREEDOM TO SPEAK TRUTH TO POWER AND FREEDOM FROM POWER'S ABUSE.
YOUR REBELS NEED TO KNOW ABOUT IT. I CAN WRITE IT DOWN FROM MEMORY IF YOU WANT.
CAP, WE'VE HEARD OF THE BILL OF RIGHTS. HOW LONG DO YOU THINK YOU WERE FROZEN?
THIS IS 2025.

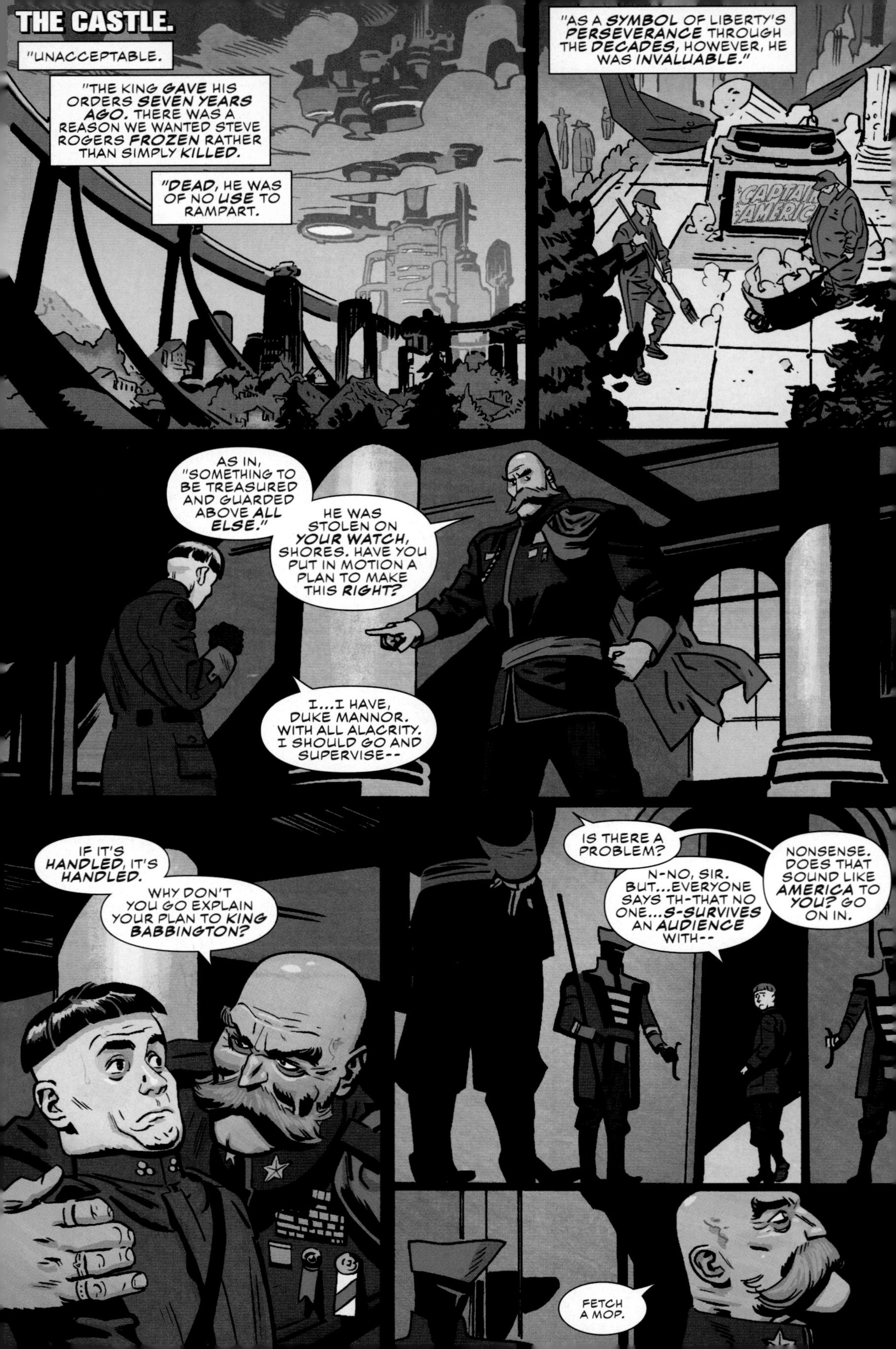
THE CASTLE.
"UNACCEPTABLE.
"THE KING GAVE HIS ORDERS SEVEN YEARS AGO. THERE WAS A REASON WE WANTED STEVE ROGERS FROZEN RATHER THAN SIMPLY KILLED.
"DEAD, HE WAS OF NO USE TO RAMPART.
"AS A SYMBOL OF LIBERTY'S PERSEVERANCE THROUGH THE DECADES, HOWEVER, HE WAS INVALUABLE."
CAPTAIN AMERICA
AS IN, "SOMETHING TO BE TREASURED AND GUARDED ABOVE ALL ELSE."
HE WAS STOLEN ON YOUR WATCH, SHORES. HAVE YOU PUT IN MOTION A PLAN TO MAKE THIS RIGHT?
I...I HAVE, DUKE MANNOR. WITH ALL ALACRITY. I SHOULD GO AND SUPERVISE--
IF IT'S HANDLED, IT'S HANDLED.
WHY DON'T YOU GO EXPLAIN YOUR PLAN TO KING BABBINGTON?
IS THERE A PROBLEM?
N-NO, SIR. BUT...EVERYONE SAYS TH-THAT NO ONE...S-SURVIVES AN AUDIENCE WITH--
NONSENSE. DOES THAT SOUND LIKE AMERICA TO YOU? GO ON IN.
FETCH A MOP.

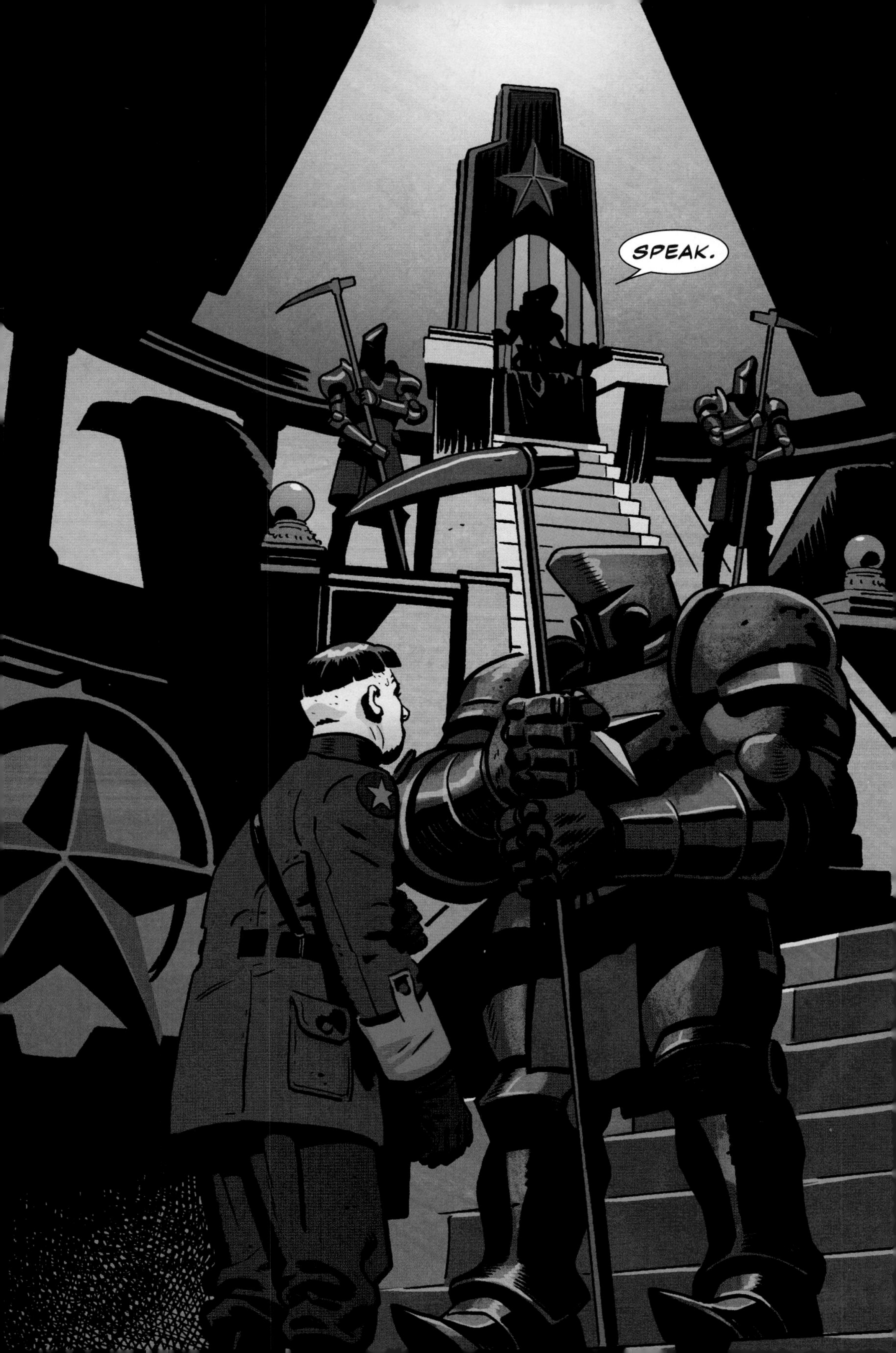
SPEAK.

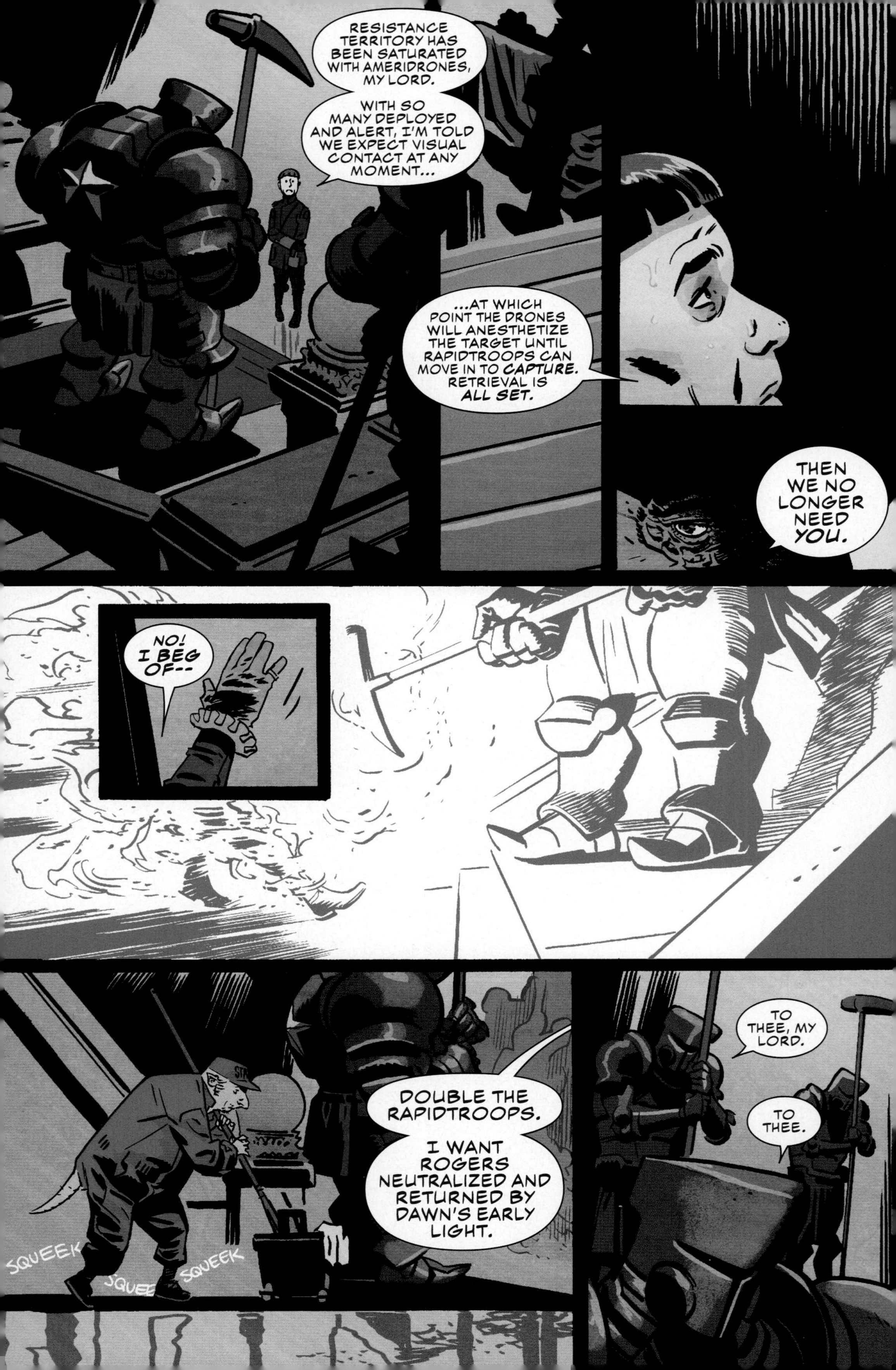
RESISTANCE TERRITORY HAS BEEN SATURATED WITH AMERIDRONES, MY LORD.
WITH SO MANY DEPLOYED AND ALERT, I'M TOLD WE EXPECT VISUAL CONTACT AT ANY MOMENT...
...AT WHICH POINT THE DRONES WILL ANESTHETIZE THE TARGET UNTIL RAPIDTROOPS CAN MOVE IN TO CAPTURE. RETRIEVAL IS ALL SET.
THEN WE NO LONGER NEED YOU.
NO! I BEG OF--
DOUBLE THE RAPIDTROOPS.
I WANT ROGERS NEUTRALIZED AND RETURNED BY DAWN'S EARLY LIGHT.
SQUEEK
SQUEE
SQUEEK
TO THEE, MY LORD.
TO THEE.

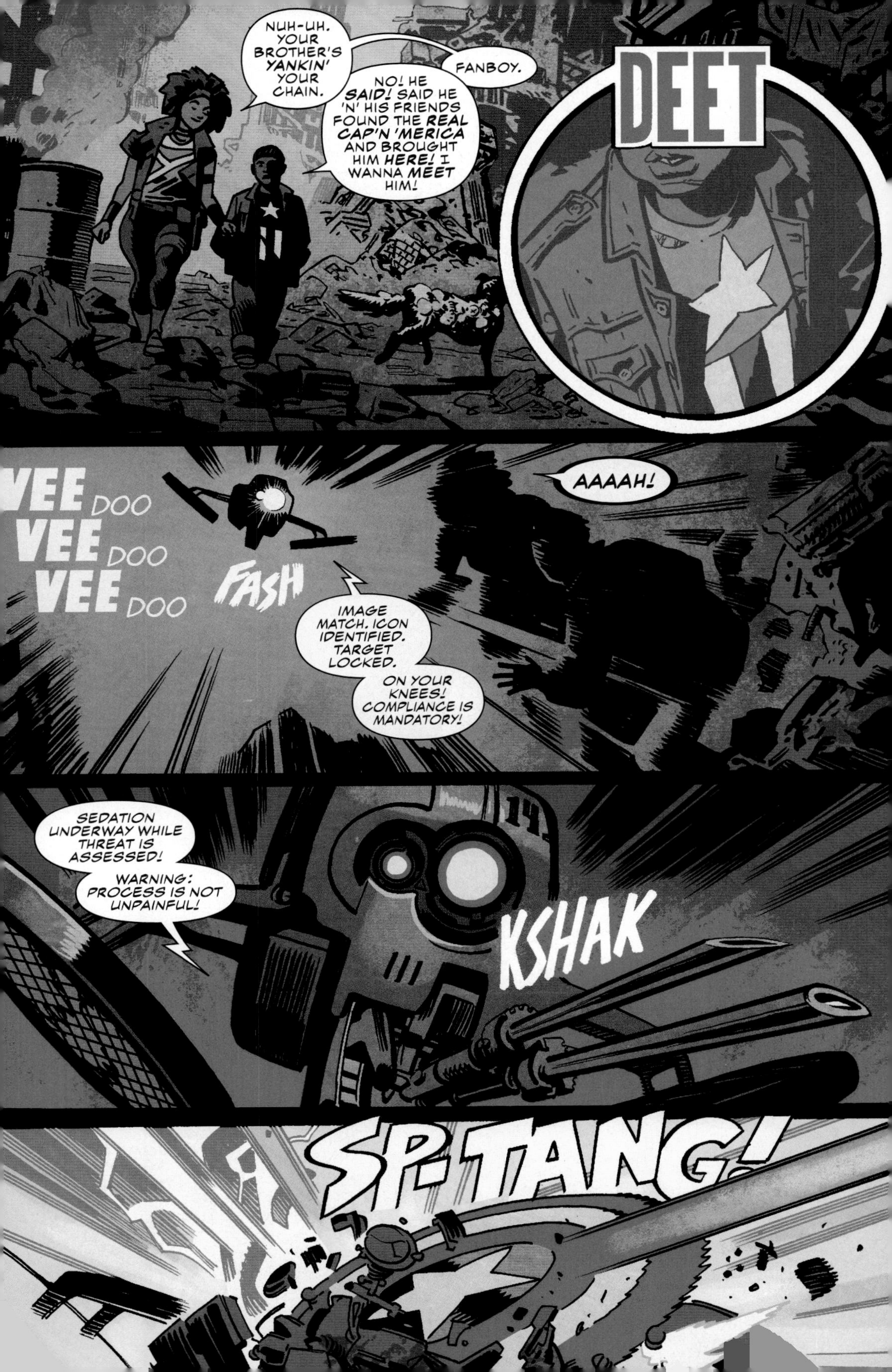
NUH-UH. YOUR BROTHER'S YANKIN' YOUR CHAIN.
FANBOY.
NO! HE SAID! SAID HE 'N' HIS FRIENDS FOUND THE REAL CAP'N 'MERICA AND BROUGHT HIM HERE! I WANNA MEET HIM!
DEET
VEE DOO VEE DOO VEE DOO
FASH
AAAAH!
IMAGE MATCH. ICON IDENTIFIED. TARGET LOCKED.
ON YOUR KNEES! COMPLIANCE IS MANDATORY!
SEDATION UNDERWAY WHILE THREAT IS ASSESSED!
WARNING: PROCESS IS NOT UNPAINFUL!
KSHAK
SP-TANG!

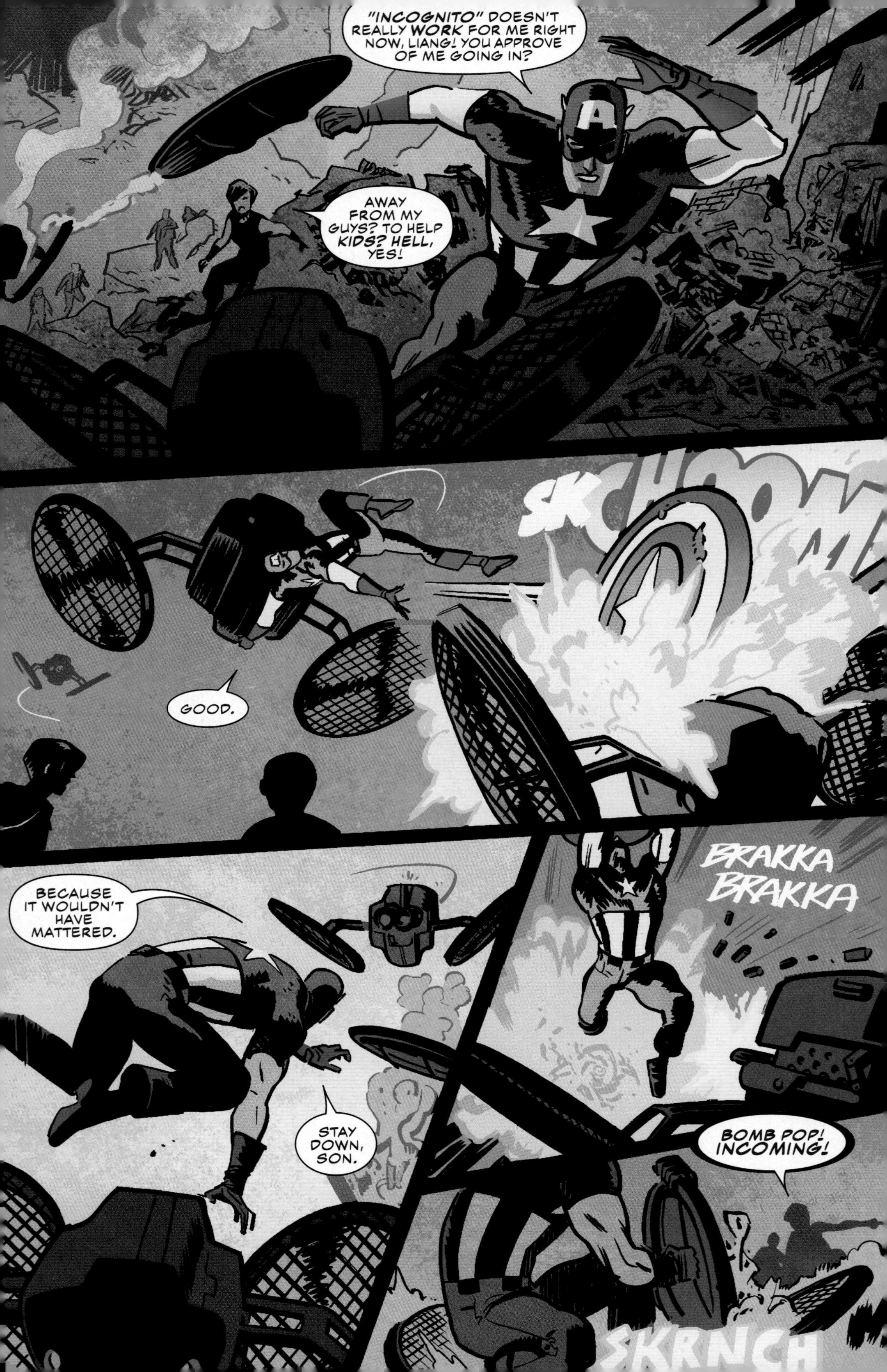
"INCOGNITO" DOESN'T REALLY WORK FOR ME RIGHT NOW, LIANG! YOU APPROVE OF ME GOING IN?
AWAY FROM MY GUYS? TO HELP KIDS? HELL, YES!
SKCHOOM
GOOD.
BECAUSE IT WOULDN'T HAVE MATTERED.
STAY DOWN, SON.
BRAKKA BRAKKA
BOMB POP! INCOMING!
SKRNCH

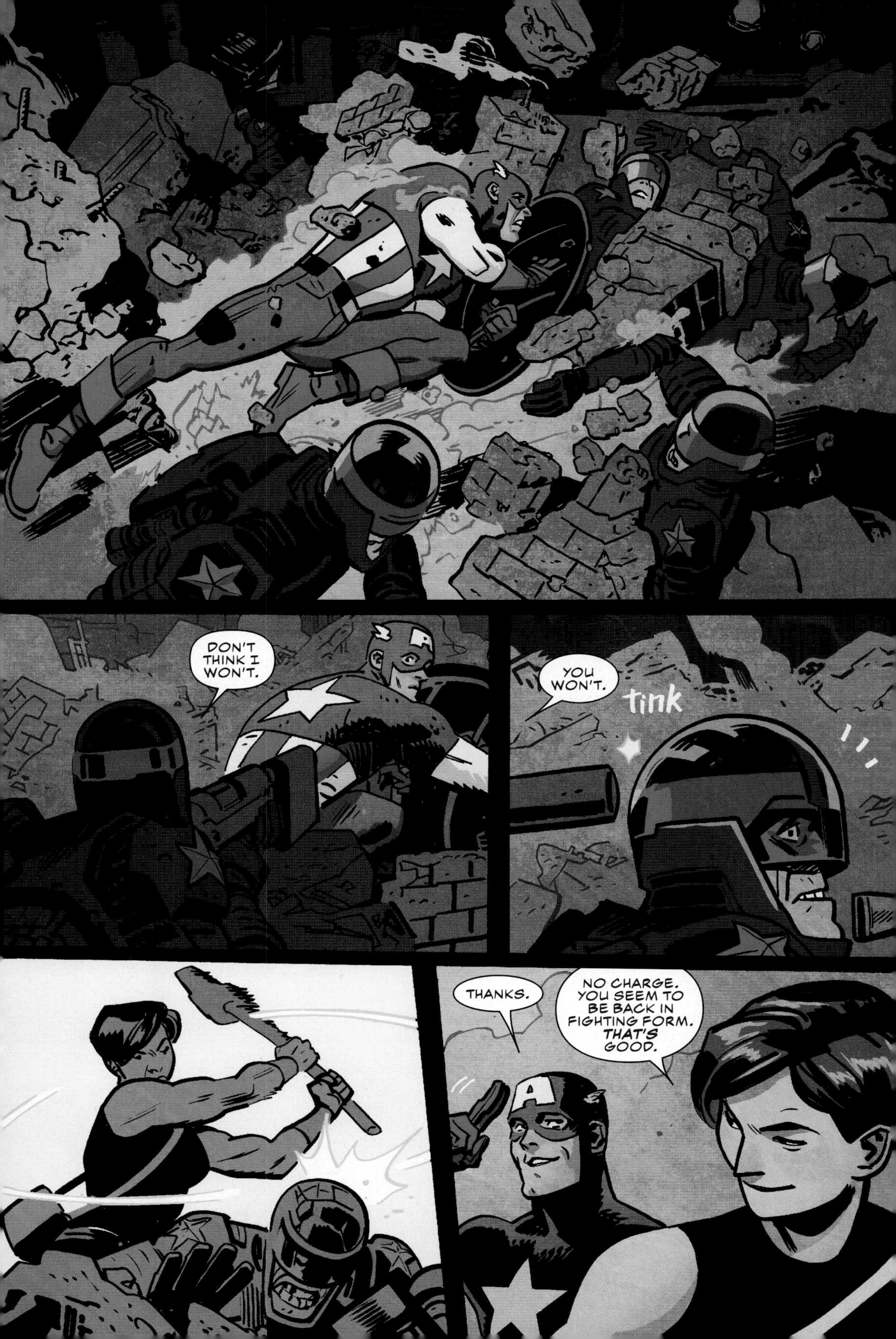

DON'T THINK I WON'T.
YOU WON'T.
tink
THANKS.
NO CHARGE. YOU SEEM TO BE BACK IN FIGHTING FORM. THAT'S GOOD.

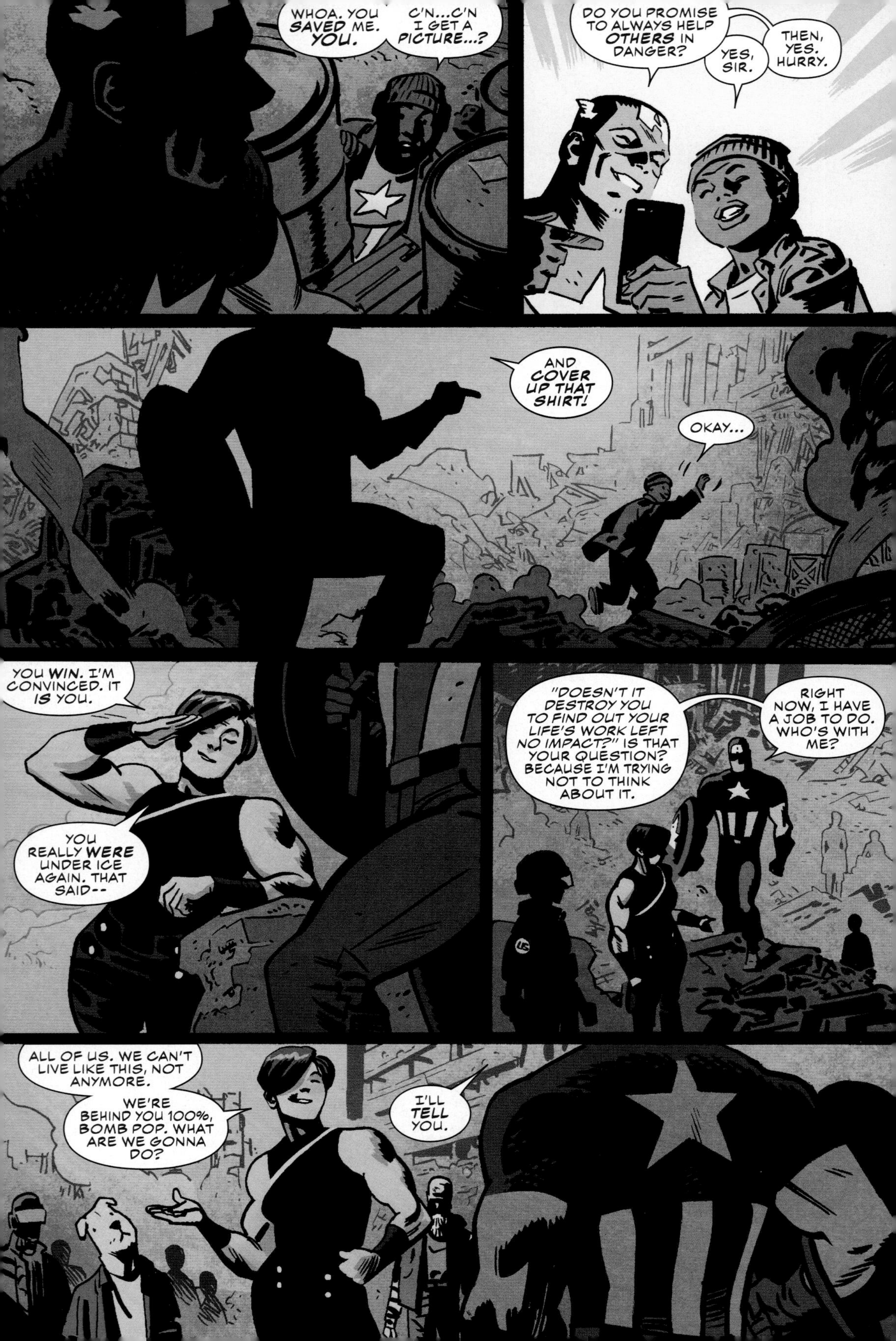
WHOA. YOU SAVED ME. YOU.
C'N...C'N I GET A PICTURE...?
DO YOU PROMISE TO ALWAYS HELP OTHERS IN DANGER?
YES, SIR.
THEN, YES. HURRY.
AND COVER UP THAT SHIRT!
OKAY...
YOU WIN. I'M CONVINCED. IT IS YOU.
YOU REALLY WERE UNDER ICE AGAIN. THAT SAID--
"DOESN'T IT DESTROY YOU TO FIND OUT YOUR LIFE'S WORK LEFT NO IMPACT?" IS THAT YOUR QUESTION? BECAUSE I'M TRYING NOT TO THINK ABOUT IT.
RIGHT NOW, I HAVE A JOB TO DO. WHO'S WITH ME?
ALL OF US. WE CAN'T LIVE LIKE THIS, NOT ANYMORE.
WE'RE BEHIND YOU 100%, BOMB POP. WHAT ARE WE GONNA DO?
I'LL TELL YOU.

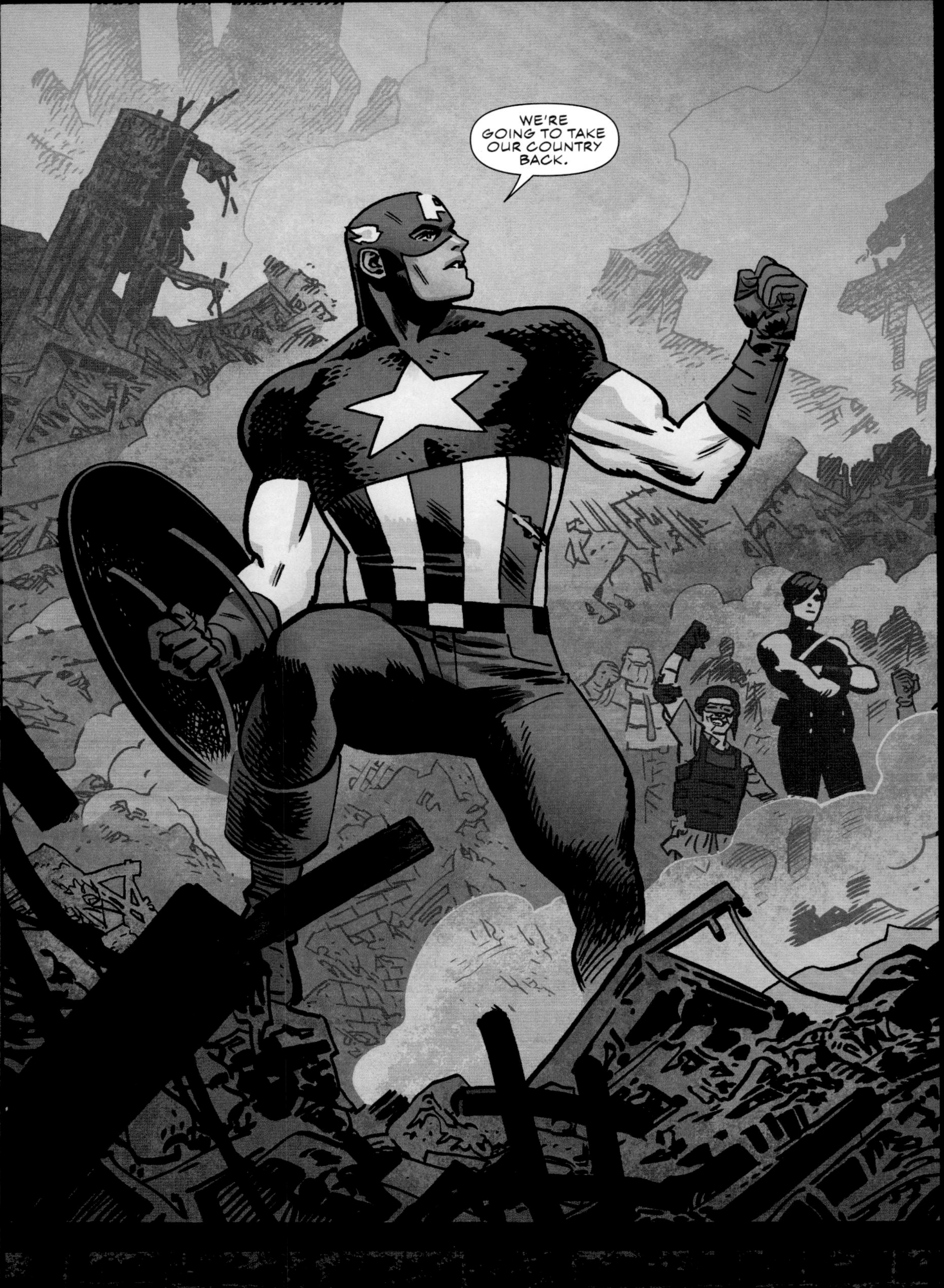
WE'RE GOING TO TAKE OUR COUNTRY BACK.

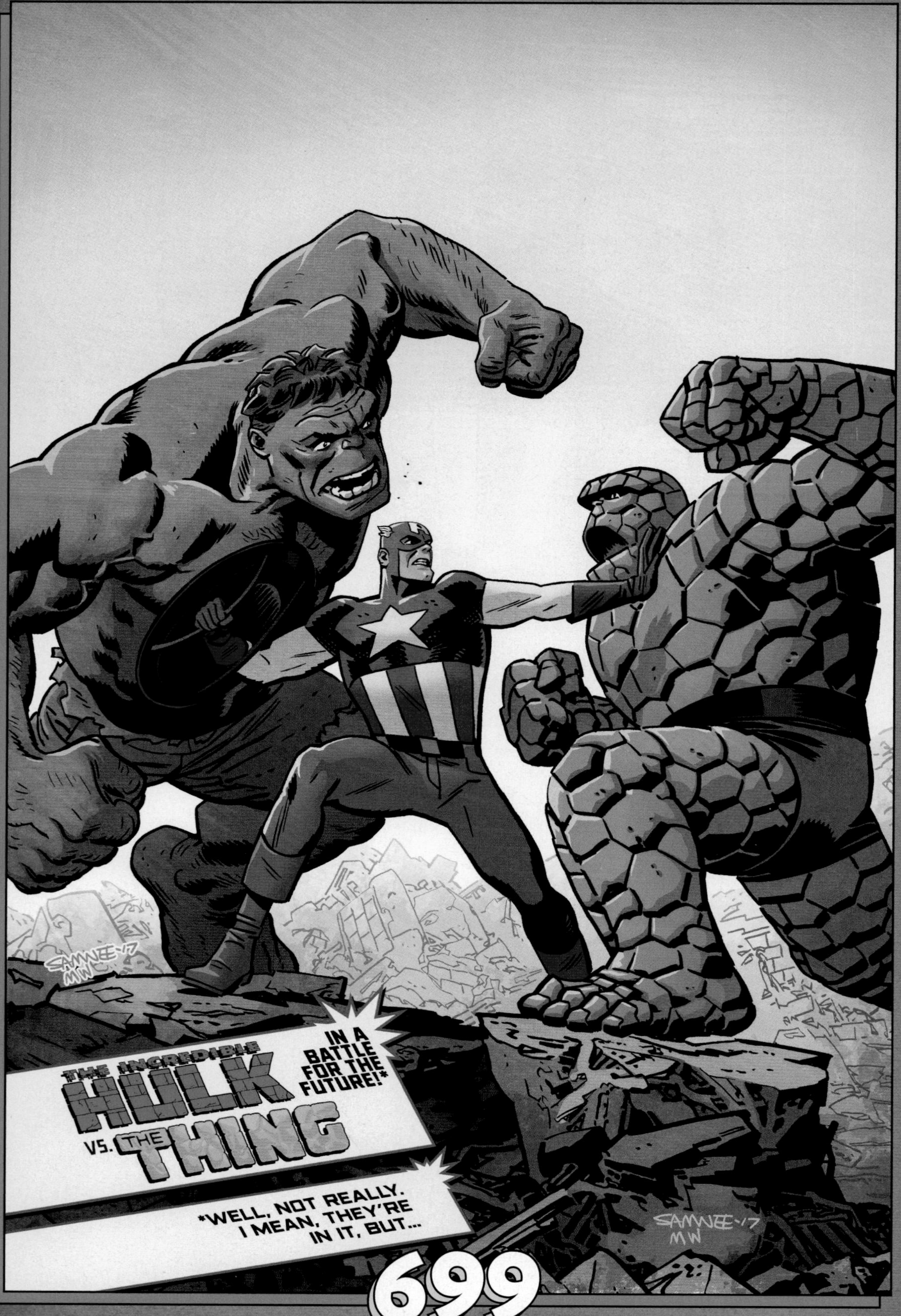

SAMNEE-'17 MW
THE INCREDIBLE HULK VS. THE THING
IN A BATTLE FOR THE FUTURE!*
*WELL, NOT REALLY. I MEAN, THEY'RE IN IT, BUT...
SAMNEE-'17 MW
699

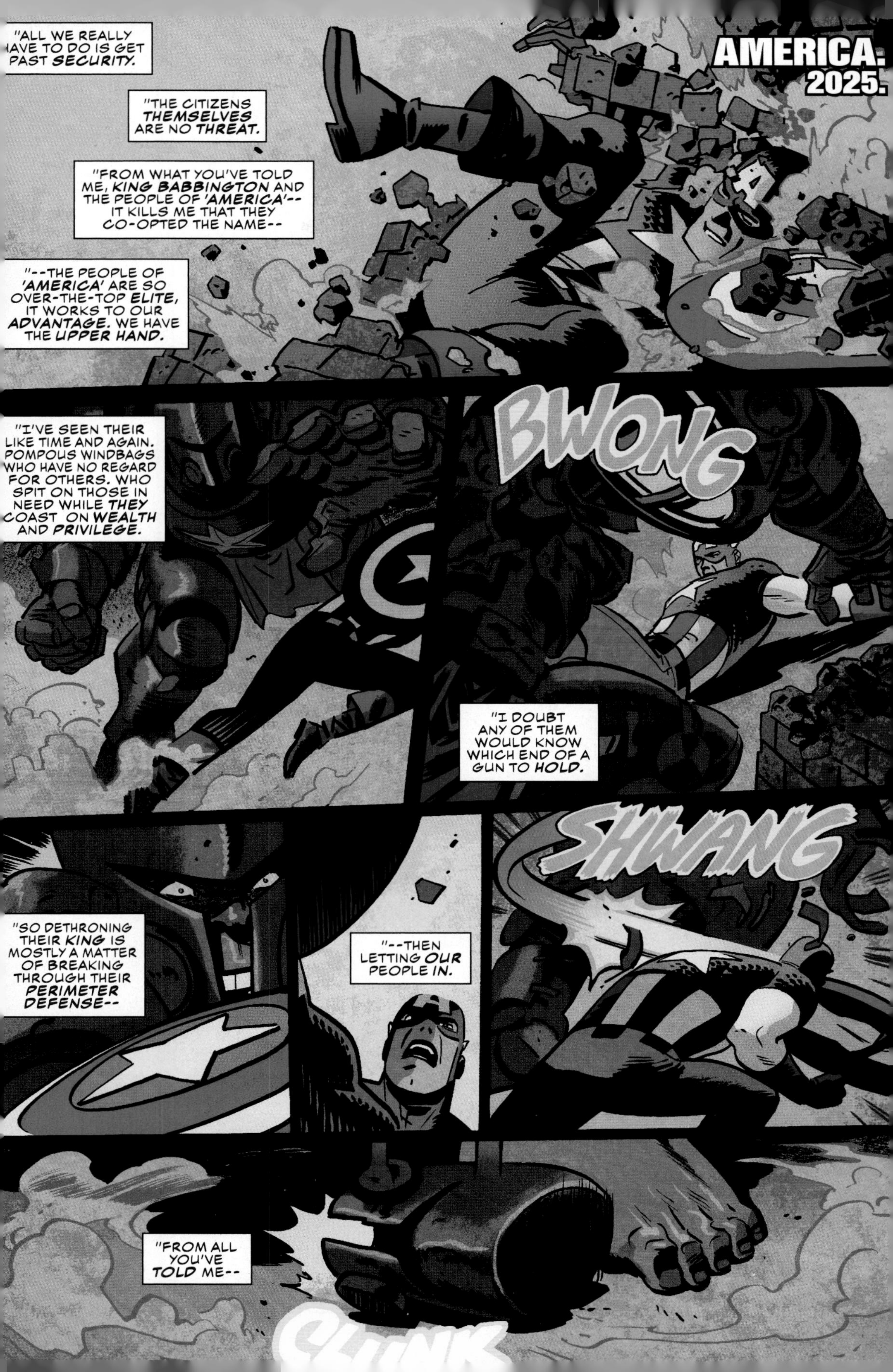
AMERICA. 2025.
"ALL WE REALLY HAVE TO DO IS GET PAST SECURITY.
"THE CITIZENS THEMSELVES ARE NO THREAT.
"FROM WHAT YOU'VE TOLD ME, KING BABBINGTON AND THE PEOPLE OF 'AMERICA'-- IT KILLS ME THAT THEY CO-OPTED THE NAME--
"--THE PEOPLE OF 'AMERICA' ARE SO OVER-THE-TOP ELITE, IT WORKS TO OUR ADVANTAGE. WE HAVE THE UPPER HAND.
"I'VE SEEN THEIR LIKE TIME AND AGAIN. POMPOUS WINDBAGS WHO HAVE NO REGARD FOR OTHERS. WHO SPIT ON THOSE IN NEED WHILE THEY COAST ON WEALTH AND PRIVILEGE.
BWONG
"I DOUBT ANY OF THEM WOULD KNOW WHICH END OF A GUN TO HOLD.
"SO DETHRONING THEIR KING IS MOSTLY A MATTER OF BREAKING THROUGH THEIR PERIMETER DEFENSE--
"--THEN LETTING OUR PEOPLE IN.
SHWANG
"FROM ALL YOU'VE TOLD ME--
CLINK

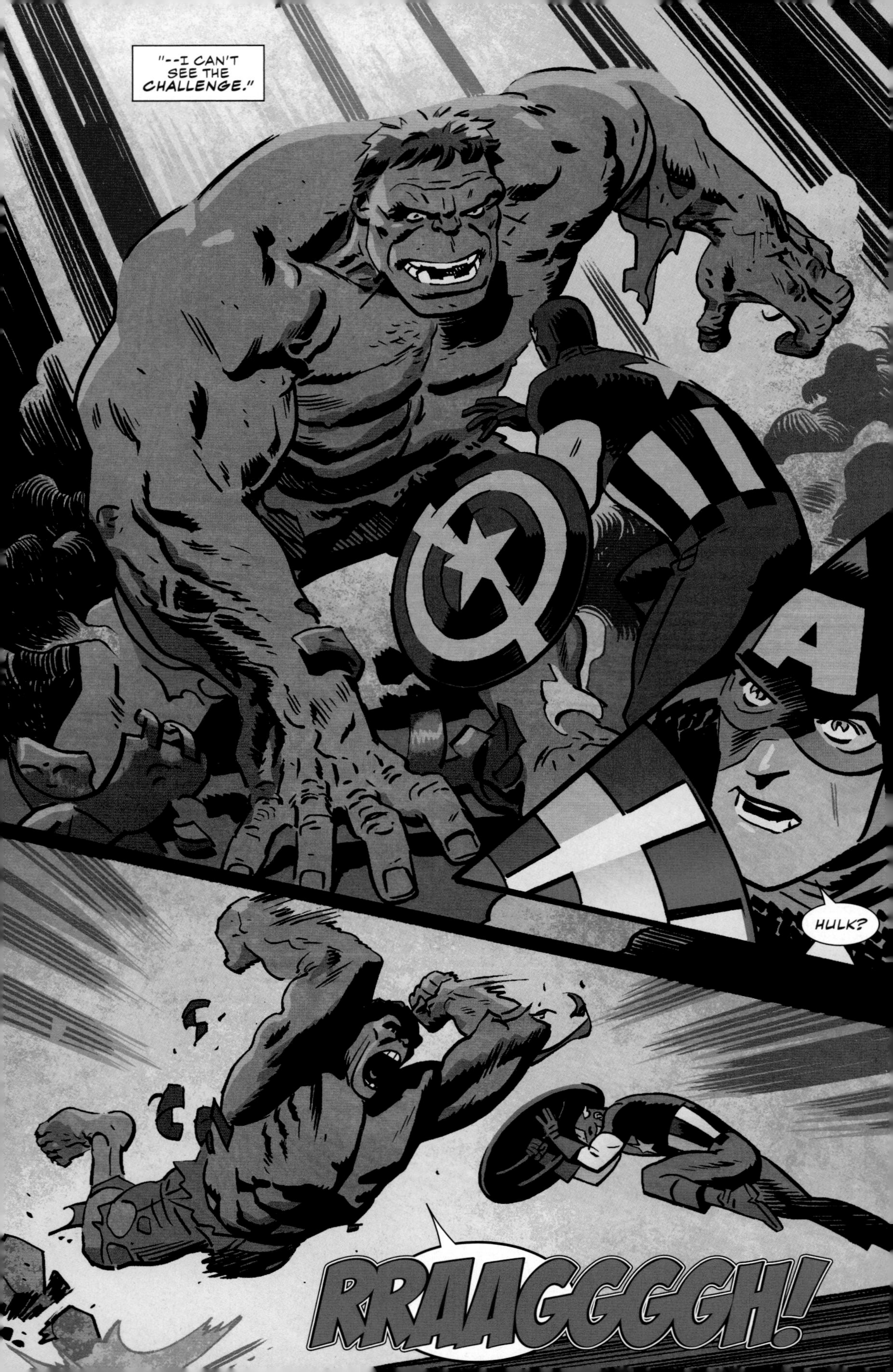
"--I CAN'T SEE THE CHALLENGE."
HULK?
RRAAGGGGH!

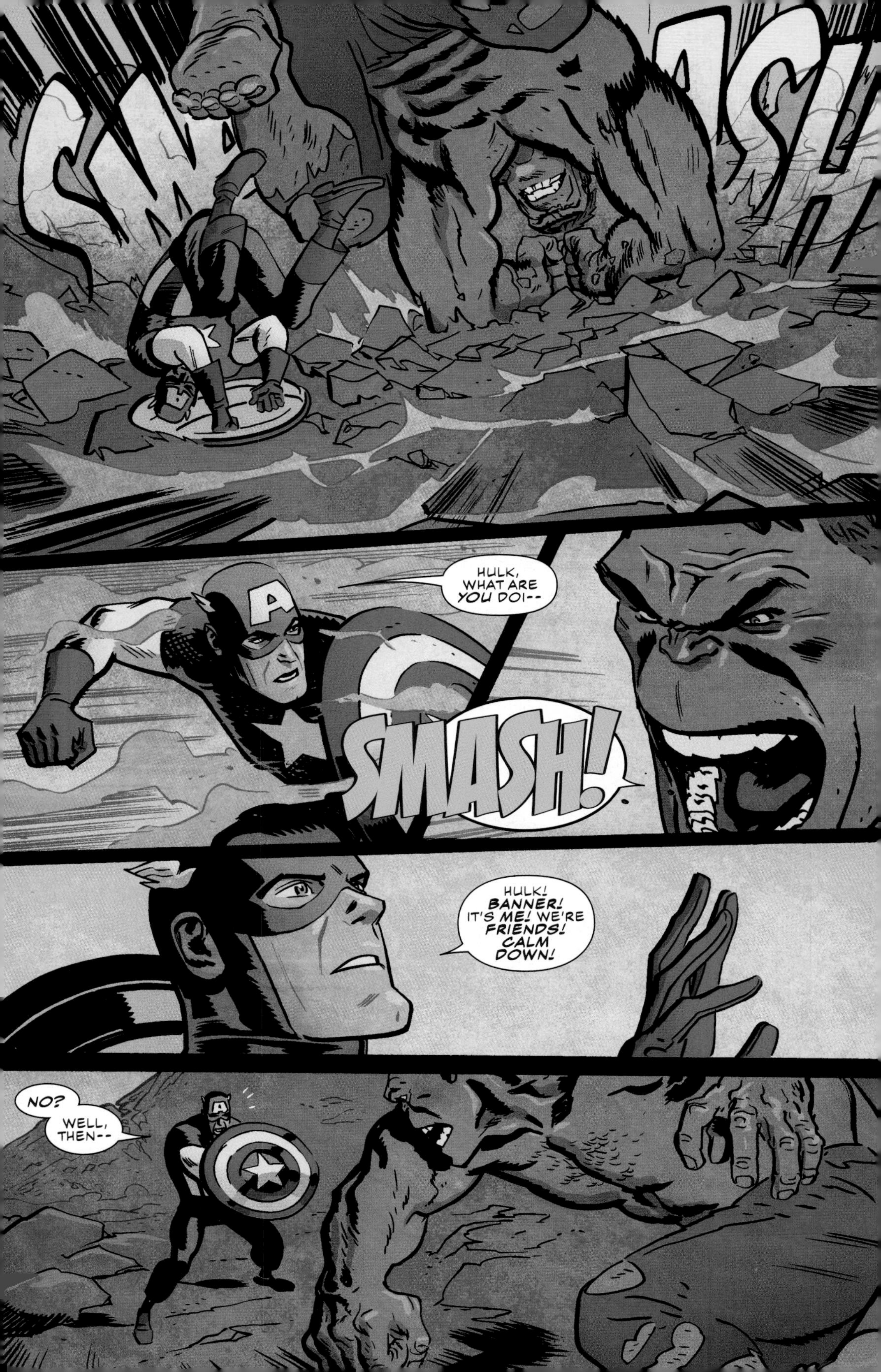
HULK, WHAT ARE YOU DOI--
SMASH!
HULK! BANNER! IT'S ME! WE'RE FRIENDS! CALM DOWN!
NO?
WELL, THEN--

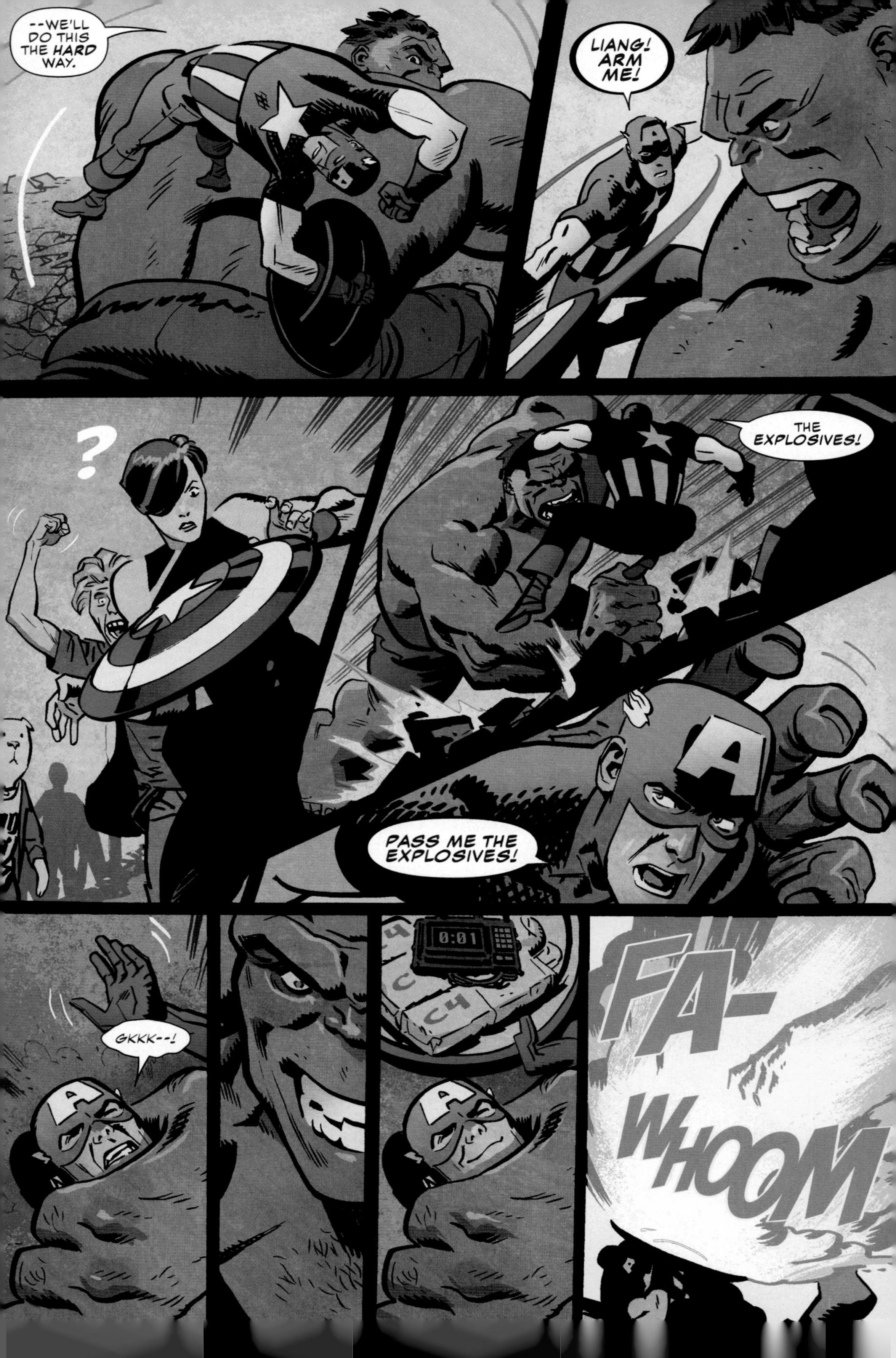
--WE'LL DO THIS THE HARD WAY.
LIANG! ARM ME!
?
THE EXPLOSIVES!
PASS ME THE EXPLOSIVES!
GKKK--!
0:01
C4
FA-WHOOM

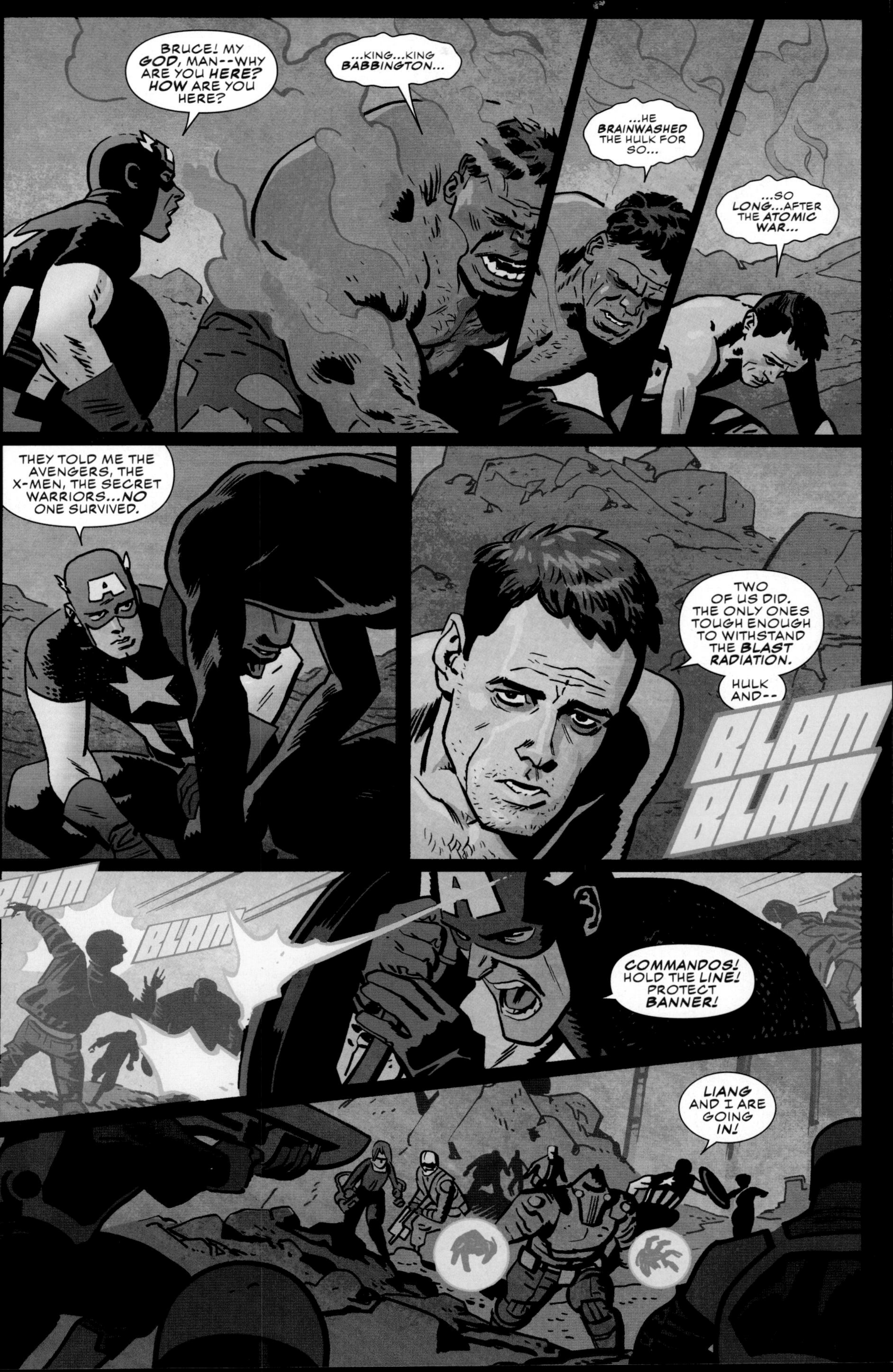
BRUCE! MY GOD, MAN--WHY ARE YOU HERE? HOW ARE YOU HERE?
...KING...KING BABBINGTON...
...HE BRAINWASHED THE HULK FOR SO...
...SO LONG...AFTER THE ATOMIC WAR...
THEY TOLD ME THE AVENGERS, THE X-MEN, THE SECRET WARRIORS...NO ONE SURVIVED.
TWO OF US DID. THE ONLY ONES TOUGH ENOUGH TO WITHSTAND THE BLAST RADIATION.
HULK AND--
BLAM BLAM
BLAM
COMMANDOS! HOLD THE LINE! PROTECT BANNER!
LIANG AND I ARE GOING IN!

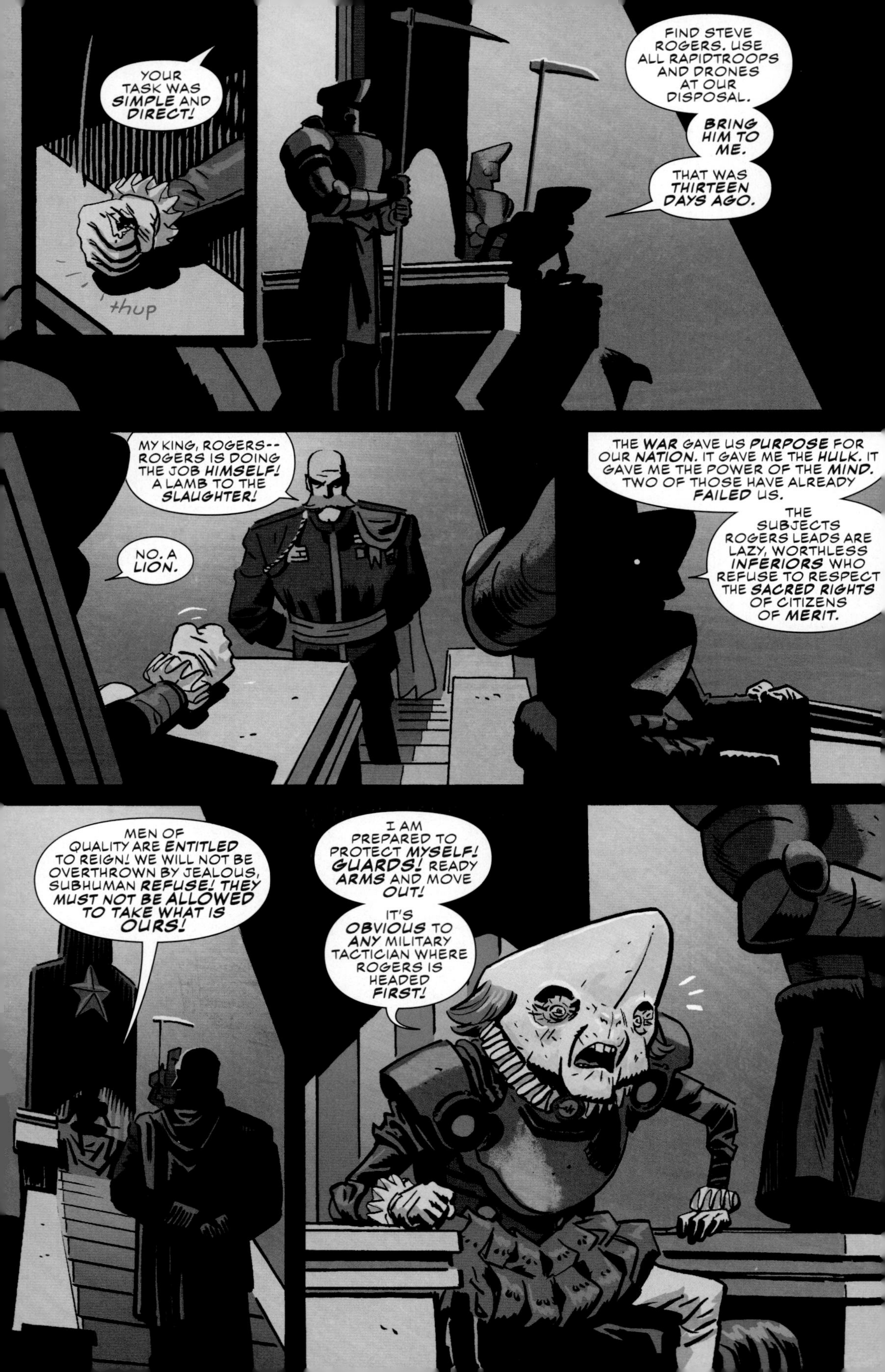
YOUR TASK WAS SIMPLE AND DIRECT!
thup
FIND STEVE ROGERS. USE ALL RAPIDTROOPS AND DRONES AT OUR DISPOSAL.
BRING HIM TO ME.
THAT WAS THIRTEEN DAYS AGO.
MY KING, ROGERS-- ROGERS IS DOING THE JOB HIMSELF! A LAMB TO THE SLAUGHTER!
NO. A LION.
THE WAR GAVE US PURPOSE FOR OUR NATION. IT GAVE ME THE HULK. IT GAVE ME THE POWER OF THE MIND. TWO OF THOSE HAVE ALREADY FAILED US.
THE SUBJECTS ROGERS LEADS ARE LAZY, WORTHLESS INFERIORS WHO REFUSE TO RESPECT THE SACRED RIGHTS OF CITIZENS OF MERIT.
MEN OF QUALITY ARE ENTITLED TO REIGN! WE WILL NOT BE OVERTHROWN BY JEALOUS, SUBHUMAN REFUSE! THEY MUST NOT BE ALLOWED TO TAKE WHAT IS OURS!
I AM PREPARED TO PROTECT MYSELF! GUARDS! READY ARMS AND MOVE OUT!
IT'S OBVIOUS TO ANY MILITARY TACTICIAN WHERE ROGERS IS HEADED FIRST!

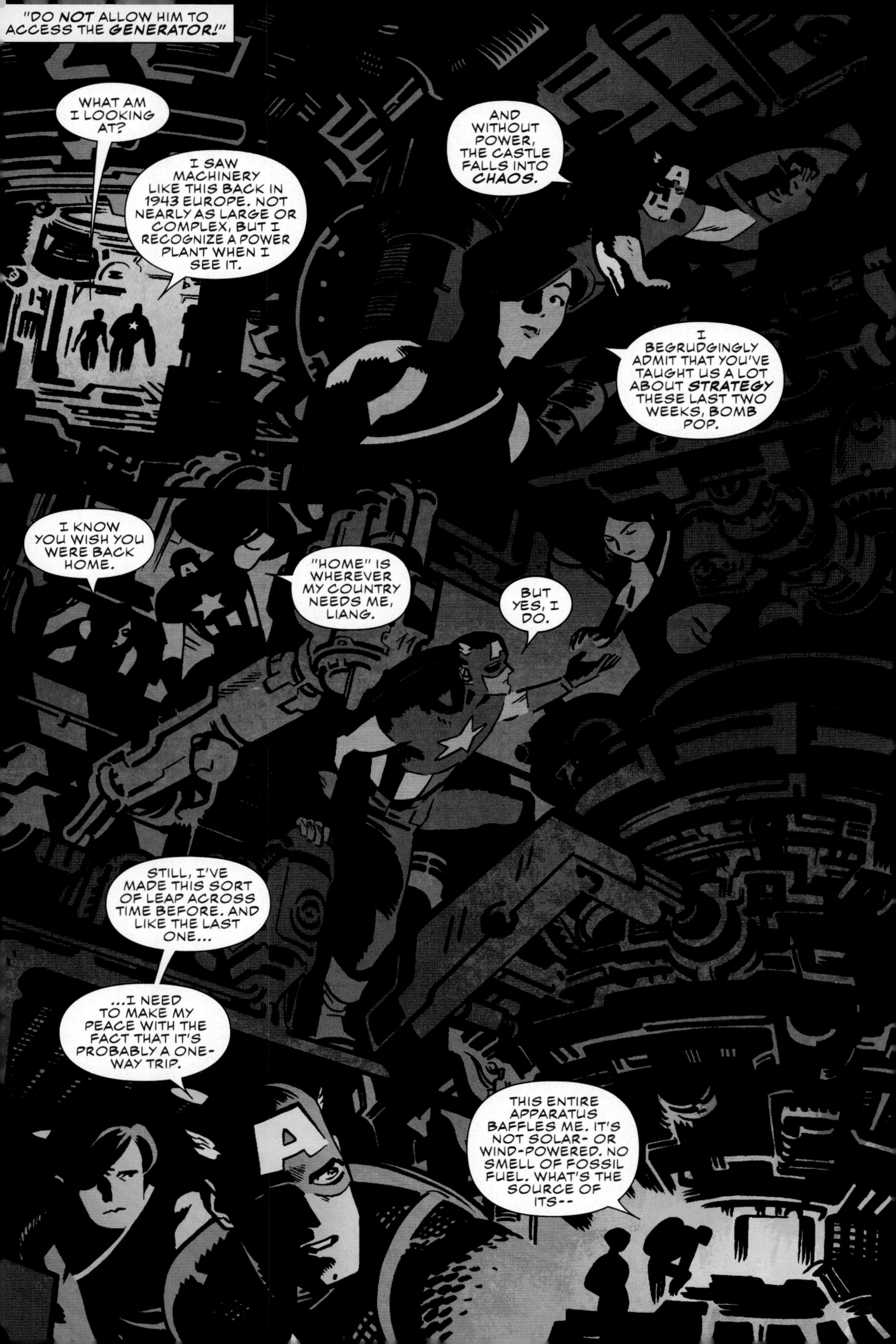
"DO NOT ALLOW HIM TO ACCESS THE GENERATOR!"
WHAT AM I LOOKING AT?
I SAW MACHINERY LIKE THIS BACK IN 1943 EUROPE. NOT NEARLY AS LARGE OR COMPLEX, BUT I RECOGNIZE A POWER PLANT WHEN I SEE IT.
AND WITHOUT POWER, THE CASTLE FALLS INTO CHAOS.
I BEGRUDGINGLY ADMIT THAT YOU'VE TAUGHT US A LOT ABOUT STRATEGY THESE LAST TWO WEEKS, BOMB POP.
I KNOW YOU WISH YOU WERE BACK HOME.
"HOME" IS WHEREVER MY COUNTRY NEEDS ME, LIANG.
BUT YES, I DO.
STILL, I'VE MADE THIS SORT OF LEAP ACROSS TIME BEFORE. AND LIKE THE LAST ONE...
...I NEED TO MAKE MY PEACE WITH THE FACT THAT IT'S PROBABLY A ONE-WAY TRIP.
THIS ENTIRE APPARATUS BAFFLES ME. IT'S NOT SOLAR- OR WIND-POWERED. NO SMELL OF FOSSIL FUEL. WHAT'S THE SOURCE OF ITS--

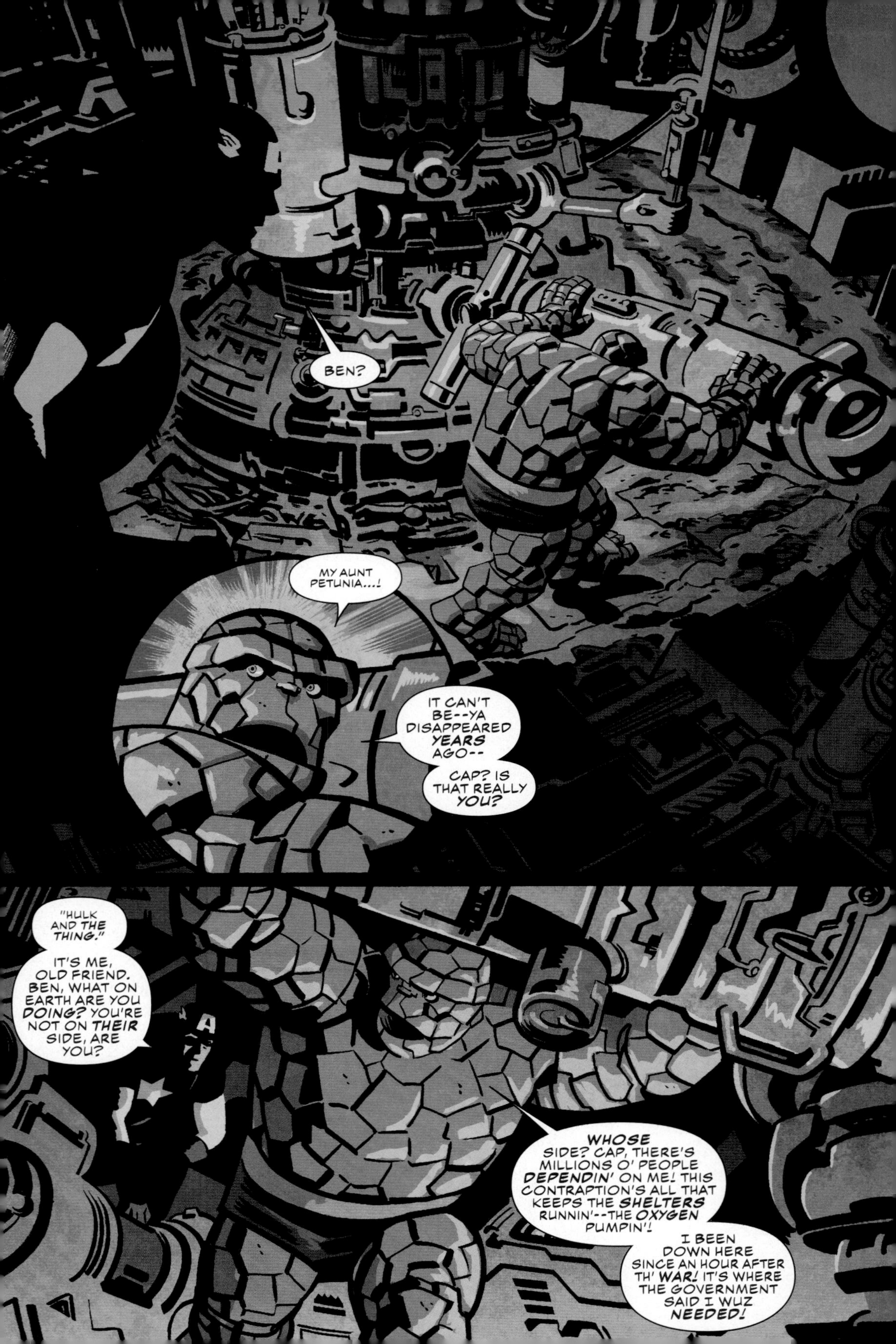
BEN?
MY AUNT PETUNIA...!
IT CAN'T BE--YA DISAPPEARED YEARS AGO--
CAP? IS THAT REALLY YOU?
"HULK AND THE THING."
IT'S ME, OLD FRIEND. BEN, WHAT ON EARTH ARE YOU DOING? YOU'RE NOT ON THEIR SIDE, ARE YOU?
WHOSE SIDE? CAP, THERE'S MILLIONS O' PEOPLE DEPENDIN' ON ME! THIS CONTRAPTION'S ALL THAT KEEPS THE SHELTERS RUNNIN'--THE OXYGEN PUMPIN'!
I BEEN DOWN HERE SINCE AN HOUR AFTER TH' WAR! IT'S WHERE THE GOVERNMENT SAID I WUZ NEEDED!

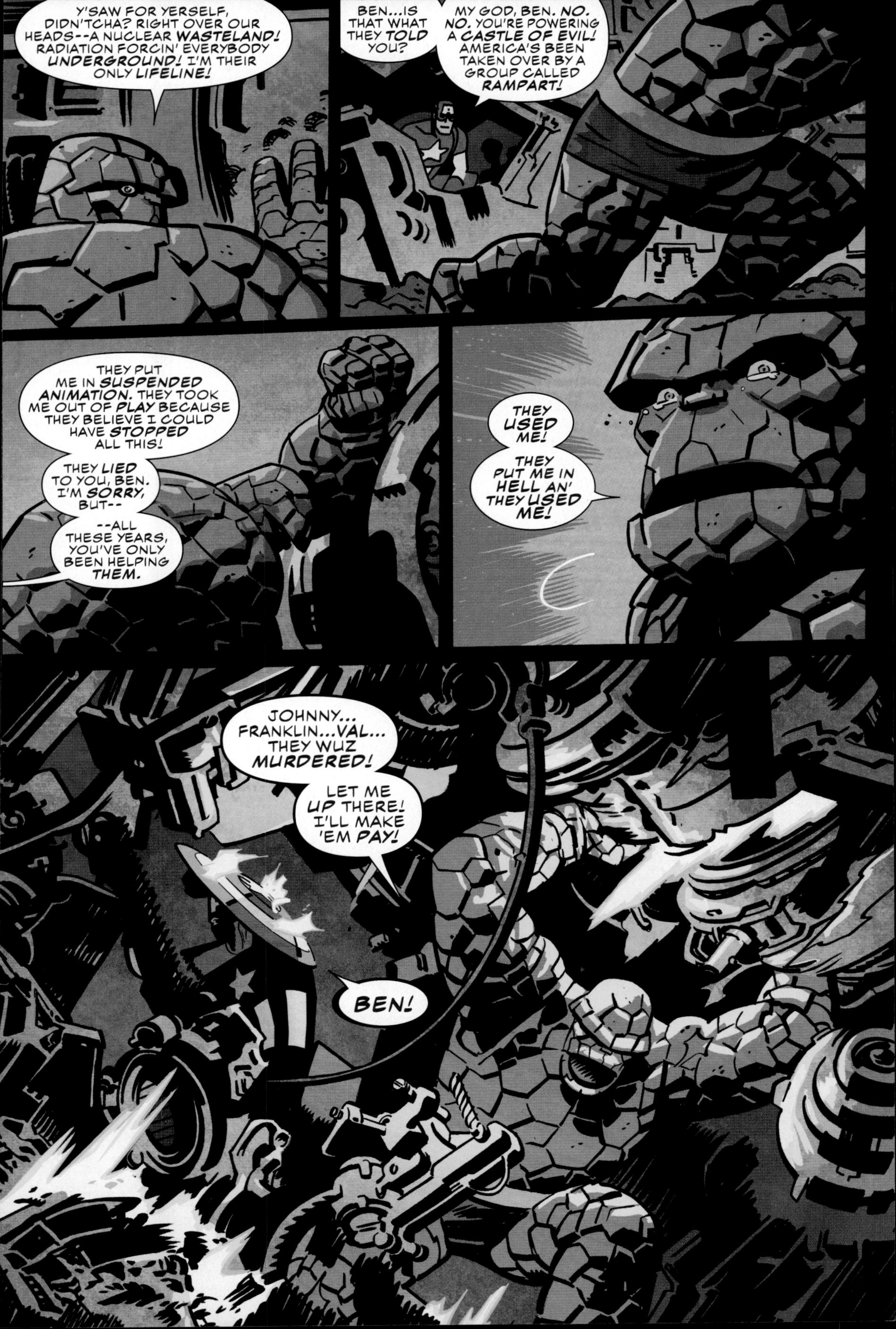

Y'SAW FOR YERSELF, DIDN'TCHA? RIGHT OVER OUR HEADS--A NUCLEAR WASTELAND! RADIATION FORCIN' EVERYBODY UNDERGROUND! I'M THEIR ONLY LIFELINE!
BEN...IS THAT WHAT THEY TOLD YOU?
MY GOD, BEN. NO. NO. YOU'RE POWERING A CASTLE OF EVIL! AMERICA'S BEEN TAKEN OVER BY A GROUP CALLED RAMPART!
THEY PUT ME IN SUSPENDED ANIMATION. THEY TOOK ME OUT OF PLAY BECAUSE THEY BELIEVE I COULD HAVE STOPPED ALL THIS!
THEY LIED TO YOU, BEN. I'M SORRY, BUT--
--ALL THESE YEARS, YOU'VE ONLY BEEN HELPING THEM.
THEY USED ME!
THEY PUT ME IN HELL AN' THEY USED ME!
JOHNNY... FRANKLIN...VAL... THEY WUZ MURDERED!
LET ME UP THERE! I'LL MAKE 'EM PAY!
BEN!

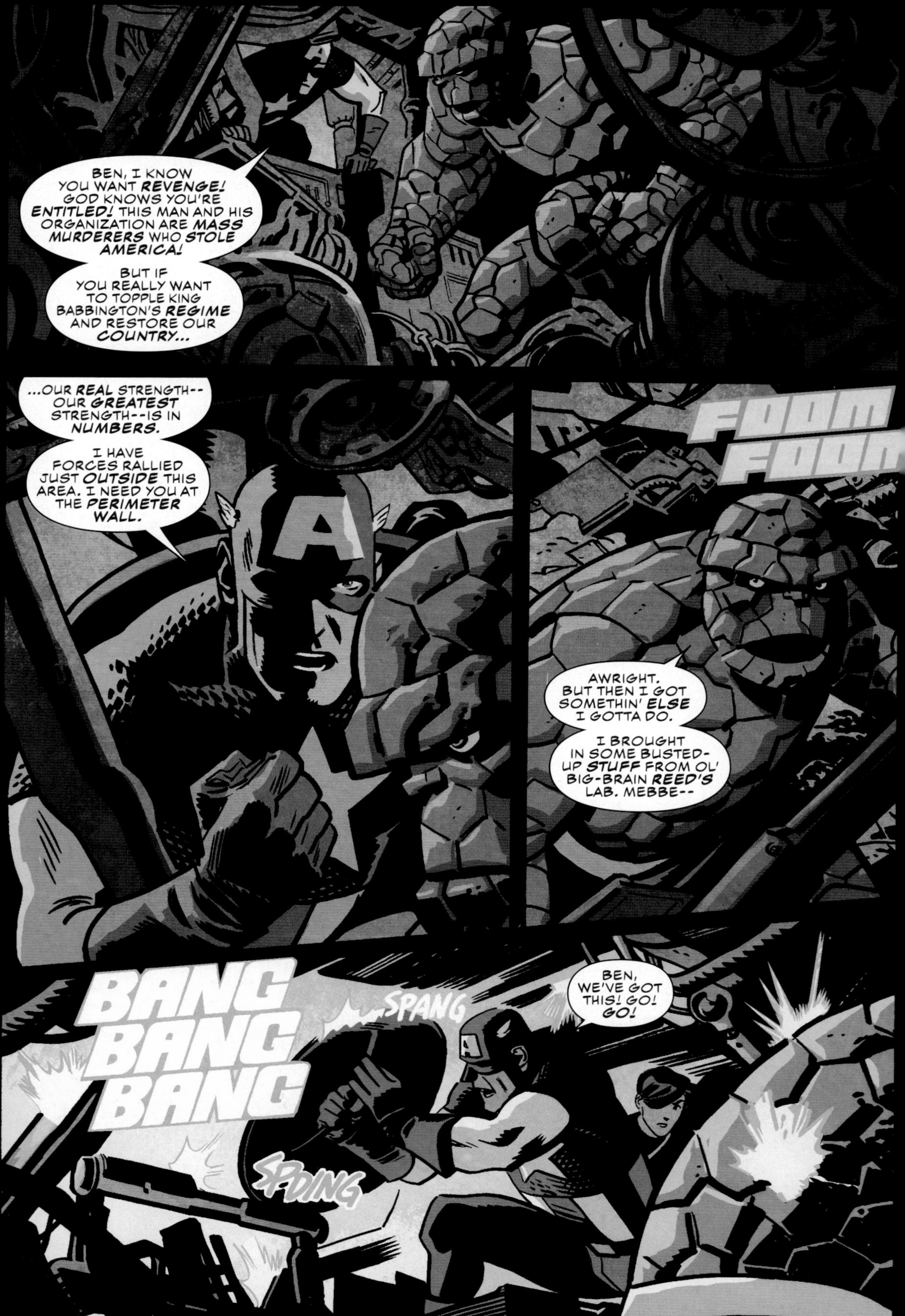
BEN, I KNOW YOU WANT REVENGE! GOD KNOWS YOU'RE ENTITLED! THIS MAN AND HIS ORGANIZATION ARE MASS MURDERERS WHO STOLE AMERICA!
BUT IF YOU REALLY WANT TO TOPPLE KING BABBINGTON'S REGIME AND RESTORE OUR COUNTRY...
...OUR REAL STRENGTH-- OUR GREATEST STRENGTH--IS IN NUMBERS.
I HAVE FORCES RALLIED JUST OUTSIDE THIS AREA. I NEED YOU AT THE PERIMETER WALL.
AWRIGHT. BUT THEN I GOT SOMETHIN' ELSE I GOTTA DO.
I BROUGHT IN SOME BUSTED-UP STUFF FROM OL' BIG-BRAIN REED'S LAB. MEBBE--
BANG BANG BANG
SPANG
SPDING
BEN, WE'VE GOT THIS! GO! GO!

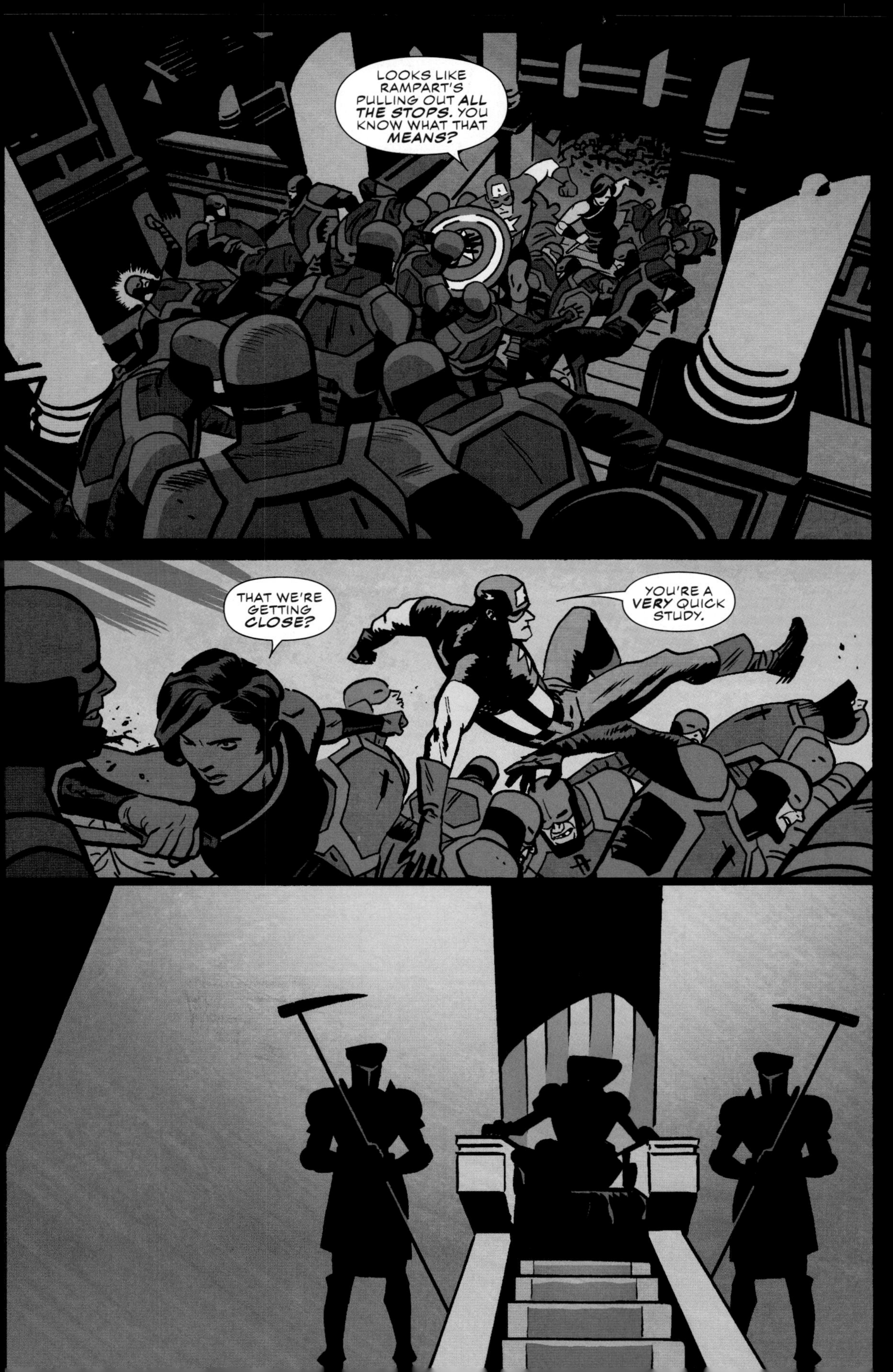
LOOKS LIKE RAMPART'S PULLING OUT ALL THE STOPS. YOU KNOW WHAT THAT MEANS?
THAT WE'RE GETTING CLOSE?
YOU'RE A VERY QUICK STUDY.

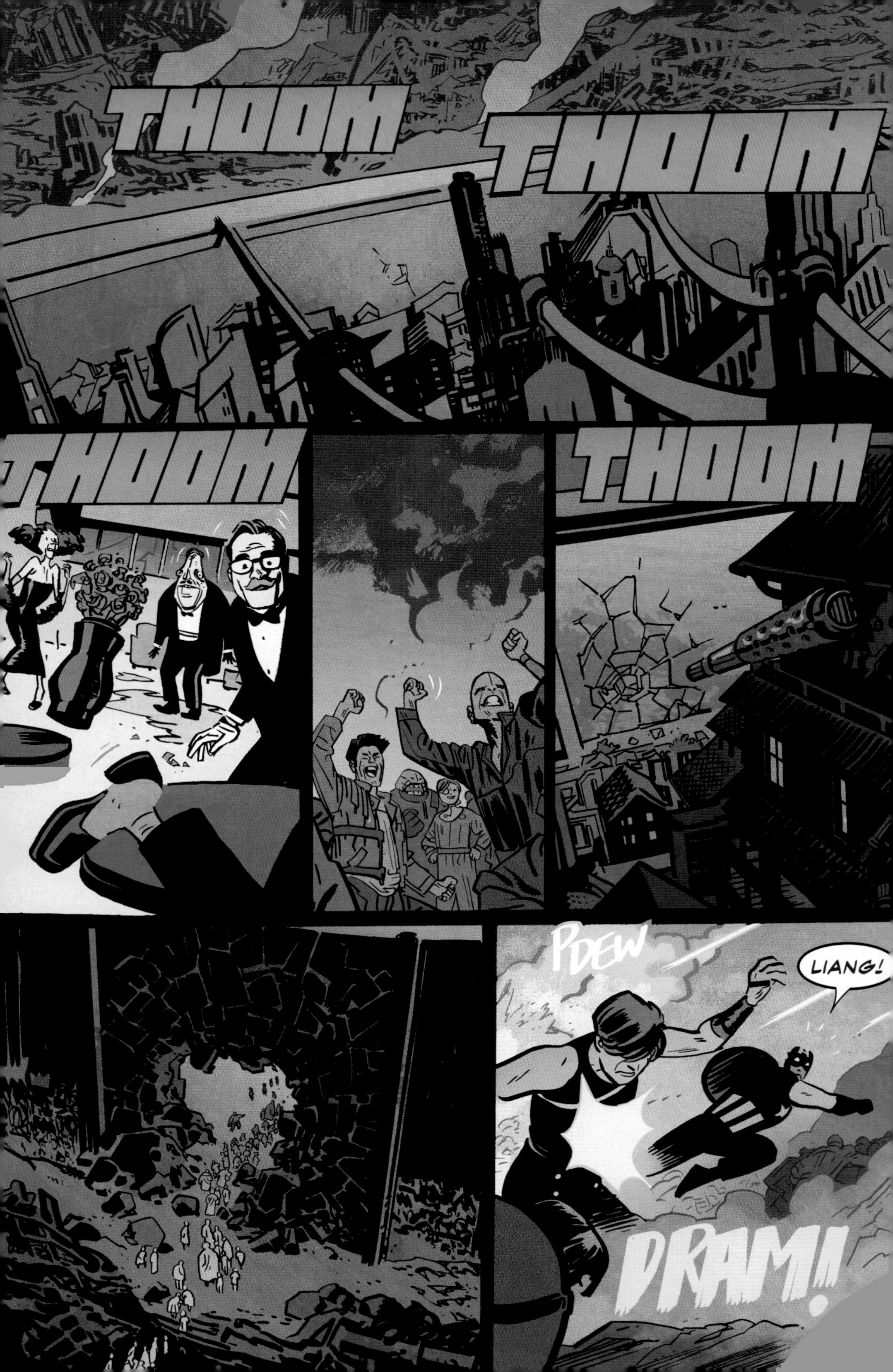
THOOM
THOOM
THOOM
THOOM
PDEW
LIANG!
DRAM!

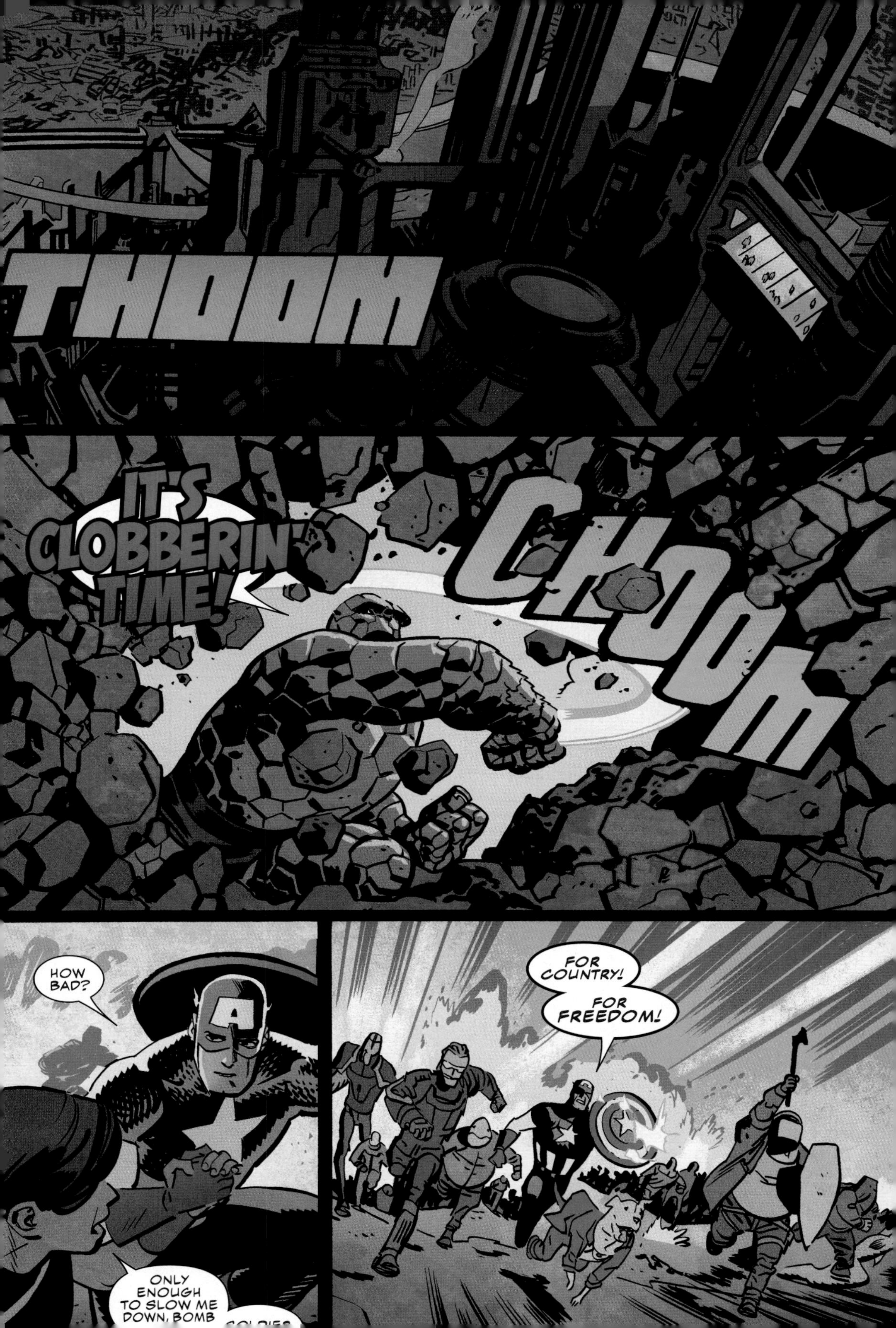
THOOM
IT'S CLOBBERIN' TIME!
CHOOM
HOW BAD?
ONLY ENOUGH TO SLOW ME DOWN, BOMB
FOR COUNTRY!
FOR FREEDOM!

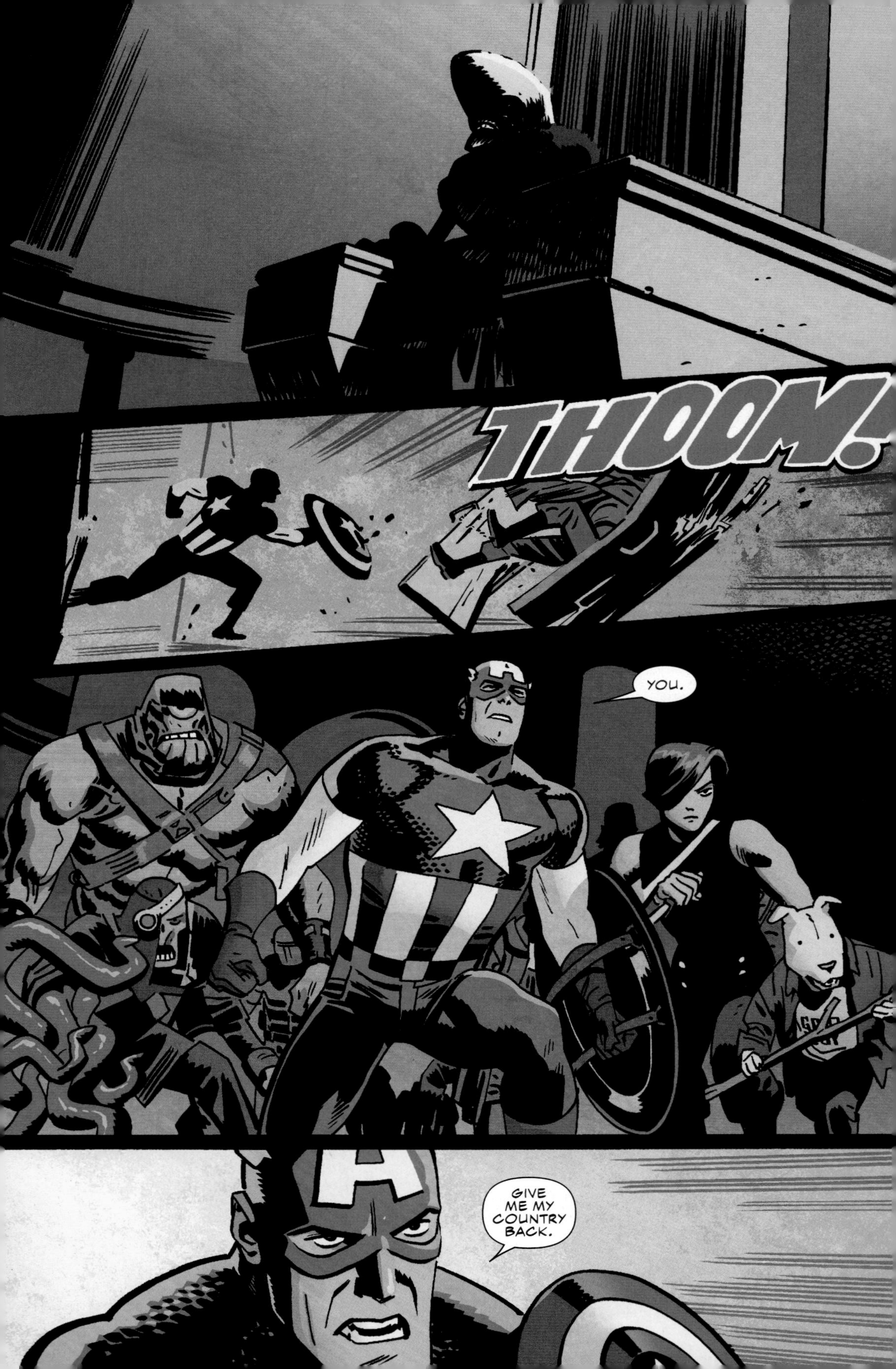
THOOM!
YOU.
GIVE ME MY COUNTRY BACK.

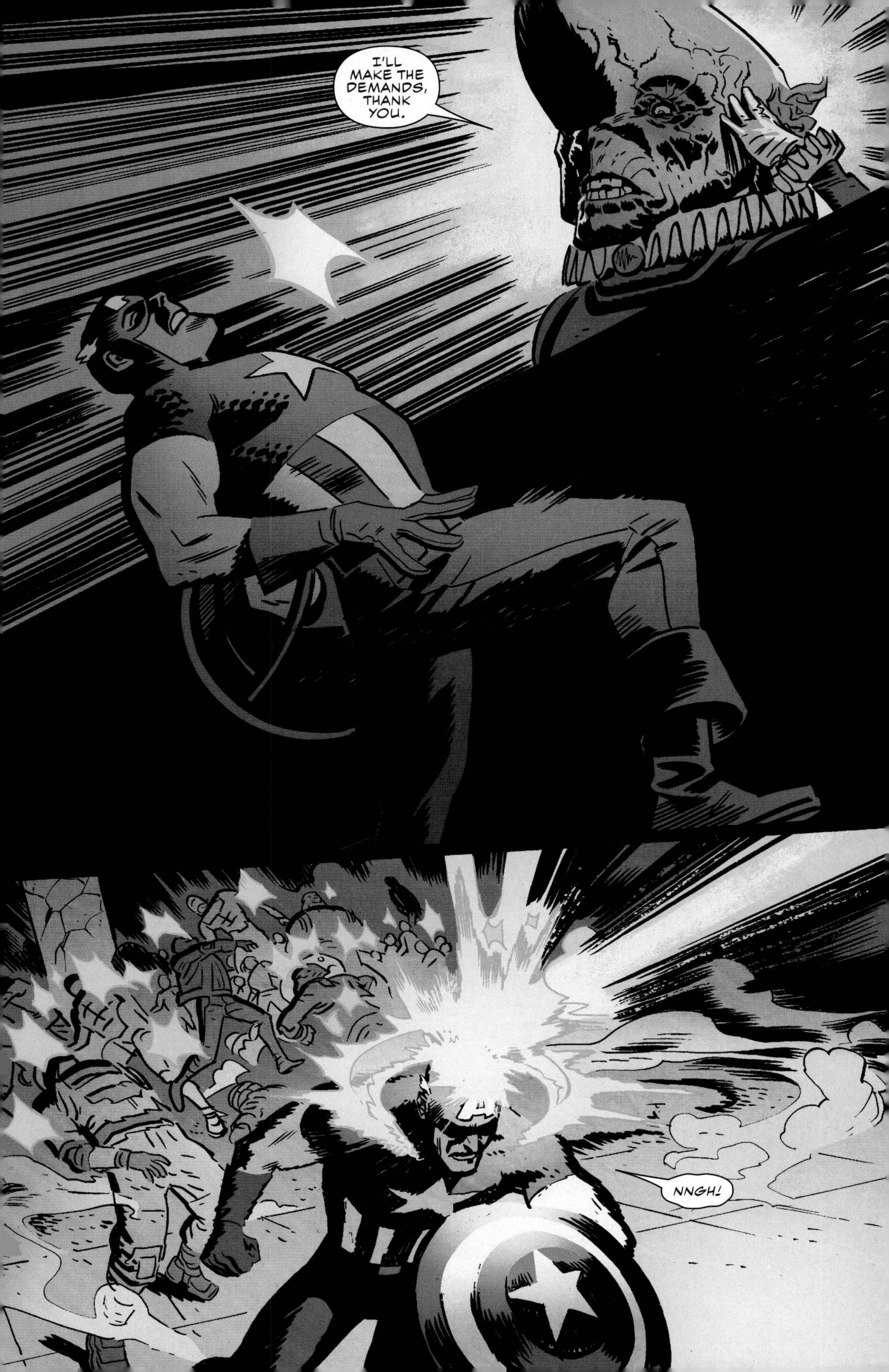
I'LL MAKE THE DEMANDS, THANK YOU.
NNGH!

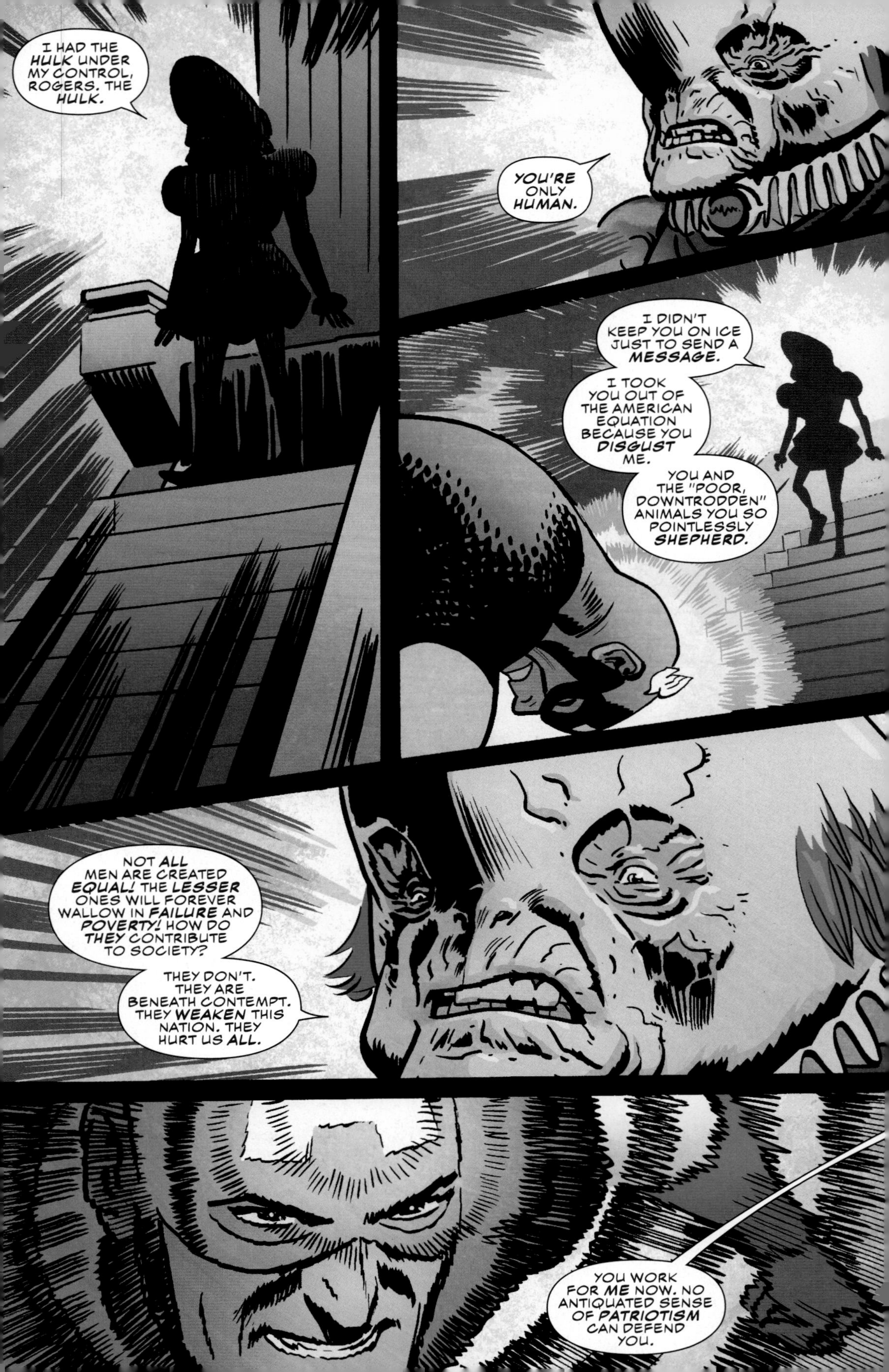
I HAD THE HULK UNDER MY CONTROL, ROGERS. THE HULK.
YOU'RE ONLY HUMAN.
I DIDN'T KEEP YOU ON ICE JUST TO SEND A MESSAGE.
I TOOK YOU OUT OF THE AMERICAN EQUATION BECAUSE YOU DISGUST ME.
YOU AND THE "POOR, DOWNTRODDEN" ANIMALS YOU SO POINTLESSLY SHEPHERD.
NOT ALL MEN ARE CREATED EQUAL! THE LESSER ONES WILL FOREVER WALLOW IN FAILURE AND POVERTY! HOW DO THEY CONTRIBUTE TO SOCIETY?
THEY DON'T. THEY ARE BENEATH CONTEMPT. THEY WEAKEN THIS NATION. THEY HURT US ALL.
YOU WORK FOR ME NOW. NO ANTIQUATED SENSE OF PATRIOTISM CAN DEFEND YOU.

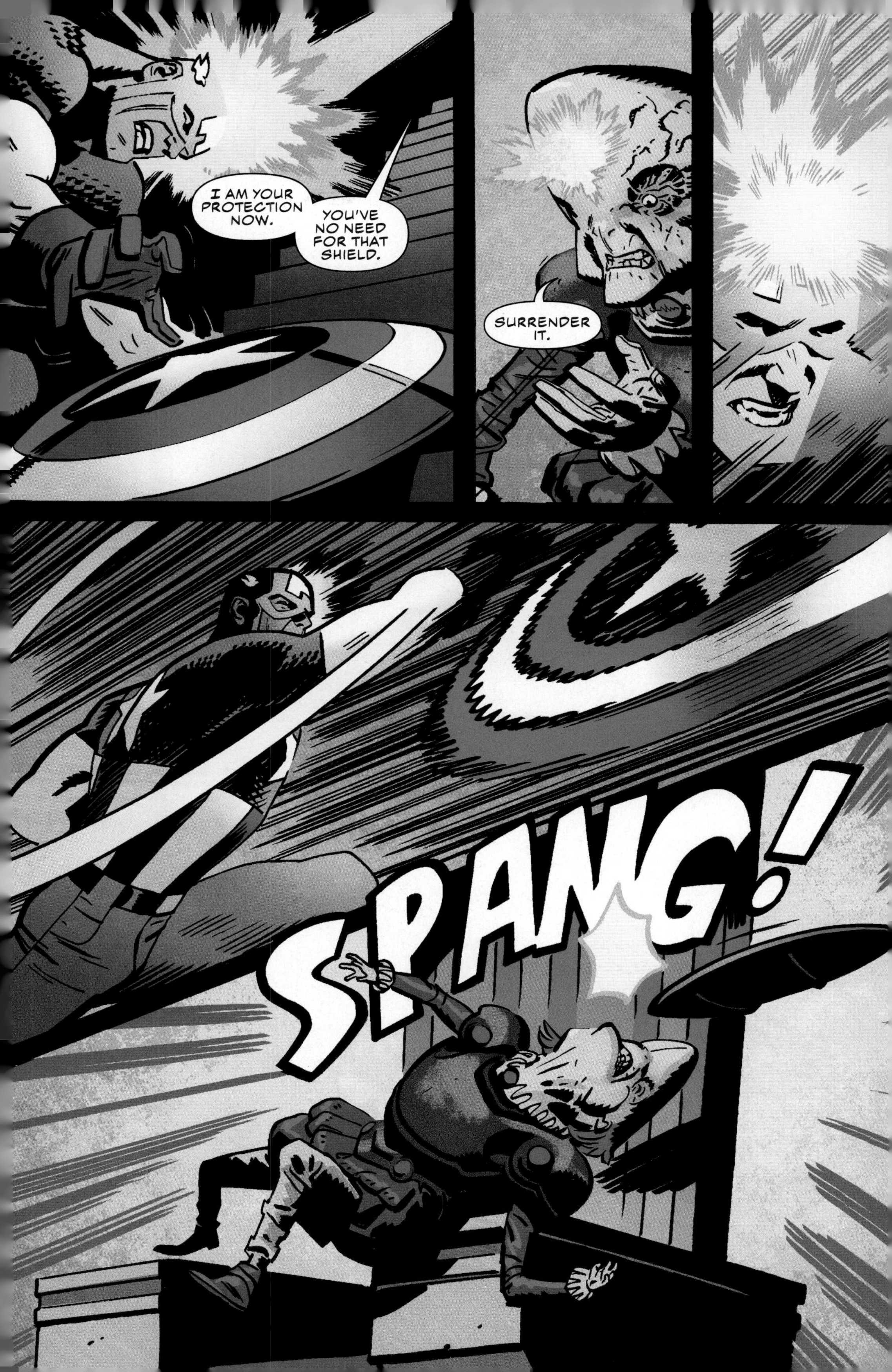
I AM YOUR PROTECTION NOW.
YOU'VE NO NEED FOR THAT SHIELD.
SURRENDER IT.
SPANG!

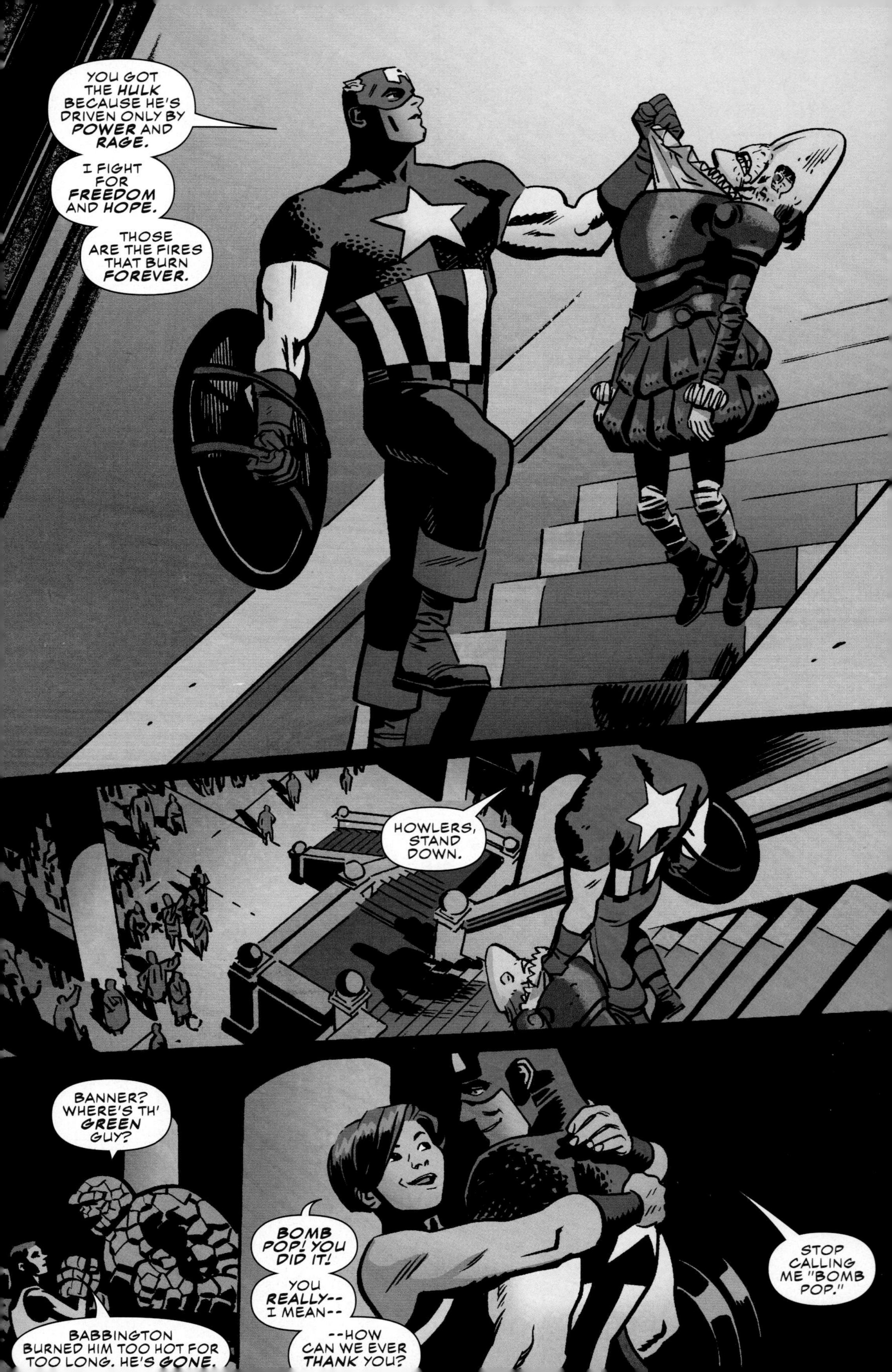
YOU GOT THE HULK BECAUSE HE'S DRIVEN ONLY BY POWER AND RAGE.
I FIGHT FOR FREEDOM AND HOPE.
THOSE ARE THE FIRES THAT BURN FOREVER.
HOWLERS, STAND DOWN.
BANNER? WHERE'S TH' GREEN GUY?
BABBINGTON BURNED HIM TOO HOT FOR TOO LONG. HE'S GONE.
BOMB POP! YOU DID IT!
YOU REALLY-- I MEAN--
--HOW CAN WE EVER THANK YOU?
STOP CALLING ME "BOMB POP."

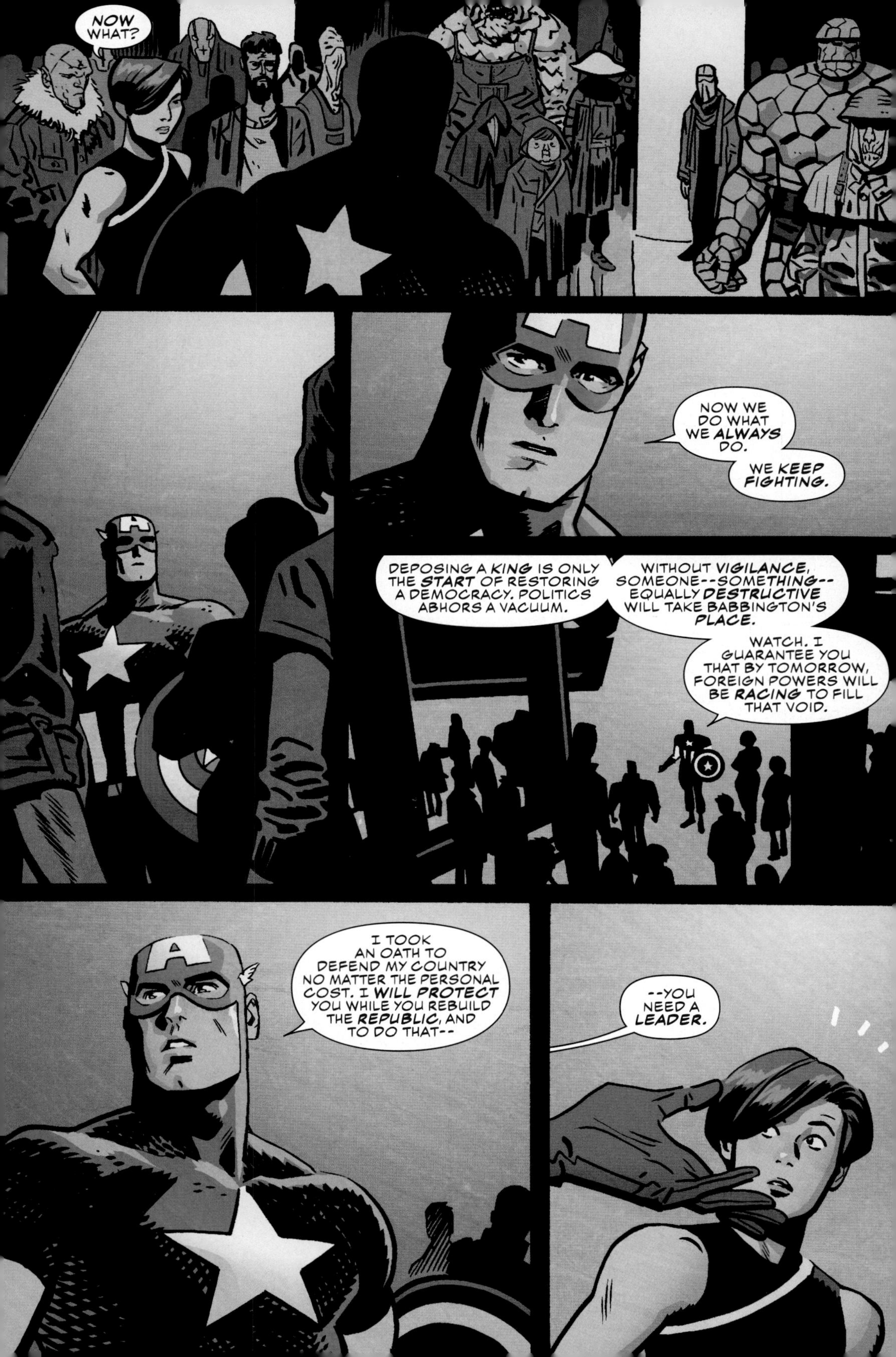
NOW WHAT?
NOW WE DO WHAT WE ALWAYS DO.
WE KEEP FIGHTING.
DEPOSING A KING IS ONLY THE START OF RESTORING A DEMOCRACY. POLITICS ABHORS A VACUUM.
WITHOUT VIGILANCE, SOMEONE--SOMETHING--EQUALLY DESTRUCTIVE WILL TAKE BABBINGTON'S PLACE.
WATCH. I GUARANTEE YOU THAT BY TOMORROW, FOREIGN POWERS WILL BE RACING TO FILL THAT VOID.
I TOOK AN OATH TO DEFEND MY COUNTRY NO MATTER THE PERSONAL COST. I WILL PROTECT YOU WHILE YOU REBUILD THE REPUBLIC, AND TO DO THAT--
--YOU NEED A LEADER.

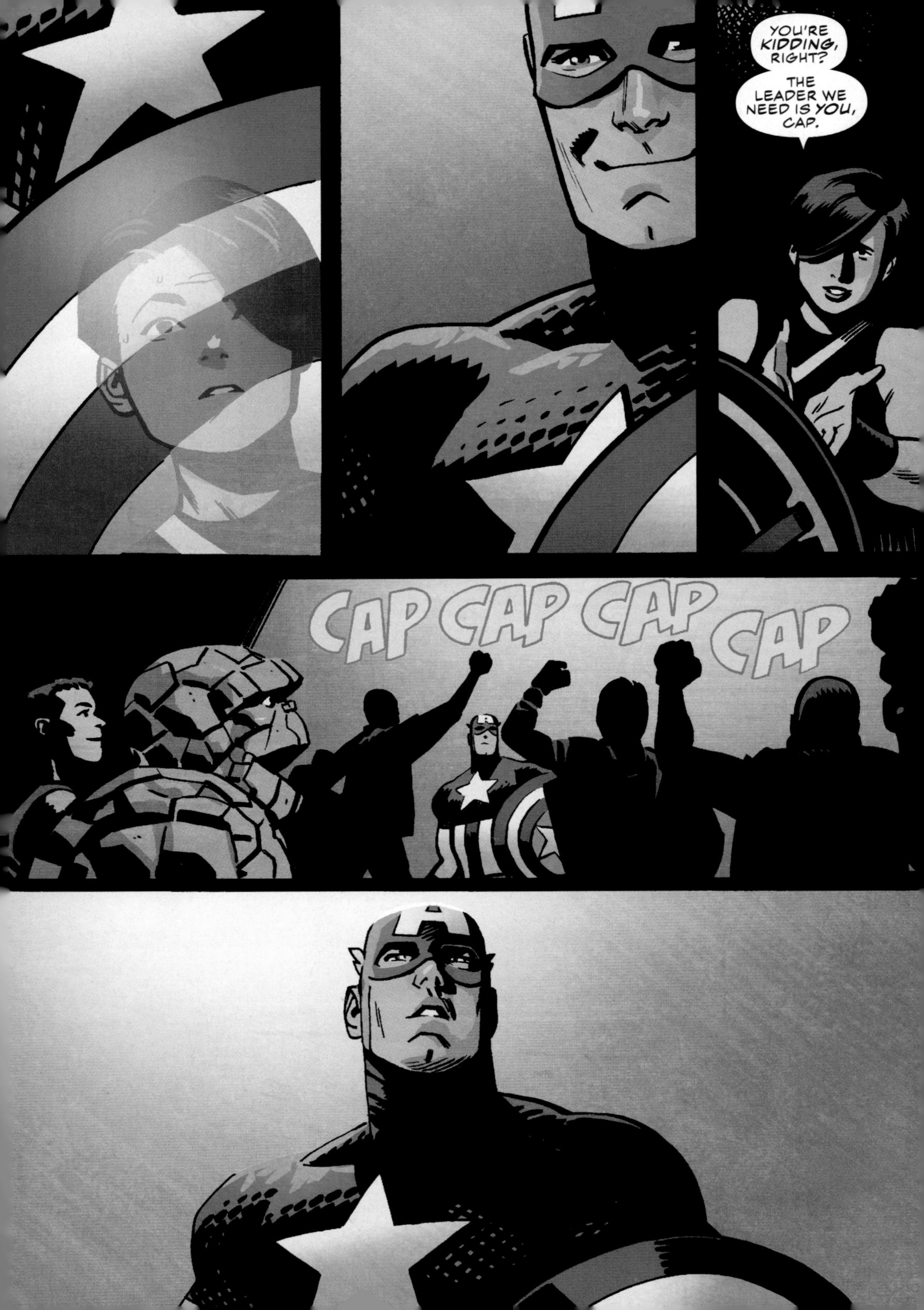
YOU'RE KIDDING, RIGHT?
THE LEADER WE NEED IS YOU, CAP.
CAP CAP CAP CAP

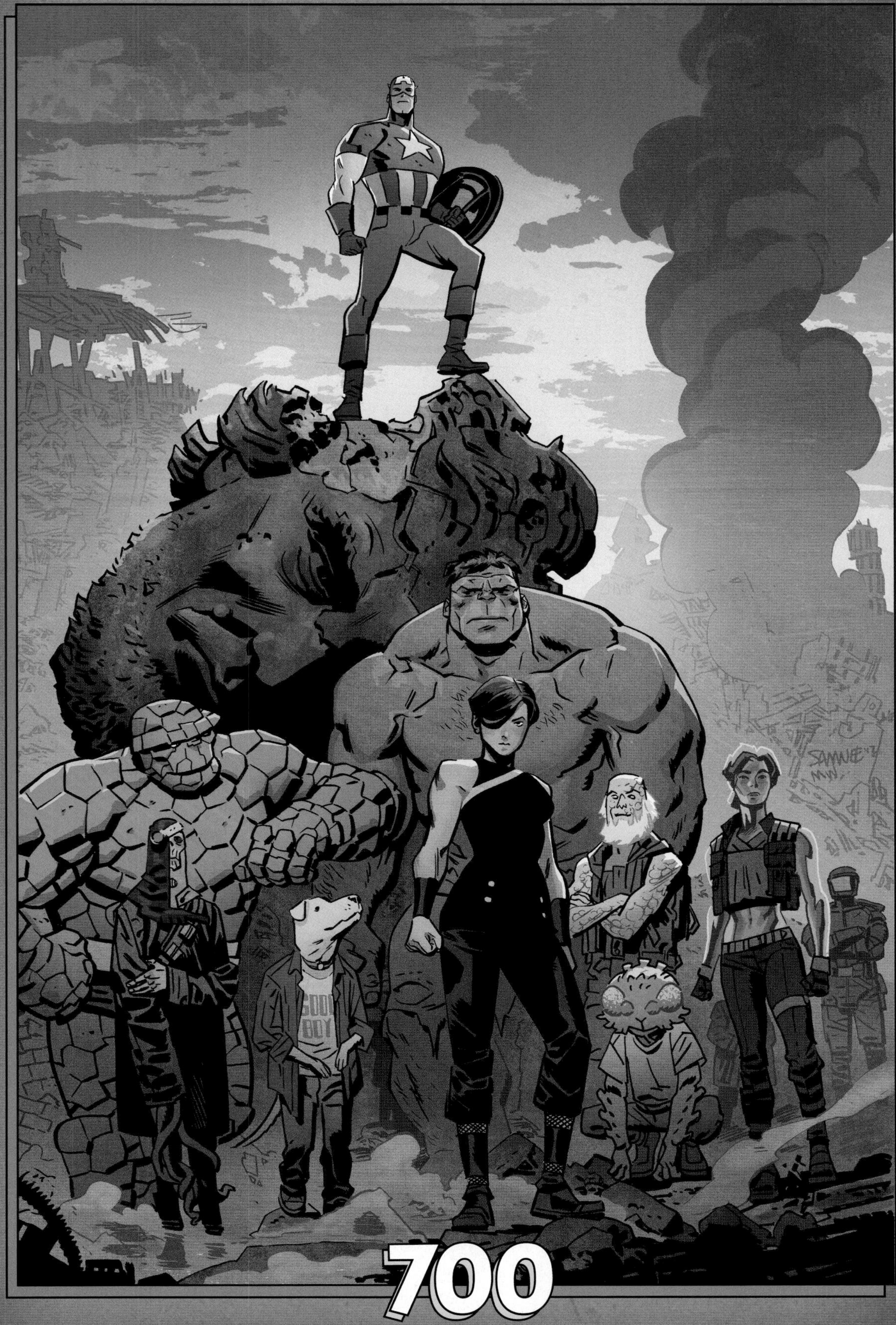
700

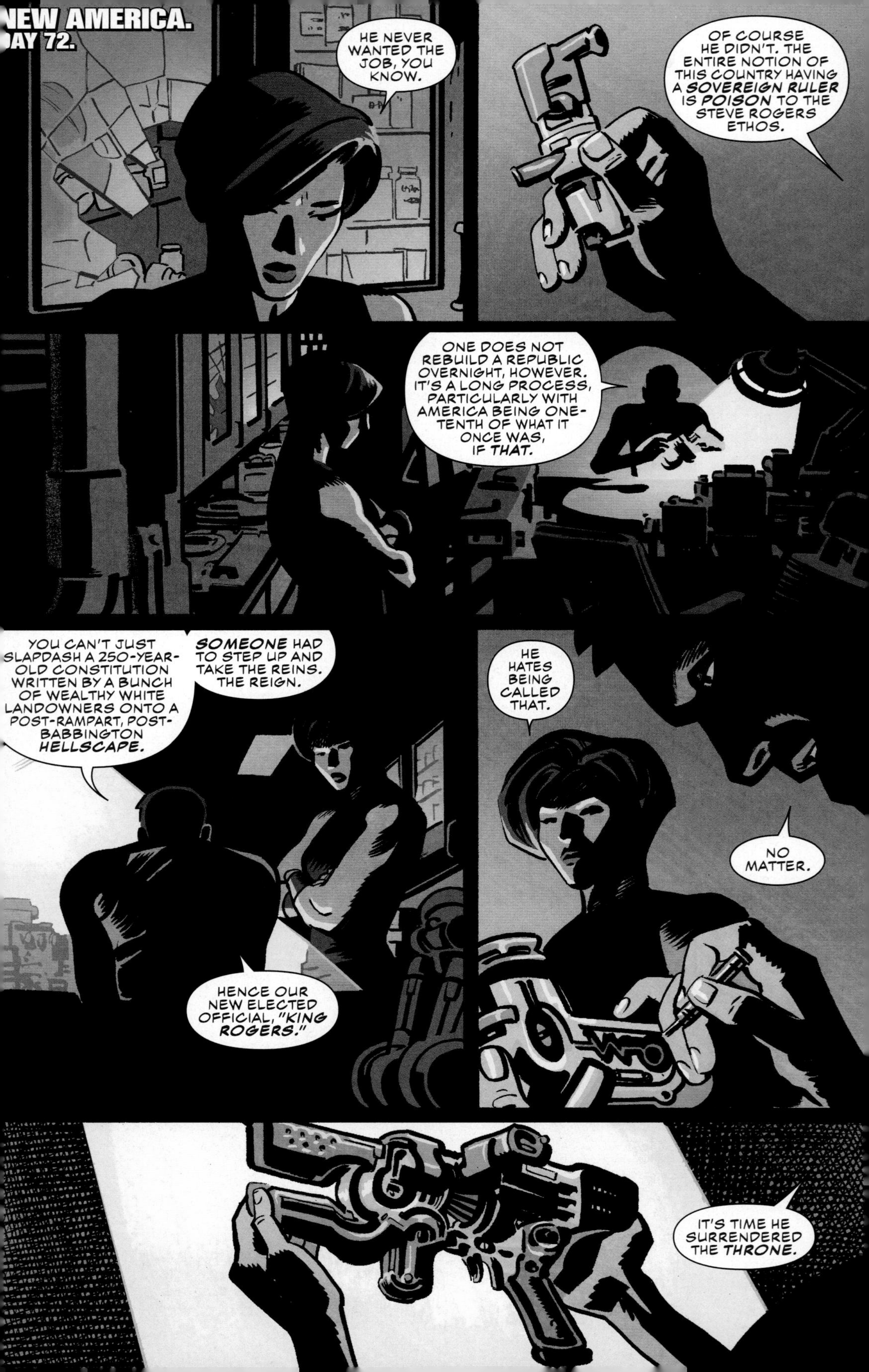
NEW AMERICA.
DAY 72.
HE NEVER WANTED THE JOB, YOU KNOW.
OF COURSE HE DIDN'T. THE ENTIRE NOTION OF THIS COUNTRY HAVING A SOVEREIGN RULER IS POISON TO THE STEVE ROGERS ETHOS.
ONE DOES NOT REBUILD A REPUBLIC OVERNIGHT, HOWEVER. IT'S A LONG PROCESS, PARTICULARLY WITH AMERICA BEING ONE-TENTH OF WHAT IT ONCE WAS, IF THAT.
YOU CAN'T JUST SLAPDASH A 250-YEAR-OLD CONSTITUTION WRITTEN BY A BUNCH OF WEALTHY WHITE LANDOWNERS ONTO A POST-RAMPART, POST-BABBINGTON HELLSCAPE.
SOMEONE HAD TO STEP UP AND TAKE THE REINS. THE REIGN.
HENCE OUR NEW ELECTED OFFICIAL, "KING ROGERS."
HE HATES BEING CALLED THAT.
NO MATTER.
IT'S TIME HE SURRENDERED THE THRONE.

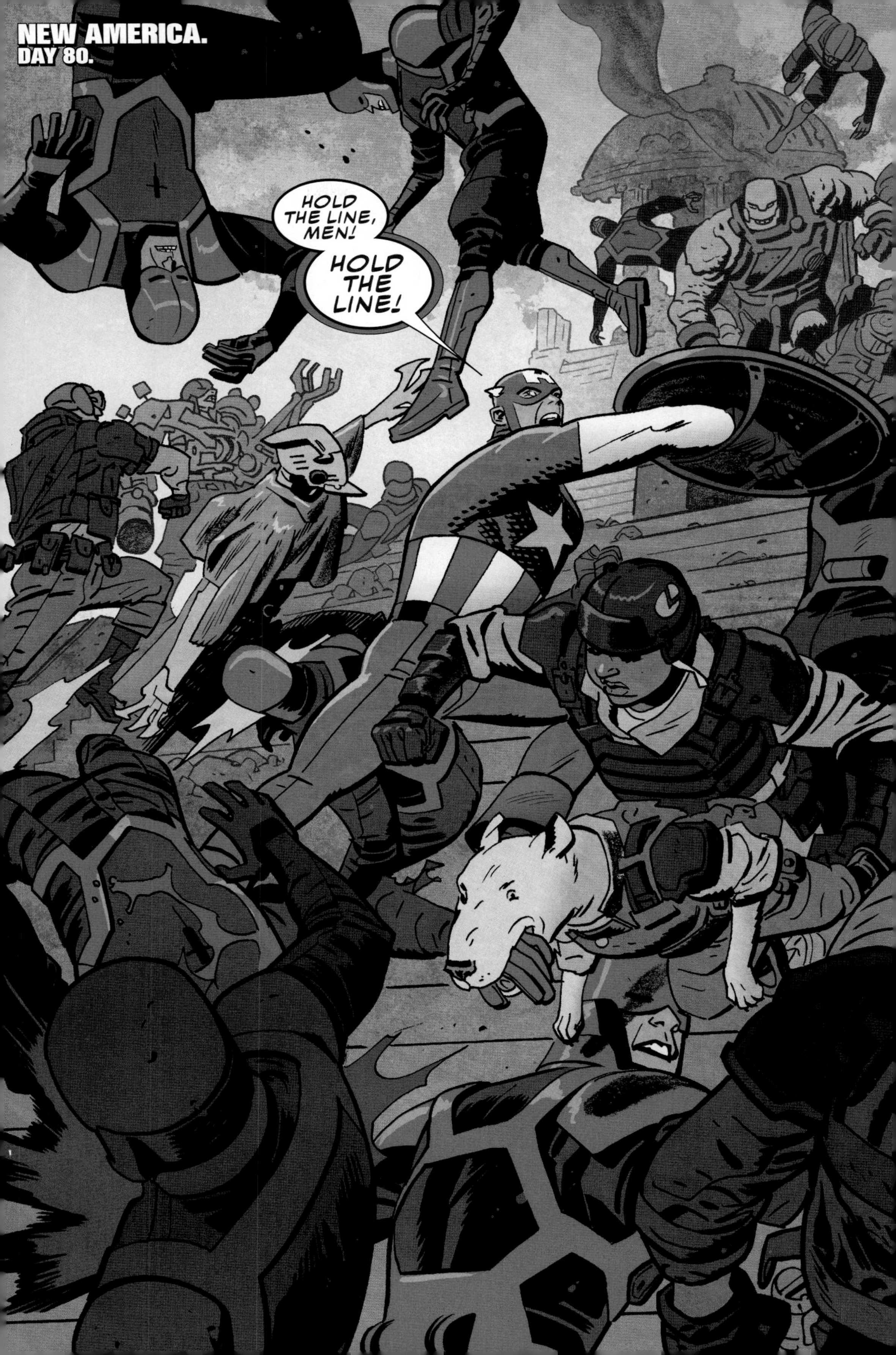
NEW AMERICA.
DAY 80.
HOLD THE LINE, MEN!
HOLD THE LINE!

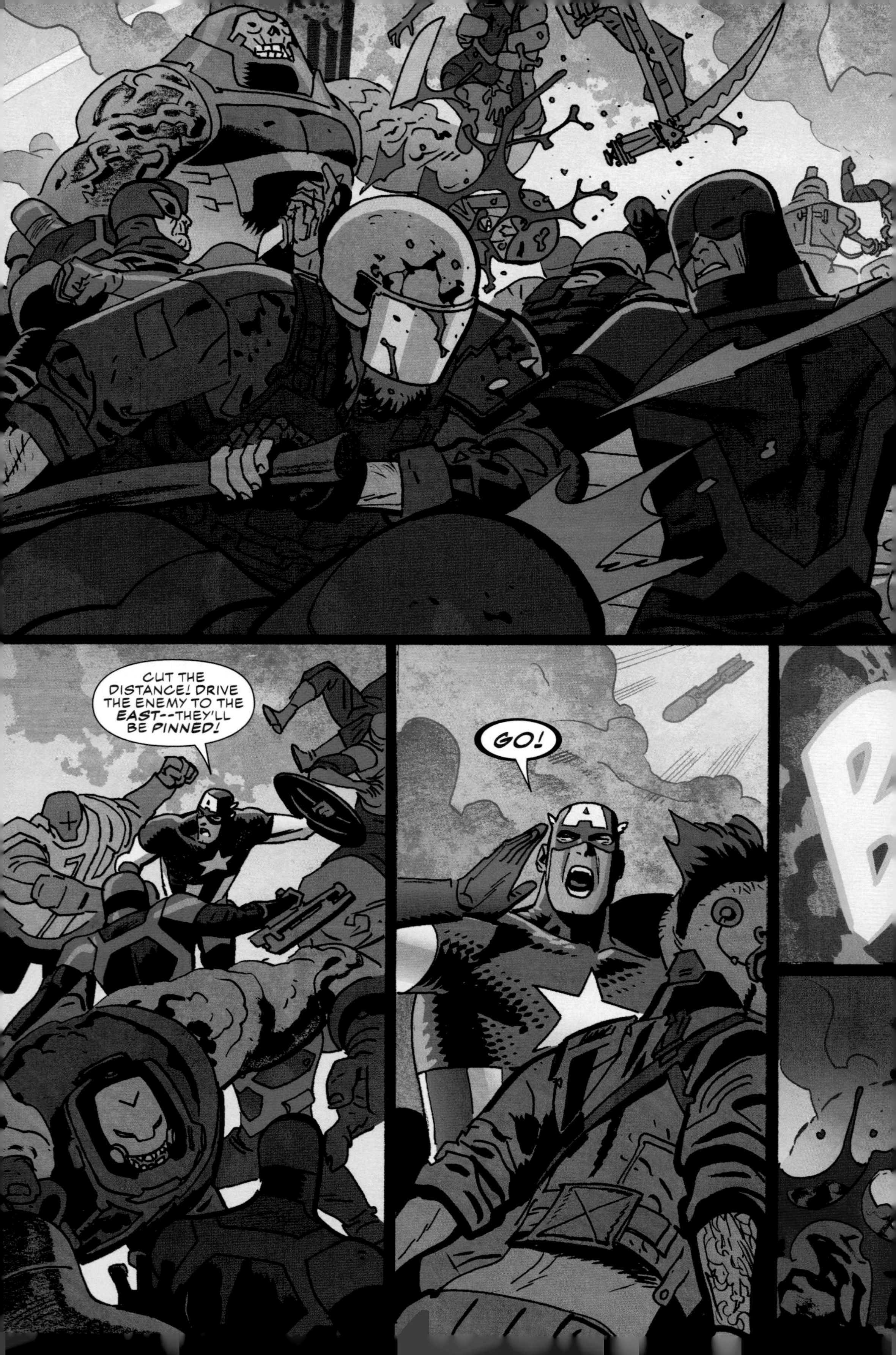
CUT THE DISTANCE! DRIVE THE ENEMY TO THE EAST--THEY'LL BE PINNED!
GO!

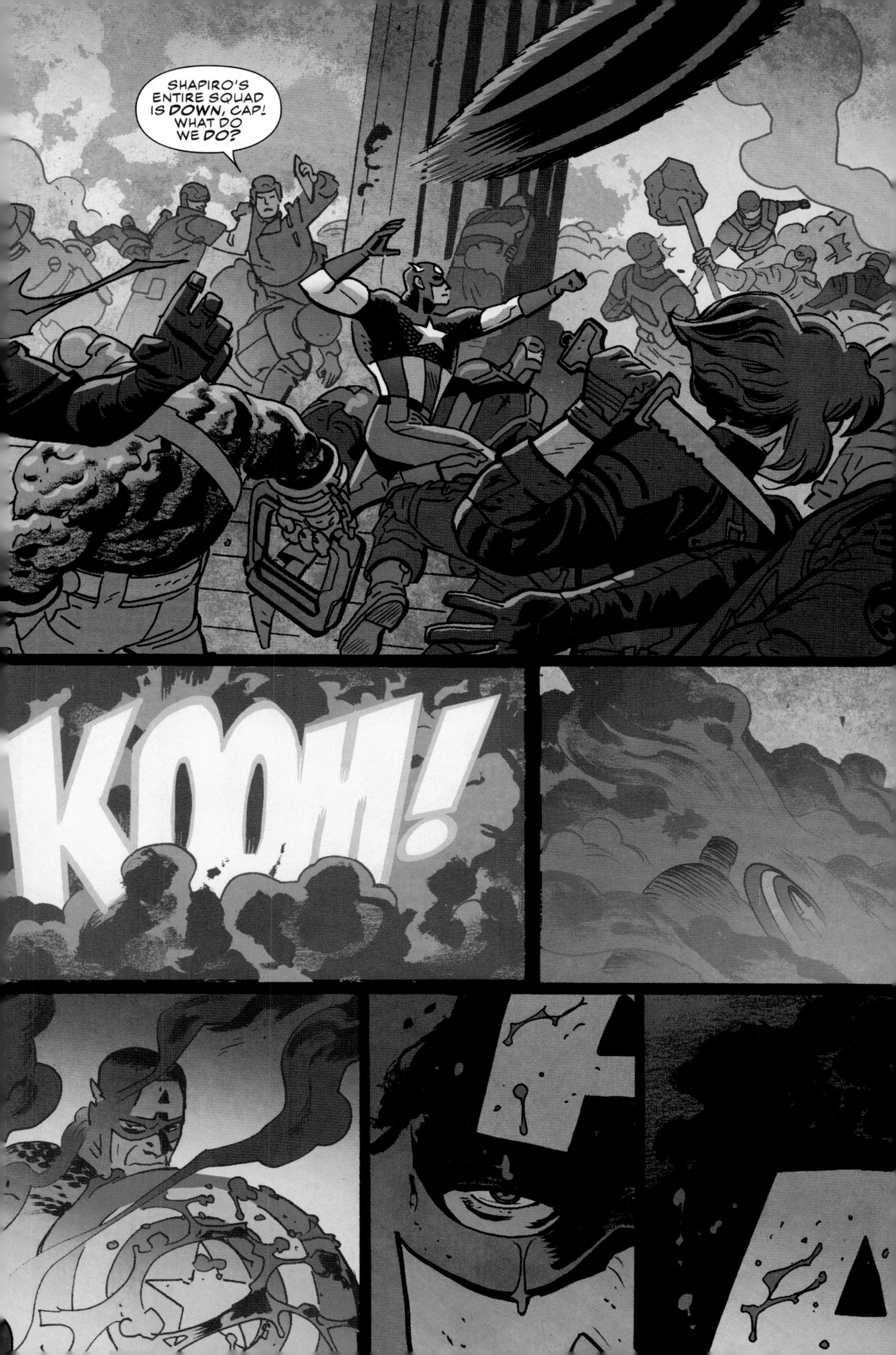
SHAPIRO'S ENTIRE SQUAD IS DOWN, CAP! WHAT DO WE DO?
KOOM!

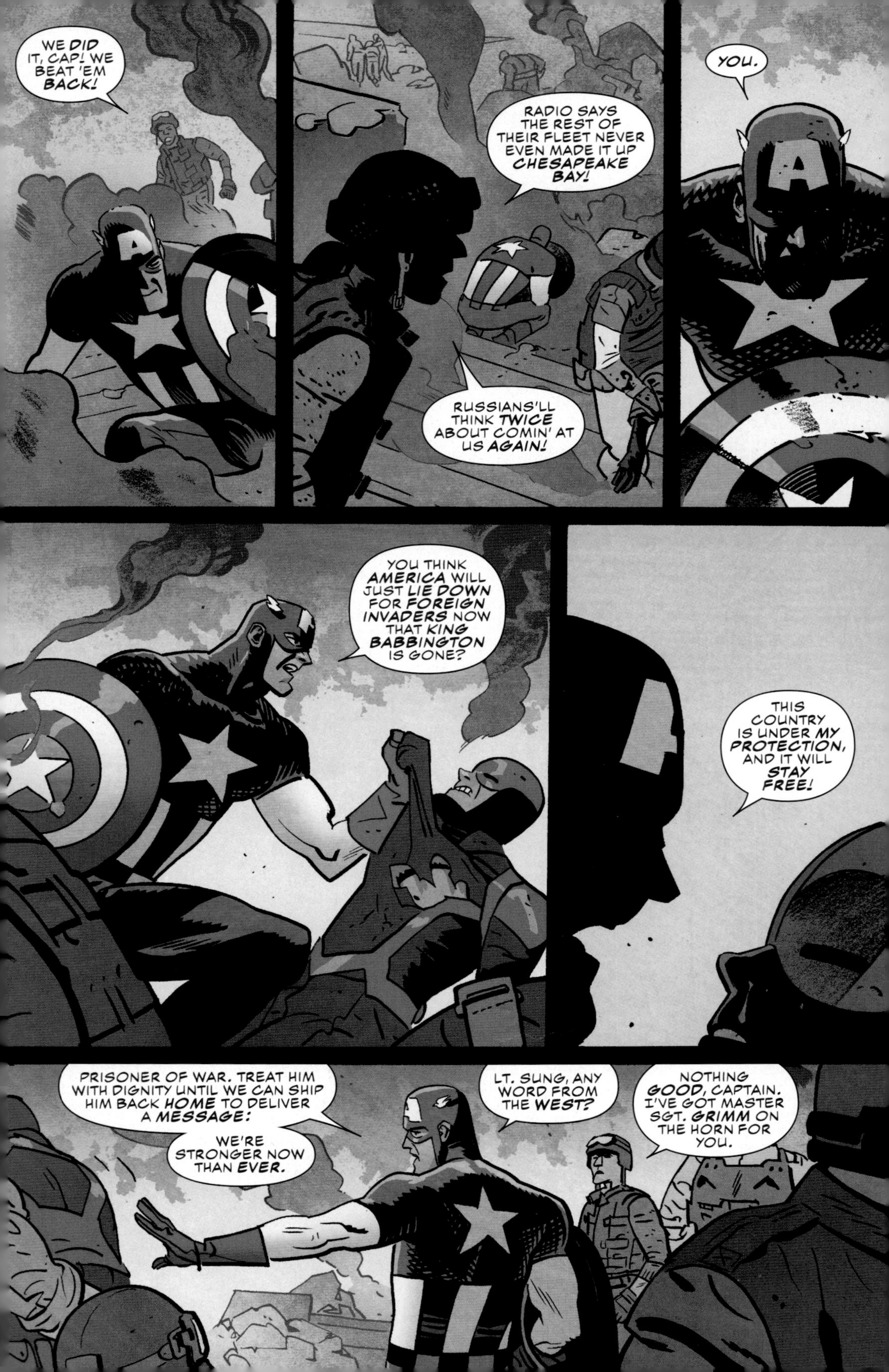
WE DID IT, CAP! WE BEAT 'EM BACK!
RADIO SAYS THE REST OF THEIR FLEET NEVER EVEN MADE IT UP CHESAPEAKE BAY!
RUSSIANS'LL THINK TWICE ABOUT COMIN' AT US AGAIN!
YOU.
YOU THINK AMERICA WILL JUST LIE DOWN FOR FOREIGN INVADERS NOW THAT KING BABBINGTON IS GONE?
THIS COUNTRY IS UNDER MY PROTECTION, AND IT WILL STAY FREE!
PRISONER OF WAR. TREAT HIM WITH DIGNITY UNTIL WE CAN SHIP HIM BACK HOME TO DELIVER A MESSAGE:
WE'RE STRONGER NOW THAN EVER.
LT. SUNG, ANY WORD FROM THE WEST?
NOTHING GOOD, CAPTAIN. I'VE GOT MASTER SGT. GRIMM ON THE HORN FOR YOU.

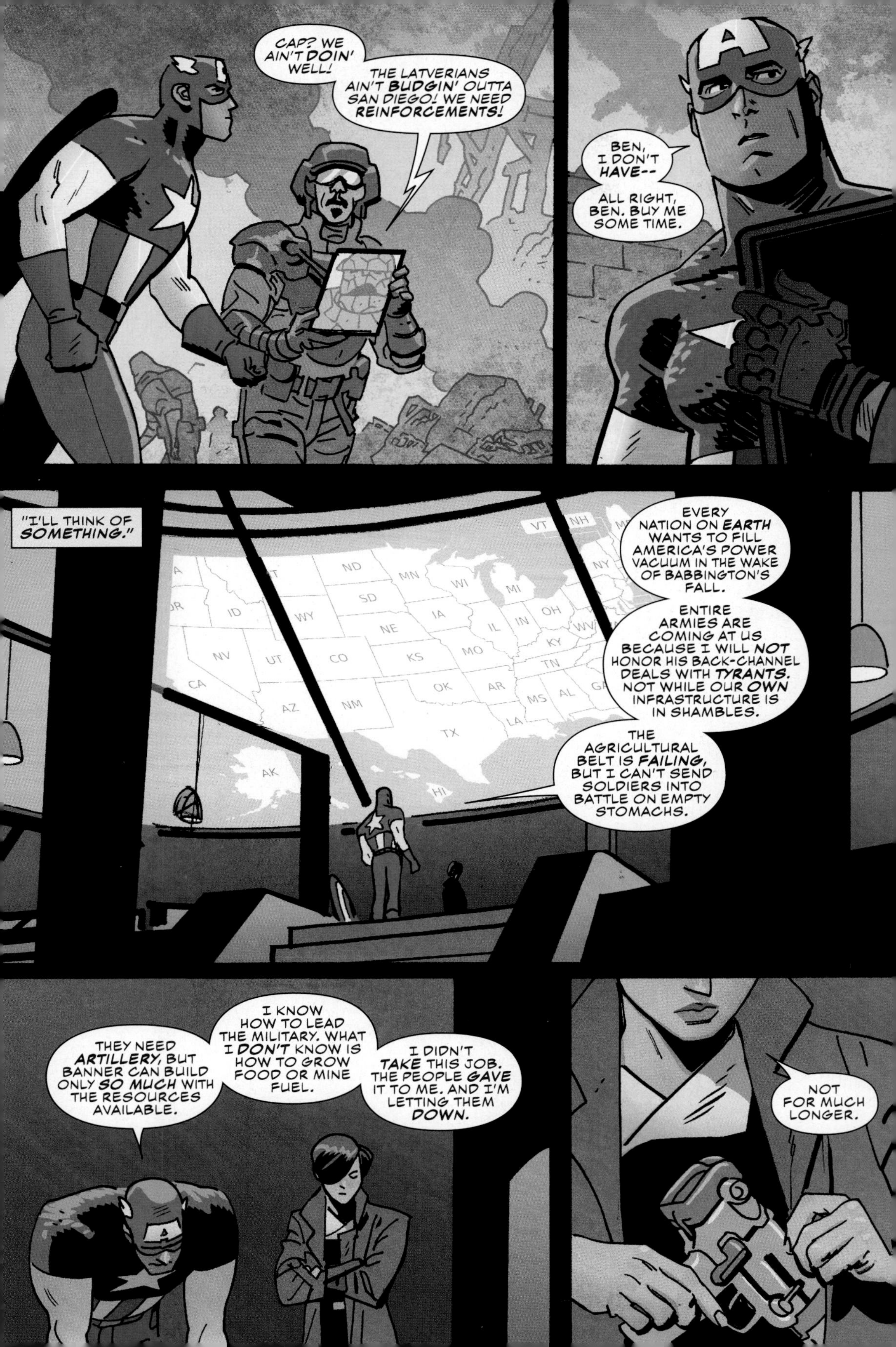
CAP? WE AIN'T DOIN' WELL!
THE LATVERIANS AIN'T BUDGIN' OUTTA SAN DIEGO! WE NEED REINFORCEMENTS!
BEN, I DON'T HAVE--
ALL RIGHT, BEN. BUY ME SOME TIME.
"I'LL THINK OF SOMETHING."
VT
NH
ND
MN
WI
MI
NY
SD
ID
WY
IA
OH
NE
IL
IN
WV
NV
UT
CO
KS
MO
KY
TN
CA
OK
AR
AZ
NM
MS
AL
LA
TX
AK
HI
EVERY NATION ON EARTH WANTS TO FILL AMERICA'S POWER VACUUM IN THE WAKE OF BABBINGTON'S FALL.
ENTIRE ARMIES ARE COMING AT US BECAUSE I WILL NOT HONOR HIS BACK-CHANNEL DEALS WITH TYRANTS. NOT WHILE OUR OWN INFRASTRUCTURE IS IN SHAMBLES.
THE AGRICULTURAL BELT IS FAILING, BUT I CAN'T SEND SOLDIERS INTO BATTLE ON EMPTY STOMACHS.
THEY NEED ARTILLERY, BUT BANNER CAN BUILD ONLY SO MUCH WITH THE RESOURCES AVAILABLE.
I KNOW HOW TO LEAD THE MILITARY. WHAT I DON'T KNOW IS HOW TO GROW FOOD OR MINE FUEL.
I DIDN'T TAKE THIS JOB. THE PEOPLE GAVE IT TO ME. AND I'M LETTING THEM DOWN.
NOT FOR MUCH LONGER.

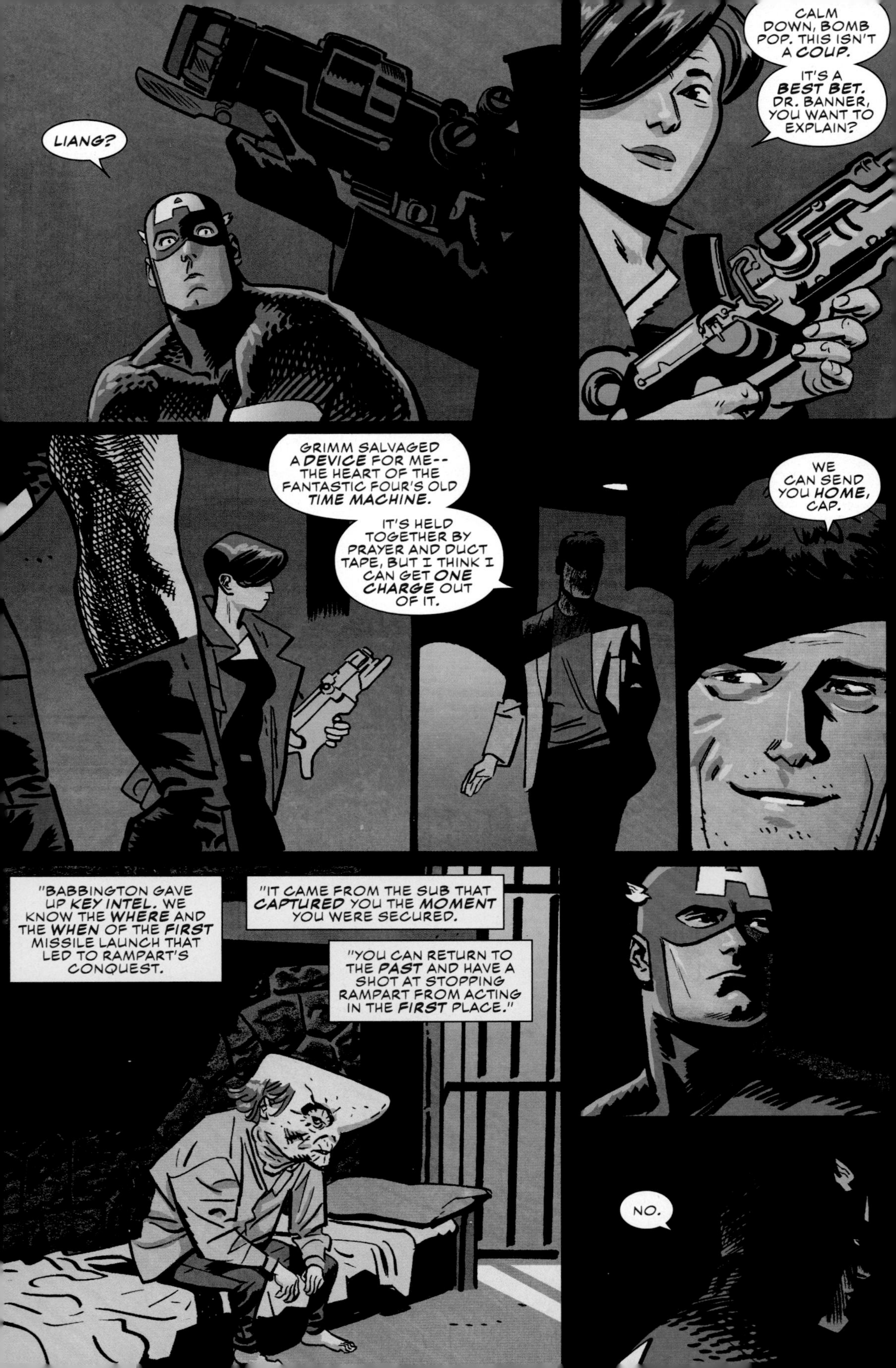
LIANG?
CALM DOWN, BOMB POP. THIS ISN'T A COUP.
IT'S A BEST BET. DR. BANNER, YOU WANT TO EXPLAIN?
GRIMM SALVAGED A DEVICE FOR ME-- THE HEART OF THE FANTASTIC FOUR'S OLD TIME MACHINE.
IT'S HELD TOGETHER BY PRAYER AND DUCT TAPE, BUT I THINK I CAN GET ONE CHARGE OUT OF IT.
WE CAN SEND YOU HOME, CAP.
"BABBINGTON GAVE UP KEY INTEL. WE KNOW THE WHERE AND THE WHEN OF THE FIRST MISSILE LAUNCH THAT LED TO RAMPART'S CONQUEST.
"IT CAME FROM THE SUB THAT CAPTURED YOU THE MOMENT YOU WERE SECURED.
"YOU CAN RETURN TO THE PAST AND HAVE A SHOT AT STOPPING RAMPART FROM ACTING IN THE FIRST PLACE."
NO.

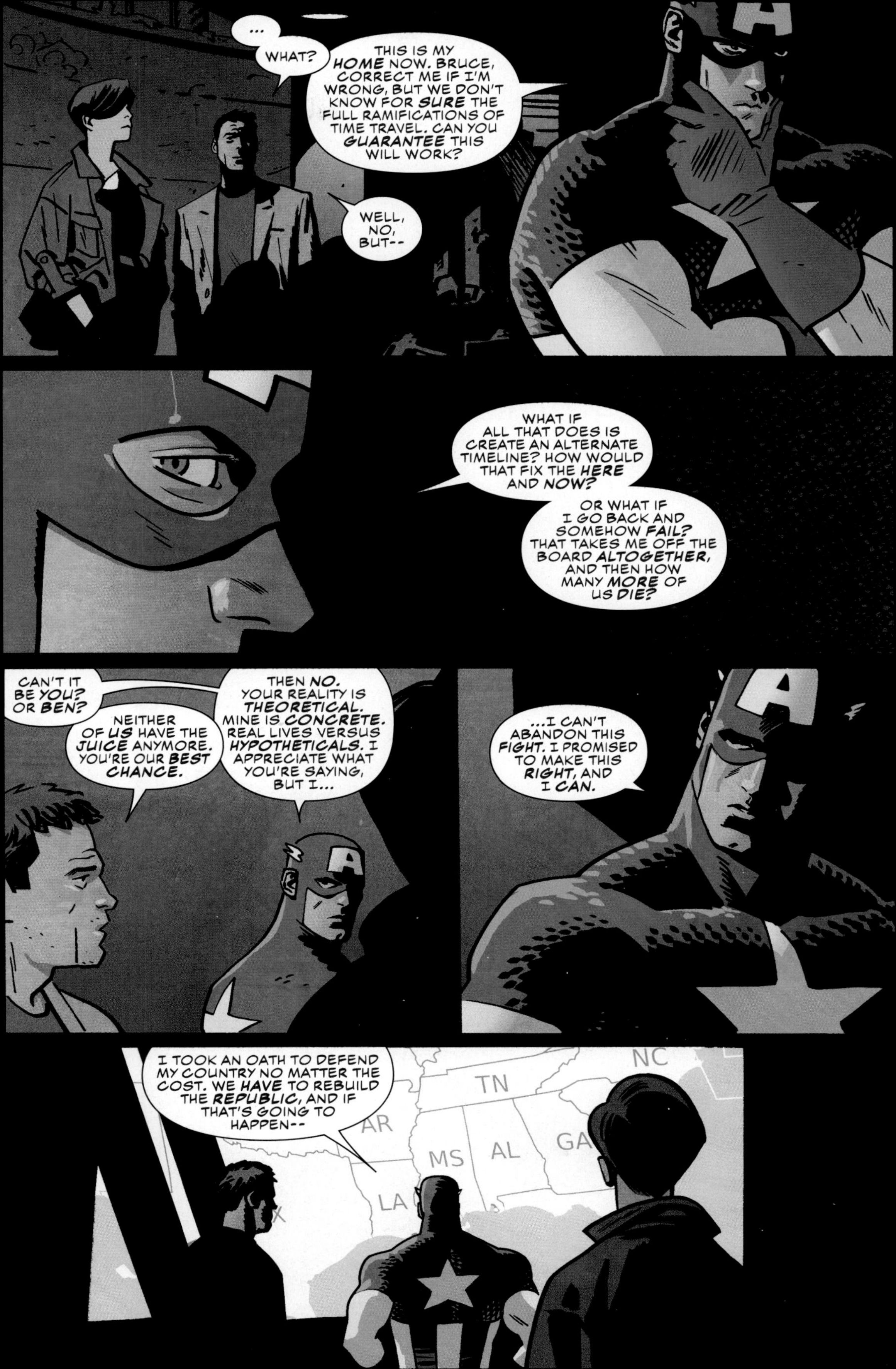
...
WHAT?
THIS IS MY HOME NOW. BRUCE, CORRECT ME IF I'M WRONG, BUT WE DON'T KNOW FOR SURE THE FULL RAMIFICATIONS OF TIME TRAVEL. CAN YOU GUARANTEE THIS WILL WORK?
WELL, NO, BUT--
WHAT IF ALL THAT DOES IS CREATE AN ALTERNATE TIMELINE? HOW WOULD THAT FIX THE HERE AND NOW?
OR WHAT IF I GO BACK AND SOMEHOW FAIL? THAT TAKES ME OFF THE BOARD ALTOGETHER, AND THEN HOW MANY MORE OF US DIE?
CAN'T IT BE YOU? OR BEN?
NEITHER OF US HAVE THE JUICE ANYMORE. YOU'RE OUR BEST CHANCE.
THEN NO. YOUR REALITY IS THEORETICAL. MINE IS CONCRETE. REAL LIVES VERSUS HYPOTHETICALS. I APPRECIATE WHAT YOU'RE SAYING, BUT I...
...I CAN'T ABANDON THIS FIGHT. I PROMISED TO MAKE THIS RIGHT, AND I CAN.
I TOOK AN OATH TO DEFEND MY COUNTRY NO MATTER THE COST. WE HAVE TO REBUILD THE REPUBLIC, AND IF THAT'S GOING TO HAPPEN--
NC
TN
AR
MS
AL
GA
LA

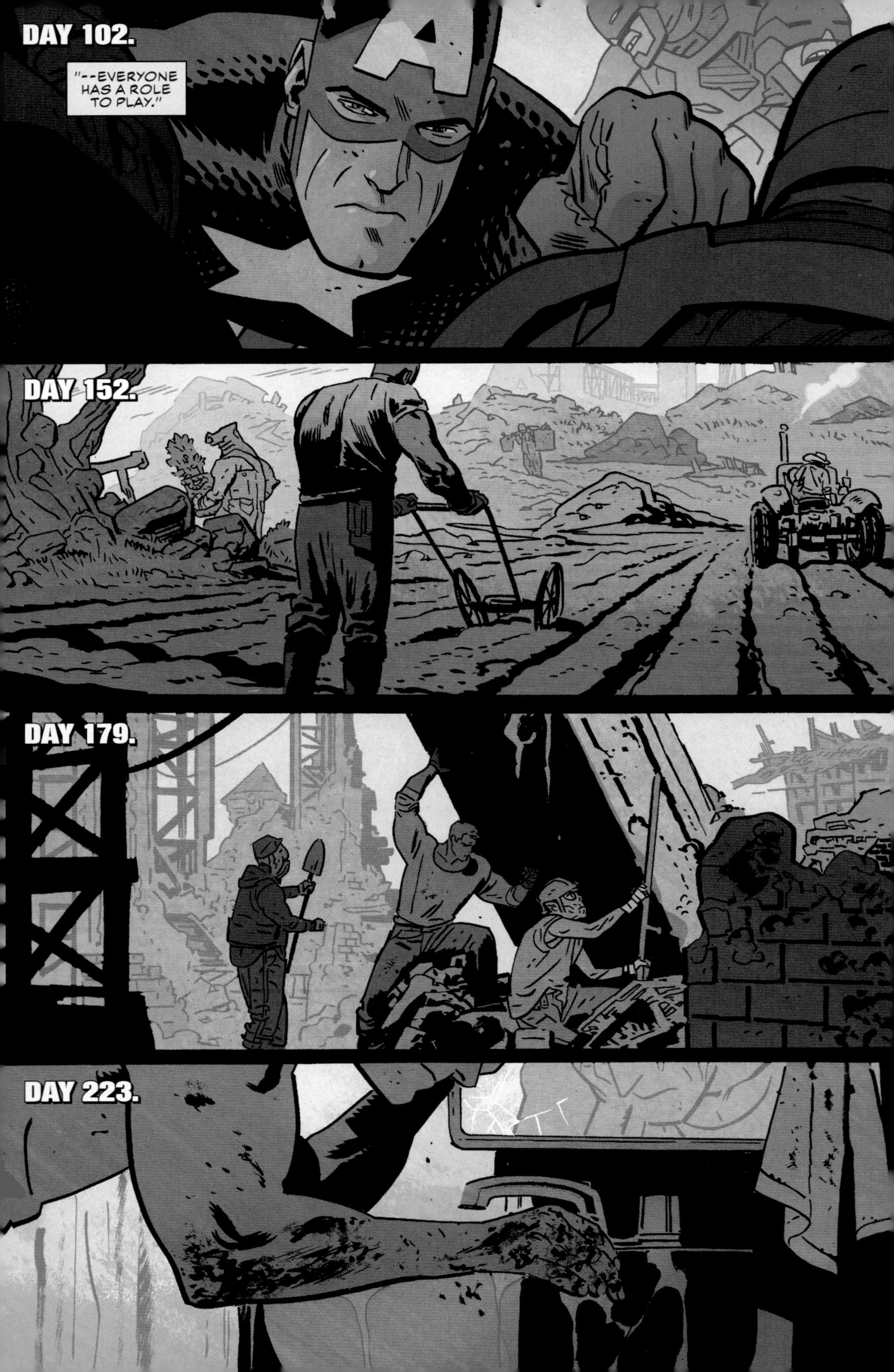
DAY 102.
"--EVERYONE HAS A ROLE TO PLAY."
DAY 152.
DAY 179.
DAY 223.

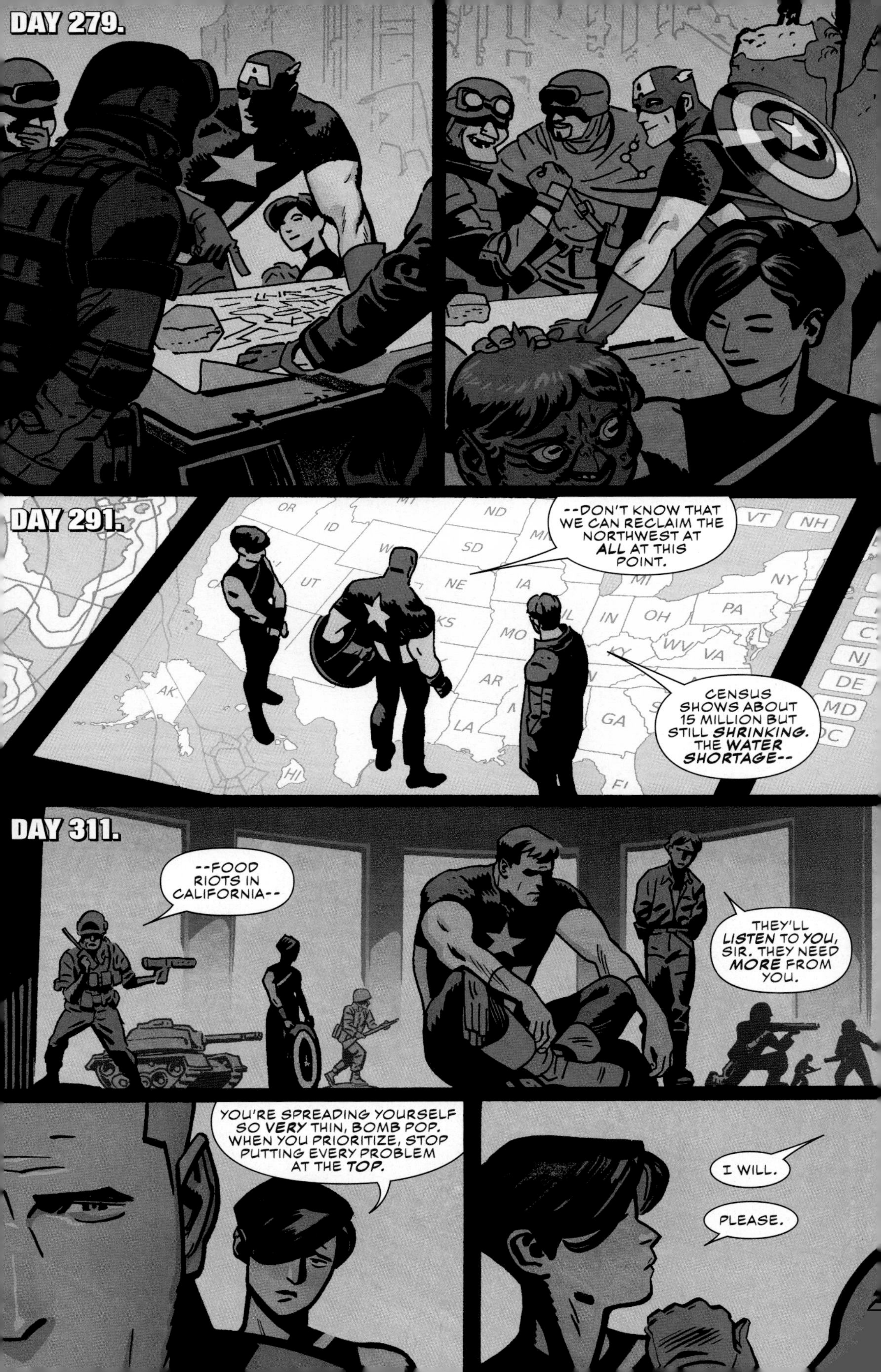

DAY 279.
DAY 291.
--DON'T KNOW THAT WE CAN RECLAIM THE NORTHWEST AT ALL AT THIS POINT.
CENSUS SHOWS ABOUT 15 MILLION BUT STILL SHRINKING. THE WATER SHORTAGE--
DAY 311.
--FOOD RIOTS IN CALIFORNIA--
THEY'LL LISTEN TO YOU, SIR. THEY NEED MORE FROM YOU.
YOU'RE SPREADING YOURSELF SO VERY THIN, BOMB POP. WHEN YOU PRIORITIZE, STOP PUTTING EVERY PROBLEM AT THE TOP.
I WILL.
PLEASE.

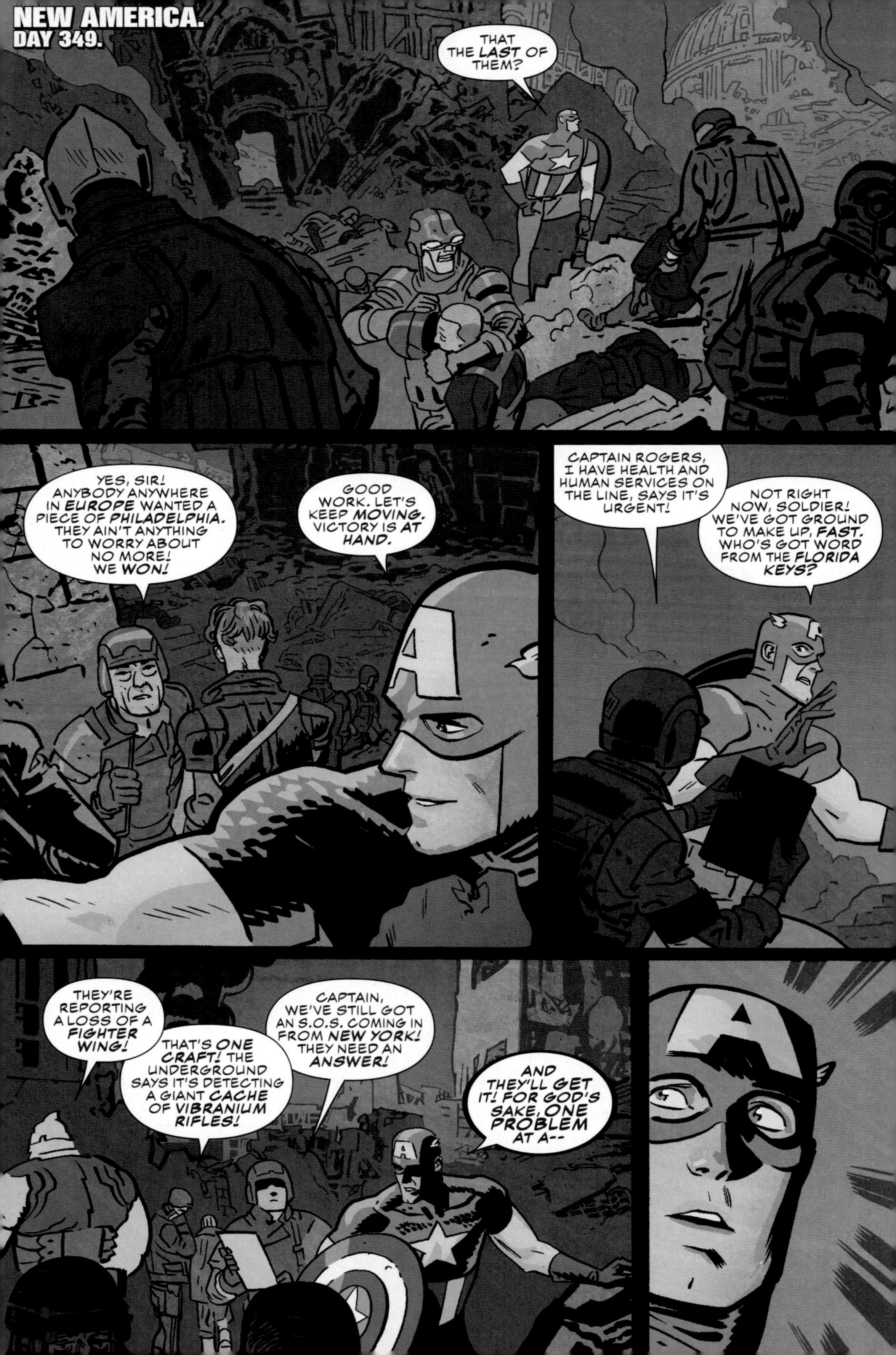
NEW AMERICA. DAY 349.
THAT THE LAST OF THEM?
YES, SIR! ANYBODY ANYWHERE IN EUROPE WANTED A PIECE OF PHILADELPHIA. THEY AIN'T ANYTHING TO WORRY ABOUT NO MORE! WE WON!
GOOD WORK. LET'S KEEP MOVING. VICTORY IS AT HAND.
CAPTAIN ROGERS, I HAVE HEALTH AND HUMAN SERVICES ON THE LINE, SAYS IT'S URGENT!
NOT RIGHT NOW, SOLDIER! WE'VE GOT GROUND TO MAKE UP, FAST. WHO'S GOT WORD FROM THE FLORIDA KEYS?
THEY'RE REPORTING A LOSS OF A FIGHTER WING!
THAT'S ONE CRAFT! THE UNDERGROUND SAYS IT'S DETECTING A GIANT CACHE OF VIBRANIUM RIFLES!
CAPTAIN, WE'VE STILL GOT AN S.O.S. COMING IN FROM NEW YORK! THEY NEED AN ANSWER!
AND THEY'LL GET IT! FOR GOD'S SAKE, ONE PROBLEM AT A--

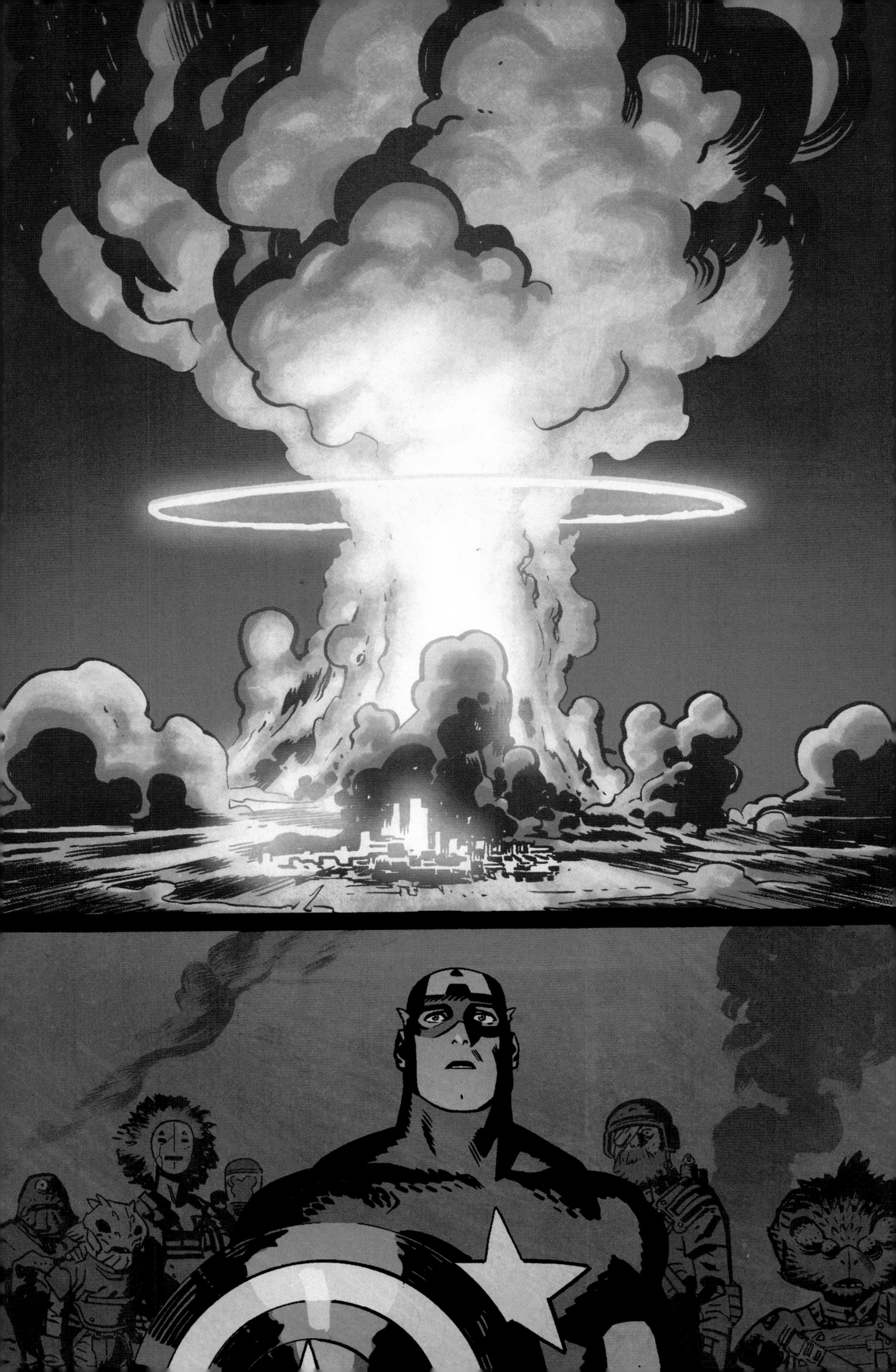

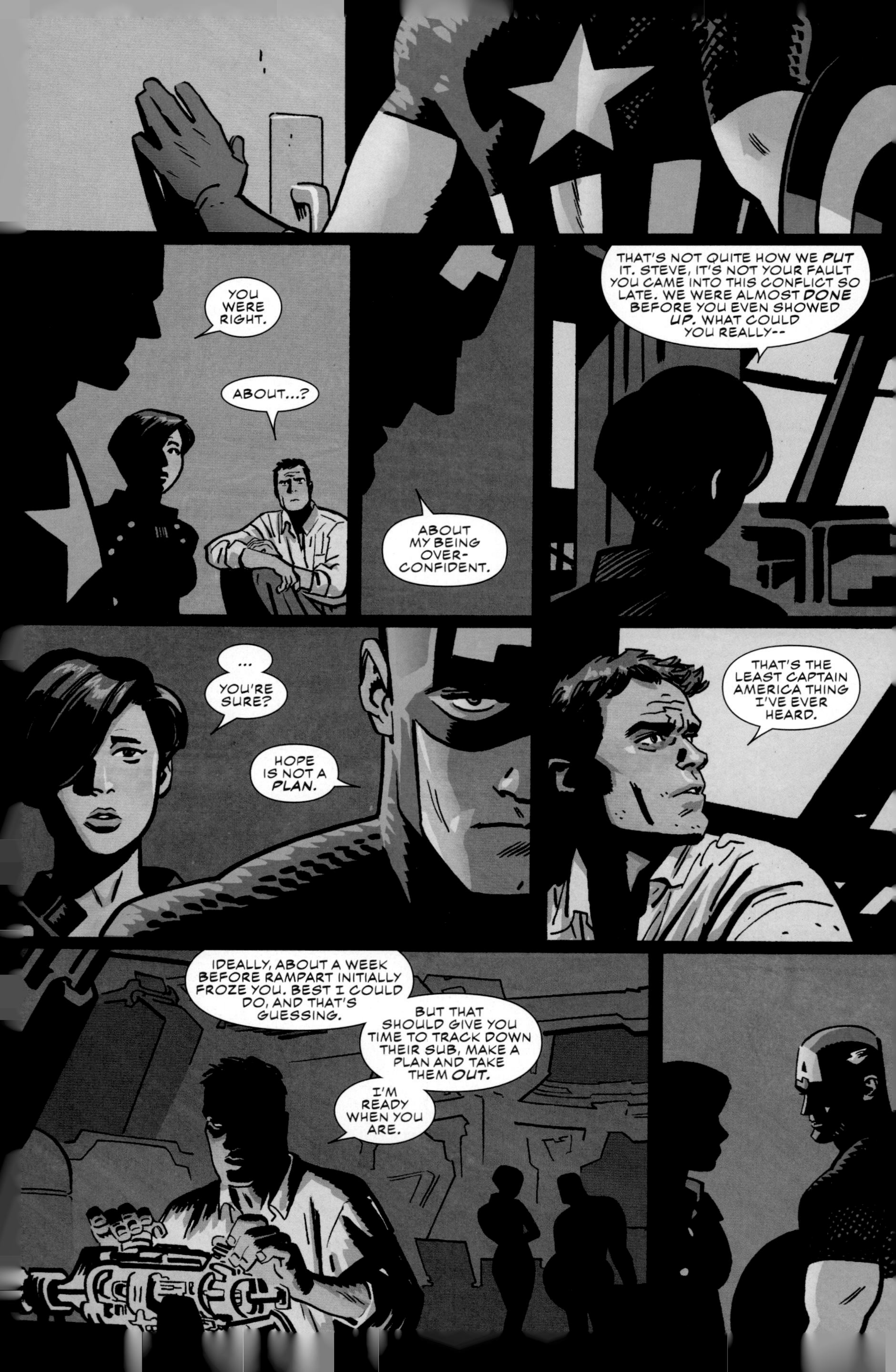
YOU WERE RIGHT.
ABOUT...?
ABOUT MY BEING OVER-CONFIDENT.
THAT'S NOT QUITE HOW WE PUT IT. STEVE, IT'S NOT YOUR FAULT YOU CAME INTO THIS CONFLICT SO LATE. WE WERE ALMOST DONE BEFORE YOU EVEN SHOWED UP. WHAT COULD YOU REALLY--
...
YOU'RE SURE?
HOPE IS NOT A PLAN.
THAT'S THE LEAST CAPTAIN AMERICA THING I'VE EVER HEARD.
IDEALLY, ABOUT A WEEK BEFORE RAMPART INITIALLY FROZE YOU. BEST I COULD DO, AND THAT'S GUESSING.
BUT THAT SHOULD GIVE YOU TIME TO TRACK DOWN THEIR SUB, MAKE A PLAN AND TAKE THEM OUT.
I'M READY WHEN YOU ARE.

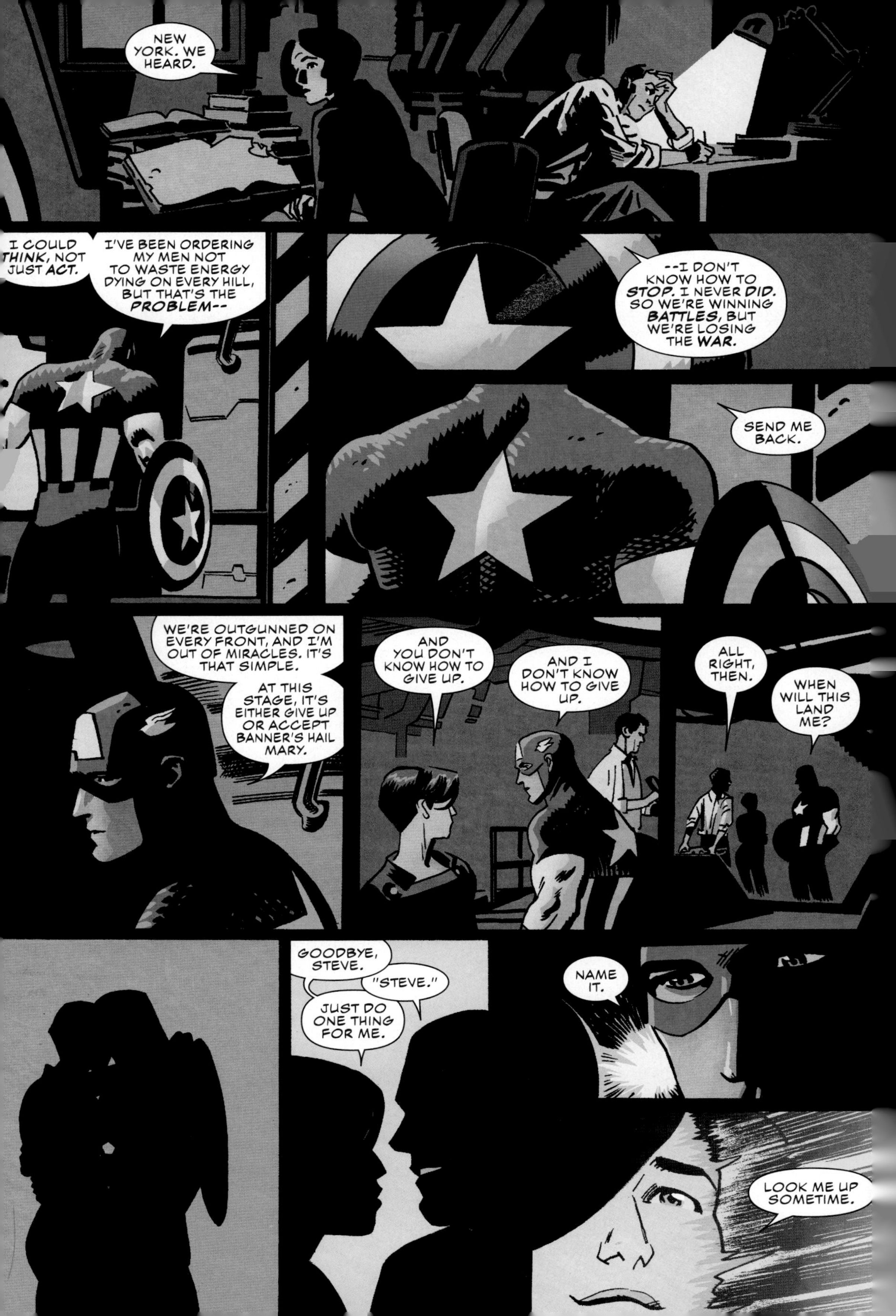

NEW YORK. WE HEARD.
I COULD THINK, NOT JUST ACT.
I'VE BEEN ORDERING MY MEN NOT TO WASTE ENERGY DYING ON EVERY HILL, BUT THAT'S THE PROBLEM--
--I DON'T KNOW HOW TO STOP. I NEVER DID. SO WE'RE WINNING BATTLES, BUT WE'RE LOSING THE WAR.
SEND ME BACK.
WE'RE OUTGUNNED ON EVERY FRONT, AND I'M OUT OF MIRACLES. IT'S THAT SIMPLE.
AT THIS STAGE, IT'S EITHER GIVE UP OR ACCEPT BANNER'S HAIL MARY.
AND YOU DON'T KNOW HOW TO GIVE UP.
AND I DON'T KNOW HOW TO GIVE UP.
ALL RIGHT, THEN.
WHEN WILL THIS LAND ME?
GOODBYE, STEVE.
"STEVE."
JUST DO ONE THING FOR ME.
NAME IT.
LOOK ME UP SOMETIME.

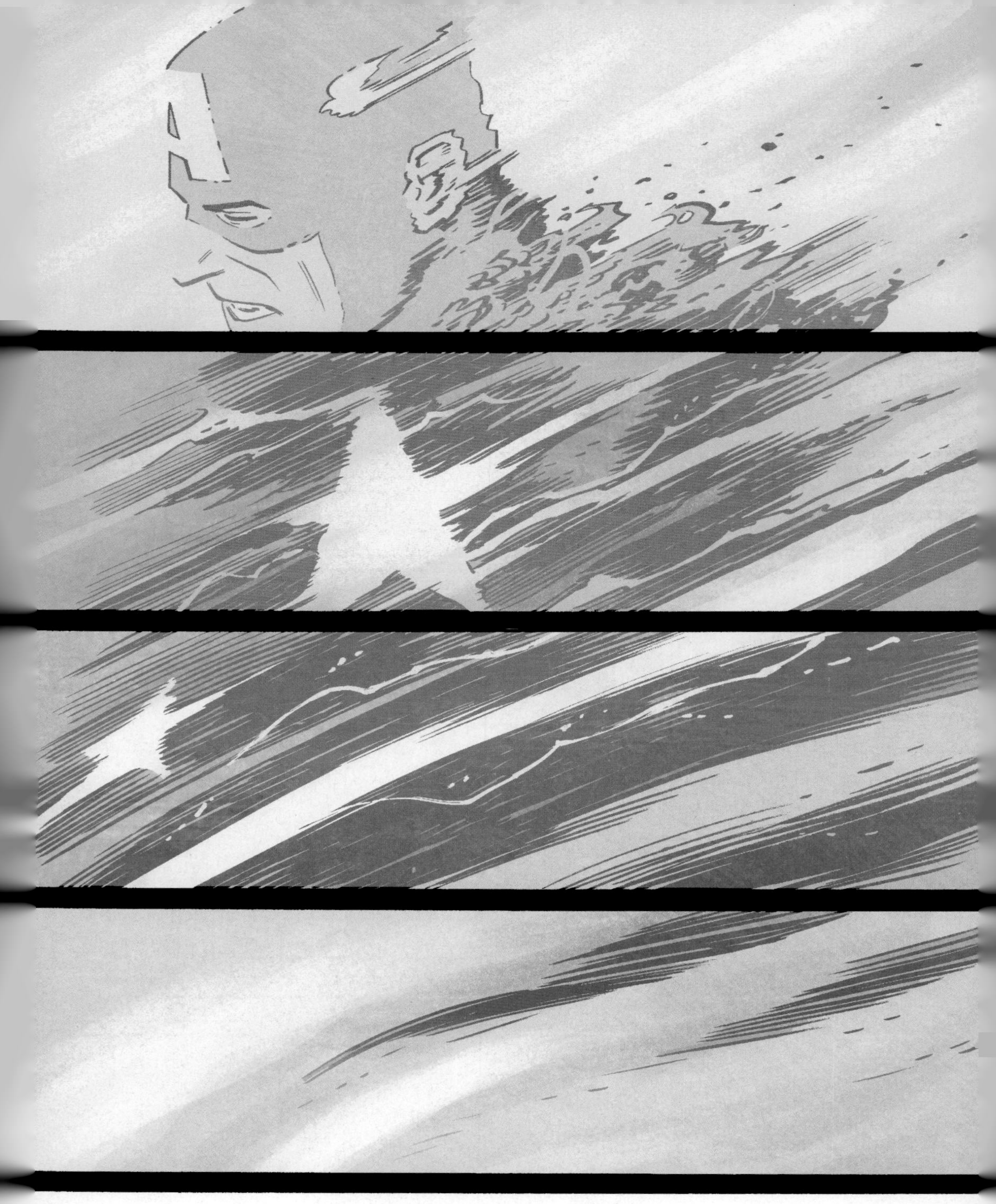

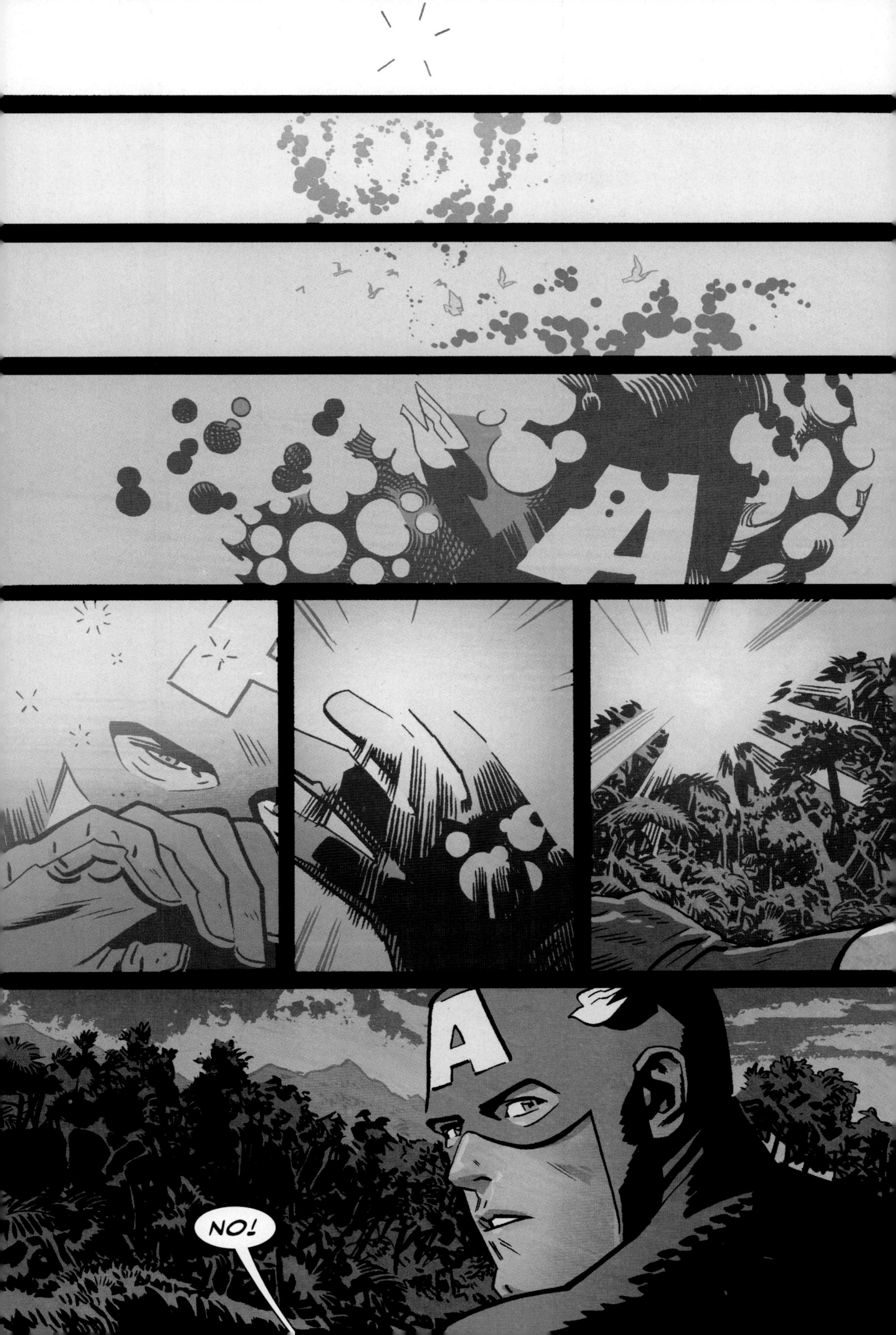
NO!

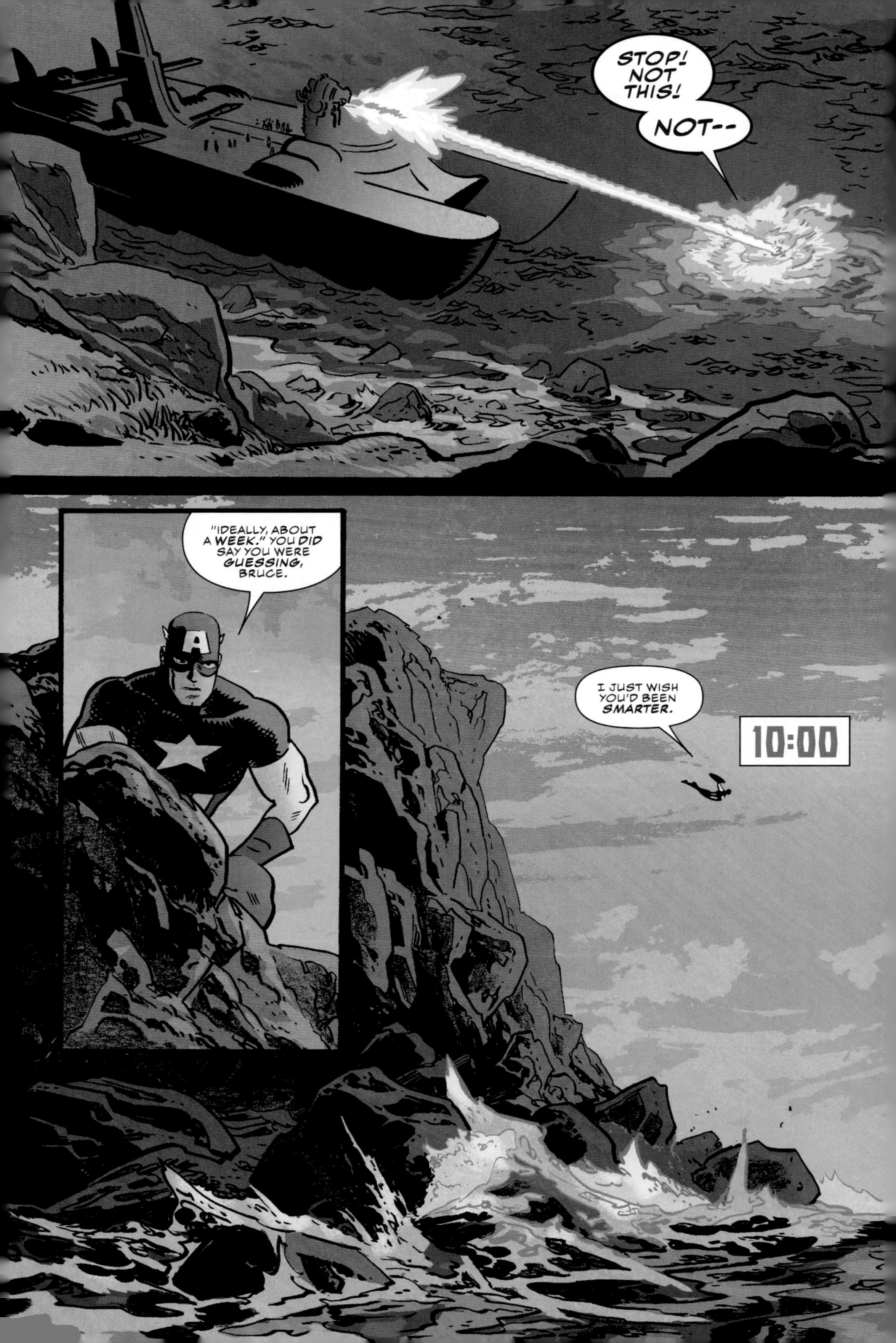
STOP! NOT THIS!
NOT--
"IDEALLY, ABOUT A WEEK." YOU DID SAY YOU WERE GUESSING, BRUCE.
I JUST WISH YOU'D BEEN SMARTER.
10:00

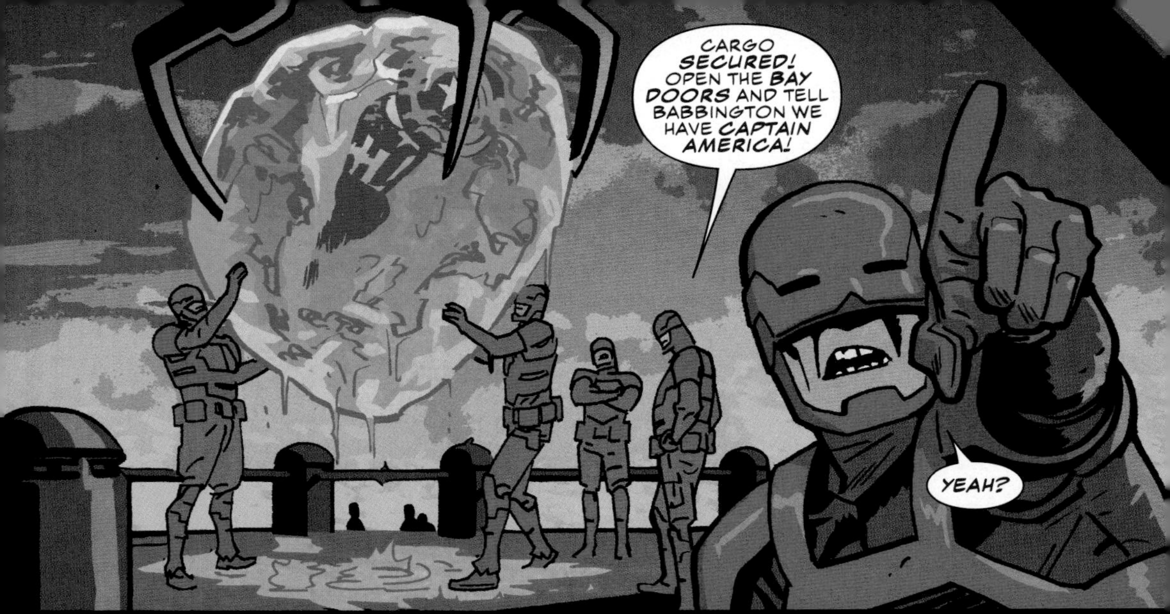
CARGO SECURED! OPEN THE BAY DOORS AND TELL BABBINGTON WE HAVE CAPTAIN AMERICA!
YEAH?

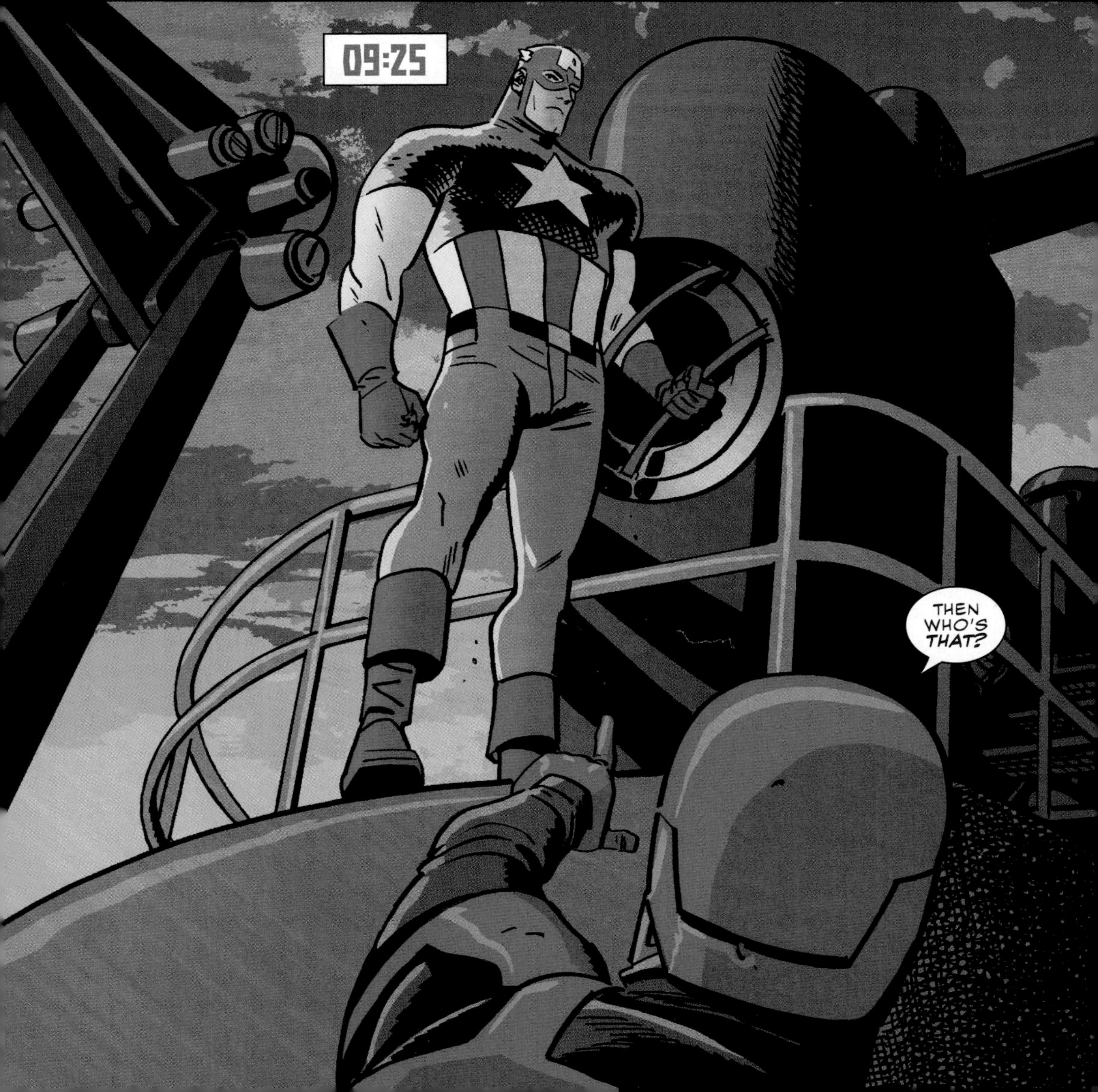
09:25
THEN WHO'S THAT?

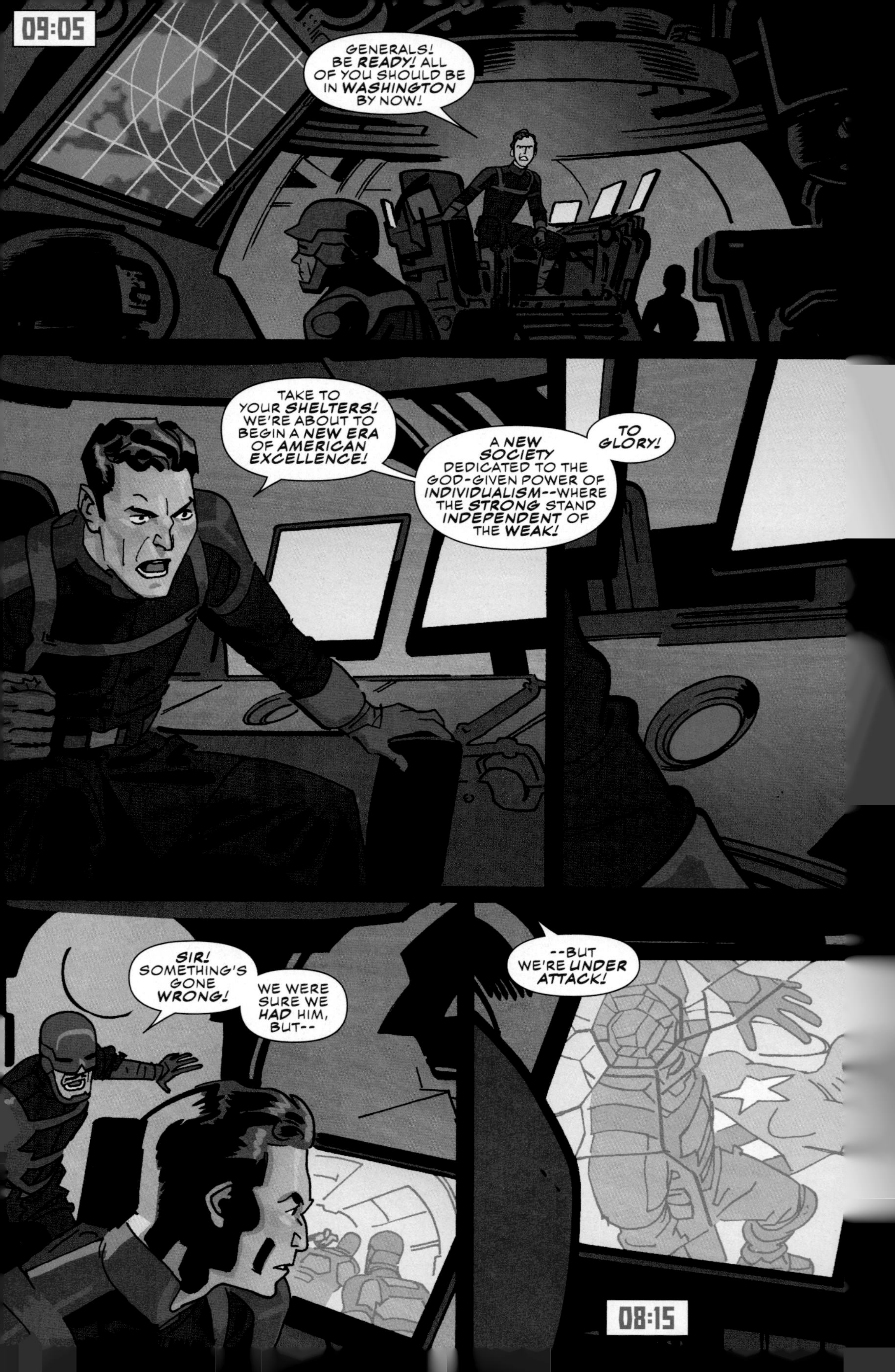
09:05
GENERALS! BE READY! ALL OF YOU SHOULD BE IN WASHINGTON BY NOW!
TAKE TO YOUR SHELTERS! WE'RE ABOUT TO BEGIN A NEW ERA OF AMERICAN EXCELLENCE!
A NEW SOCIETY DEDICATED TO THE GOD-GIVEN POWER OF INDIVIDUALISM--WHERE THE STRONG STAND INDEPENDENT OF THE WEAK!
TO GLORY!
SIR! SOMETHING'S GONE WRONG!
WE WERE SURE WE HAD HIM, BUT--
--BUT WE'RE UNDER ATTACK!
08:15

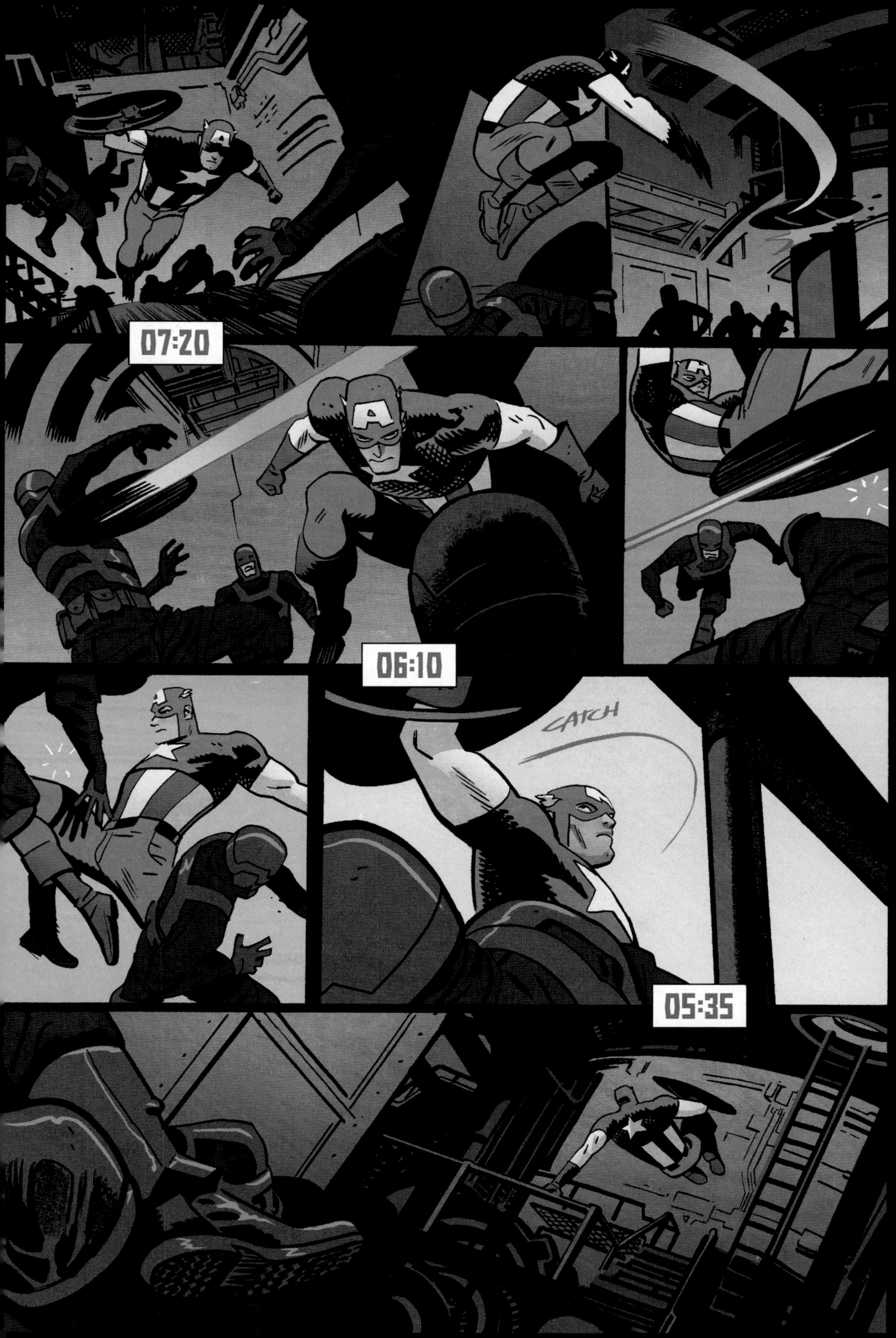
07:20
06:10
CATCH
05:35

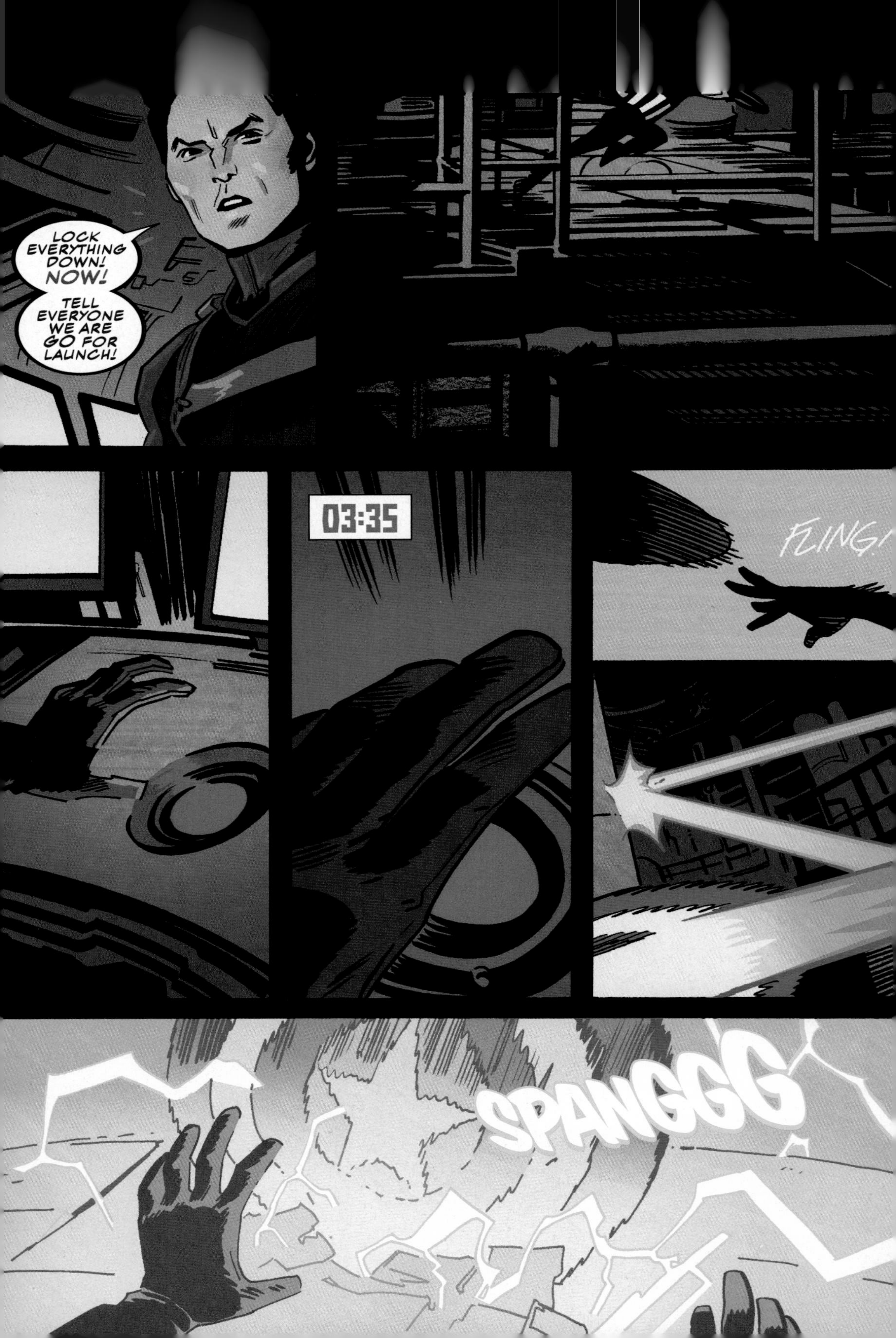
LOCK EVERYTHING DOWN! NOW!
TELL EVERYONE WE ARE GO FOR LAUNCH!
03:35
FLING!
SPANGGG

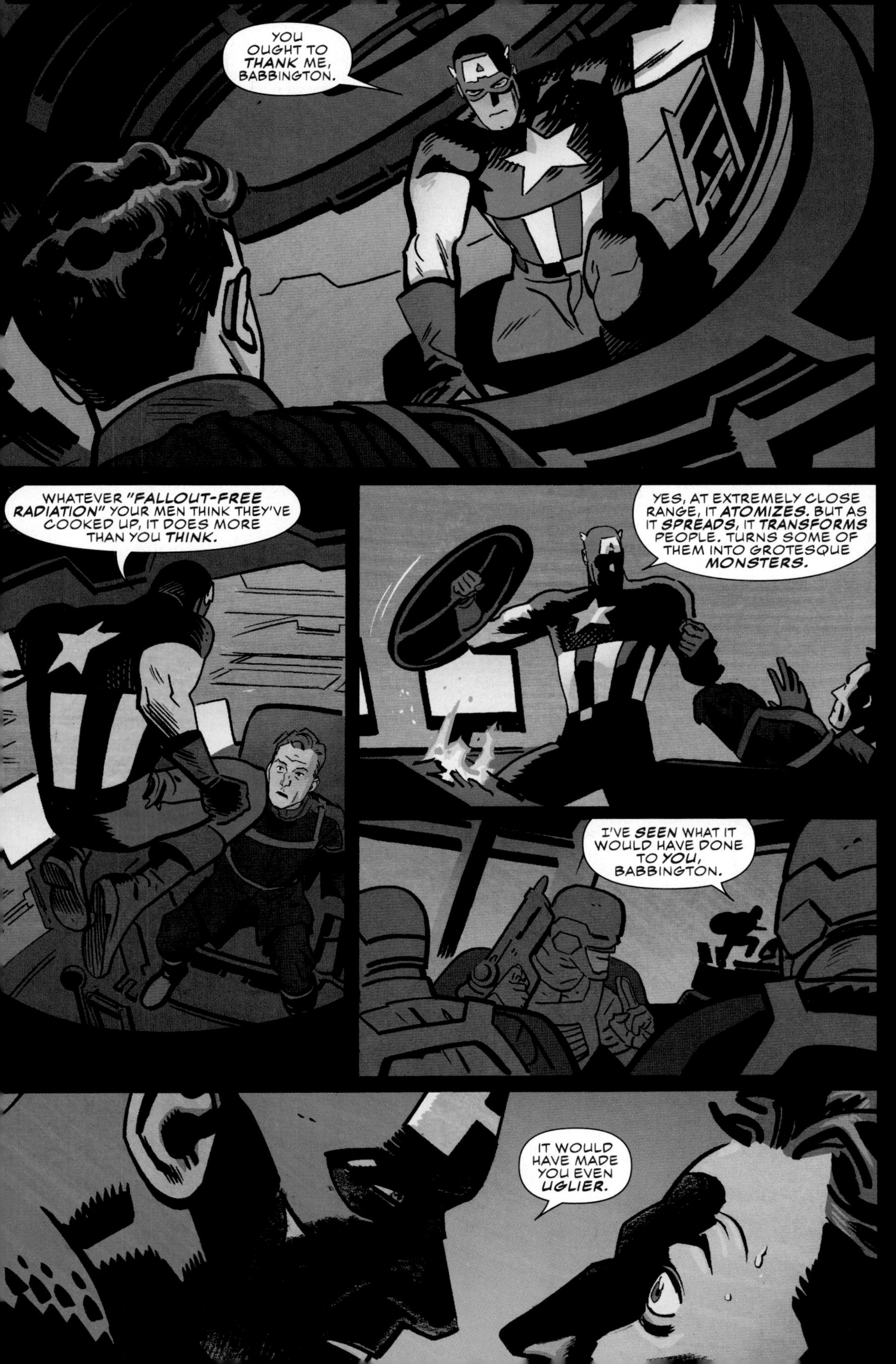
YOU OUGHT TO THANK ME, BABBINGTON.
WHATEVER "FALLOUT-FREE RADIATION" YOUR MEN THINK THEY'VE COOKED UP, IT DOES MORE THAN YOU THINK.
YES, AT EXTREMELY CLOSE RANGE, IT ATOMIZES. BUT AS IT SPREADS, IT TRANSFORMS PEOPLE. TURNS SOME OF THEM INTO GROTESQUE MONSTERS.
I'VE SEEN WHAT IT WOULD HAVE DONE TO YOU, BABBINGTON.
IT WOULD HAVE MADE YOU EVEN UGLIER.

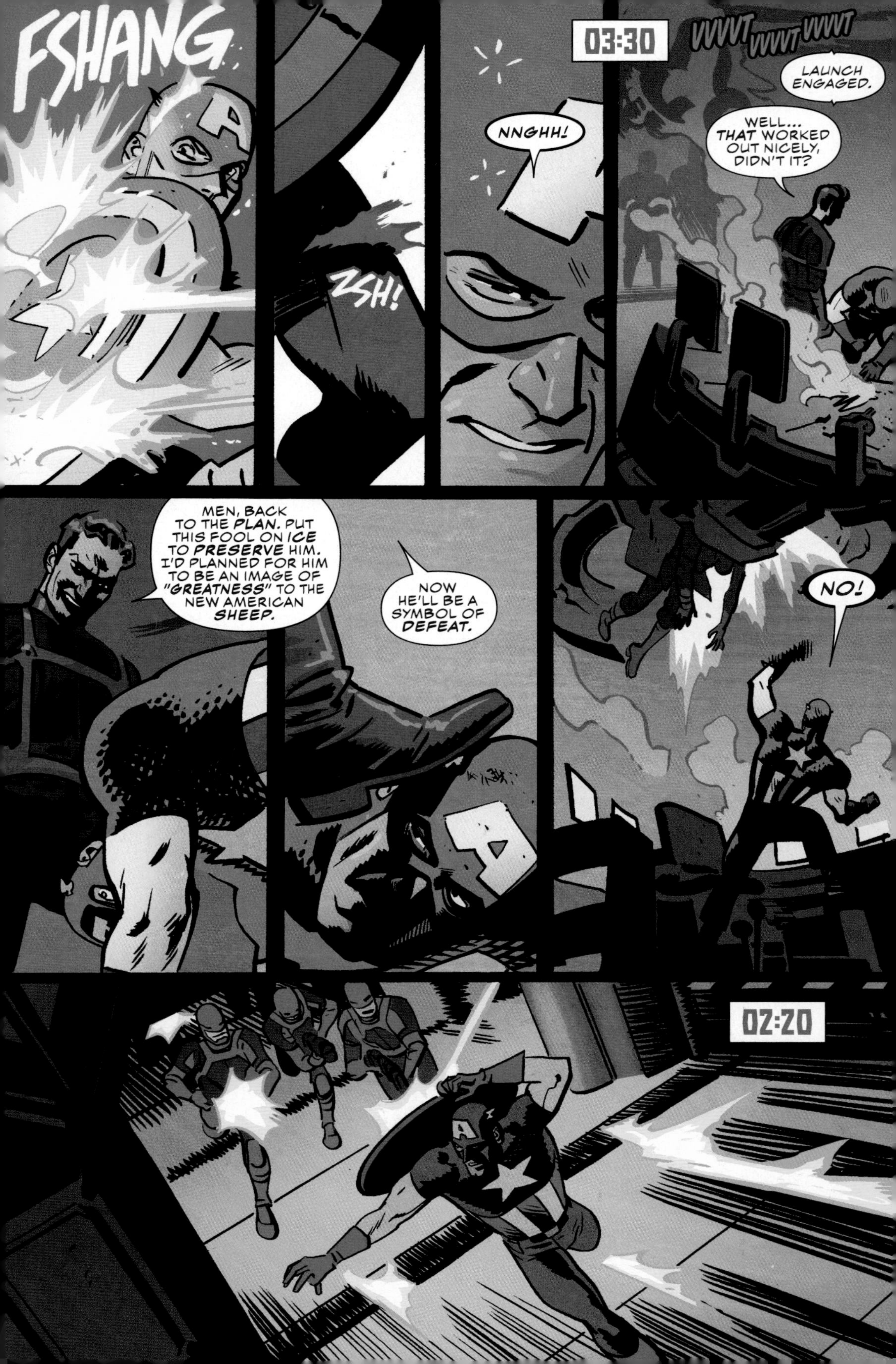
FSHANG
ZSH!
NNGHH!
03:30
VVVVT VVVVT VVVVT
LAUNCH ENGAGED.
WELL... THAT WORKED OUT NICELY, DIDN'T IT?
MEN, BACK TO THE PLAN. PUT THIS FOOL ON ICE TO PRESERVE HIM. I'D PLANNED FOR HIM TO BE AN IMAGE OF "GREATNESS" TO THE NEW AMERICAN SHEEP.
NOW HE'LL BE A SYMBOL OF DEFEAT.
NO!
02:20

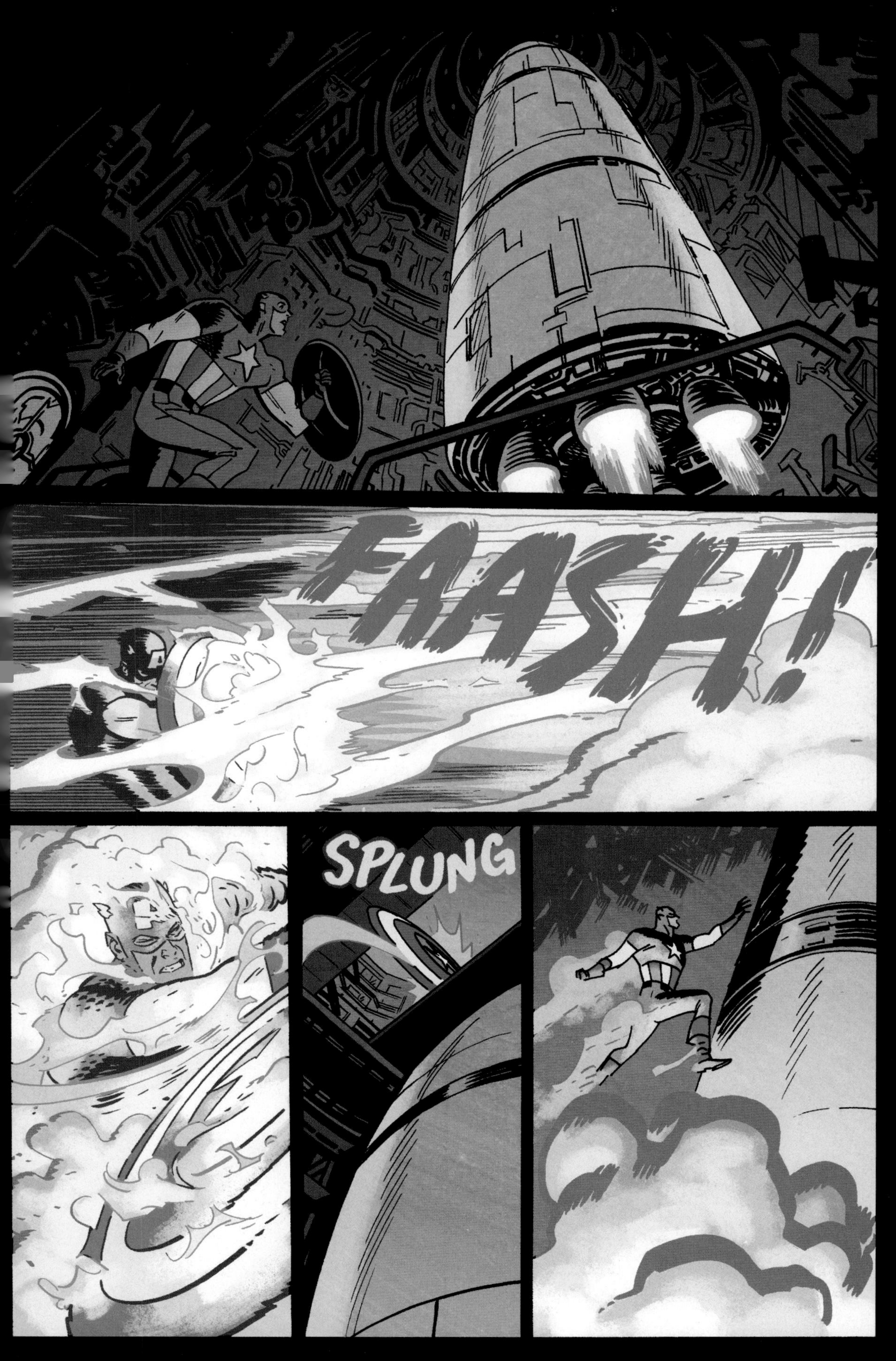
FAASH!!
SPLUNG

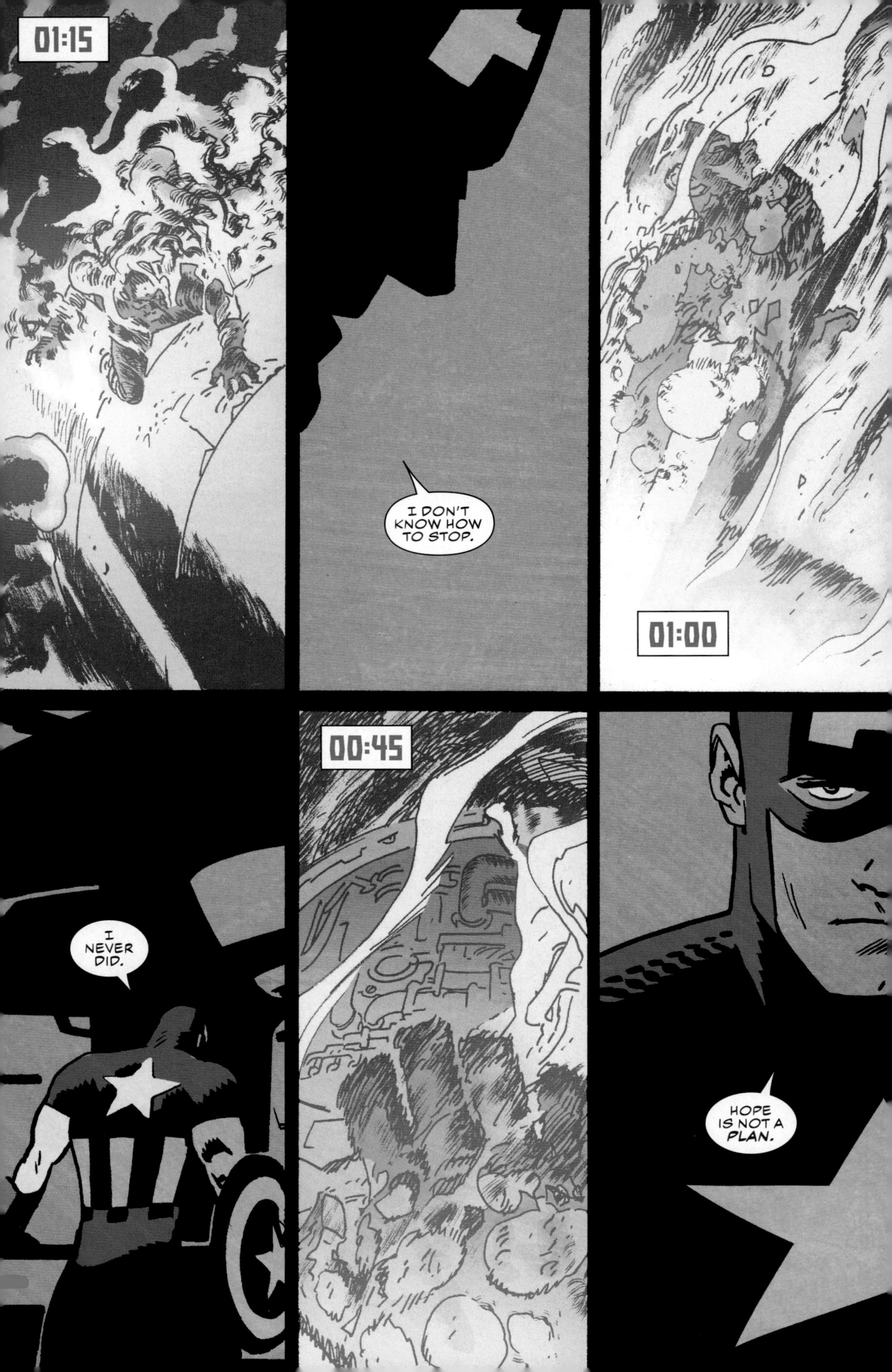
01:15
I DON'T KNOW HOW TO STOP.
01:00
I NEVER DID.
00:45
HOPE IS NOT A PLAN.

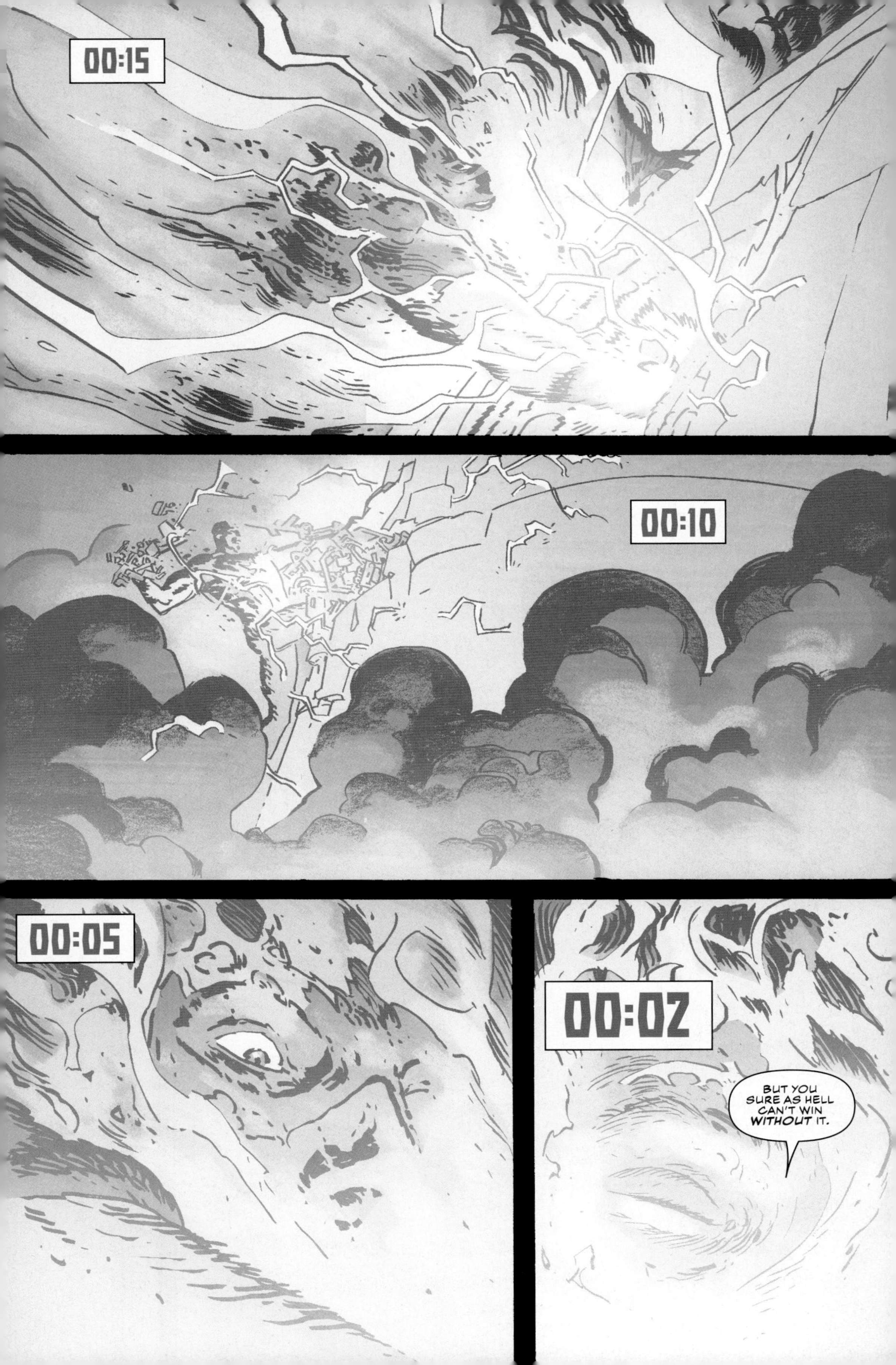
00:15
00:10
00:05
00:02
BUT YOU SURE AS HELL CAN'T WIN WITHOUT IT.

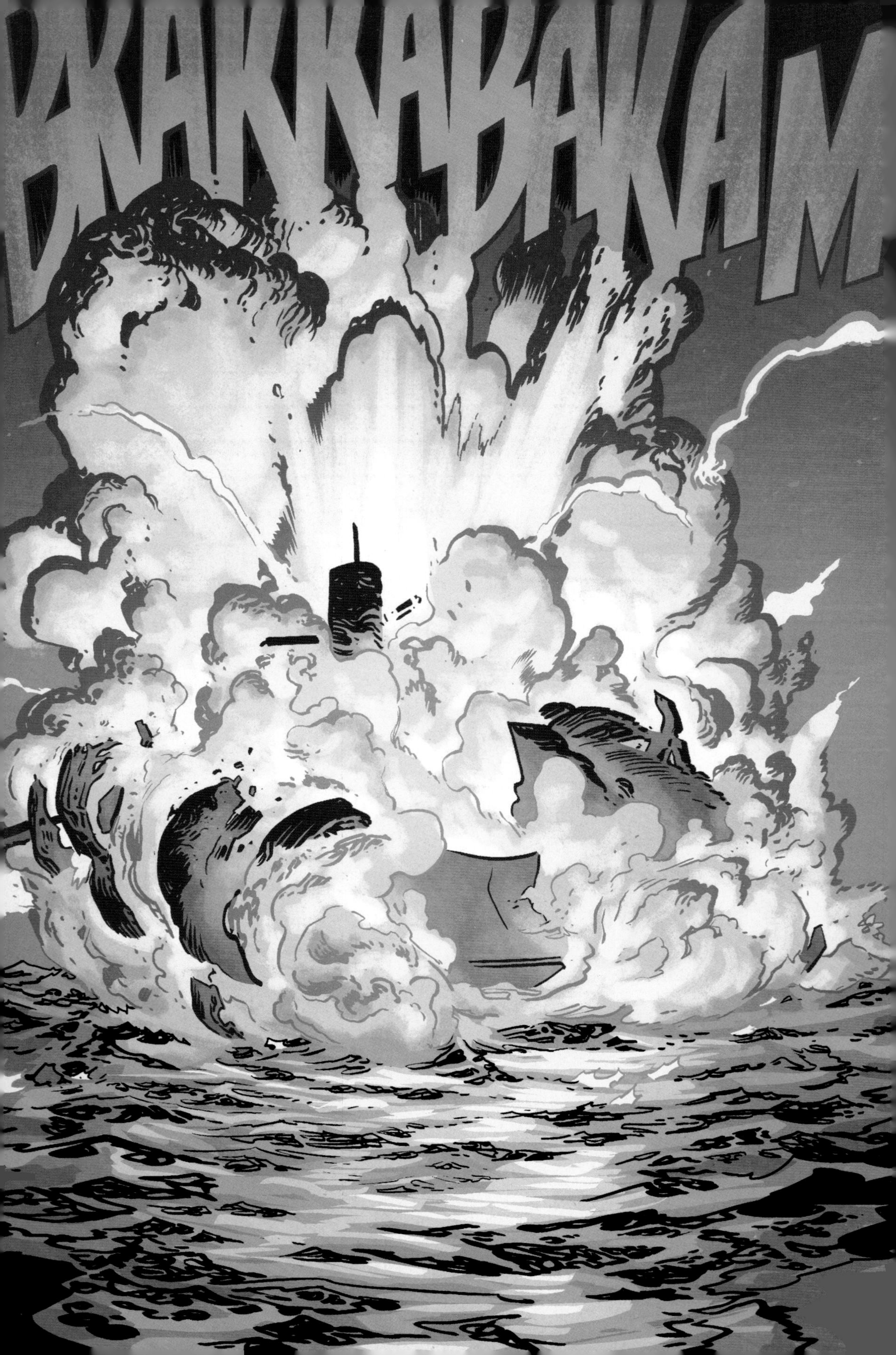

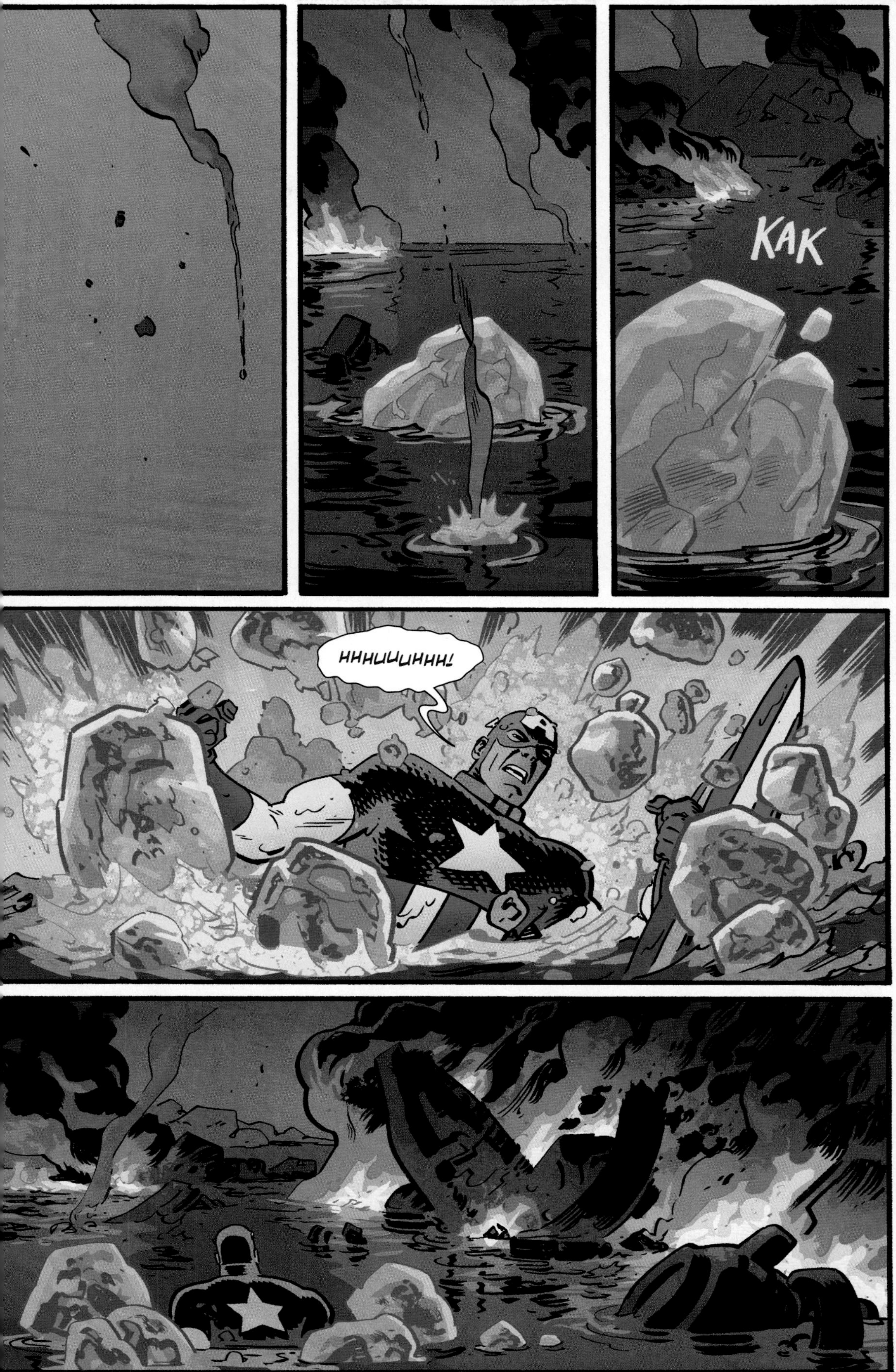
KAK
HHHUUUHHH!

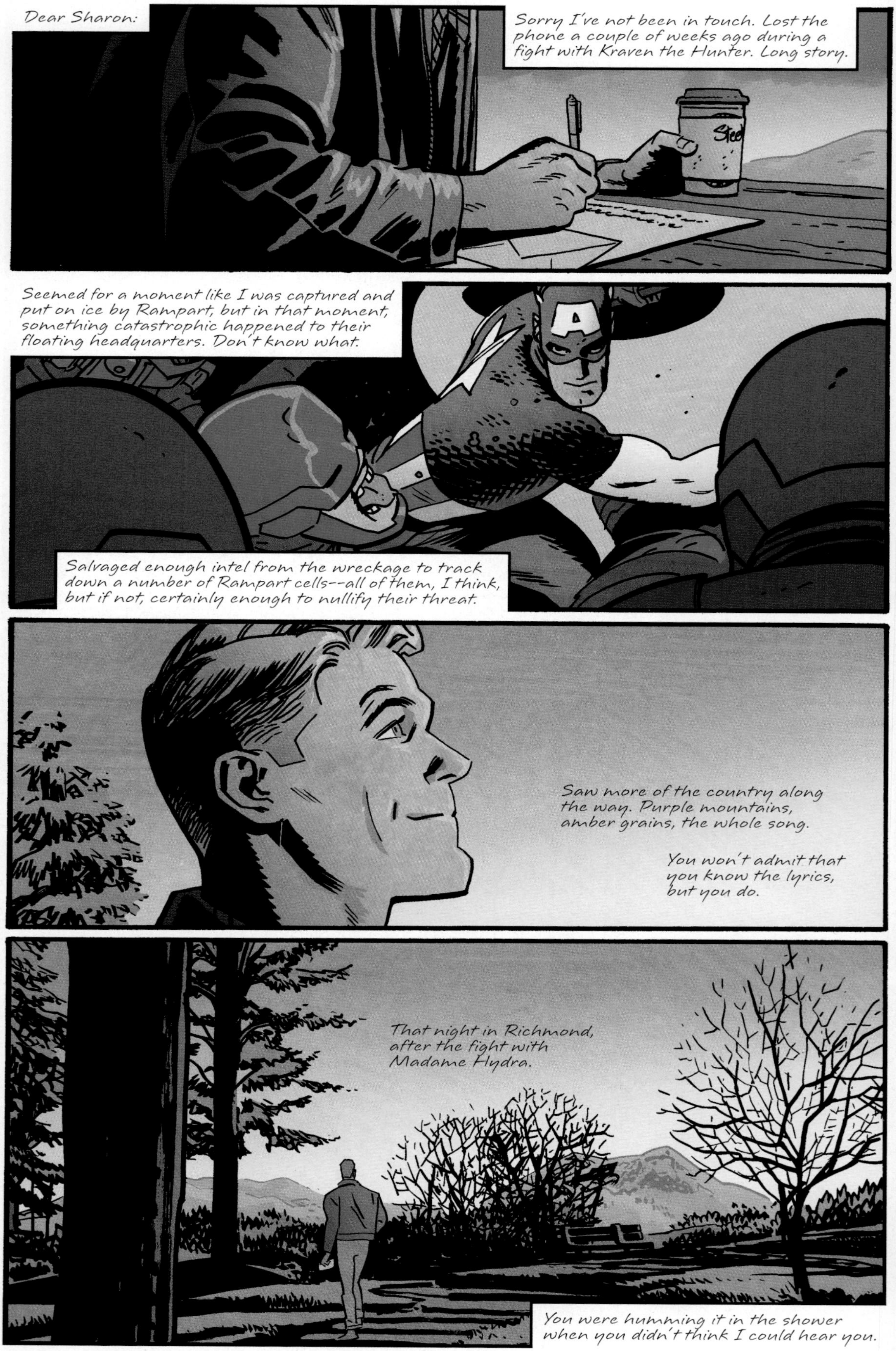
Dear Sharon:
Sorry I've not been in touch. Lost the phone a couple of weeks ago during a fight with Kraven the Hunter. Long story.
Steve
Seemed for a moment like I was captured and put on ice by Rampart, but in that moment, something catastrophic happened to their floating headquarters. Don't know what.
Salvaged enough intel from the wreckage to track down a number of Rampart cells--all of them, I think, but if not, certainly enough to nullify their threat.
Saw more of the country along the way. Purple mountains, amber grains, the whole song.
You won't admit that you know the lyrics, but you do.
That night in Richmond, after the fight with Madame Hydra.
You were humming it in the shower when you didn't think I could hear you.

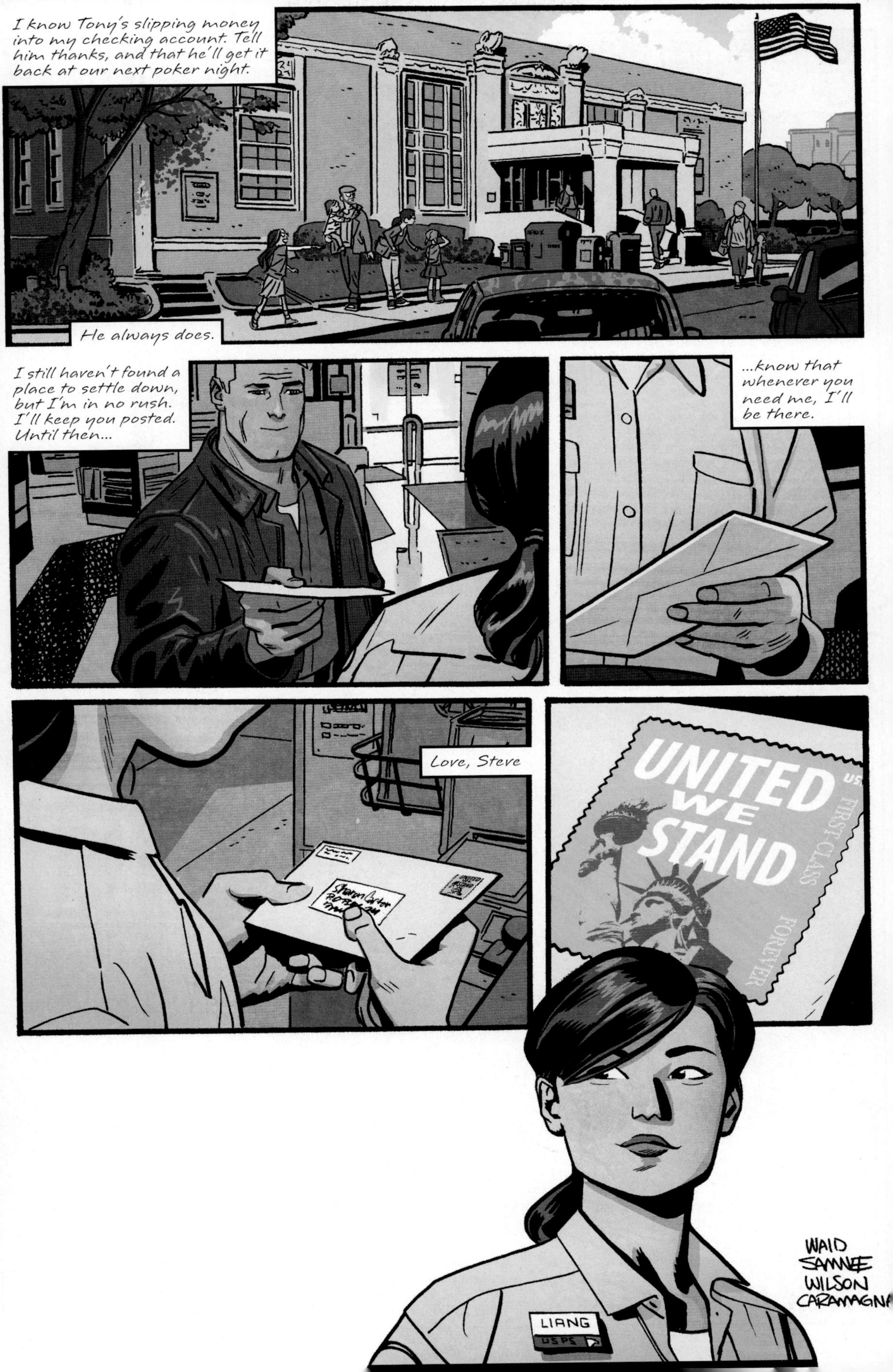

I know Tony's slipping money into my checking account. Tell him thanks, and that he'll get it back at our next poker night.
He always does.
I still haven't found a place to settle down, but I'm in no rush. I'll keep you posted. Until then...
...know that whenever you need me, I'll be there.
Love, Steve
UNITED WE STAND
FIRST-CLASS
FOREVER
WAID
SAMNEE
WILSON
CARAMAGNA
LIANG
USPS

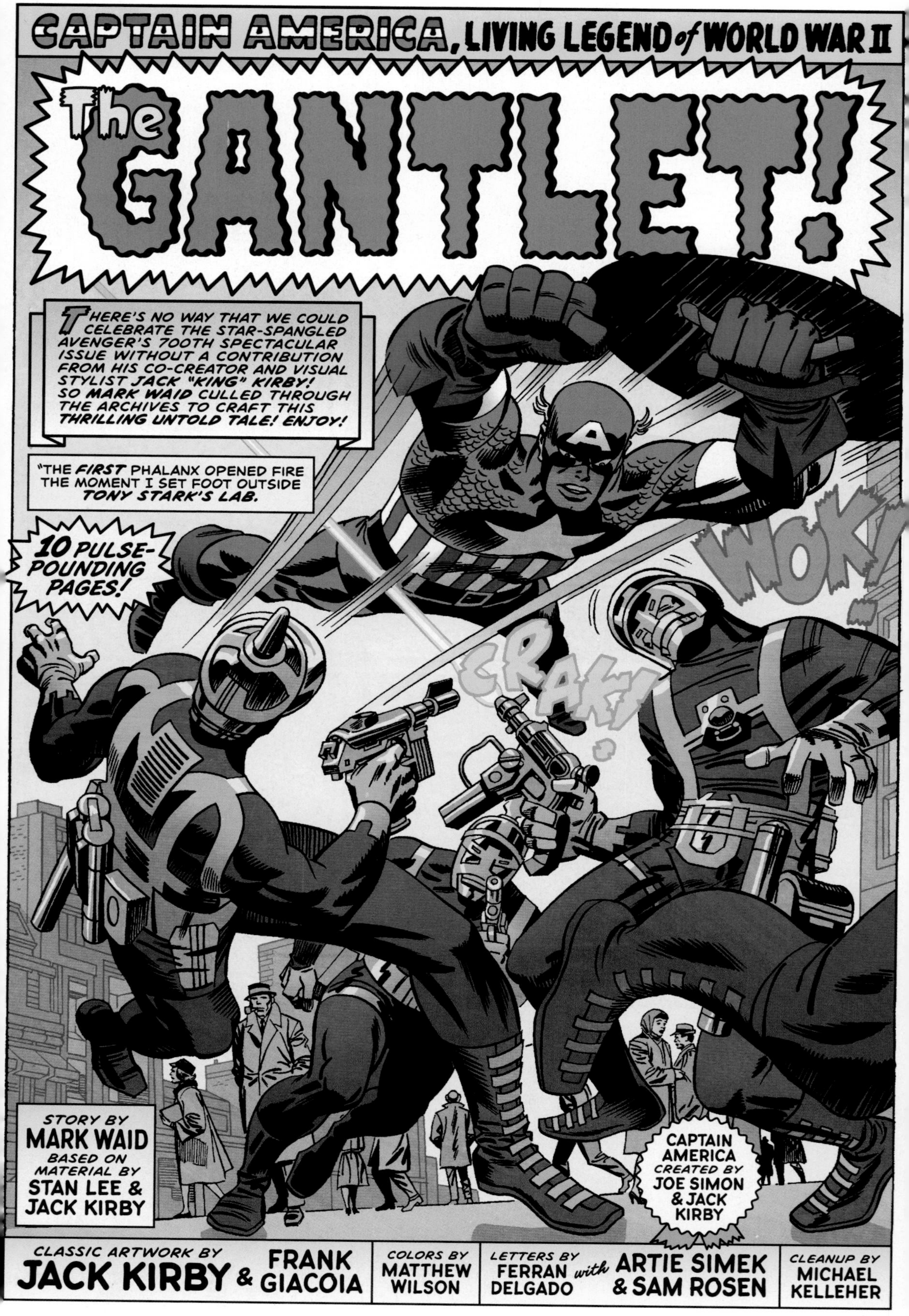

CAPTAIN AMERICA, LIVING LEGEND of WORLD WAR II
The GANTLET!
THERE'S NO WAY THAT WE COULD CELEBRATE THE STAR-SPANGLED AVENGER'S 700TH SPECTACULAR ISSUE WITHOUT A CONTRIBUTION FROM HIS CO-CREATOR AND VISUAL STYLIST JACK "KING" KIRBY! SO MARK WAID CULLED THROUGH THE ARCHIVES TO CRAFT THIS THRILLING UNTOLD TALE! ENJOY!
"THE FIRST PHALANX OPENED FIRE THE MOMENT I SET FOOT OUTSIDE TONY STARK'S LAB.
10 PULSE-POUNDING PAGES!
WOK
CRAK!
STORY BY MARK WAID BASED ON MATERIAL BY STAN LEE & JACK KIRBY
CAPTAIN AMERICA CREATED BY JOE SIMON & JACK KIRBY
CLASSIC ARTWORK BY JACK KIRBY & FRANK GIACOIA
COLORS BY MATTHEW WILSON
LETTERS BY FERRAN DELGADO with ARTIE SIMEK & SAM ROSEN
CLEANUP BY MICHAEL KELLEHER

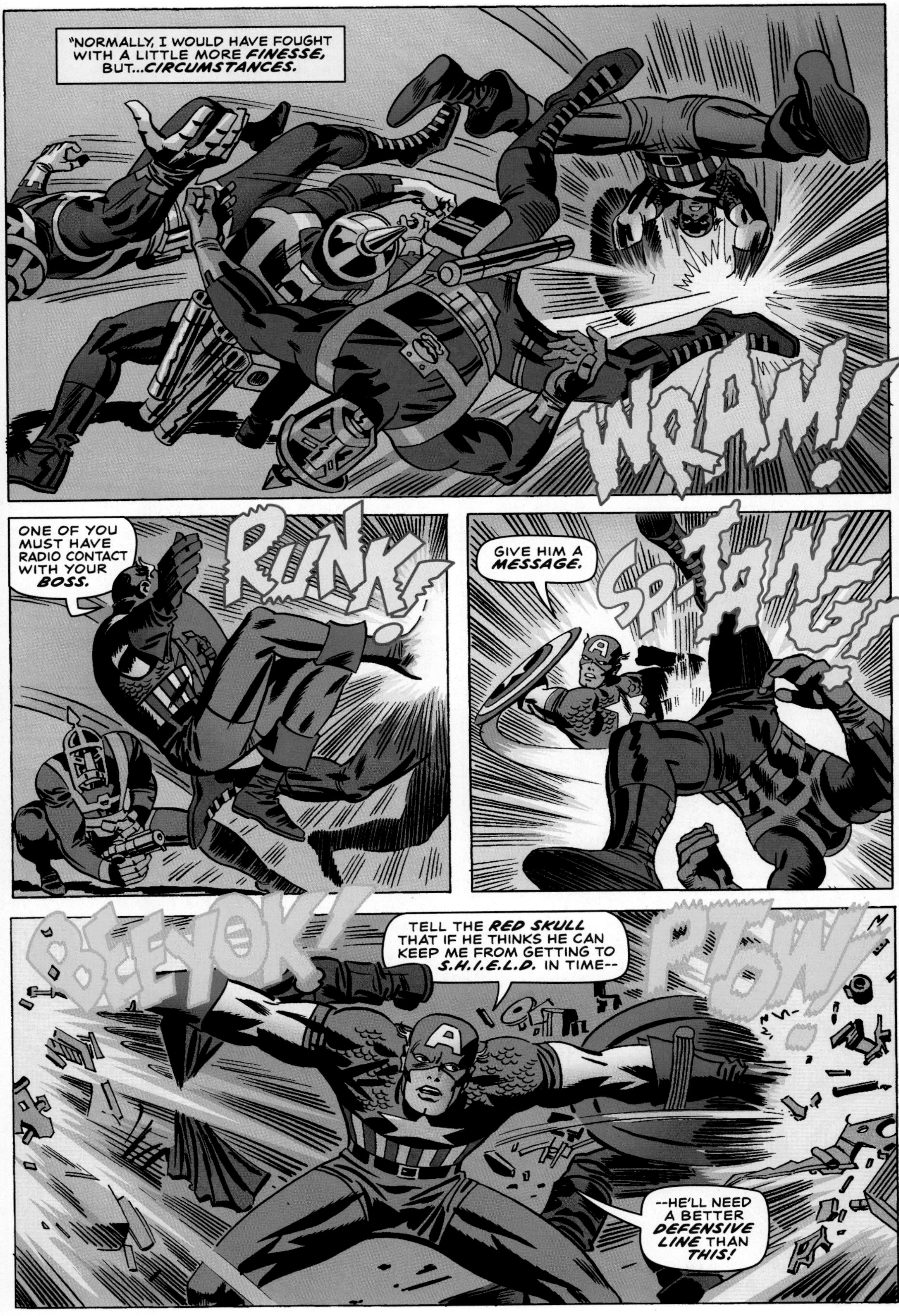
"NORMALLY, I WOULD HAVE FOUGHT WITH A LITTLE MORE *FINESSE*, BUT...*CIRCUMSTANCES*.
WRAM!
ONE OF YOU MUST HAVE RADIO CONTACT WITH YOUR *BOSS*.
RUNK!
GIVE HIM A *MESSAGE*.
SP-TANG!
BEEYOK!
TELL THE *RED SKULL* THAT IF HE THINKS HE CAN KEEP ME FROM GETTING TO *S.H.I.E.L.D.* IN TIME--
PTOW!
--HE'LL NEED A BETTER *DEFENSIVE LINE* THAN *THIS!*

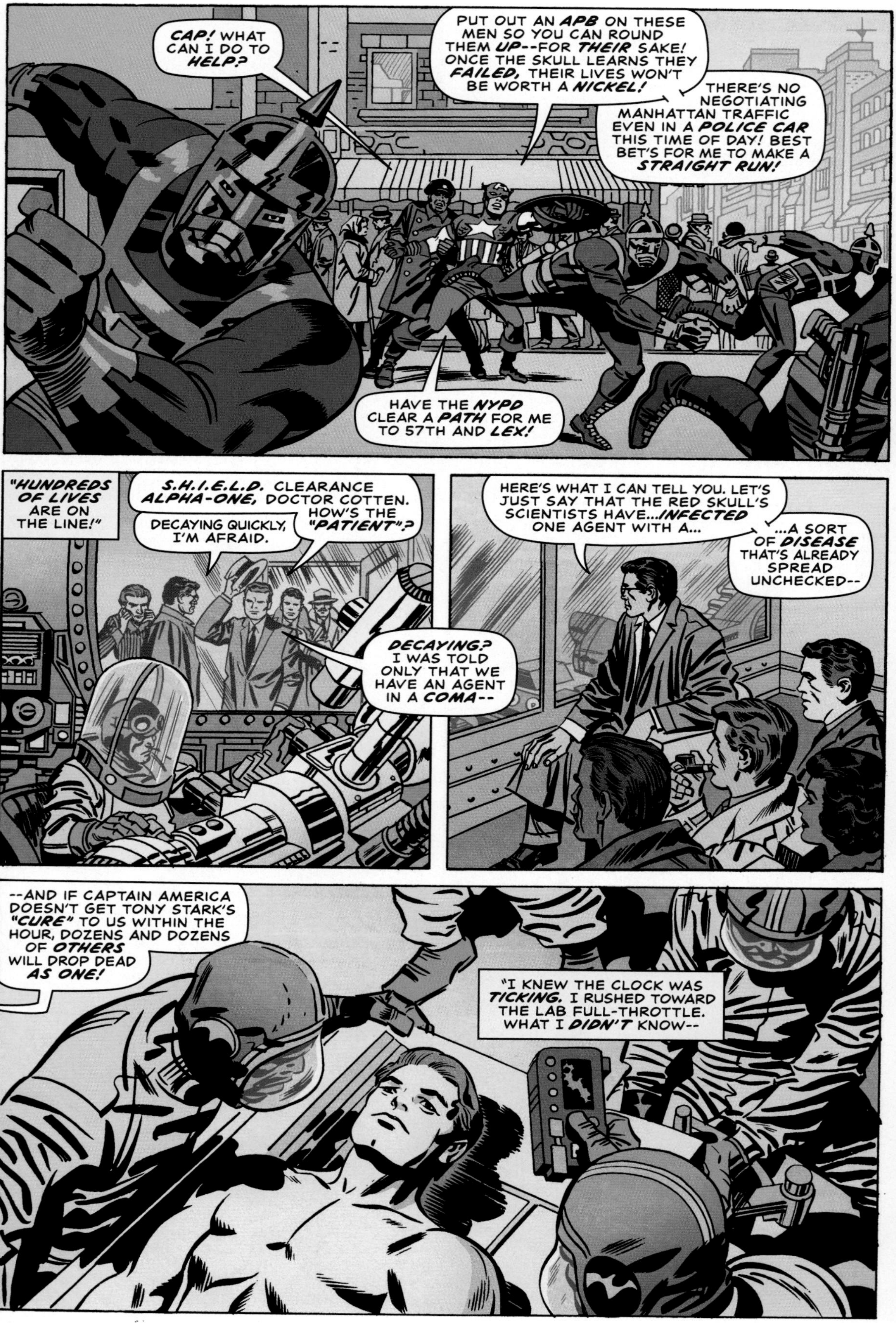

CAP! WHAT CAN I DO TO HELP?
PUT OUT AN APB ON THESE MEN SO YOU CAN ROUND THEM UP--FOR THEIR SAKE! ONCE THE SKULL LEARNS THEY FAILED, THEIR LIVES WON'T BE WORTH A NICKEL!
THERE'S NO NEGOTIATING MANHATTAN TRAFFIC EVEN IN A POLICE CAR THIS TIME OF DAY! BEST BET'S FOR ME TO MAKE A STRAIGHT RUN!
HAVE THE NYPD CLEAR A PATH FOR ME TO 57TH AND LEX!
"HUNDREDS OF LIVES ARE ON THE LINE!"
S.H.I.E.L.D. CLEARANCE ALPHA-ONE, DOCTOR COTTEN. HOW'S THE "PATIENT"?
DECAYING QUICKLY, I'M AFRAID.
DECAYING? I WAS TOLD ONLY THAT WE HAVE AN AGENT IN A COMA--
HERE'S WHAT I CAN TELL YOU. LET'S JUST SAY THAT THE RED SKULL'S SCIENTISTS HAVE...INFECTED ONE AGENT WITH A...
...A SORT OF DISEASE THAT'S ALREADY SPREAD UNCHECKED--
--AND IF CAPTAIN AMERICA DOESN'T GET TONY STARK'S "CURE" TO US WITHIN THE HOUR, DOZENS AND DOZENS OF OTHERS WILL DROP DEAD AS ONE!
"I KNEW THE CLOCK WAS TICKING. I RUSHED TOWARD THE LAB FULL-THROTTLE. WHAT I DIDN'T KNOW--

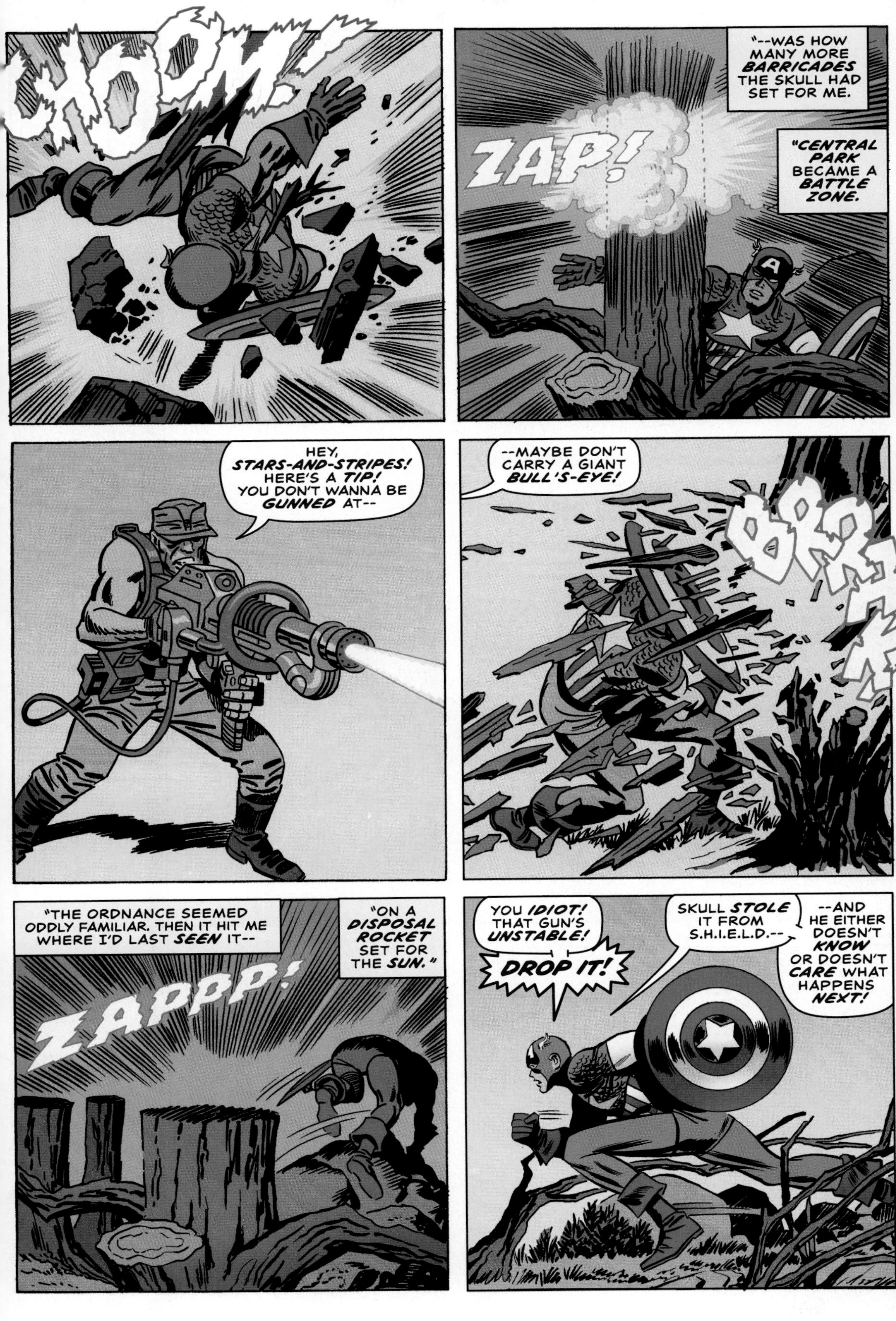
CHOOM!
"--WAS HOW MANY MORE BARRICADES THE SKULL HAD SET FOR ME.
"CENTRAL PARK BECAME A BATTLE ZONE.
ZAP!
HEY, STARS-AND-STRIPES! HERE'S A TIP! YOU DON'T WANNA BE GUNNED AT--
--MAYBE DON'T CARRY A GIANT BULL'S-EYE!
BRRRK
"THE ORDNANCE SEEMED ODDLY FAMILIAR. THEN IT HIT ME WHERE I'D LAST SEEN IT--
"ON A DISPOSAL ROCKET SET FOR THE SUN."
ZAPPP!
YOU IDIOT! THAT GUN'S UNSTABLE!
DROP IT!
SKULL STOLE IT FROM S.H.I.E.L.D.--
--AND HE EITHER DOESN'T KNOW OR DOESN'T CARE WHAT HAPPENS NEXT!

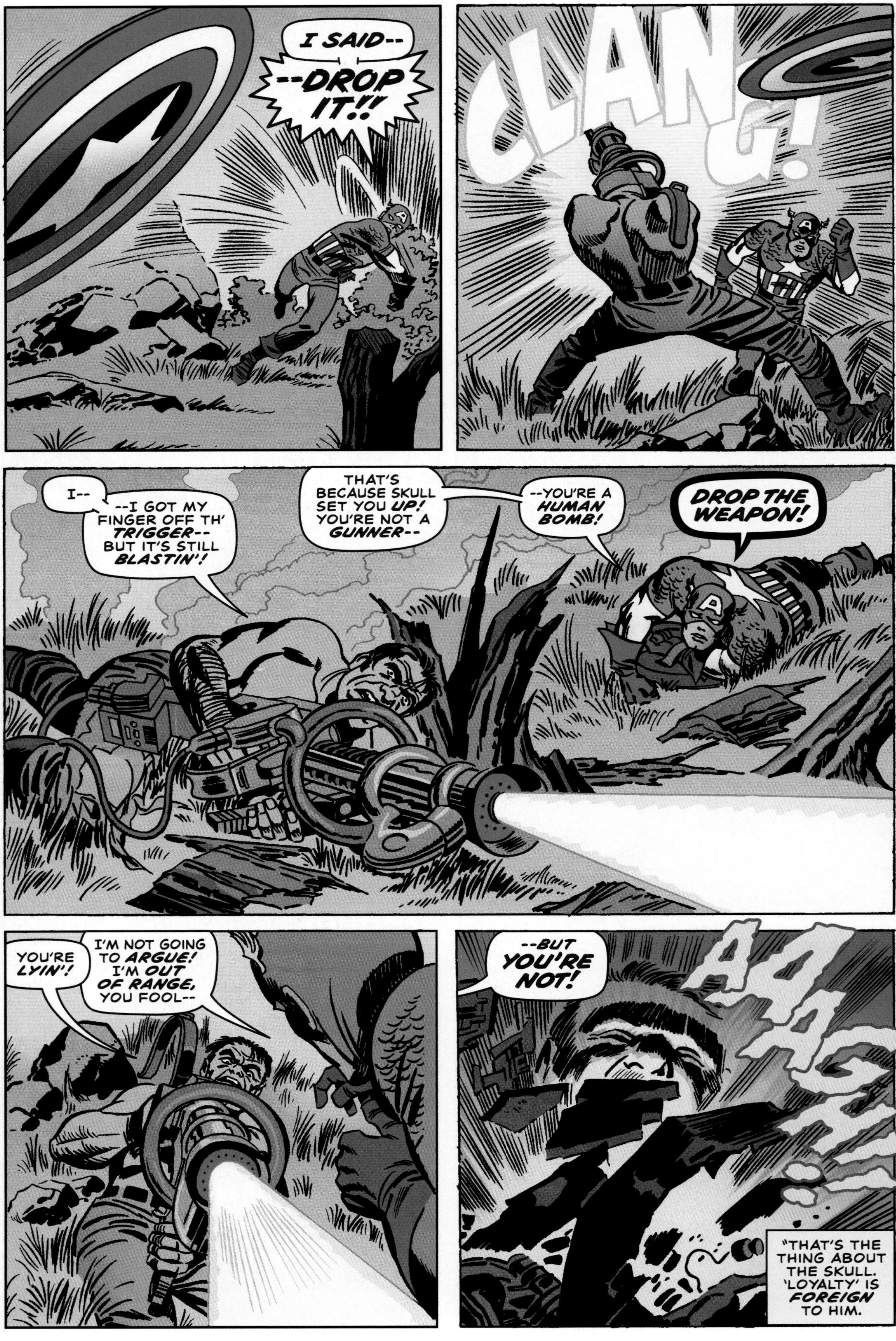
I SAID--
--DROP IT!!
CLANG!
I--
--I GOT MY FINGER OFF TH' TRIGGER--BUT IT'S STILL BLASTIN'!
THAT'S BECAUSE SKULL SET YOU UP! YOU'RE NOT A GUNNER--
--YOU'RE A HUMAN BOMB!
DROP THE WEAPON!
YOU'RE LYIN'!
I'M NOT GOING TO ARGUE! I'M OUT OF RANGE, YOU FOOL--
--BUT YOU'RE NOT!
AAGH
"THAT'S THE THING ABOUT THE SKULL. 'LOYALTY' IS FOREIGN TO HIM.

"HE'LL SACRIFICE *ANYONE* TO FUEL HIS SICK AGENDAS.

HERR SKULL, WE HAVE DRONE FOOTAGE OF CENTRAL PARK.

I'M AFRAID THE CAPTAIN REMAINS ON THE MOVE.

I SAID--

SILENCE!

GIVE ME A MOMENT OR CHOOSE YOUR COFFIN!

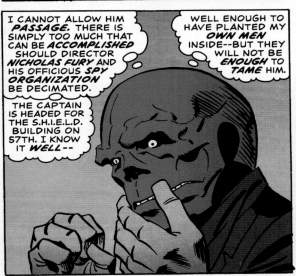

I CANNOT ALLOW HIM *PASSAGE.* THERE IS SIMPLY TOO MUCH THAT CAN BE *ACCOMPLISHED* SHOULD DIRECTOR *NICHOLAS FURY* AND HIS OFFICIOUS *SPY ORGANIZATION* BE DECIMATED.

THE CAPTAIN IS HEADED FOR THE S.H.I.E.L.D. BUILDING ON 57TH. I KNOW IT *WELL*--

WELL ENOUGH TO HAVE PLANTED MY *OWN MEN* INSIDE--BUT THEY WILL NOT BE *ENOUGH* TO *TAME* HIM.

I HAVE UNDERESTIMATED THE CAPTAIN FOR THE LAST TIME. HE RESPECTS ONLY *STRENGTH?* ONLY *COMBAT?* VERY WELL.

SEND THE BRAWLER!

"INSIDE THE BUILDING, I KNEW BETTER THAN TO RELAX. THE SKULL HADN'T *WON* YET--

"--AND *RELENTLESSNESS* IS HIS POINT OF *PRIDE.*

FIRE!

DON'T TELL ME YOU LIGHTWEIGHTS ARE THE SKULL'S *A-TEAM!*

BRAK!

SKLAK!

MERELY AN ADVANCE SQUAD.

BATROC--?

UNGHH!

BYONG!

MY POOR *CAPITAINE.* I AM FRESH AND ENERGIZED FOR *BATTLE. YOU,* HOWEVER...

BIANNG!

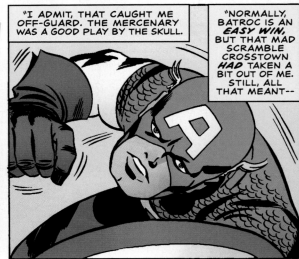

"I ADMIT, THAT CAUGHT ME OFF-GUARD. THE MERCENARY WAS A GOOD PLAY BY THE SKULL.

"NORMALLY, BATROC IS AN *EASY WIN,* BUT THAT MAD SCRAMBLE CROSSTOWN *HAD* TAKEN A BIT OUT OF ME. STILL, ALL THAT MEANT--

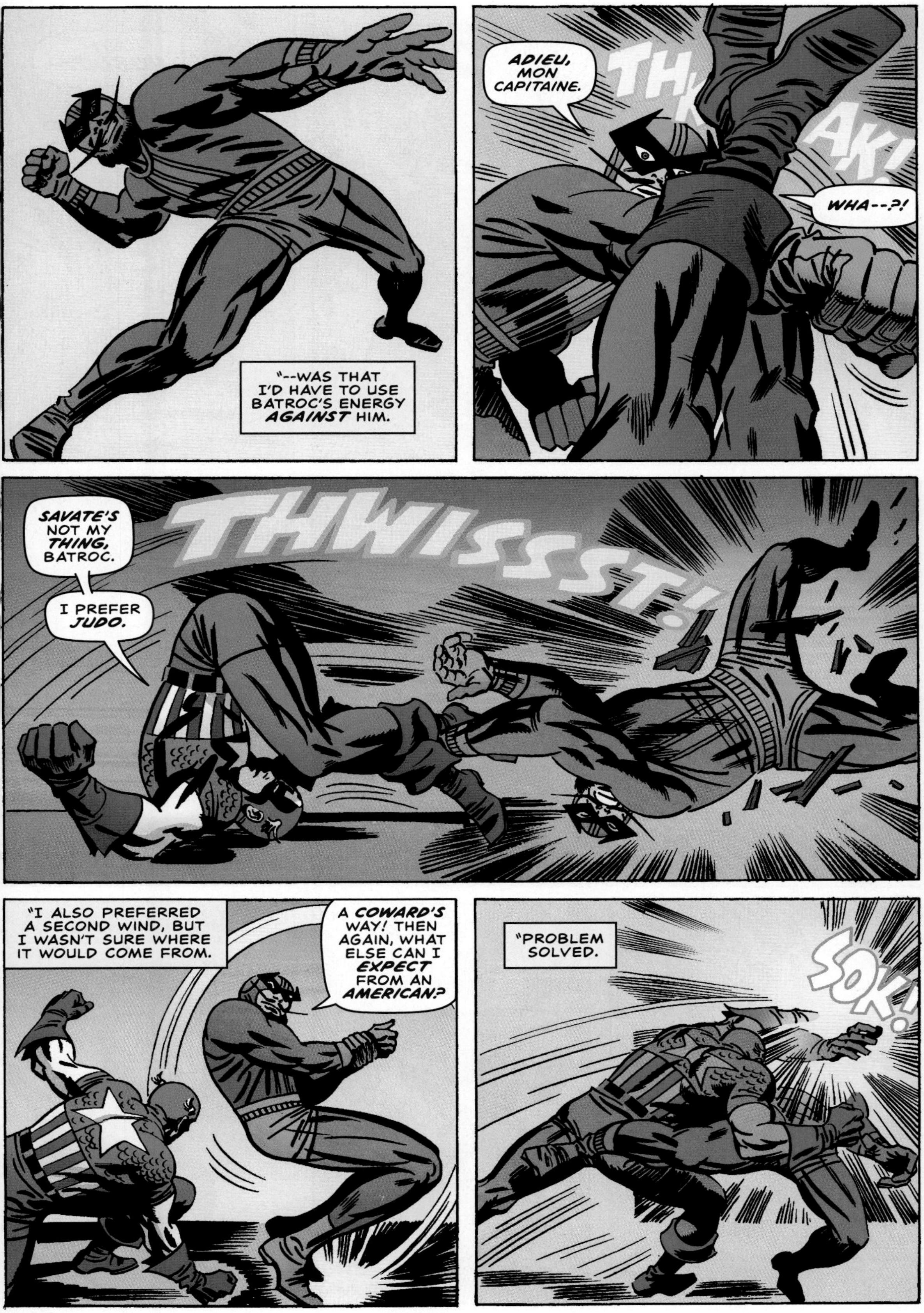

"--WAS THAT I'D HAVE TO USE BATROC'S ENERGY AGAINST HIM.
ADIEU, MON CAPITAINE.
THWAK!
WHA--?!
SAVATE'S NOT MY THING, BATROC.
I PREFER JUDO.
THWISSST!
"I ALSO PREFERRED A SECOND WIND, BUT I WASN'T SURE WHERE IT WOULD COME FROM.
A COWARD'S WAY! THEN AGAIN, WHAT ELSE CAN I EXPECT FROM AN AMERICAN?
"PROBLEM SOLVED.
SOK!

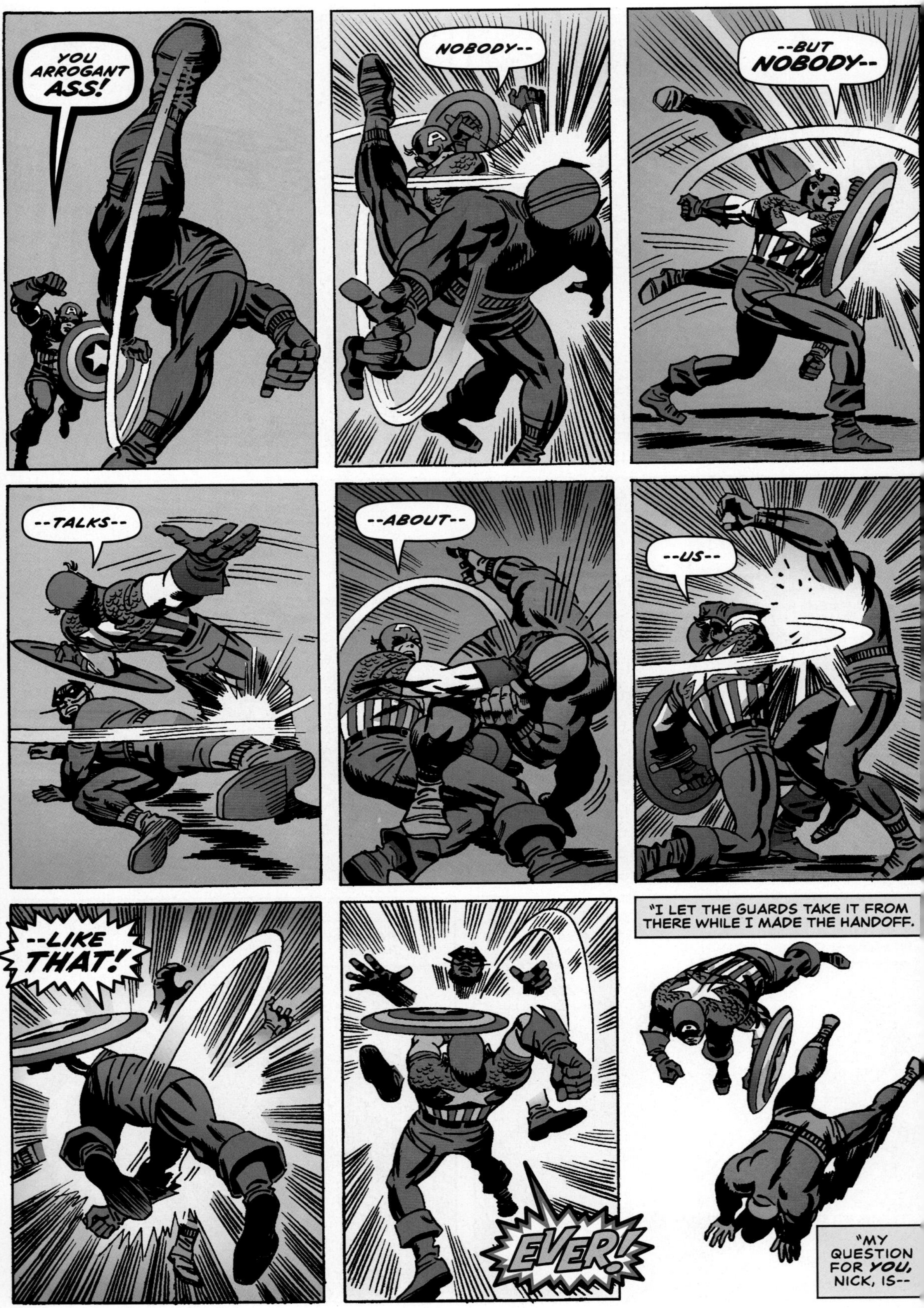
YOU ARROGANT ASS!
NOBODY--
--BUT NOBODY--
--TALKS--
--ABOUT--
--US--
--LIKE THAT!
EVER!
"I LET THE GUARDS TAKE IT FROM THERE WHILE I MADE THE HANDOFF.
"MY QUESTION FOR YOU, NICK, IS--

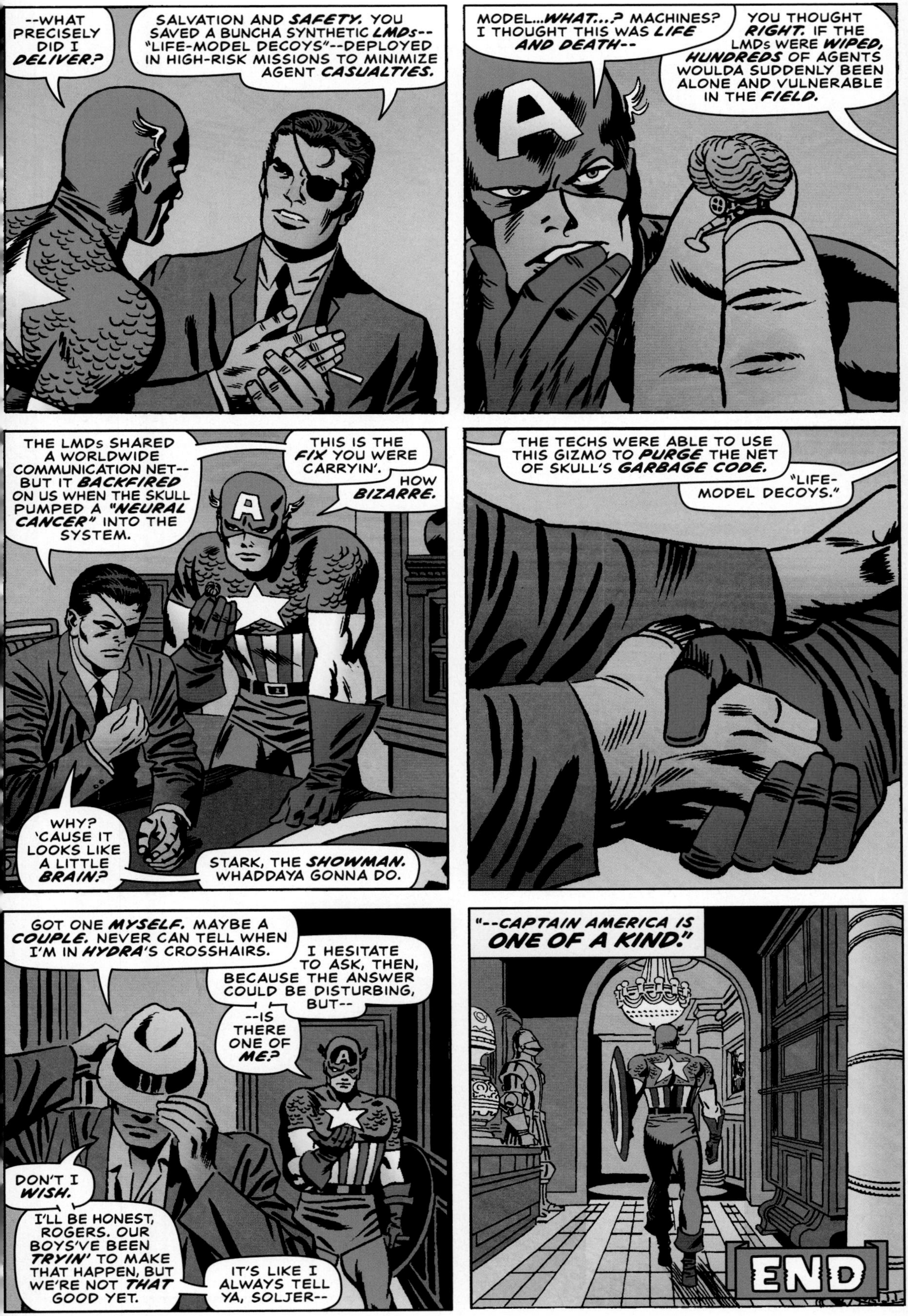

--WHAT PRECISELY DID I DELIVER?
SALVATION AND SAFETY. YOU SAVED A BUNCHA SYNTHETIC LMDs--"LIFE-MODEL DECOYS"--DEPLOYED IN HIGH-RISK MISSIONS TO MINIMIZE AGENT CASUALTIES.
MODEL...WHAT...? MACHINES? I THOUGHT THIS WAS LIFE AND DEATH--
YOU THOUGHT RIGHT. IF THE LMDs WERE WIPED, HUNDREDS OF AGENTS WOULDA SUDDENLY BEEN ALONE AND VULNERABLE IN THE FIELD.
THE LMDs SHARED A WORLDWIDE COMMUNICATION NET--BUT IT BACKFIRED ON US WHEN THE SKULL PUMPED A "NEURAL CANCER" INTO THE SYSTEM.
THIS IS THE FIX YOU WERE CARRYIN'.
HOW BIZARRE.
WHY? 'CAUSE IT LOOKS LIKE A LITTLE BRAIN?
STARK, THE SHOWMAN. WHADDAYA GONNA DO.
THE TECHS WERE ABLE TO USE THIS GIZMO TO PURGE THE NET OF SKULL'S GARBAGE CODE.
"LIFE-MODEL DECOYS."
GOT ONE MYSELF. MAYBE A COUPLE. NEVER CAN TELL WHEN I'M IN HYDRA'S CROSSHAIRS.
I HESITATE TO ASK, THEN, BECAUSE THE ANSWER COULD BE DISTURBING, BUT--
--IS THERE ONE OF ME?
DON'T I WISH.
I'LL BE HONEST, ROGERS. OUR BOYS'VE BEEN TRYIN' TO MAKE THAT HAPPEN, BUT WE'RE NOT THAT GOOD YET.
IT'S LIKE I ALWAYS TELL YA, SOLJER--
"--CAPTAIN AMERICA IS ONE OF A KIND."
END

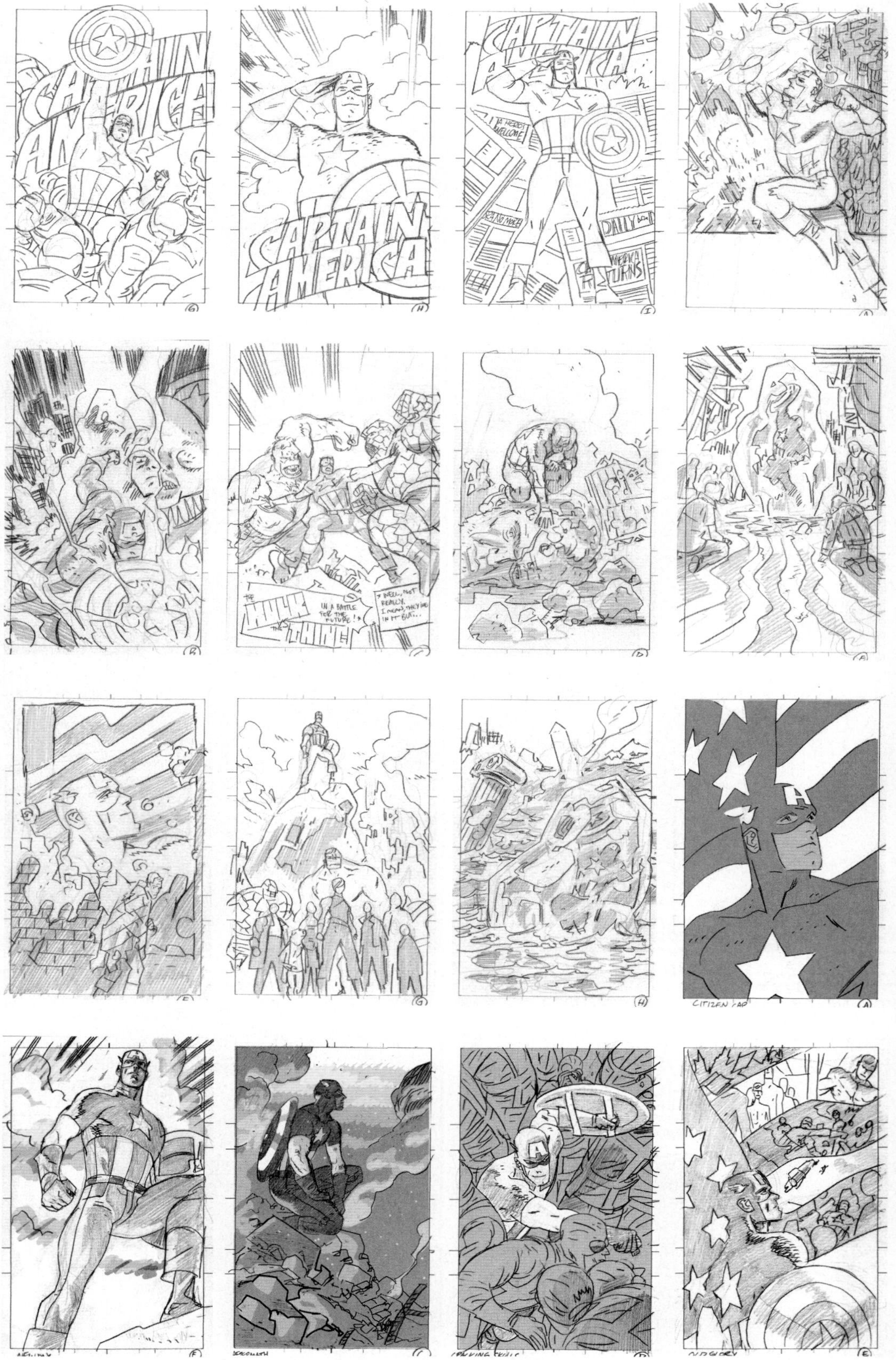
CAPTAIN AMERICA
CAPTAIN AMERICA
CAPTAIN AMERICA
DAILY
CITIZEN CAP

COVER SKETCHES BY **CHRIS SAMNEE**

B. MARTIN AFTER McFARLANE
delgado

#695 VARIANT
BY **BILLY MARTIN** & **EDGAR DELGADO**

STERANKO

#695 VARIANT
BY **JIM STERANKO**

#695 LEGACY HEADSHOT VARIANT
BY **MIKE McKONE** & **RACHELLE ROSENBERG**

CAPTAIN AMERICA
MARVEL
LEGACY
CAPTAIN AMERICA
695

#695 TRADING CARD VARIANT
BY **JOHN TYLER CHRISTOPHER**

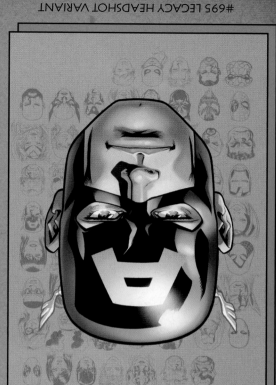

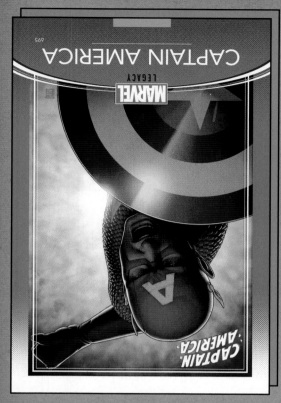

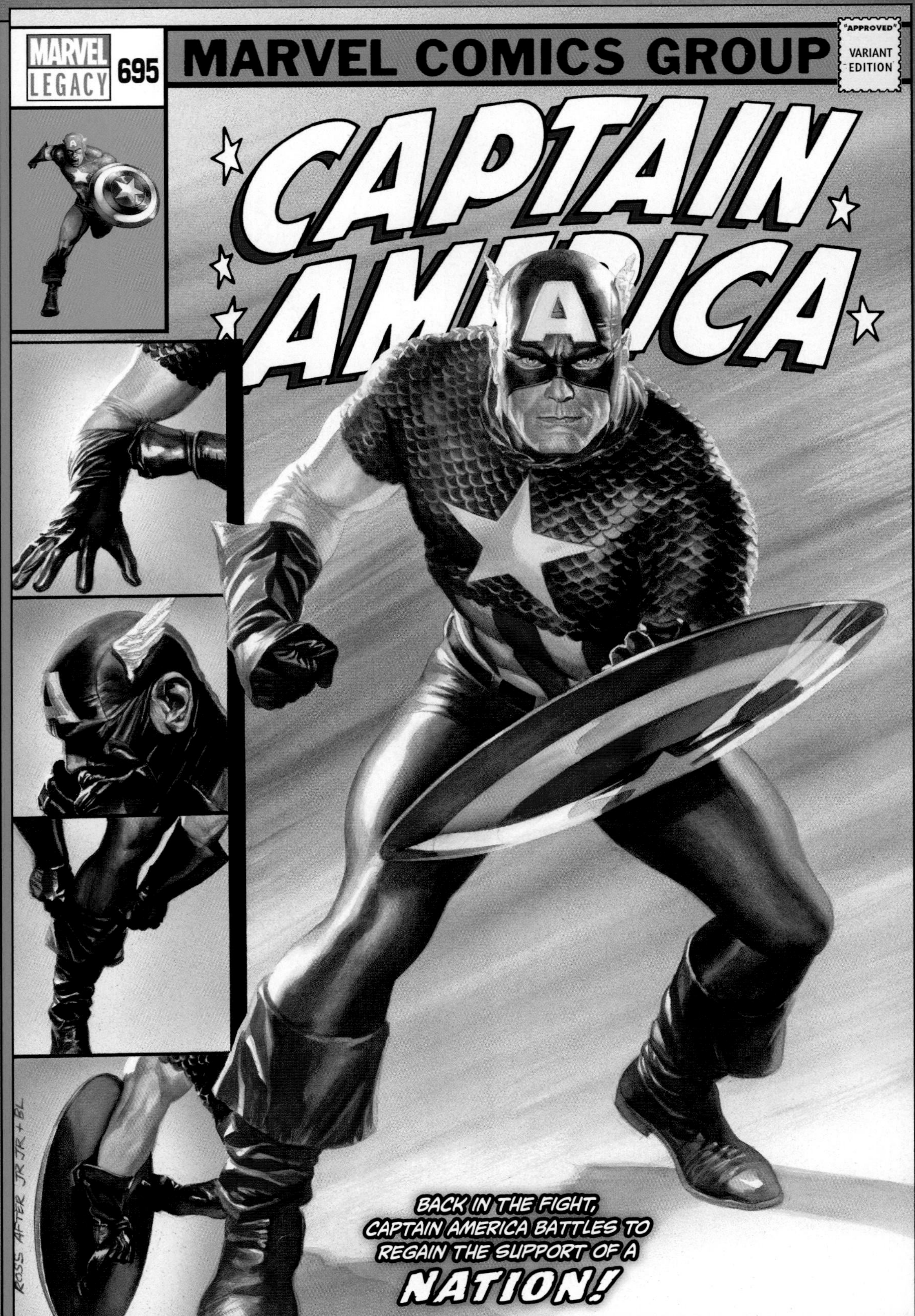
MARVEL LEGACY
695
MARVEL COMICS GROUP
"APPROVED" VARIANT EDITION
CAPTAIN AMERICA
ROSS AFTER JR JR + BL
BACK IN THE FIGHT, CAPTAIN AMERICA BATTLES TO REGAIN THE SUPPORT OF A NATION!

#695 HOMAGE VARIANT BY **ALEX ROSS**